# THE CHEF'S KITCHEN COMPANION

by BARBARA GRUNES

The author gratefully acknowledges the help of the American Egg Board, the National Fisheries Institute, and the National Live Stock and Meat Board.

Photographs, in order of appearance:
Citrus Punch (81); Spicy Chicken Liver Paté (93) and Tangy Meatballs (144); Barbecued Pecans (153), Curried Nuts (154) and Toasted Nuts (155); Cheese Ball (157); Old-Fashioned Vegetable Soup (225); French Onion Soup (232); Roast Turkey with Cumberland Sauce (298); Chicken Pie (281); Trout Amandine (334); Tuna Mousse with Cucumber Sauce (326); Beef Stroganoff (364); Beef Kabobs (366); Pecos Chili with a Touch of Honey (382); Hollandaise Sauce (441); Large Layered Salad (495); Hot Potato Salad (480); Marinated Vegetables (476); Jelly Omelet (569); Seafood Crepes (594); Glazed Lemon Bread (720); Egg Braid Bread (694); Christmas Stollen (712); Irish Soda Bread (726); Spinach Lasagna (756); Spaghetti with Meat Sauce (761): Enchiladas with Sour Cream (780); Babas Au Rhum (840); Coffee Cake with Nuts (836); Southern Pecan Pie (892); Boston Cream Pie (872); Cornish Hens on a Spit (959); Hamburgers (957).

ISBN 0-8249-3045-2

Published by Ideals Publishing Corporation
11315 Watertown Plank Road
Milwaukee, Wisconsin 53226
Published simultaneously in Canada

# TABLE OF CONTENTS

## —COOKING BASICS—

# RECIPES

# RECIPES

# COOKING BASICS

# COOKING
# BASICS

## Equipping the Kitchen

Depending on the size of your family and your individual
needs you can build on the following basic kitchen supply list.

| | |
|---|---|
| Basting bulb | Casseroles |
| Bottle opener | Corkscrew |
| Bread pans | Double boiler |
| Can opener | Deep frying thermometer |
| Candy thermometer | Egg Beater |
| Cake pans | Funnel |
| Cookie sheets | Good knives |
| Colander | Grater |

# Equipping the Kitchen

| | |
|---|---|
| Knife sharpener | Pastry board |
| Ladle | Rolling pin and cover |
| Measuring cups | Roasting pan |
| Measuring spoons | Saucepans and covers |
| Mixing bowls | Skillets and covers |
| Mixing spoons | Sieve |
| Muffin pans | Spatulas |
| Meat thermometer | Slotted spoon |
| Nutcracker | Teapot |
| Parchment paper | Whisks |
| Pastry cloth | Timer |
| Potato peeler | Tester |

## SPECIAL KITCHEN EQUIPMENT

**Food processors** are very special and talented machines. Depending on the brand and model, it can chop, mix, slice, shred, grate, julienne, cream, puree, knead, and emulsify. The machine contains a motor housed in either a plastic or metal base, a plastic bowl that fits onto a base, and a plastic lid with a food chute that fits over the bowl. Most machines come equipped with two blades. Since features vary from brand to brand, it is a good idea to become familiar with available features before you start shopping for your processor. Once you have mastered the basics of a processor it can make your life in the kitchen easier. It does take some adjustment to get the most out of it.

Look for the differences between a belt or a direct drive motor. On a belt driven machine the motor loses a little efficiency and the belt may require occasional changing. Braking action is an important feature: the action helps stop the movement of the blades, making the machine safer to operate. Pulsing action or a pulse switch is helpful, but not essential. Automatic cutoff is an important feature.

**Toaster ovens** are most useful as a supplement to the kitchen range, but they can come in handy as a range substitute in a dorm room, tiny apartment, or vacation home.

Toasters are essential in every kitchen. You can cook a variety of foods in your toaster, such as frozen waffles and pastries, but the toaster is still basically used to toast bread.

**Blenders** perform a variety of functions. They can mix, beat, chop, grate, and crush. Consider your blender needs before you invest. Make sure that the cap fits tightly.

**Automatic drip coffee makers** seem to be very popular. Available in a wide variety of sizes and styles, all basically perform the same function. Water poured into the holding tank is heated and then passed through the top of the unit into a filter containing the coffee grounds. The coffee then drips into the pot. Make sure the coffee maker you choose is not too noisy.

**Electric coffee pots** should be immersible for easy cleaning.

**Electric mixers** are either free-standing or portable. Standing mixers are easy to operate and perform special mixing and blending tasks. Portable mixers can be carried around the kitchen and are easily stored.

# Kitchen Techniques

## HIGH ALTITUDE ADJUSTMENT

**Candy Making**

To adjust sugar recipes for altitude, reduce the finish temperature. If you use a candy thermometer, first test the temperature at which water boils. While there will be minor changes from day to day due to weather conditions, the range is usually slight. At 5,000 feet altitude, water boils at approximately 202°F, or 10° less than at sea level. Therefore, correct the finish temperature for the candy by subtracting the 10°. For example, if a sea level recipe for creamy fudge gives a finish temperature for syrup at 238°, at 5,000 feet the thermometer reading would be 228°.

**Vegetables**

Cooking time will be increased from 2 to 10 minutes. Thick vegetables, such as beets, turnips, and onions may require even longer time.

**Baking Temperatures**

Layer cakes and cupcakes are best baked at 360° to 370° F. Above 5,000 feet, oven temperatures may be increased from 3-4 degrees.

## HINTS FOR ORIENTAL COOKING

If the meat is slightly frozen until stiff, it is easier to slice in small pieces.

It is important to prepare both soup broth and stocks in advance. The broth is generally used instead of water for cooking, adding flavor to the foods.

All cutting of ingredients should be done in advance. All ingredients should be placed within reach.

Gravy is always prepared before cooking and is generally made from cornstarch dissolved with water. Sometimes seasoning is added.

Dried ingredients are usually reconstituted in water until softened. After they are squeezed dry, cut away the unwanted parts.

Flavors and seasonings (that is, salt, oil, and pepper) should be harmonized and adjusted to individual taste.

As a rule, a maximum amount of time is spent in preparation—that is, the chopping, mincing and dicing—and a minimum of time is spent actually cooking.

## CARVING HINTS

The bones get in your way if you don't know where to expect them, therefore a little investigation tells you just where they are.

Convention doesn't forbid your standing up to carve, so if it is easier, by all means, stand up and carve.

A sharp knife is a must.

Always cut across the grain. If you cut with the grain, long meat fibers give a stringy texture to the slice. Steaks are the exception.

Let meat stand for about 10 to 15 minutes before carving.

Be sure that the platter is large enough to allow room to carve.

A heated platter is a nice touch.

# MAKING COFFEE

1. START WITH A THOROUGH-LY CLEAN COFFEEMAKER. Rinse coffeemaker with hot water before using. Wash thoroughly after each use and rinse with hot water.
2. FRESH COFFEE IS BEST. Buy coffee in the size can or package which will be used within a week.
3. START WITH FRESHLY DRAWN COLD WATER.
4. NEVER BREW LESS THAN ¾ OF THE CAPACITY OF THE COFFEEMAKER.
5. COFFEE SHOULD NEVER BE BOILED.
6. SERVE COFFEE AS SOON AS POSSIBLE AFTER BREWING. If necessary to keep coffee hot, hold at serving temperature by placing pot in pan of hot water or over very low heat.

## COFFEE-MAKING CHART

Here are the amounts of ground coffee and fresh water needed to make any given number of servings of coffee. These proportions apply to all methods of brewing coffee. The basis is one standard measure* of coffee and ¾ of a measuring cup (6 fluid ounces) of water.

| Average 5½-Ounce Servings | Standard Measures of Coffee | Level Tablespoons | Standard Measuring Cups of Water |
|---|---|---|---|
| 2 | 2 | 4 | 1½ |
| 4 | 4 | 8 | 3 |
| 6 | 6 | 12 | 4½ |
| 8 | 8 | 16 | 6 |

*A standard coffee measure equals two level measuring tablespoons.

# Glossary of Cooking Techniques

**Bake**   To cook with dry heat, as in the oven.

**Barbecue**   To broil or roast food. Can be done on a revolving frame. It also refers to thin slices of meat or ribs in a seasoned sauce.

**Baste**   To moisten with liquid during cooking.

**Beat**   To make a smooth mixture by stirring briskly, introducing air.

**Blanch**   To pour boiling water over food, which is left in the water for a short time.

**Blend**   To mix two or more ingredients together until mixture is smooth.

**Boil**   To cook in water or in another liquid that is to be kept in continuous motion by heating. The boiling point for liquid is 212° F.

**Braise**   To cook slowly with moist heat.

**Broil**   To cook by exposing the food directly to the heat source.

**Candy**   To conserve or preserve by boiling the food with sugar, encrusting the food with sugar.

**Caramelizing**   To heat dry sugar or foods containing sugar until they are light brown and have a caramel flavor.

**Chop**   To cut into small, medium or large pieces.

**Combine**   To mix ingredients together.

**Cream**   To mix ingredients, usually shortening, sugar and eggs or a combination of these, until they are light and fluffy.

**Cut**   To incorporate shortening into flour with a pastry knife.

**Dice**   To cut food into small pieces of equal size, usually quarter-inch cubes.

**Dissolve**   To melt or liquefy an ingredient.

**Dredge**   To coat food with flour, or to sprinkle it with flour.

**Fricassee**   To stew in gravy.

**Fry**   To cook food in fat. Pan-fry refers to cooking food in a small amount of fat; deep-frying refers to cooking by immersing food in hot fat.

**Glacé**   To coat food with a thin sugar syrup that has been cooked to the crack stage.

**Grate**   To reduce food in size by rubbing with a rough surface.

**Grill**   To broil food on a grill.

**Grind**   To process foods in a food chopper, grinder, or food processor.

**Knead**   To manipulate dough with a pressing, folding and stretching motion.

**Lard**   To insert fat in meat, or lay strips of fat on the surface of meat.

**Marinate**   To let food stand in a mixture of oil and vinegar or in a lemon based sauce.

**Melt**   To liquefy by heat.

**Mince**   To chop or cut food as finely as possible.

**Mix**   To combine foods by stirring.

**Parch**   To brown grains by means of dry heat.

**Pare**   To cut off the outside covering of fruits and vegetables.

**Peel**   To strip off the outer covering of fruits with thick skins or rinds, such as oranges or bananas.

**Poach**   To cook slowly in water to just below the boiling point.

**Pot Roast**   To cook slowly with moist heat.

**Puree**   To cook food until it is very soft; then mash or process until very smooth and thick. Cream, stock or milk may be added.

**Render**   To free fat from connective tissue by heating until the fat melts and drains.

**Roast**   To cook with dry heat, usually in an oven.

**Scald**   To heat liquid to temperature just below the boiling point.

**Score**   To cut lightly so as to mark the food with a thin line.

**Shirr**   To break eggs into a dish with cream and bake.

**Shred**   To cut into thin slices, then cut across the slices to make $1/8$-inch strips.

# Ingredients

## KITCHEN STAPLES

| | |
|---|---|
| Onions | Baking soda |
| Garlic | Baking powder |
| Eggs, 1 dozen | **Vinegars:** |
| Milk, 1 quart | Red wine vinegar |
| Butter, unsalted | Cider |
| Cheese | White Distilled |
| Vegetable oil | **Extracts:** |
| Peanut oil | Vanilla |
| Olive oil | Almond |
| Flour | Lemon |
| Cake flour | Cream of Tartar |
| Unbleached flour | Unflavored gelatin |
| Cornmeal | **Condiments:** |
| **Sugar:** | Mustard: Dijon |
| Granulated sugar | Ketchup |
| Confectioners' sugar | Worcestershire sauce |
| Brown sugar | Tabasco sauce |
| Honey | **Liquors:** |
| Cornstarch | |

White wine

Brandy

Sherry

Rum

**Beverages:**

Tea

Coffee

Juice

**Paper Goods:**

Napkins

Paper towels

Plastic storage bags

Plastic wrap

Aluminum foil

Parchment paper

Waxed paper

Kitchen string

Cheesecloth

**Herbs and Spices:**

Salt

Pepper

Basil

Parsley

Marjoram

Sage

Thyme

Paprika

Ginger

Cinnamon

Allspice

Nutmeg

Curry powder

Garlic powder

Onion salt

Chili powder

Cumin

Caraway seeds

# SPICES AND HERBS

**Allspice**  The dried berry of the pimento tree of the West Indies. Used to compliment cinnamon, resembles cinnamon, cloves and nutmeg together.

**Anise**  The fruit of a small annual plant. Grown in Spain, Mexico and India. Used on breads, cakes, cookies and all licorice flowers.

**Basil**  An annual plant, cultivated in Western Europe. Leaves are dried, ground and powdered. Used to flavor soups, sauces, and forms a wonderful combination with tomatoes.

**Bay Leaves**  The flavorful leaf of the laurel tree. It is dried whole and used to flavor soups, meats and pickles.

**Capers**  Grown in the Mediterranean countries. It is a flower bud of the Capparis spinosa. It is pickled and used as a condiment.

**Caraway**  A member of the parsley family, a biennial herb with an aromatic fruit usually known as caraway seeds. Holland is the largest commercial source.

**Cardamom**  Grown in Ceylon, India and Central America. Sold as ground seeds, whole seeds and whole pods. Used in cookies, bread and as a condiment.

**Cayenne Pepper**  A hot, savory flavor used in meat dishes and gravies. Grown in Africa.

**Chervil**  Aromatic leaves used to flavor soups and salads.

**Chili**  A hot pepper. Used as a base for chili sauces.

**Cinnamon**  The inner bark of Cinnamon zeylancium which grows only in Ceylon. It has a very milky flavor. Cassia cinnamon grown in the Far East is most generally used and has a more full-bodied flavor. The dried bark is sold in sticks or ground.

**Cloves**  The clove of the myrtle family, an evergreen tree that is grown 30 feet high. It is the dried unexpanded, nail-shaped flower bud, which is picked just before the blossom opens out and turns a deep red. Of spices that may be classified as flower spices, the clove is most important. Sold whole or ground.

**Coriander**  An herb of the parsley family. The aromatic seeds are used for confections, cookies, pickles and meat products. Indigenous to southern Europe and the Mediterranean region.

**Cumin Seed**  A small annual herb of the parsley family. It is believed to be a native of upper Egypt, Turkistan, and the eastern Mediterranean region. Used to flavor meats, sausage, pickles and used in curry powder.

**Curry Powder**  A yellow condiment from India containing various spices.

**Dill**  An annual herb grown for its aromatic seed. Used in pickles, sauces and with fish.

**Fennel**  An herb, the seeds are ground and used to flavor fish, sauces.

**Garlic**  Is a strong flavored plant of the lily family. The cloves are used to flavor meats, salads and a wide variety of foods.

**Ginger**  Is the root of an herbaceous perennial grown in semitropical countries.

**Leek**  Is a strong flavored plant similar to the onion.

**Mace**  Is the network around the nutmeg kernel. It is a vivid red when it is fresh and dries to a light orange. It is sold whole or ground and is used to flavor sauces, gravies, cakes and pies. The aroma is similar to nutmeg but the flavor is different.

**Marjoram** Is the fragrant annual of the mint family. The leaves are dried and used whole or powdered to flavor soups, salads, stuffings, meats and sausage. The best marjoram comes from France, although it is grown in other areas of the world.

**Mint** Is a fragrant plant. The leaves are used fresh or dried to flavor certain soups, vegetables, fruits and beverages.

**Mustard** It is the second largest consumed spice in the United States next to pepper. The seeds are used whole or ground. It is combined with spices and vinegar to make a moist product known as prepared mustard.

**Nutmeg** The kernel of the fruit of the Myristica tree grown in the East and West Indies. It has divisions, the outer husk, the mace, the inner shell and the seed or nutmeg. Sold whole or ground, it is best to grind your own.

**Onion** Is a strong pungent flavored plant of the lily family. The bulb is used to flavor meats, fish, poultry and salad.

**Paprika** Is a sweet red pepper which is dried and ground after the seeds and stem are removed. It has a mild flavor. The most popular paprika is grown in Spain and Hungary.

**Parsley** Is a biennial herb used to flavor meats, vegetables and salads. Used widely as a garnish.

**Pepper** Made from peppercorns which are the dried berries of a vine, Pepper Nigrum. Black pepper is made from the whole berry. White pepper is made from what is left of the fully ripened berry after the outer coat has been removed. Green pepper is the underripe peppercorn.

**Pimento** Is the fleshy fruit of the Spanish paprika. It is canned and used in meats, vegetable dishes and salads.

**Poppy Seed** Is the seed of one variety of the poppy plant. It is not the opium poppy. It is used for breads, rolls, cakes and cookies. It is imported from Central Europe.

**Rosemary** Is an evergreen plant. The leaves and flowers are used to flavor and garnish fish, stews and sauces.

**Saffron** The stigma of a flower that is similar to a crocus, Crocus sativus. Dried and used to flavor breads and meats, it has a rich orange-yellow color and is very costly, so use sparingly.

**Sage** A perennial mint plant. The leaves are dried, used in stuffing and to flavor meats.

**Sesame Seeds** The seeds of an herb used to flavor rolls and cookies and for flavoring oriental oil. It is sold hulled. The preferred seeds are grown in Turkey.

**Soy Sauce** Is an oriental sauce made from fermented soy beans. There is a light and dark variety.

**Tabasco Sauce** A highly seasoned sauce made with cayenne peppers and other flavorful ingredients.

**Tarragon** A perennial herb, the fresh or dried leaves are used to flavor salads, pickles, vinegar and sauces.

**Thyme** An herb, the powdered leaves are used to season meats, poultry and some fish.

## SUBSTITUTIONS

**IF YOU'RE OUT OF**
Vegetables
I lb. fresh mushrooms

1 cup canned tomato sauce

1 cup tomato juice

Broccoli flowerets
Cooked pumpkin

Fruits
1 cup raisins

1 cup sliced strawberries

Meat
1/2 pound ground pork
1 1/2 cups diced cooked ham

**YOU CAN SUBSTITUTE**

3 ounces dried mushrooms or 6-8 ounces canned mushrooms, drained

8–ounce can stewed tomatoes blended in blender or 1 cup tomato puree, seasoned

1/2 cup tomato sauce plus 1/2 cup water

Cauliflower or Brussels sprouts
Cooked squash

1 cup cut-up dates, currants, dried prunes or chopped apricots

10-ounce package frozen strawberries, reducing sugar in recipe to 1/3 cup.

1/2 pound sausage meat
12 ounces pork luncheon meat, diced

½ pound shrimp, cooked, shelled and deveined

5-ounce can shrimp, drained

**Nuts**
1 pint nuts
Cashews

Sunflower seeds
Peanuts

**Miscellaneous**
½ cup ketchup or chili sauce

½ cup tomato sauce plus 2 tablespoons sugar, 1 tablespoon vinegar and ⅛ teaspoon cloves

½ cup tartar sauce

6 tablespoons mayonnaise or salad dressing and 2 tablespoons pickle relish

White wine
1 cup chicken or beef broth

Apple cider or juice
1 cup water plus 1 bouillon cube or 1 teaspoon instant bouillon

# Glossary of Common Cooking Terms

**Appetizer**   A small amount of food served before dinner.

**Aspic**   A transparent jelly, usually made of stock.

**Batter**   A beaten combination of liquid, flour and other ingredients; used in baking.

**Bisque**   A rich, thick cream soup usually having a fish base.

**Bonbon**   A candy that has been dipped into fondant.

**Bouillabaisse**   A chowder made of many varieties of fish with tomatoes and wine.

**Bouillon**   A clear, delicately seasoned soup.

**Charlotte** Usually a gelatin dessert with flavored whipped cream, molded and lined with a sponge cake or lady fingers.

**Cider**   Juice pressed from apples; and used as a drink or to make vinegar.

**Cobbler**   A deep-dish fruit pie with a pastry of rich biscuit dough.

**Cocktail**   A drink, usually alcoholic, served before dinner or independently of meals.

**Compote**   A sweetened stewed fruit, keeping the fruit as whole as possible.

**Condiments**   Food seasonings.

**Consommé**   A highly seasoned, clear soup.

**Cracklings**   Crisp particles left after the fat has been dried.

**Cream sauce**   A white sauce made with cream.

**Croquettes**   A mixture of chopped foods held together by eggs or sauce; then shaped, dipped, and fried.

**Croutons**   Cubes of toasted or fried bread.

**Custard**   A cooked or baked mixture of sweetened eggs and milk.

**Deep-dish pie**   A fruit pie with top crust only.

**Dough**   A mixture of liquid and flour, used for baking that is stiff enough to be kneaded.

**Entree**   Main dish of a meal.

**Fondant**   A sugar and water mixture cooked to the soft-ball stage (234° F.), then cooled and baked.

**Frosting**   A cooked or uncooked sugar mixture used to cover and decorate cakes, cookies, and other foods.

**Gelatin**   A purified protein made from connective tissues and bones of animals.

**Giblets**   The liver, heart, and gizzard of poultry.

**Goulash**   A thick meat stew.

**Gumbo**  A soup containing okra.

**Hollandaise**  A rich sauce made of eggs and butter.

**Julienne**  Food cut into match-like strips.

**Marinade**  An oil and acid mixture in which food is allowed to stand.

**Marzipan**  A paste of sweet almonds and sugar.

**Meringue**  A mixture of stiffly beaten egg whites, flavoring and sugar, used on pies.

**Mocha**  A flavoring made with coffee and chocolate.

**Mousse**  A mixture of whipped cream, sugar and flavoring. It can be frozen, or it can be made with gelatin and combined with meat, poultry, fish, fruits or vegetables.

**Muffin**  A drop batter baked in individual pans and served as a quick bread.

**Pilaf**  Rice boiled with meat, poultry or fish, and highly seasoned.

**Ragout**  A thick, highly seasoned stew.

**Relish**  A seasoned food used as an accompaniment to other foods.

**Roe**  Fish eggs.

**Roux**  A smooth blend of fat and flour used for thickening.

**Sherbet**  A frozen mixture of fruit juice, sugar, egg whites and milk, or water.

**Souffle**   An entrée or dessert made with white sauce, egg yolks, whipped egg whites and flavorings.

**Stock**   The liquid in which meat or poultry has been cooked.

**Suet**   The firm white fat of beef.

# TABLES

# HERB CHART

| USE THIS HERB → | BASIL | BAY LEAF | CHIVE | CURRY POWDER | DILL |
|---|---|---|---|---|---|
| When You Fix: ↓ | Aromatic odor, warm sweet flavor used whole or ground | A pungent flavor. Available as whole leaf | Mild flavor of onion | Blend of spices in proper proportion | Aromatic odor with delicate caraway flavor |
| MEATS CASSEROLES | Beef stew Steak, Veal Lamb Venison | Meats, Stews, Sauerbraten | | Curries of meat Veal Mildly hot casseroles | Veal Pork spareribs Lamb stew |
| POULTRY SEAFOOD | Chicken Duck Fish Seafood cocktails | Poached fish | Fish dishes | Chicken Fish Shrimp Chicken salad | Fish dishes Chicken salad |
| VEGETABLES PICKLES PRESERVES | Tomatoes Potatoes Peas Squash Herb butter | Pickled beets Relishes | Potato dishes Vegetable garnish | Various vegetables Pickled carrots Green bean sticks | Potatoes baked or boiled Tomatoes Beans Pickles Garnish |
| EGGS AND CHEESE | Cheeses Welsh rabbit and Egg dishes | | Omelets and Egg dishes Cream and cottage cheese | Egg salad Egg dishes Cheese fillings Sour cream | Sour cream Cream and Cottage cheese Scrambled eggs |
| RICE SPAGHETTI NOODLES | Spanish rice Spaghetti dishes | | | Oriental touch to rice | Buttered noodles |
| SOUPS SALADS SAUCES | Bean Mock turtle Potato soups Tossed salads | Vegetable and Fish soups Tomato sauces and Gravies Marinades | Various Soups and Salads | Gravies Flavor teaser in soups Chili sauce Shrimp sauce | Fish and Vegetable salads Butter sauce Cream sauce |

# HERB CHART

| USE THIS HERB → | GINGER | MARJORAM | OREGANO | SAGE | TARRAGON |
|---|---|---|---|---|---|
| When You Fix: ↓ | Aromatic, pungent root with warm flavor-sold fresh, dried or ground | Aromatic odor, potent flavor | Strong aromatic odor, bitter taste, whole or ground | Pleasant aromatic odor and warm, bitter taste. Used fresh & dried | Aromatic leaves, with hot pungent flavor |
| MEATS CASSEROLES | Pot roast Pork, Veal Beef Casseroles | Stuffing for all meats Ragouts, Stew Beef, Veal Pork Roasts Lamb Sausage | Pork, Veal and Lamb dishes Meat loaf Stews Chili | Stuffing for meat dishes Veal and Pork dishes Pork roast Sausage Hamburgers | Beef and Veal dishes |
| POULTRY SEAFOOD | | Chicken and fish dishes Stuffed fish Fish chowder | Roast duck Fish chowder | Poultry | Fish and Chicken dishes Chicken cacciatore Lobster |
| VEGETABLES PICKLES PRESERVES | Pickles Preserves Chutney Vegetable combos | Scalloped potatoes and tomatoes Dressing for broccoli cabbage spinach | Hash brown potatoes Dried beans Lentils | Vegetable loaves Beans Tomatoes | Potatoes Tomatoes Beets Spinach Pickles |
| EGGS AND CHEESE | | Egg salad Egg dishes Cheese dishes | Sprinkle on top of dishes with cheeses | Fresh cheese Cheese combo dishes | Eggs Benedict Egg and Cheese dishes |
| RICE SPAGHETTI NOODLES | | Spaghetti sauce | Spaghetti with meat sauce Pizza | | |
| SOUPS SALADS SAUCES | Soups Chicken broth Gravies Fruit salad Whipped cream | Soups Salad dressing Green vegetables salads | Vegetable and Fish salads | Salads | Tartar sauce Sweet-sour sauce Fish Sauces Green salads Aspics |

# METRIC CONVERSION

**Cup Equivalents (volume)**

| | | |
|---|---|---|
| ¼ cup | = | 60 ml. |
| ⅓ cup | = | 85 ml. |
| ½ cup | = | 125 ml. |
| ⅔ cup | = | 170 ml. |
| ¾ cup | = | 180 ml. |
| 1 cup | = | 250 ml. |
| 1¼ cups | = | 310 ml. |
| 1½ cups | = | 375 ml. |
| 2 cups | = | 500 ml. |
| 3 cups | = | 750 ml. |
| 5 cups | = | 1250 ml. |

**Spoonful Equivalents (volume)**

| | | |
|---|---|---|
| ⅛ teaspoon | = | .5 ml. |
| ¼ teaspoon | = | 1.5 ml. |
| ½ teaspoon | = | 3 ml. |
| ¾ teaspoon | = | 4 ml. |
| 1 teaspoon | = | 5 ml. |
| 1 tablespoon | = | 15 ml. |
| 2 tablespoons | = | 30 ml. |
| 3 tablespoons | = | 45 ml. |

**Oven Temperatures**

| | | |
|---|---|---|
| 275° F | = | 135° C |
| 300° F | = | 149° C |
| 325° F | = | 165° C |
| 350° F | = | 175° C |
| 375° F | = | 190° C |
| 400° F | = | 205° C |
| 425° F | = | 218° C |
| 450° F | = | 230° C |
| 500° F | = | 260° C |

# METRIC CONVERSION

**Cup Equivalents (volume)**

| | | |
|---|---|---|
| ¼ cup | = | 60 ml. |
| ⅓ cup | = | 85 ml. |
| ½ cup | = | 125 ml. |
| ⅔ cup | = | 170 ml. |
| ¾ cup | = | 180 ml. |
| 1 cup | = | 250 ml. |
| 1¼ cups | = | 310 ml. |
| 1½ cups | = | 375 ml. |
| 2 cups | = | 500 ml. |
| 3 cups | = | 750 ml. |
| 5 cups | = | 1250 ml. |

**Spoonful Equivalents (volume)**

| | | |
|---|---|---|
| ⅛ teaspoon | = | .5 ml. |
| ¼ teaspoon | = | 1.5 ml. |
| ½ teaspoon | = | 3 ml. |
| ¾ teaspoon | = | 4 ml. |
| 1 teaspoon | = | 5 ml. |
| 1 tablespoon | = | 15 ml. |
| 2 tablespoons | = | 30 ml. |
| 3 tablespoons | = | 45 ml. |

**Oven Temperatures**

| | | |
|---|---|---|
| 275° F | = | 135° C |
| 300° F | = | 149° C |
| 325° F | = | 165° C |
| 350° F | = | 175° C |
| 375° F | = | 190° C |
| 400° F | = | 205° C |
| 425° F | = | 218° C |
| 450° F | = | 230° C |
| 500° F | = | 260° C |

# METRIC CONVERSION

**Pan Sizes (linear & volume)**

| | | |
|---|---|---|
| 1 inch | = | 2.5 cm. |
| 8-inch square | = | 20-cm. square (baking pan) |
| 13 x 9 x 1½-inch | = | 33 x 23 x 4 cm. |
| 10 x 6 x 2-inch | = | 25 x 15 x 5 cm. |
| 13 x 9 x 2-inch | = | 33 x 23 x 5 cm. |
| 12 x 7½ x 1½-inch | = | 30 x 18 x 4 cm. (baking pans & dishes) |
| 9 x 5 x 3-inch | = | 23 x 13 x 8 cm. (loaf pan) |
| 10-inch | = | 25 cm. (skillet) |
| 12-inch | = | 30 cm. (skillet) |
| 1 quart | = | 1 liter (baking dishes) |
| 2 quarts | = | 2 liters |
| 5 to 6 cups | = | 1.5 liters (ring mold) |

**Weight (meat, can, and package sizes)**

| | | |
|---|---|---|
| 1 ounce | = | 28 g. |
| ½ pound | = | 225 g. |
| ¾ pound | = | 340 g. |
| 1 pound | = | 450 g. |
| 1½ pounds | = | 675 g. |
| 2 pounds | = | 900 g. |
| 3 pounds | = | 1.4 kg. (larger amounts will be weighed in kilograms) |
| 10 ounces | = | 280 g. (most frozen vegetables) |
| 10½ ounces | = | 294 g. (most condensed soups) |
| 15 ounces | = | 425 g. |
| 16 ounces | = | 450 g. |
| 1 pound, 24 ounces | = | 850 g. (can sizes) |

# SUBSTITUTIONS

## SPICES/FLAVORINGS

| | |
|---|---|
| 1/2 tsp. cayenne or red pepper | few drops Tabasco |
| 1 T. chopped fresh herbs | 1 T. dried herbs |
| 1 tsp. dry mustard | 2-3 tsp. prepared mustard |
| 1 T. lemon juice | 2 tsp. vinegar |
| 1 tsp. grated fresh ginger | 1/4 tsp. ground ginger |
| 1 clove garlic, pressed or minced | 1/4 tsp. each oregano, basil, thyme and rosemary plus dash of cayenne |
| 1 tsp. pumpkin pie spice | 1/2 tsp. cinnamon, 1/4 tsp. giner, 1/8 tsp. each nutmeg and cloves |
| 1 tsp. marjoram | 1 tsp. oregano |
| 1 tsp. Worcestershire sauce | 1 tsp. bottled steak sauce |
| fresh parsley | fresh celery leaves |

## FLOUR/STARCHES

| | |
|---|---|
| 2 3/4 c. cake flour | 2 1/2 c. all-purpose or unbleached flour |
| 1 T. cornstarch or 1 1/2 tsp. arrowroot | 2 T. flour |

## LEAVENING AGENT

| | |
|---|---|
| 1 tsp. baking powder | 1 tsp. cream of tartar plus scant tsp. baking soda |

**SWEETENERS**

| | |
|---|---|
| 1 c. honey | 1¼ c. sugar plus ½ c. water |
| 1½ c. corn syrup | 1 c. sugar plus ½ cup water |
| 1 c. sugar | ⅔ c. honey plus ½ tsp. baking soda |
| ¼ c. cinnamon-sugar | ¼ c. granulated sugar plus ½ tsp. cinnamon |

**CHOCOLATE**

| | |
|---|---|
| 1 (1 oz.) square unsweetened chocolate | 3 T. cocoa plus 1 T. fat |
| 1 square semisweet chocolate | 1 square unsweetened chocolate plus 1 T. sugar |
| 4 oz. bar German's sweet chocolate | ¾ c. real chocolate chips |

**DAIRY PRODUCTS**

| | |
|---|---|
| 1 c. whole milk (fresh) | ½ c. evaporated milk plus ½ c. water or 1 c. reconstituted nonfat dry milk plus 2 T. butter or oil |
| 1 c. buttermilk or soured milk | 1 T. vinegar or lemon juice plus whole milk to make 1 cup (let stand 5 minutes) |
| 1 c. dairy sour cream | 1 c. plain yogurt or 1 c. evaporated milk plus 1 T. vinegar or 1 c. cottage cheese mixed in blender with 2 T. milk and 1 T. lemon juice |

**SHORTENING**

| | |
|---|---|
| 1 c. butter or margarine | ⅞ c. oil or lard or ¾ c. rendered chicken fat |

# Oven Chart

**General Oven Chart**
{
Very Slow Oven — 250° to 300°F.
Slow Oven — 300° to 325°F.
Moderate Oven — 325° to 375°F.
Med. Hot Oven — 375° to 400°F.
Hot Oven — 400° to 450°F.
Very Hot Oven — 450° to 500°F.
}

## Breads
| | |
|---|---|
| Baking Powder Biscuits | 450°F. 12 — 15 min. |
| Muffins | 400° to 425°F. 20 — 25 min. |
| Quick Breads | 350°F. 40 — 60 min. |
| Yeast Bread | 375° to 400°F. 45 — 60 min. |
| Yeast Rolls | 400°F. 15 — 20 min. |

## Cakes
| | |
|---|---|
| Butter Loaf Cakes | 350°F. 45 — 60 min. |
| Butter Layer Cakes | 350° to 375°F. 25 — 35 min. |
| Cup Cakes | 375°F. 20 — 25 min. |
| Chiffon Cakes | 325°F. 60 min. |
| Sponge Cakes | 325°F. 60 min. |
| Angel Food Cakes | 325°F. 60 min. |

## Cookies
| | |
|---|---|
| Bar Cookies | 350°F. 25 — 30 min. |
| Drop Cookies | 350° to 375°F. 8 — 12 min. |
| Rolled and Ref. Cookies | 350° to 400°F. 8 — 12 min. |

## Pastry
| | |
|---|---|
| Meringues | 350°F. 12 — 20 min. |
| Pie Shells | 450°F. 12 — 15 min. |
| Filled Pies | 450°F. 10 min. lower to 350°F. 40 min. |

## Roasts
| | |
|---|---|
| Beef Roast | 325°F. Rare 18 — 20 min. per lb. Medium 22 — 25 min. per lb. Well done — 30 min. per lb. |
| Chicken | 325°F - 350°F. 30 min. per lb. |
| Duck | 325°F. - 350°F. 25 min. per lb. |
| Fish Fillets | 500°F. 15 - 20 min. |
| Goose | 325°F. - 350°F. 30 min. per lb. |
| Ham | 350°F. 20 - 30 min. per lb. |
| Lamb | 300°F. - 350°F. 35 min. per lb. |
| Meat loaf | 375°F. 60 min. for 2 lb. loaf |
| Pork Roast | 350°F. 30 min. per lb. |
| Turkey | 250°F. - 325°F. 15 - 25 min. per lb. |
| Veal Roast | 300°F. 30 min. per lb. |
| Venison | 350°F. 20 - 25 min. per lb. |

# CAN SIZES

| CONTAINER INDUSTRY TERM | APPROXI-MATE NET WEIGHT (Check label) | APPROXIMATE CUPS | PRODUCTS |
|---|---|---|---|
| 8-ounce | 8 ounces | 1 | Fruits, vegetables, *specialties |
| Picnic | 10½ ounces | 1¼ | Condensed soups, small quantities of fruits, vegetables, meat and fish products, *specialties |
| 12-ounce (vacuum) | 12 ounces | 1½ | Used largely for vacuum-packed corn |
| No. 300 | 1 pound | 1¾ | Pork and beans, baked beans, meat products, cranberry sauce, *specialties |
| No. 303 | 16-17 ounces | 2 | Fruits, vegetables, meat products, ready-to-serve soups, *specialties |
| No. 2 | 1 pound, 4 ounces, or 20 ounces, or 18 fluid ounces | 2½ | Juices, fruits, vegetables, ready-to-serve soups, *specialties |
| No. 2½ | 1 pound, 13 ounces, or 29 ounces | 3½ | Fruits, some vegetables (pumpkin, sauerkraut, spinach, and other greens, tomatoes) |
| No. 3 Cyl. | 3 pounds, 3 ounces, or 46 fluid ounces | 5¾ | Fruit and vegetable juices, whole chicken |

*SPECIALTIES: Usually a food combination such as macaroni, spaghetti, Spanish-style rice, Mexican-type foods, Chinese foods, tomato aspic, etc.

# COOKING FOR CROWDS

| RELISHES (combine several) | | | |
|---|---|---|---|
| Carrot strips | 25 | 2-3 strips | 1 pound |
| Celery | 25 | 1 2- to 3-inch piece | 1 pound |
| Olives | 25 | 3 to 4 olives | 1 quart |
| Pickles | 25 | 1 ounce | 1 quart |
| **SALADS** | | | |
| Fruit | 24 | ⅓ cup | 2 quarts |
| Potato | 24 | ½ cup | 3 quarts |
| Tossed Vegetable | 25 | ¾ cup | 5 quarts |
| Salad dressing | 32 | 1 tablespoon | 1 pint |
| **SOUP** | 25 | 1 cup (main course) | 1½ gallons or 10 10½- to 11-ounce cans condensed or 2 50-ounce cans condensed |
| **VEGETABLES** | | | |
| Canned | 28 | ½ cup | 4 1-lb. 11 ounce to 1 lb. 13-ounce cans |
| | 25 | ½ cup | 1 6½ to 7¼ lb. cans |
| Fresh: | | | |
|    Lettuce, for salad, Iceberg | 24 | ⅙ head, raw | 4 heads |
|    Onions | 25 | ⅓ cup, small whole or pieces | 6¼ pounds |
|    Potatoes, mashed | 24 | ½ cup, mashed | 6 pounds, raw |
| Frozen: | | | |
|    Beans, green or wax | 25 | ⅓ cup | 5¼ pounds |
|    Carrots | 25 | ⅓ cup, sliced | 5 pounds |
|    Corn, whole kernel | 25 | ⅓ cup | 5 pounds |
|    Peas | 25 | ⅓ cup | 5 pounds |
|    Potatoes, French fried | 25 | 10 pieces | 3¼ pounds |

# COOKING FOR CROWDS

| Foods | Servings | Serving Unit | Amount to Purchase |
|---|---|---|---|
| **BEVERAGES** | | | |
| Coffee, ground | 40 to 50 | ¾ cup | 1 pound (5 cups) |
| Milk | 24 | 1 cup | 1½ gallons |
| Tea, instant, iced | 40 | ¾ cup | 1 cup |
| Tea, leaves | 50 | ¾ cup | 1 cup |
| **DESSERTS** | | | |
| Cake | 24 | 2½-inch squares | 1 15½x10½x1-inch sheet cake |
| Ice cream | 24 | ½ cup or 1 slice | 3 quarts |
| Pie | 30 | ⅙ of pie | 5 9-inch pies |
| **FRUIT** | | | |
| Canned | 24 | ½ cup | 1 6½- to 7½-lb. can |
| **MEAT** | | | |
| Beef roast, chuck | 25 | 4 ounces | 12¼ pounds, bone in |
| Ground beef | 25 | 3-ounce patty | 6¾ pounds |
| Ham, baked, sliced | 25 | 4 ounces | 10 pounds, boneless |
| Chicken | 24 | ¼ chicken | 6 chickens |
| Turkey | 25 | 3 ounces | 15 pounds |
| **PASTA, RICE** | | | |
| Rice, long-grain | 24 | ½ cup, cooked | 1½ pounds uncooked |
| Spaghetti and noodles | 25 | ¾ cup, cooked | 2½ pounds uncooked |

# Meal Planning and Menus

## NEW YEAR'S DAY BRUNCH

Anchovies and Pimientos
Finnan Haddie
Oatmeal Quick Bread
Pasta Salad
Lemon Angel Pie
Fruit Fondue

# NEW YEAR'S DINNER

Vegetable Croustades
Herbed Cucumbers
Molded Salad
Salisbury Steak
Broccoli Casserole
Praline Mousse

# VALENTINE SURPRISE

Flat Mushroom Crepe
Croissant
or
Noodle Buddin
Apple Butter
Strawberry Custard Ice Cream
or
Floating Island
Caramel-Coated Marshmallows

## FEBRUARY FANTASY

Cheese in Crust
Waldorf Salad
Ziti
Stuffed Sweet Peppers
Apple Charlotte
or
Orange Chiffon Cake
English Toffee

## MARCH MIXINGS

Salmon Steak Tartare
or
Chicken Gumbo
Stuffed Pork Chops
Potato Pancakes
Dilly Bread
Creme Brulee
or
Australian Pavlova
Chocolate Truffles

# EASTER BRUNCH

Apricot Bran Bread
Ham Deviled Eggs
Stuffed Baked Potatoes
Zucchini Custard Casserole
Eggs Benedict
Hot Cross Buns
Banana Mocha Cake

# EASTER DINNER

Waldorf Salad
Spiced Walnuts
Baked Ham
Spicy Sweet Cherry Sauce for Ham
or
Stuffed Leg of Lamb
Easter Egg Braid
Artichokes with Hollandaise Sauce
Frozen Peach Pie

# APRIL APPETITE

Olive Cheese Ball
Beef Wellington with Truffle Sauce
Hearts of Palm Salad
Egg Braid Bread
Lemon Meringue Pie
or
Strawberry Cream Puffs

# MAY MASTERPIECES

Lasagna
or
Veal Parmigiana
Spinach Salad
Bread Sticks
or
Spinach Pasta
Key Lime Pie
or
Meringue Kisses

# MOTHER'S DAY BREAKFAST

Banana Breakfast Drink
Chocolate Omelet
Fruit Salad
Orange Sponge Cake with
Whipped Chocolate Frosting

# FATHER'S DAY

Beef Wellington
7–Layer Salad
Fried Sauerkraut
Dinner Rolls
Chocolate Cake
Punch
English Toffee

## JUNE JAMBOREE

Mexican Nachos
Cole Slaw
Southern Fried Chicken
Apple Muffins
Cranberry Relish
Deep Dish Apple Pie
or
Individual Grand Marnier Souffles

## JULY JAMBALAYA

Lemon Ice Drink
Yogurt Avocado Dip
Tomato, Roquefort and Pistachio Salad
Jambalaya
Buttermilk Rolls
Blueberry Pie
Pineapple Italian Ice

# FOURTH OF JULY CELEBRATION

Pate´ with Green Peppercorns
Red, White and Blue Salad
Charcoal Broiled Sirloin Steak
Deep-Dish Apple Pie
Spiced Ice Tea

# FOURTH OF JULY GARDEN PARTY

Chilled Mint Pea Soup
Blueberry Mold
Salmon Mousse
or
Poached Salmon with Dill Sauce
or
Barbecued Spareribs
Deep Dish Apple Pie

# AUGUST ASSORTMENT

Iced Coffee
Vegetable Strudel
Poached Trout with Wine Sauce
or
Cheese Souffle
or
Greek Style Fish
Floating Island
or
Flan Flan

# SEPTEMBER SIMMERINGS

Mushroom Salad
Apple Soup
Salad
Chicken Jubilee
Rye Bread with Caraway
Banana Cream Pie
or
Marbled Cheesecake

## OCTOBER OFFERINGS

Chilled Apricot Soup
Curry Walnut Cheese Mold
Potato Rolls
Trout Armendine
Chocolate Chiffon Cake
or
Praline Apple Bread Pudding

## NOVEMBER NATURALS

Pate' with Green Peppercorns
Chicken Tetrazzini
Stuffed Zucchini
Sourdough Bread
or
Limpa Bread
Pecan Pie
or
Jelly Roll

## DECEMBER DEEP DISHES

French Onion Soup
Choucroute Alsacienne
Buttermilk Rolls
or
Sourdough Bread
Chocolate Souffle´

## CANDLELIGHT DINNER

Strawberry-Raspberry Soup
Chicken Croquettes
Croissants
Baked Alaska
or
Individual Orange Souffles

# V.I.P. BRUNCH

Mint Julep
Barbecued Pecans
Cheese Sticks
Quiche
or
Cheese Souffle´
Mexican Coffee
Lemon Crepe Souffle´

# ORIENTAL PICNIC

Mint Tea
Chinese Pork Balls
Rumaki
Chinese Steamed Dumplings
Chicken with Peanuts
or
Smoked Tea Chicken
Rice
Preserved Watermelon Rind
Apricot Bars

# LOW-CALORIE BRIDGE PARTY

Vegetable Soup
Stuffed Rock Cornish Hens
Steamed Asparagus
Creamy Salad Dressing over Lettuce Wedges
Egg Custard

# PATIO PARTY

Chick Pea Spread
Pita Bread
Pickled Scallops
Pickled Crab apples
Chicken Drumsticks (on the grill)
Grilled Salmon
Caesar Salad
Flourless Chocolate Cake
or
Lemon Angel Pie

# FAMILY DINNER

Cheese in Crust
Ham Steak (on the grill)
Oatmeal Bread
or
Banana Bread
Large Layered Salad
White Layer Cake with Candy Cane Frosting

# GRADUATION LUNCH FOR 12-16

Citrus Punch
Tiny German Meatballs
Miniature Hot Dogs
Lamb Curry
Cantaloupe Preserves
Mushroom Salad
Upside Down Cake
Butter Cookies
English Toffee

# NEW ENGLAND STYLE BRUNCH

Pate' with Walnuts
Boston Fish Chowder
Finnan Haddie
English Muffins
or
Steamed Brown Bread
Applesauce
Blueberry Muffins

# SOUTHWEST DINNER

Sangria
Nachos
Gazpacho
Red Chili
Cornbread with Bacon
Jicama Salad
Strawberry Salad
Raspberry Chiffon Pie

# AFTER THE FOOTBALL GAME

Eggnog
Squash Soup
Chili
Cornbread
Chocolate Cupcakes
Oatmeal Cookies

# HIGH TEA

Cheese Ball with Pineapple
Country Style Herb Cheese
Scones
Peach Jam
Apricot Nut Bread
Banana Nut Bread
Marshmallow Meringues
Walnut Torte
Fudge

## LADIES' DAY LUNCHEON

Steamed New Potatoes with Yellow Caviar
Avocado Salad
Salmon Loaf
Brioche
Carrot Cake with Cream Cheese Frosting
or
Prune Spice Cake

## ST. PATRICK'S DAY

Emerald Pear Salad
Irish Soda Bread
Corned Beef and Cabbage
Parslied New Potatoes
Spinach Souffle'
Pistachio Torte
Irish Coffee

# V.I.P. DINNER

Artichoke Squares
Waldorf Salad
Toned Seafood Mousseline with Sauce Vert
Roast Loin of Veal
Babas au Rhum
or
Apple Crepes

# LET'S CELEBRATE

Ceviche
Hot Sherry Consommé
Butterflied Leg of Lamb
Fettucini Alfredo
Herb Bread
Sour Cream Chocolate Cake

# BEVERAGES AND APPETIZERS

# Beverages
## And
# Appetizers

## BEVERAGES

## CREAMY STRAWBERRY NOG _

**Makes 2 servings**

   1 cup strawberries, cut in half
   1 cup strawberry ice cream
   1 egg
½ cup cream or milk

Combine all ingredients in blender or food processor fitted with steel blade. Process 30 seconds or until blended. Pour mixture into tall chilled glasses.

# HOT CRANBERRY PUNCH _____

4 cups water
1/2 pound cranberries
2 cups sugar
1 large orange
1 1/2 teaspoon whole cloves
1 quart apple juice
1 pint apple wine

Combine water, cranberries and sugar in a saucepan. Cut orange into quarters and add. Combine spices in a cheesecloth bag; add. Bring mixture to a boil and simmer for 5 minutes, constantly crushing berries with a spoon. Remove spices and orange sections. Strain cranberry mixture. Set berries aside for use as a relish. Combine liquid and apple juice; heat to boiling. Add apple wine and heat but do not boil. Serve immediately in a heated bowl. Note: When making this punch as a gift, prepare as above except do not add wine. Give punch and wine in separate bottles; include directions for heating and serving.

# MOCK CHAMPAGNE PUNCH

1 can (6 ounces) frozen lemonade
1 can (6 ounces) frozen pineapple juice
1 cup water
3 cups ginger ale, chilled
1 cup sparkling water, chilled

In a tall pitcher or blender, stir together lemonade, pineapple juice, and water until blended. Just before serving, add ginger ale and sparkling water. Stir gently. Serve over ice.

# CLARET CUP

**Makes 8 to 10 servings**

1 quart claret
1 ounce Maraschino liqueur
2 ounces curacao
2 tablespoons fine granulated sugar

Use a large glass pitcher. Combine all the ingredients. Serve with ice in tall glasses and garnish each glass with a long toothpick skewered with a slice of orange, a chunk of pineapple and a sprig of fresh mint, if desired.

# SANGRIA WINE PUNCH _____

**Makes 6 servings**

- 1 bottle, $^4/_5$ quart, sweetened wine
- 3 cups sparkling water
- 1 cup raspberries, fresh or frozen
- 1 cup superfine sugar
- $^1/_4$ cup orange juice

In a chilled pitcher mix red wine and sparkling water. Mix in remaining ingredients. Stir to combine. Serve over ice in tall chilled glasses.

# ORANGE LEMONADE _____

**Makes 8 servings**

- 5 large lemons
- 2 large oranges
- 1 cup superfine sugar
- 2 quarts cold water

Squeeze lemons and oranges, remove seeds. Pour mixture into chilled pitcher. Stir in sugar and water. Stir until ingredients are combined. Refrigerate until ready to serve. Pour over ice cubes in chilled glasses.

# GLOGG _____

2 cups golden raisins
6 whole cardamon seeds, crushed
2 teaspoons whole cloves
2 cinnamon sticks
Grated peel of 1 orange
2¹/₄ cups sugar
6 cups water
1 gallon dry red wine
¹/₂ cup whole unblanched almonds

In a large saucepan, stir together raisins, cardamon, cloves, cinnamon sticks, orange peel, sugar, and water. Bring mixture to a boil over medium heat. Reduce heat, cover to simmer for 20 minutes. Strain, reserving raisins and cinnamon sticks. Return mixture to saucepan. Add wine. Heat until just beginning to simmer. Add almonds just before serving.

# SOUTH OF THE BORDER CHOCOLATE _____

**Makes 4 servings**

    3 **ounces Mexican chocolate, crushed or grated into small pieces for easy melting**
    4 **cups milk**
  1/4 **teaspoon ground cinnamon**
  1/8 **teaspoon ground nutmeg**

In a heavy medium saucepan, over low heat, melt chocolate. Blend in remaining ingredients. Mixture will foam. Pour into individual coffee mugs. Sprinkle with cinnamon and nutmeg.

# CRANBERRY WASSAIL PUNCH

**Makes 18 servings**

- 5 cinnamon sticks
- 10 whole cloves
- 1 quart tea
- 1 quart cranberry juice
- 1 quart apple juice
- 1 cup superfine sugar
- 2 cups freshly squeezed orange juice
- 1 cup freshly squeezed lemon juice

Tie cinnamon sticks and cloves in a cheesecloth bag. In a large heavy saucepan combine all ingredients. Simmer uncovered for 30 minutes. Remove cinnamon sticks and cloves. Pour into a punch bowl. Serve warm.

# CHRISTMAS SYLLABUB

**Makes 16 servings**

- 2 cups milk
- 3 cups cream
- 1 cup superfine sugar
- 1 bottle (⁴/₅ quart) dry white wine
- 2 tablespoons grated lemon peel
- 1 tablespoon grated orange peel
- 5 tablespoons freshly squeezed orange juice
- 5 egg whites
  Ground cinnamon

In a punch bowl, combine milk and cream. Blend in half of the sugar, whisking until the sugar is dissolved. Add dry white wine, lemon peel, orange peel, and orange juice. In a deep mixing bowl, beat egg whites until soft peaks form. Sprinkle remaining 1/2 cup sugar over egg whites. Continue beating until sugar is incorporated and the egg whites form stiff peaks. Fold egg whites into syllabub mixture. Sprinkle with ground cinnamon.

# HOT MULLED WINE ____

**Makes 6 servings**

- ½ cup boiling water
- ½ cup superfine sugar
- 1 small lemon, sliced thin
- ½ teaspoon ground cinnamon
- 5 whole cloves
- 1 bottle (⅘ quart) port wine
  Nutmeg
- 6 cinnamon sticks

In a medium saucepan combine water, sugar, lemon slices, cinnamon, and cloves. Simmer over low heat until sugar dissolves. Stir in port wine and continue simmering 15 minutes. Strain into mugs, garnish with ground nutmeg, and serve with cinnamon sticks.

# ICED COFFEE _____

**Makes 6 servings**

- 5 cups hot coffee
- 4 tablespoons sugar
- $1/2$ teaspoon cinnamon
- $1/4$ cup coffee-flavored liqueur (or to taste)

In a large mixing bowl combine hot coffee, sugar and cinnamon; cool. Pour coffee into 6 tall ice drink glasses, over crushed ice. Drizzle coffee-flavored liqueur over coffee.

# LEMON ICE _____

**Makes 6 servings**

- 1 can, 6 ounces, frozen lemonade
- 4 cups finely crushed ice
- Pointed paper cups

Using a blender or a food processor fitted with a steel blade, pour in contents of frozen lemonade can. Add ice, 1 cup at a time and process. It will be noisy. Add 1 cup at a time until all the ice has been used. Serve immediately in paper cups. Cool and refreshing.

# MOROCCAN MINT TEA

**Makes 6-8 servings**

1/2 cup sugar
3/4 cup packed fresh crushed mint leaves
1 cup boiling water
6 cups hot tea
Fresh mint leaves

In a large bowl combine sugar, fresh crushed mint leaves, and boiling water; stir, and let stand 5 minutes. Strain mixture into a chilled pitcher half filled with ice. Add tea, stir. Pour into individual glasses. Garnish with fresh mint leaves.

# IRISH COFFEE

1/4 cup instant coffee
3 cups hot brewed coffee
1/4 cup Irish whiskey (or use 1 teaspoon brandy extract
1/4 cup sugar
1/2 cup sweetened heavy cream, whipped

Dissolve instant coffee in the brewed coffee. Add whisky and sugar. Pour into large goblets or stemmed coffee cups. Sweeten with additional sugar and top with sweeten heavy cream or thawed frozen whipped topping.

# MINT JULEP _____

**Makes 6 servings**

- 24 sprigs fresh mint
- 6 teaspoons confectioners' sugar
- 3 tablespoons water
- 12 ounces Kentucky Bourbon whiskey
- 6 orange slices
- 6 mint sprigs

For each mint julep arrange 4 sprigs of fresh crushed mint into a tumbler. Mix with 1 teaspoon confectioners' sugar and 2 teaspoons of water. Add ½ glass of shaved ice and 2 ounces Bourbon whiskey. Stir gently until the glass becomes frosted. Decorate with a slice of orange and a mint sprig. Serve with straws.

# CAFÉ BRULOT _____

- 2 tablespoons grated orange peel
- ¾ cup sugar
- 6 cinnamon sticks
- 16 whole cloves
- ½ cup brandy, heated
- ¼ cup orange-flavored liqueur, heated
- 8 cups hot strong coffee

In a heatproof serving bowl, stir together orange peel and sugar; press together so that sugar absorbs orange flavor. Stir in cinnamon and cloves. In a saucepan over low heat, heat brandy and liqueur until warm. Stir in coffee; pour into small demitasse cups.

# CITRUS PUNCH ____

**Makes 16 servings**

    2 cups freshly squeezed orange juice
    2 cups freshly squeezed lemon juice
 1/2 cup grenadine syrup
 1/2 cup sugar
    2 quarts ginger ale, chilled
    1 orange, sliced
    1 lemon, sliced
    1 quart orange sherbet

In a punch bowl combine orange juice, lemon juice, grenadine syrup, and sugar over ice cubes or block of ice. When guests arrive, pour the ginger ale around the sides of the punch bowl. Float scoops of sherbet in the punch.

# DIPS

# YOGURT
# AVOCADO DIP _____

**Makes 8 servings**

2 medium ripe avocados, peeled
1 cup plain low fat yogurt
1 teaspoon Worcestershire sauce

In a medium mixing bowl, mash avocado. Blend in low fat yogurt and Worcestershire sauce. Cover and chill 1 hour. Serve with vegetables and crackers.

# CHUTNEY
# APPETIZER _____

1/3 cup chutney
1/4 pound cheddar cheese, grated
4 English muffins, split

In a small bowl, combine chutney and cheddar cheese; blend well. Spread chutney mixture on English muffins. Place on a cookie sheet. Broil until bubbly, about 1 minute. Cut each muffin into quarters. Serve hot.

# FRESH GARDEN DIP _____

**Makes 8-10 servings**

> 1 package (8 ounces) cream cheese, room temperature
> 1 can (10¾ ounces) condensed tomato soup
> 1 clove garlic, minced
> 2 stalks celery, diced
> 2 sprigs parsley, minced
> 3 green onions, minced
> 1 carrot, grated
> 2 teaspoons white horseradish
> ¼ teaspoon salt and pepper

In a large bowl blend cream cheese and tomato soup. Mix in remaining ingredients; blend well. Cover dip and chill 1 hour. Mix again and serve with crackers or chips.

# SMOKED BEEF DIP __

> 1 teaspoon minced onion
> 1 tablespoon sherry
> 1 8-ounce package cream cheese
> 2 tablespoons mayonnaise
> ¼ cup stuffed olives, minced
> 1 3-ounce package smoked beef, minced

Soak onion in sherry until soft. Add remaining ingredients.

# CAVIAR RING _____

1 jar, 4 ounces salmon caviar
1 jar, 3¹/₂ ounces, whitefish caviar
2 packages, 8 ounces each, cream cheese, room temperature
2 tablespoons freshly squeezed lemon juice
1 green onion, chopped
1 teaspoon Worcestershire sauce
Fresh chopped parsley for garnish

Drain caviars. Cream the cheese and seasonings. Place cheese mixture in center of a serving plate and shape into a circle about 7-inches in diameter and 1-inch thick, similar to a layer cake. Cover 1 4-inch circle in the center with salmon caviar. Cover the remaining 1¹/₂ inches on top and the sides with whitefish caviar. Place small sprigs of parsley around edges of salmon caviar. Garnish base of cheese mixture with parsley. Serve with party breads or melba toast.

# TANGY DILL DIP IN A BREAD CONTAINER

**Makes 12 servings**

   1 round loaf dark rye bread, unsliced
 3/4 cup mayonnaise
 1/2 cup chili sauce
 1/4 teaspoon salt
 1/4 cup fresh dill weed, minced or substitute dried dill weed.
   Raw prepared vegetables: cauliflower, cucumbers, green onions, cherry tomatoes, broccoli and carrots.

Cut top off dark rye bread, hollow out the center. Break bread into one-inch size pieces, reserve. Place rye bread in the center of a serving dish. In a medium mixing bowl, combine mayonnaise, chili sauce, salt, and dill weed. Place dill dip in bread shell, surround the bread with chunks. Arrange cut vegetables around bread. Serve dip with the chunks of bread and vegetables.

# SANDWICH WREATH

20 **party rye slices**
20 **party pumpernickel slices**
   **Butter**

Butter 10 rye slices and 10 pumpernickel slices. Spread deviled ham on buttered rye. Spread Chicken Salad on buttered pumpernickel. Top with remaining bread slices. To form wreath, arrange sandwiches around rim of a large round plate. Decorate with a velvet or satin bow.

# DEVILED HAM SPREAD

1 **can (4½ ounces) deviled ham**
¼ **cup chopped celery**
½ **teaspoon Worcestershire sauce**

In a small bowl, mix together all ingredients.

# CHICKEN SALAD SPREAD

1 can, 4³/₄ ounces, chicken spread
¹/₄ cup chopped apples
1 tablespoon sour cream

In a small bowl, mix together all ingredients.

# GREEN GODDESS DIP

**Makes 8 servings**

1 can (2 ounces) anchovy fillets, drained
2 cloves garlic, peeled and minced
3 green onions, minced
1 tablespoon tarragon vinegar
¹/₂ cup sour cream
1 cup mayonnaise
¹/₄ cup parsley, minced
Salt and pepper to taste

Chop anchovies; place in a deep bowl. Add remaining ingredients; blend thoroughly. Cover and chill. Let stand at room temperature ¹/₂ hour before serving.

# CAVIAR DIP _____

1 jar (2 ounces) red caviar, lumpfish
2 cups mayonnaise
1 tablespoon freshly squeezed lemon juice
1 small onion, minced

Rinse and drain caviar. In a large deep bowl stir together all ingredients, being careful not to crush the caviar. Cover and chill dip 1 hour. Serve with small blini or chips.

# CRAB DIP _____

1 can (7 ounces) crab meat, shredded
2 eggs, hard boiled and peeled
3 green onions, minced
2 teaspoons horseradish
1/4 teaspoon salt
1/4 teaspoon pepper
1 cup commercial sour cream
1 package (3 ounces) cream cheese, room temperature

In a large deep glass bowl combine all ingredients. Cover and chill 1 hour. Serve with crackers or raw pared vegetables.

# SPREADS and PATÉS

## CARAWAY ANCHOVY SPREAD

**Makes 6-8 servings**

- 2 packages (3 ounces) cream cheese, room temperature
- ½ cup butter
- 2 green onions, minced
- 1 teaspoon caraway seeds
- 2 teaspoons capers, drained
- 1 can (2 ounces) anchovy fillets, drained and mashed

In a large mixing bowl combine all ingredients until mixture is smooth and well blended. Cover spread. Chill 1 hour. Serve with celery and carrot sticks.

# BILOXI BUTTER _____

$^1/_2$ **pound cooked, peeled, cleaned shrimp fresh or frozen or 2 cans, 4$^1/_2$ ounces each, shrimp**
$^1/_2$ **cup butter, room temperature**
 2 **tablespoons freshly squeezed lemon juice**
 2 **teaspoons horseradish**
$^1/_8$ **teaspoon nutmeg**
$^1/_8$ **teaspoon liquid hot pepper sauce**
   **Tiny shrimp for garnish**

Thaw, drain and rinse shrimp; grind. Cream butter; add seasonings and shrimp, blend together. Pack shrimp butter into a 1$^1/_2$ cup mold or two 6-ounce custard cups. Chill. Remove shrimp butter from mold and arrange on serving plate. Garnish with tiny shrimp, serve with bread, crackers or vegetables.

# WALNUT ANCHOVY SPREAD _

**Makes 8 servings**

- 1 package (8 ounces) cream cheese, room temperature
- 2 tablespoons anchovy paste
- 1 tablespoon milk
- 1/2 cup black olives, pitted and chopped
- 1/4 cup chopped walnuts

In a deep medium-sized mixing bowl, beat cream cheese, anchovy paste, and milk until well blended. Mix in remaining ingredients. Chill 1 hour; stir. Serve with cocktail bread or raw, pared vegetables.

# MUSTARD BUTTER _

- 1/4 cup butter, room temperature
- 1 tablespoon Dijon mustard
- 2 teaspoons chopped fresh parsley
- 1/4 teaspoon crushed thyme

Whisk together all ingredients in a small bowl. Place in a covered container. Refrigerate until ready to serve. Good on steak or ham.

# ANCHOVY BUTTER __

**¹/₂ cup butter, room temperature**
**¹/₄ cup anchovy paste**

In a deep bowl soften butter. Mix in anchovy paste until well blended. Serve over fish.

# ORANGE HONEY BUTTER _____

**Makes 1¹/₄ cup**

**¹/₂ cup butter or margarine**
**¹/₂ cup honey**
**¹/₂ cup freshly squeezed orange juice**

In a small saucepan melt butter; stir in honey and orange juice, stir occasionally. Continue simmering over medium heat until mixture combines and is warm.

# SPICY CHICKEN LIVER PATÉ

**Makes 8 servings**

2½ pounds chicken livers, cut in half, gristle removed
 ½ cup butter, room temperature
 1 large onion, minced
 ½ teaspoon cinnamon
 1 teaspoon curry powder
 ¼ teaspoon salt
 ¼ teaspoon pepper
 1 cup butter, room temperature
 4 tablespoons sherry

In a medium saucepan combine all ingredients except 1 cup butter and sherry. Simmer, covered for 10 minutes. Puree in a blender or a food processor fitted with steel blade. Blend in the softened butter and sherry. Place the paté in a covered dish; chill until firm. Serve with crackers or French bread.

# LIPTAUER
# CHEESE SPREAD ___

**Makes 8 servings**

- 1 package (8 ounces) cream cheese, room temperature
- 1/2 cup butter, room temperature, cut into 1/2-inch pieces
- 1/2 teaspoon salt
- 1/4 teaspoon pepper
- 1/4 teaspoon caraway seeds
- 2 teaspoons capers, drained
- 3 green onions, chopped
- 1 can (2 ounces) anchovies, drained, chopped
- 1 tablespoon Roquefort cheese or blue cheese

In a deep mixing bowl beat cream cheese and butter until light and fluffy. Blend in remaining ingredients and continue beating until smooth. Serve with crackers or cocktail rye.

# OLIVE NUT SPREAD

**3 cups whole pitted ripe olives, finely chopped**
**1 cup finely chopped walnut pieces, lightly toasted**
**¼ cup mayonnaise**
**¼ teaspoon thyme**
**Black pepper to taste**
**Sliced white bread to brioche**
**Ripe olive slices or wedges**

In a mixing bowl, stir together olives, nuts and mayonnaise. Blend in thyme and pepper. Use mixture as a spread for cut or pinwheel party sandwiches. Garnish sandwiches with olives slices or wedges.

Cut Party Sandwiches: Remove crusts from a thinly sliced standard loaf. Cut bread into squares, triangles, fingers and ribbons. For a more unusual look, cut out with hors d'oeuvre or cookie cutters. Spread with olive mixture.

Pinwheel Sandwiches: Trim crust from a loaf of unsliced bread. Cut into seven ½-inch horizontal slices. Lightly press each slice with a rolling pin. Spread with mixture. Roll up tightly jelly-roll fashion. Wrap rolls in plastic wrap or foil and refrigerate 8 hours or longer before slicing. Cut each roll into 8 to 12 crosswise slices.

Quick pinwheels: Substitute a thinly sliced standard loaf for the unsliced loaf. Proceed as above.

# MIDDLE EAST CHICKPEA SPREAD _

**Makes 8 servings**

- 1 can (15½ ounces) garbanzo beans
- 2 tablespoons freshly squeezed lemon juice
- 2 cloves garlic, peeled, minced
- 2 tablespoons olive oil
- 3 tablespoons Tahini (available in Middle East food stores)

Drain garbanzo beans. In a large mixing bowl combine garbanzo beans, lemon juice, garlic olive oil, and Tahini; blend to a smooth paste. Mound the spread onto a serving dish. Serve at room temperature with warm pita bread.

# OLD WORLD CHOPPED LIVER ____

**Makes 8-10 servings**

    3 medium onions, chopped
  ¼ cup butter
1½ pounds trimmed chicken livers
    Salt, pepper, and garlic salt to taste
  1 teaspoon prepared mustard

Sauté in a large skillet onions in butter over medium heat, stirring occasionally. Mix in chicken livers; continue to sauté until livers are no longer pink. Season with salt, pepper and garlic salt to taste. Mix in mustard. Roughly chop liver mixture. Place in covered container; chill until ready to serve. Serve with pickled gherkins and dark rye bread.

# PATÉ WITH GREEN PEPPERCORNS

10 bacon slices, blanched
3/4 pound beef, chopped
1/2 pound calves' liver, gristle removed, minced
1/4 pound pork fat, ground
3 tablespoons green peppercorns, drained
1 medium onion, minced
1/2 cup cream
3 tablespoons brandy
2 eggs
1/4 teaspoon salt
1/4 teaspoon pepper

Line a small paté terrine, 11 inches x 4 1/2 inches x 3 inches, with overlapping bacon slices. Set aside. In a large deep bowl, combine beef, liver, pork fat, peppercorns, onion, cream, brandy, eggs, salt, and pepper. Mound paté mixture into bacon-lined paté terrine. Fold bacon slices over the top of the terrine. Place terrine in a pan; fill pan halfway with hot water. Bake terrine at 350°F. for 1 1/2 hours. Drain fat off. Cool paté completely; chill overnight. Serve with pared vegetable and crusty bread.

# HERBED MUSHROOM PATÉ

**Makes 6 servings**

- 1 tablespoon butter
- 1 small onion, minced
- 2 tablespoons butter, melted
- 1 pound mushrooms, chopped
- 1/4 cup chopped fresh parsley
- 3 stalks celery, chopped
- 2 eggs, slightly beaten
- 1/2 cup ricotta cheese
- 3/4 cup bread crumbs
- 1 teaspoon chopped fresh basil
- 1/2 teaspoon oregano
- 1/2 teaspoon salt
- 1/4 teaspoon pepper

Heat butter in a large skillet over medium heat. Sauté onions until soft. In a large mixing bowl add onions and remaining ingredients. Mound into a 4-cup mold lined with buttered wax paper. Place mold in a pan half-filled with water. Bake at 350°F. for 1 1/2 hours or until cooked; cool. Invert onto serving dish. Gently remove paper. Chill and serve with dark bread.

# PATÉ
# WITH WALNUTS ____

**Makes 10-12 servings**

- ½ pound bacon, sliced
- 2 tablespoons butter
- 3 ounces walnuts, roughly chopped
- 2 cloves garlic,peeled, minced
- 1 medium onion, minced
- ½ pound veal, minced
- ½ pound chicken, chopped
- ½ pound pork, chopped
- ¼ pound chicken livers, gristle removed, minced
- ½ pound pork fat, diced,
- 2 eggs
- ½ teaspoon cinnamon
- ½ teaspoon nutmeg
- ½ teaspoon, crushed dried savory
- ½ teaspoon salt
- ½ teaspoon pepper
- 1 chicken breast, boned and cut into ½-inch strips

Blanch bacon in large skillet; simmer 5 minutes. Drain; set aside. Lightly sauté walnuts; set aside. Melt remaining butter in skillet; sauté garlic and onion in butter until soft; set aside. In a large mixing bowl, combine veal, chicken, pork, chicken livers, pork fat and eggs. Stir in walnuts, onion mixture, and spices. Arrange blanched bacon strips so they overlap and are draped over a 4-cup terrine or baking dish. Spoon half of paté mixture into prepared terrine. Arrange chicken pieces over bottom layer. Fill terrine with remaining paté. Cover top with bacon strips. Cover with aluminum foil; place in pan, fill halfway with hot water. Bake at 250°F. for 1½ hours or until paté tests done. Remove terrine; drain juices. Cool to room temperature. Chill overnight before serving. Serve with gherkins and crusty French bread.

# HOT CRABMEAT SPREAD _____

1 8 ounce package cream cheese
1 tablespoon milk
6½ ounces crabmeat
2 tablespoons instant chopped onion
½ teaspoon cream-style horseradish
½ teaspoon salt
½ teaspoon pepper

Soften cream cheese with the milk. Combine all ingredients in a baking dish. Bake at 375° for 15 minutes. Serve hot on crackers.

# BACON PATÉ WITH PEPPERCORNS ___

¹/₂ pound lean pork
¹/₂ pound veal
¹/₄ pound cooked ham
¹/₄ pound liver
¹/₄ pound pork fat, diced
2 cloves garlic, crushed
1 teaspoon salt
¹/₄ teaspoon black peppercorns, coarsely ground
¹/₂ teaspoon green peppercorns, coarsely ground
¹/₄ teaspoon allspice, thyme, nutmeg, cloves
3 tablespoons Cognac
4 slices bacon

Chop pork, veal, ham and liver coarsely. Mix with diced pork fat and garlic. Add remaining ingredients except sliced bacon and combine. Mound mixture into a ovenproof ceramic or glass terrine. Cover top of terrine with bacon slices. Place terrine in a larger pan filled halfway with hot water. Bake at 350° for 1¹/₂ hours. Cool. Unmold on serving platter. Garnish with olives and cut vegetables. Serve with crusty bread.

# VEGETABLES

## MARINATED BROCCOLI

**Makes 8 servings**

2 pounds fresh broccoli, broken into floweretes
3 tablespoons freshly squeezed lemon juice
1 bottle (8 ounces) Italian dressing

In a large saucepan cook broccoli in salted water until tender but still firm. Drain broccoli and place on paper toweling. Place broccoli into a glass mixing bowl. Cover with lemon juice and Italian dressing. Cover and chill, 24 hours, stirring occasionally. Drain broccoli and serve with toothpicks.

# ASPARAGUS ROLL-UPS

**Makes 12 servings**

24 asparagus stalks, trimmed to 4 inches long
24 slices white bread
$1/2$ cup butter, room temperature
 4 green onions, minced
$1/2$ teaspoon salt
$1/2$ teaspoon pepper

In a saucepan, cook asparagus until just tender; drain on paper towels, chill. Remove crusts from white bread. With a rolling pin, flatten bread slices. In a mixing bowl, combine butter, green onions, salt, and pepper. Spread over bread slices. Arrange one asparagus stalk on each slice of bread. Roll bread jelly roll style and secure with wooden pick. Brush remaining butter mixture over asparagus roll-ups. Cut each one into thirds. Arrange on cookie sheet. Broil 4 minutes, 4 to 5 inches from the heat.

# CHEESY STUFFED MUSHROOMS

**Makes 8 servings**

- 1 **pound mushrooms with 2-inch caps**
- 2 **tablespoons corn oil**
- 2 **tablespoons butter**
- 1 **small onion, minced**
- 1 **clove garlic, peeled and minced**
- 1/4 **teaspoon salt**
- 1/4 **teaspoon crushed tarragon**
- 1/2 **cup lightly-seasoned bread crumbs**
- 4 **tablespoons freshly grated Parmesan cheese**
- 2 **tablespoons chopped fresh parsley**

Carefully remove the stems from mushrooms. Arrange the caps open side up on a lightly oiled cookie sheet. Mince mushroom stems. Heat oil and butter in large skillet. Add mushroom stems, onion, and garlic; sauté until tender. Mix in salt, tarragon, bread crumbs, and cheese. Mound mixture lightly in the inverted caps. Bake at 400°F. for 12-15 minutes or until the mushrooms are tender and the tops are lightly brown. Top with parsley before serving.

# HERB MARINATED MUSHROOMS

**Makes 10-12 servings**

- 1/2 cup salad oil
- 2/3 cup tarragon wine vinegar
- 2 cloves garlic, minced
- 3 tablespoons sugar
- 1/2 teaspoon salt
- 2 tablespoons water
- 3 tablespoons chopped crushed basil
- 2 tablespoons chopped crushed tarragon
- 3 green onions, minced
- 1 1/2 pounds mushrooms, trimmed
- 1 tablespoon chopped parsley

In a large glass bowl, combine all ingredients; toss gently to mix. Cover with plastic wrap and refrigerate for 3 to 4 hours. Toss marinated mushrooms before serving. This makes a fine addition to a summer picnic.

# FRIED MUSHROOMS AND CAULIFLOWER

**Makes 8 servings**

- 1 cup all-purpose flour
- 1 teaspoon baking powder
- 1/2 teaspoon salt
- 1/2 teaspoon garlic powder
- 1 egg, beaten
- 1/2 cup milk
- 1 tablespoon shortening, melted
- 1/2 pound cauliflower, broken into floweretes
- 1/2 pound small mushrooms, trimmed
  Vegetable oil

In a large mixing bowl combine flour, baking powder, salt, garlic powder, egg, milk, and shortening. Let mixture sit 20 minutes at room temperature; stir. Heat oil to 375°F. in a heavy saucepan or ten-inch skillet. Dip cauliflower and mushrooms into batter. Deep-fry, a few pieces at a time, until golden brown. Drain on paper toweling.

# MUSHROOM ROLLS

**Makes 6 servings**

- 1/2 loaf white bread, crusts removed
- 1/4 cup butter
- 1/2 pound mushrooms, minced
- 3 tablespoons all-purpose flour
- 1/2 teaspoon salt
- 1 cup light cream
- 3 green onions, minced
- 1 teaspoon freshly squeezed lemon juice

With rolling pin, roll each slice of bread until very thin; set aside. Heat butter in a 12-inch heavy skillet; add mushrooms. Sauté for 4 minutes or until soft. Blend in flour, salt, and cream. Continue stirring until mixture begins to thicken. Mix in green onions and lemon juice. Spread mixture evenly on each slice of the bread. Roll up jelly roll style. Arrange seam side down on a cookie sheet. Bake at 400°F. for 10 minutes. Slice and serve.

# LIGHT EGGPLANT APPETIZER

**Makes 8 servings**

- 1 **eggplant**
- 1 **medium onion, minced**
- 2 **cloves, peeled, minced**
- 4 **stalks celery, chopped**
- 1/2 **cup mushrooms, chopped**
- 1 **tomato, peeled and chopped**
- 2 **tablespoons freshly squeezed lemon juice**
- 6 **tablespoons tomato juice**
- 1/2 **teaspoon salt**
- 1/2 **teaspoon pepper**
- 1/2 **teaspoon crushed basil**
- 1/2 **teaspoon crushed oregano**
  **Dark rye bread**

Pierce the eggplant with tines of a fork. Place eggplant on aluminum foil. Bake in preheated oven at 400°F. for 10 minutes. Cool eggplant; peel. Mince eggplant and place in a large mixing bowl. Add remaining ingredients; mix well. Check for seasonings. Cover; chill. Stir before serving. Serve with dark rye bread.

# CAPONATA (EGGPLANT RELISH)

**Makes 8-10 servings**

- 1 large eggplant, cut into $1/2$-inch cubes
- 4 tablespoons olive oil
- 1 medium onion, minced
- 2 cloves garlic, peeled and minced
- 2 green peppers, seeded and chopped
- 4 stalks celery, chopped
- 1 can (8 ounces) pitted black olives, drained, chopped
- 1 cup mushrooms, trimmed and minced
- $1/2$ cup tomato paste
- 2 tablespoons wine vinegar
- 4 tablespoons dark brown sugar
- $1/2$ teaspoon salt
- $1/4$ teaspoon freshly ground pepper

Soak eggplant in salted water for 20 minutes; drain. Pat dry with paper toweling. In a large heavy skillet, heat olive oil. Sauté onion and garlic over medium heat until onion is soft. Add eggplant, green peppers, and celery. Cover and cook, stirring occasionally, for 15 minutes. Add remaining ingredients. Simmer uncovered for 15 minutes. Check seasonings. Transfer caponata to a serving bowl. Cover and refrigerate. Serve at room temperature with pared vegetables.

# CHEESE

## ARTICHOKE CHEESE MELTS

**Makes 8 servings**

- 1 can (8½ ounces) artichoke hearts, drained and cut into quarters
- 1 cup mayonnaise
- 1 cup freshly grated Parmesan cheese
- Crackers

In a large bowl, combine all ingredients except crackers. Spread and arrange artichoke mixture on crackers so that each cracker has one piece of the artichoke on it. Place crackers on a cookie sheet. Bake at 350°F. for 5 minutes or until the cheese is warm.

# APPETIZER CHEESE TRAY

A simple cheese tray is one of the easiest of appetizers to create. Begin with a centerpiece of club cheese in its attractive brown crock. Surround with slices of tangy blue or smoky provolone.

Add cubes of milk brick, Jack or Muenster cheese. Slices or wedges of cheddar and colby cheese, along with nutlike Swiss, add to an interesting selection.

Garnish with crisp vegetables such as radishes, cucumber slices, celery and carrot sticks and olives. Crackers and sesame sticks add sparkle and contrast. For special occasions, make balls of Edam and serve in the cheese's own bright red shell.

# PIMIENTO CHEESE SPREAD

**Makes 8 servings**

- 1 pound grated Cheddar cheese
- 1/4 cup dry white wine
- 1/4 cup mayonnaise
- 1/2 cup chopped pimiento
- 2 tablespoons chopped fresh parsley
- 1 teaspoon grated onion
- 1 teaspoon catsup
- 1/2 teaspoon celery salt

In a large bowl combine all ingredients. Gather together into a ball. Place on a serving plate. Chill 1 hour. Serve with crackers and raw pared vegetables.

# MEXICAN NACHOS _

**Makes 12 servings**

 10  corn tortillas
       Peanut oil for deep-frying
 1/2  pound Cheddar cheese, grated

Cut each tortilla into 6 wedges. In a 10-inch skillet, add oil to a depth of 1 inch. Deep–fry tortilla wedges a few pieces at a time until cooked, about 10-15 seconds; drain on paper toweling. Arrange the wedges in a 9-inch pie plate; sprinkle with grated cheese. Broil for 2 minutes or until the cheese melts. Serve hot.

# CHEDDAR CHEESE BALL

 1  8 ounce package cream cheese, softened
 4  ounces sharp cheddar cheese, grated
 1  tablespoon chopped pimiento
 1/4  teaspoon cayenne pepper
 1/4  teaspoon salt
 1  tablespoon chopped green pepper
 1  teaspoon chopped onion
 1 1/2  teaspoon Worcestershire sauce
       Walnuts

Put cream cheese into small mixing bowl; beat until smooth and creamy. Add remaining ingredients except Walnuts. Blend well. Shape into a ball, roll in nuts and chill.

# OLIVES, ONIONS, AND CHEESE ON CRACKERS ___

**Makes 12 servings**

- ½ pound Cheddar cheese, grated
- 5 green onions, minced
- 3 tablespoons mayonnaise
- 1 cup sliced black olives, drained

In a large deep bowl, combine Cheddar cheese, green onions, mayonnaise, and black olives. Spread cheese mixture on sesame crackers or cocktail rye. Place on cookie sheet. Bake at 350°F. for 10 minutes. Serve hot.

# CHEESE POPCORN __

- Vegetable oil
- Popcorn
- 1 teaspoon paprika
- 1 teaspoon salt or onion or garlic salt
- ⅓ cup grated cheese

Pour oil to depth of about ⅛ inch in pan. Pour in enough popcorn to cover bottom of pan 1 kernel deep. Cover tightly and place over high heat, shaking until corn stops popping. Combine paprika, salt and grated cheese. Sprinkle over hot corn, mixing so that all kernels are coated.

# CHEESE ARTICHOKE SQUARES

**Makes 8 servings**

    2  tablespoons butter
    4  green onions, minced
    2  jars (6 ounces each) marinated artichokes, drained
  1/2  pound sharp Cheddar cheese, grated
    6  crackers, crushed
  1/4  teaspoon salt
  1/4  teaspoon pepper
  1/4  teaspoon Tabasco
    4  eggs, slightly beaten

In a medium skillet, heat butter over medium heat; sauté green onions until softened. In a large mixing bowl, add green onions and remaining ingredients, except eggs. Pour mixture into an 8 x 8-inch baking pan. Top with beaten eggs. Bake at 350° for 35 minutes. Cut into small squares.

# CHEESE PUFFS ____

**Makes 12 servings**

1¼ cups water
3½ ounces butter
½ teaspoon Worcestershire sauce
1¼ cups cake flour
3 eggs
1½ cups Gouda or Swiss cheese, grated

In a medium saucepan, bring water and butter to boiling point. Mix in Worcestershire sauce and flour; remove from heat. With the back of a wooden spoon, quickly blend in flour. Add eggs, one at a time, blending well with each addition. Divide grated cheese in half. Mix ½ of the cheese into batter. Shape mixture into 1-inch balls. Roll balls in remaining cheese. Arrange cheese balls on a cookie sheet. Bake at 375°F. for 25 minutes or until golden. The puffs will almost double in size.

# OLIVE CHEESE BALLS _____

**Makes 3 dozen**

- 1/4 **pound Cheddar cheese, grated**
- 4 **tablespoons butter, room temperature**
- 3/4 **cup all-purpose flour**
- 1/4 **teaspoon salt**
- 1/4 **teaspoon pepper**
- 36 **stuffed green olives or pitted black olives**

In a large mixing bowl, combine cheese, butter, flour, salt, and pepper to yield a soft dough. Pinch off 1 teaspoon of dough and flatten out with fingers. Arrange 1 olive in the center of dough and cover it, sealing well. Arrange cheese balls on cookie sheet. Bake at 400°F. for 12 to 14 minutes.

# CHEESE BUDS _____

- 2 **cups flour**
- 1/2 **pound butter or margarine**
- 1/2 **pound grated cheese**
- **Salt and ground red pepper to taste**

Soften cheese and butter and mix in with the flour. Season to taste. Pinch off small bits (does not raise) and place on a cookie sheet. Top with a pecan half. Bake at 400°F. approximately 15 minutes or until brown. Cool. Makes 60 cheese buds the size of a half dollar.

# TIROPITES (CHEESE TRIANGLES)

**Makes 12 servings**

- 1/2 pound feta cheese, crumbled
- 1/2 pound ricotta or dry cottage cheese
- 3 eggs
- 1 package (1 pound) phyllo (strudel) sheets
- 1/2 pound butter, melted

In a large mixing bowl, combine feta cheese and ricotta cheese; add eggs and blend. Working quickly, cut phyllo dough into 2-inch wide strips. Brush one strip at a time with melted butter. Place 1 teaspoon of filling on corner of the phyllo strip and fold the corner over to form a triangle. Continue folding from side to side, keeping the triangle shape (as if folding a flag). Continue folding until all of the dough has been used. Arrange the triangles on a lightly buttered cookie sheet. Brush once more with the melted butter. Bake at 375°F. for 10 minutes or until cheese triangles are a golden brown. Serve hot.

# CHEESE AND BACON LOG

**Makes 12 servings**

- ³/₄ pound sharp Cheddar cheese, grated
- 8 slices bacon, chopped
- ¹/₂ teaspoon Worcestershire sauce
- 1 medium onion, minced
- 1 teaspoon dry mustard
- 1 tablespoon mayonnaise

In a large bowl, combine all ingredients. On a sheet of waxed paper, roll cheese mixture into a long log 1¹/₂ inches in diameter. Wrap log securely with waxed paper; freeze. When ready to serve, slice and arrange on crackers. Place crackers on a cookie sheet. Broil until cheese has melted.

# CHEESE IN CRUST

**Makes 8 servings**

- 1 11-ounce tube refrigerator biscuits
- 7 ounces Edam cheese

On a lightly floured board, roll out the biscuits, overlapping, forming a 14-inch circle. Remove wax from Edam cheese. Arrange cheese in center of rolled dough. Wrap dough to cover cheese. Place seam side down on cookie sheet. Bake at 350°F. for 30 minutes. Cool 10 minutes before serving.

# CHEESE STICKS ——

**Makes 6 servings**

    4 tablespoons butter, cut into ¹/₂-inch cubes
    4 tablespoons Cheddar cheese, grated
    ³/₄ cup all-purpose flour
    ¹/₂ teaspoon garlic powder
    1 egg
    1 egg white, slightly beaten
    Sesame seeds

In a large mixing bowl combine butter, cheese, flour, and garlic powder. Mix in egg, gather dough together, cover with plastic wrap. Refrigerate 45 minutes. On a lightly floured board roll out dough into a rectangle about 12 inches long. Sprinkle lightly with flour if dough is sticky. Using a sharp knife, cut ¹/₂-inch strips, 3¹/₂-4 inches long. With a spatula, transfer to cookie sheet. Brush with egg white; sprinkle with sesame seeds. Bake at 400°F. for 8 minutes or until cheese sticks are firm. Cool, serve.

# SNAPPY CHEESE BALL

- 1 pound Cheddar cheese, shredded
- 1 package (8 ounces) cream cheese, room temperature
- 1 green bell pepper, chopped
- 1 medium onion, minced
- 1 teaspoon Worcestershire sauce
- ½ teaspoon garlic powder
- 1 cup chopped pecans

Combine all ingredients, except pecans, in a large bowl. Gather mixture together into a ball. Place pecans on a plate; roll cheese ball in nuts. Refrigerate until ready to serve. Serve with crackers and cut raw vegetables.

# BLUE CHEESE MOUSSE _____

**Makes 12 servings**

1½ **envelopes unflavored gelatin**
 ¼ **cup cold water**
  6 **egg yolks**
  2 **cups heavy cream, divided**
 ¾ **pound blue cheese**
  3 **egg whites, stiffly beaten**

In a small bowl, sprinkle gelatin over cold water to soften. In a small heavy saucepan, combine egg yolks and ½ cup of the heavy cream. Cook over low heat; whisk until mixture is creamy and has begun to thicken. Mix in gelatin and continue whisking until gelatin has completely dissolved. Pour mixture into a large bowl; set aside. Crumble cheese through a sieve; add to gelatin mixture. Cool until the mixture is partially set. Whip the remaining cream and fold into blue cheese mixture. Fold in stiffly beaten egg whites. Mound mixture into a lightly oiled 2-quart mold. Chill. When ready to serve, unmold onto a chilled serving platter. Garnish with raw vegetables.

# CLASSIC FONDUE __

**Makes 6 servings**

- 1 large clove garlic
- 2 tablespoons butter
- 1/4 cup all-purpose flour
- 1 1/2 cups milk
- 1/4 teaspoon cayenne pepper or to taste
- 4 cups grated Swiss cheese
- 1/4 cup dry white wine
- 1 loaf French bread, cut into 1-inch cubes

Rub the inside of the fondue pot with garlic. Melt butter; whisk in the flour until smooth. Slowly mix in milk. Stir constantly until the milk thickens. Stir in the cayenne. Gradually add the Swiss cheese, 1/4 cup at a time. Stir until fondue is melted. Blend in wine. Continue simmering for 5 minutes. Serve with French bread and/or cut vegetables.

# SANTA FE CHILE CON QUESO _

**Makes 2 servings**

- 2 tablespoons peanut oil or bacon drippings
- 3 large onions, chopped
- 3 cloves garlic, minced
- 2 cup canned green chilies
- 2 medium tomatoes, chopped
- 1 teaspoon oregano
- 1/2 teaspoon sugar
- 2 tablespoons ground cumin
- 1 pound Cheddar cheese, cut into 1/2-inch cubes
- 1 pound Monterey Jack cheese, cut into 1/2-inch cubes

In a heavy iron skillet or electric skillet, heat peanut oil; add onions and garlic; sauté until onions are tender. Add chilies, tomatoes, oregano, sugar, and cumin. Cover skillet, bring mixture to a boil. Reduce heat to simmer and continue cooking 15 minutes. Add cheese to sauce. Simmer until cheese is melted.

# CAMEMBERT CHEESE BALLS ——

**Makes 8 servings**

- ¹/₂ pound Camembert cheese, room temperature
- 1 package (8 ounces) cream cheese, room temperature
- 1 tablespoon all-purpose flour
- ¹/₂ cup milk
- 1 egg
- 1 cup bread crumbs

In a large deep bowl, combine all ingredients except egg and bread crumbs. Blend until mixture is smooth. With buttered hands roll mixture into one-inch balls. Dip Camembert cheese balls into slightly beaten egg. Roll balls in the bread crumbs. Chill one hour.

# FISH AND SEAFOOD

# EASY TAPENADE ___

**Makes 12 servings**

    2 cans (2 ounces each) anchovy fillets with oil
    4 cloves garlic, peeled and minced
    1/4 cup olive oil
    1/2 cup pitted black olives
      Freshly squeezed juice of 1/2 lemon
    1 can (6 1/2 ounces) tuna fish with oil
      Raw prepared vegetables: celery, cucumbers, carrots, radishes, green peppers, green onions

In a food processor fitted with steel blade or blender, process all ingredients until smooth. Cover and refrigerate 1 hour. Mix tapenade well, serve with cut raw vegetables.

# PICKLED SHRIMP ___

**Makes 10-12 servings**

    2 pounds medium-large shrimp
  1/2 teaspoon salt
    4 tablespoons mixed pickling spices
    2 large onions, sliced into rings
1 1/4 cups salad oil
  3/4 cup wine vinegar
    1 teaspoon salt
  1/4 teaspoon freshly ground pepper
    2 teaspoons capers and juice

Shell, devein, and rinse shrimp. Fill a large saucepan half full with water; bring water to a boil, reduce heat to a simmer. Add shrimp, salt, and mixed pickling spices. Continue simmering until the shrimp are cooked, about 5 minutes. Drain shrimp. Discard spices and water. Arrange shrimp in a deep glass bowl. Combine remaining ingredients in a small mixing bowl. Add marinade to shrimp, toss together. Cover, chill shrimp 24 hours, toss occasionally.

# SHRIMP REMOULADE ___

**Makes 10-12 servings**

   2  **pounds shrimp**
   1  **cup mayonnaise**
   1  **teaspoon crushed tarragon**
   1  **clove garlic, peeled, minced**
   1  **teaspoon dry mustard**
   2  **teaspoons capers**
   3  **small sour pickles, minced**

Shell, devein and rinse shrimp. Fill a saucepan $2/3$ full with water; bring to a boil. Carefully lower shrimp into water. Reduce heat to a simmer; continue cooking only until shrimp have cooked, no longer than 5 minutes. Drain shrimp; arrange in a glass bowl. Combine remaining ingredients in a small mixing bowl. Mix sauce with shrimp. Chill overnight, toss occasionally. Serve cold.

# CRAB DABS _____

1 can, 12 ounces, dungeness crabmeat or other crabmeat, fresh or frozen
2 cans, 6$^{1}/_{2}$ or 7$^{1}/_{2}$ ounces each, crabmeat
$^{1}/_{3}$ cup fine soft bread crumbs
2 tablespoons dry sherry
1 teaspoon chopped chives
1 teaspoon dry mustard
$^{1}/_{4}$ teaspoon salt
10 slices bacon, cut in thirds

Thaw, drain, remove shell or cartilage and chop crabmeat.
Combine all ingredients except bacon. Mix thoroughly, chill 30
minutes. Portion crab mixture with a tablespoon. Shape into
small rolls. Wrap bacon around crab rolls and secure with a
toothpick. Place crab rolls on a broiler pan. Broil about 4-
inches from heat for 8-10 minutes or until bacon is crisp. Turn
carefully. Broil 4-5 minutes longer or until bacon is crisp.

# PICKLED SCALLOPS

**Makes 10-12 servings**

4 tablespoons olive oil
2 tablespoons butter
2 pounds small scallops
1 large onion, sliced into rings
2 cloves garlic, peeled and minced
3/4 cup freshly squeezed orange juice
1/2 cup freshly squeezed lime juice
1/4 teaspoon hot pepper sauce
1 orange, sliced thin, seeds removed
1 lime, sliced thin, seeds removed

In a large skillet, heat olive oil and butter. Sauté scallops lightly until tender. Place scallops in a deep glass mixing bowl. Layer onion rings and garlic over scallops. In a small mixing bowl combine orange juice, lime juice, hot pepper sauce, and orange and lime slices. Pour over scallops. Cover, chill up to 24 hours. Toss occasionally. Serve chilled.

# CAVIAR PIE _____

**Makes 8 servings**

- 6 eggs, hard–boiled, peeled and chopped
- 1/4 pound butter, room temperature
- 1 package (8 ounces) cream cheese
- 1 carton (8 ounces) commercial sour cream
- 1/4 teaspoon Tabasco sauce, or to taste
- 5 green onions, chopped
- 1/4 teaspoon freshly squeezed lemon juice
- 2 jars (2 ounces each) black caviar lumpfish
- 1 jar (2 ounces) red caviar lumpfish
- 1/2 cup chopped fresh parsley

In a large mixing bowl combine hard boiled eggs and butter. Spoon over the bottom layer of a 9-inch pie plate. In a large mixing bowl combine cream cheese, sour cream, Tabasco sauce, chopped green onions and lemon juice. Gently arrange cheese mixture over egg layer. Decorate top of caviar pie with both black and red caviar and the chopped parsley. Refrigerate 1 hour. Serve with thinly sliced dark bread.

# BARBECUED SHRIMP

**Makes 10-12 servings**

1½ pounds shrimp
 1 pound bacon slices, strips cut in half
   Chili sauce

Shell, devein, and rinse shrimp. Pat dry with paper toweling. Wrap each shrimp in a bacon strip, securing it with a toothpick. Dip in chili sauce. Arrange shrimp in a wire barbecue basket on the grill or arrange shrimp on a broiler pan. Broil, 4 inches from heat. Turn shrimp occasionally; broil until done, about 5 minutes.

# CLAM DIP

   1 8 ounce package cream cheese
   1 8 ounce can minced clams
   1 tablespoon mayonnaise
 ½ teaspoon garlic salt
   1 tablespoon Worcestershire sauce
 ¼ teaspoon seasoned salt

Mix all ingredients together, adding clam juice for consistency desired. Refrigerate. This dip can be made a week ahead and refrigerated for later use.

# ESCARGOTS _____

**Makes 4 servings**

- 1 medium onion, minced
- 8 cloves garlic, peeled, minced
- 1 bunch parsley, trimmed, minced
- 1/4 pound butter, room temperature, cut into small pieces
- 2 dozen escargots, drained
- 2 dozen escargot shells

With a food grinder or a food processor fitted with a steel blade, finely chop onion, garlic and parsley. Add butter in pieces and puree. Place one escargot in each shell. Generously mound butter mixture into each shell. Place escargots on cookie sheet; bake at 375°F. for 30 minutes. Serve hot with small forks and French bread.

# SARDINE-STUFFED EGGS _____

- 6 hard-cooked eggs, cut lengthwise in half
- 1 4³/₈-ounce tin boneless, skinless, oil-packed sardines, drained
- 1/4 cup mayonnaise
- 2 teaspoons lemon juice
- Seasoned salt to taste

Carefully scoop out egg yolks. Mash the yolks and mix well with the other ingredients. Refill the whites. These eggs may be prepared 1 to 2 days in advance, wrapped with plastic wrap, and refrigerated.

# HOT OYSTER APPETIZER

**Makes 12 servings**

- 1 tablespoon vegetable oil
- 4 tablespoons butter
- 24 white bread rounds, 1½ inches in diameter
- 1 medium onion, minced
- 2 cloves garlic, peeled and minced
- 4 tablespoons parsley, minced
- ¼ teaspoon salt
- ¼ teaspoon freshly ground pepper
- ½ teaspoon freshly squeezed lemon juice
- 24 medium-large oysters
- 6 strips bacon, cut into 4 pieces each
  Toothpicks

In a 12-inch heavy skillet, melt butter with oil. Sauté the white bread rounds until lightly browned. Drain bread rounds on paper toweling. Sprinkle each round with onion, garlic, parsley, salt, pepper and lemon juice. Arrange an oyster on top of each round. Place a square of bacon over oyster and secure with a toothpick. Place rounds onto a broiler tray. Broil 4 inches from heat until the bacon is crisp. Remove toothpicks, serve hot.

# HERRING WITH GRAPES AND APPLES

**Makes 6 servings**

- 1 pint herring in wine sauce
- 1/2 pint commercial sour cream
- 1/2 teaspoon celery seeds
- 1 cup seedless green grapes, cut in half
- 2 large Red Delicious apples; quartered, cored, and cut into 1/2-inch chunks

In a large deep glass bowl drain herring, cut each piece in half. Blend in remaining ingredients. Cover; chill 2 hours. Serve with dark rye bread slices.

# SMOKY SALMON ___

  1 can (7³/₄ ounces) salmon
¹/₄ cup mayonnaise
  1 tablespoon freshly squeezed lemon juice
  1 teaspoon horseradish
  1 teaspoon grated onion
¹/₄ teaspoon liquid smoke
    Pastry for a 9-inch crust

Drain and flake salmon. Add remaining ingredients, except pastry. Blend together. Divide pastry in half. Roll very thin in circles about 9 inches in diameter. Spread each circle with ¹/₂ cup salmon mixture. Cut into 16 wedge-shaped pieces. Roll in jelly-roll fashion, beginning at the round edge. Place rolls on cookie sheet. Prick top to allow steam to escape. Bake at 350°F. for 10 to 15 minutes or until lightly browned.

# SALMON STEAK TARTARE ___

**Makes 6-8 servings**

   4 eggs
   1 large onion, minced
   1 pound very fresh red salmon fillets, ground
   1/4 teaspoon Tabasco
   3 tablespoons freshly squeezed lemon juice
   1/4 teaspoon salt
   1/4 teaspoon freshly ground pepper
   Anchovy fillets for garnish
   1/4 cup minced parsley
   1 lemon, sliced
   1 large onion, minced

Hard boil eggs, peel, mince; place eggs in deep mixing bowl. Mix in onion and salmon. Add Tabasco, lemon juice, salt and pepper. Shape salmon mixture into a ball; place on a chilled plate. Decorate with anchovy fillets. Cover salmon with parsley. Garnish salmon with lemon slices and minced onion. Serve with crusty bread.

# CLAMS CASINO ____

**Makes 6 servings**

- 6 tablespoons butter
- 1 green bell pepper, seeded, chopped
- 1 small onion, minced
- 3/4 cup bread crumbs
- 1 tablespoon chopped fresh parsley
- 1/2 teaspoon salt
- 1/4 teaspoon pepper
- 1 tablespoon freshly squeezed lemon juice
- 1 1/2 dozen cherrystone clams on the half shell
- 2 slices bacon, cut into 1-inch pieces

In a large skillet melt butter over medium heat. Sauté pepper and onion until soft. Stir in bread crumbs; mix in parsley, salt, pepper and lemon juice. Sauté only until combined. Arrange clams on a cookie sheet. Spoon stuffing lightly over clams. Top with bacon strips. Bake clams at 400°F. for 10 minutes or until bacon is crisp. Serve hot.

# BAKED CLAMS _____

**Makes 8 servings**

> ¹/₂ cup butter, room temperature
> 2 cans (7¹/₂ ounces each) minced clams
> 2 cups flavored bread crumbs
> ¹/₂ teaspoon garlic powder
> ¹/₂ teaspoon oregano

In a 12-inch skillet, melt butter over medium heat. Drain liquid from 1 can of the clams and blend clams into the butter. Add remaining clams and liquid from extra can. Stir in remaining ingredients. Stir to blend. Divide mixture among clam shells. Arrange clam shells on a cookie sheet. Bake at 350°F. for 5 minutes.

# MEAT AND POULTRY

# MINIATURE HOT DOGS

**Makes 8 servings**

  2/3 cup prepared mustard
  1 cup currant jelly
  1 pound cocktail hot dogs

Combine prepared mustard and currant jelly in the top of a double boiler over hot, not boiling, water. Cook over medium heat until mixture is combined and warmed. In a separate saucepan, fill halfway with water; bring to a boil, reduce heat to a simmer. Add hot dogs, simmer 10 minutes, drain. Stir hot dogs into simmering tangy mixture; heat thoroughly.

# CHINESE PORKBALLS

**Makes 6-8 servings**

- 2 cups bread cubes
- 1/2 cup milk
- 1 1/4 pounds ground pork
- 3 green onions, minced
- 2 cloves garlic, minced
- 2 tablespoons soy sauce
- 1 can, 5 ounces, water chestnuts, drained and minced
- 1/4 cup peanut oil

In a small bowl soak bread cubes in milk; squeeze out excess milk. Add bread to ground pork in large mixer bowl. Mix in remaining ingredients except oil. Shape into 1-inch balls. Heat oil in a wok or heavy 12-inch skillet. Brown porkballs over medium heat, drain, serve with sauce.

# TINY GERMAN MEATBALLS _____

**Makes 8 servings**

1¼ pounds ground beef
½ teaspoon salt
¼ teaspoon pepper
1 medium onion, chopped
¼ cup bread crumbs
⅔ cup evaporated milk
3 tablespoons peanut oil
3 tablespoons butter

**Sauce**

1 cup water
2 tablespoons wine vinegar
2 tablespoons tomato sauce
½ teaspoon salt
¼ teaspoon pepper
½ cup gingersnap crumbs
½ cup raisins

In a large mixer bowl combine ground beef, salt, pepper, onion, bread crumbs, and evaporated milk. Form into 1-inch balls, reserve. Heat peanut oil and butter in a 3-quart saucepan and brown meatballs. Combine sauce ingredients. Bring to a boil, reduce heat to simmer; continue cooking 5 minutes. Add sauce to meatballs, combine, simmer for 15 minutes or until meatballs are cooked. Serve warm.

# TANGY MEATBALLS _

**Makes 8 servings**

1¼ pounds ground beef
  2 green onions, minced
  2 tablespoons peanut oil
  1 carrot, grated
  1 cup celery, diced
  2 tablespoons cornstarch
  2 tablespoons water
  1 cup pineapple chunks with ½ cup pineapple juice
½ cup vinegar
  3 tablespoons soy sauce
½ cup sugar
½ teaspoon salt
½ teaspoon pepper
½ teaspoon minced ginger

In a large bowl combine ground beef and green onions, form into 1-inch balls, reserve. In a large saucepan heat oil. Stir-fry carrots and celery in oil until tender. Push vegetables to one side. Fry meatballs until cooked. Dissolve cornstarch with water in a small saucepan. Add remaining ingredients, simmer 5 minutes, stirring often. Add sauce to meatballs; heat until warm.

# SPICY PORK STRIPS ———

**Makes 8-10 servings**

- 1/2 cup soy sauce
- 2 tablespoons sugar
- 3 green onions, chopped
- 1/2 teaspoon powdered ginger
- 1/2 teaspoon salt
- 1/2 teaspoon pepper
- 2 pounds pork tenderloin
- 3 tablespoons sesame seeds

In a large shallow mixing bowl combine first 6 ingredients for a marinade. Turn pork tenderloin in the marinade and marinate for 2 hours. Drain and reserve marinade. Arrange tenderloin on an oiled broiling pan; roast at 325°F. for 45 minutes. Cool 5 minutes. Cut into paper thin pieces. In a medium saucepan heat remaining marinade; pour sauce over hot pork slices. Sprinkle with sesame seeds. Serve with thin bread and small pickles.

# COLD COOKED BEEF SLICES

**Makes 6-8 servings**

- 1/2 **head lettuce**
- 1 **pound sirloin steak, cooked and cut into thin strips**
- 1/2 **teaspoon salt**
- 1/4 **teaspoon ground pepper**
- 2 **tablespoons freshly squeezed lemon juice**
- 1 **cup commercial sour cream**
- 1 **medium onion, sliced into rings**

Decoratively arrange lettuce on a serving platter. Place sirloin steak strips over lettuce. In a small bowl, combine salt, pepper, lemon juice and sour cream; stir. Drizzle sauce over sirloin steak. Sprinkle with onion slices.

# PARTY WIENERS

- **Frankfurters, Vienna sausages or cocktail wieners**
- 1/3 **cup prepared mustard**
- 1/2 **cup currant jelly**

Cut meat in bite-size pieces. Mix mustard and jelly in 1-quart saucepan. Add meat. Cover and cook at low heat for 10 minutes. Serve on toothpicks with crackers. Makes 3/4 cup sauce.

# BAKED SAUSAGES

**Makes 6 servings**

3 eggs
1/4 teaspoon salt
1/4 teaspoon pepper
1/4 teaspoon crushed oregano leaves
1 1/2 cups all-purpose flour
1 1/2 cups milk
1 1/2 pounds sausages, cut into 1-inch pieces

In a large deep mixing bowl beat eggs and spices until light and fluffy. Sprinkle flour over eggs, incorporate. Add milk in a slow steady stream and continue beating until blended. Cover, chill 30 minutes. In a large skillet over medium heat, fry sausages until cooked, turning often. Divide sausages and drippings into individual custard cups. Divide and pour batter over sausages. Bake at 400°F. for 30 minutes. Serve warm.

# APPETIZER PORK RIBS

3 pounds pork loin back ribs, cut into rib sections
1 cup chili sauce
2/3 cup catsup
1/4 cup freshly squeezed lemon juice
2 tablespoons brown sugar
2 teaspoons Worcestershire sauce
1/2 teaspoon garlic salt
   Dash of hot sauce

Place ribs in a baking pan, 13 x 9 x 2 inches. Bake, uncovered, at 425° for 30 minutes. Drain off drippings. Combine remaining ingredients in saucepan; mix well. Cook over medium heat for 5 to 10 minutes, stirring often. Pour sauce over ribs; cover with aluminum foil. Reduce heat to 325° and bake for 45 to 55 minutes, basting once with sauce. To serve transfer to chafing dish and keep warm.

# SMALL STEAK SANDWICHES

**Makes 8-10 servings**

  1 package salad dressing
  1 cup peanut oil
  ½ teaspoon Worcestershire Sauce
2½- 3 pounds beef tenderloin

In a small bowl, combine salad dressing, peanut oil and Worcestershire sauce, stir to blend. Rub tenderloin with marinade. Marinate tenderloin 1 hour at room temperature. Place tenderloin in a shallow baking dish, reserve marinade. Bake uncovered at 325°F. for 20 minutes per pound. Baste occasionally with marinade. Turn once. Cool 5 minutes. Slice thin. Serve with miniature rolls.

# SZECHWAN CHICKEN WINGS

**Makes 8 servings**

3 pounds chicken wings
4 tablespoons peanut oil
2 teaspoons chili paste with garlic (available at Oriental food stores)
6 tablespoons soy sauce
2 tablespoons honey, or to taste

Carefully, with a sharp knife, cut the bony tips off the chicken wings. Reserve wing tips to make chicken stock. Cut the remaining chicken wings into 2 pieces each. Heat peanut oil in a large heavy skillet; sauté chicken wings until they are golden brown. In a small mixer bowl combine remaining ingredients. Pour sauce over the chicken wings, mix well. Cover and simmer the chicken wings 20 minutes, stirring occasionally.

# LIVERS WITH MUSTARD SAUCE

**Makes 6-8 servings**

> 1 pound chicken livers
> 1 cup bread crumbs
> 1 teaspoon garlic powder
> 1/4 cup butter, melted

Cut livers in half. In a medium mixer bowl, combine bread crumbs, garlic and melted butter. Dredge livers in crumb mixture, coating evenly. Arrange coated livers in a shallow baking pan; bake at 350°F. for 30 minutes or until golden brown. Serve hot with mustard sauce.

**Mustard Sauce**

> 1/2 cup powdered mustard
> 1/2 cup water
> 2 tablespoons chives, minced

In a medium mixer bowl, combine all ingredients. Refrigerate 1 hour or until ready to serve.

# RUMAKI ——————————

**Makes 10-12 servings**

12 chicken livers
12 water chestnuts, drained, cut in half
 6 slices bacon, cut in half
½ cup plum sauce (available in Oriental food stores)
½ teaspoon powdered ginger
   Toothpicks

Cut the chicken livers in half. Arrange each half on top of a water chestnut piece. Wrap a strip of bacon lengthwise around the liver and water chestnut. Secure with a toothpick. In a medium mixer bowl combine plum sauce and powdered ginger. Marinate rumaki 45 minutes. Drain rumaki, arrange on a broiler pan. Broil, turning frequently until the bacon is cooked, about 5 minutes. Serve hot.

# BACON-CHESTNUT APPETIZERS ——————

**Makes 30 servings**

15 slices bacon, halved
30 canned water chestnuts

Wrap halved bacon slices around chestnuts. Fasten with toothpicks. Broil until bacon is done.

# OTHER APPETIZERS

# BARBECUED PECANS

**Makes 8 servings**

- 2 tablespoons butter
- 2 tablespoons A-1 sauce
- 2 cups pecan halves
- 1/2 teaspoon coarse salt
- Dash cayenne pepper

In small saucepan, melt butter. Add A-1 sauce and pecans, toss until well coated. Arrange on a cookie sheet; bake at 325°F. for 20 minutes. Shake the pan often to prevent burning. Place in serving bowl; sprinkle with salt and pepper.

# CURRIED NUTS _____

**Makes 4 cups**

        4  cups mixed nuts
        4  tablespoons butter or margarine
        2  teaspoons curry powder
        1  teaspoon salt
     1/4  teaspoon garlic powder
          Cayenne powder to taste

Preheat oven to 325°F. In a rimmed cookie sheet or 9 x 13-inch baking pan, melt butter with seasonings. Mix well. Add nuts, tossing to coat. Bake 30 minutes or until golden brown, stirring occasionally.

# NIBBLE MIX _____

        1  pound butter, melted
        6  tablespoons Worcestershire sauce
        2  teaspoons garlic salt
        2  teaspoons onion salt

Place butter in a baking dish and put in roaster or oven to melt. Stir in Worcestershire sauce. Add small boxes of the following.

| | |
|---|---|
| Rice Chex | Wheat Chex |
| Cheerios | Pretzel sticks |
| 1 can mixed nuts | |

Sprinkle with the garlic and onion salts. Mix. Bake at 225°F. for 1 hour, stirring occasionally.

# TOASTED NUTS ____

**Makes 10-12 servings**

  2 **cups walnut halves**
  2 **cups pecan halves**
  1 **cup superfine sugar**
¼ **teaspoon salt**
  2 **egg whites**
½ **teaspoon cinnamon**
½ **cup butter**

On a cookie sheet toast pecans and walnuts for 8 minutes or until nuts are lightly browned. In a deep bowl beat egg whites until soft peaks form. Sprinkle sugar, salt and cinnamon over egg whites, incorporate. Fold nuts into egg whites. Melt butter in a jelly roll pan with sides. Place nut mixture in pan. Bake at 325°F. for 30 minutes or until all the butter has been absorbed and the mixture is lightly browned; cool. Break into bite-sized pieces. Store in an airtight plastic container or tin.

# CHINESE STEAMED DUMPLINGS

**Makes 24**

1/2 pound ground pork
1/2 cup raw shrimp, shelled, deveined, minced
1/4 cup water chestnuts, drained, minced
 4 Chinese mushrooms, reconstituted in hot water, stems removed, minced
 2 tablespoons soy sauce
1/2 teaspoon salt
 1 pound won ton wrappers (available in Oriental food stores)

In a large mixing bowl combine ground pork, shrimp, water chestnuts, Chinese mushrooms, soy sauce and salt. Cut won-ton wrappers into a circle shape with the top of a glass or a cookie cutter. Place 1 heaping teaspoon of the pork mixture in the center of a won-ton wrapper. Turn in sides of skin, forming pleats, and leaving the top open. Arrange dumplings in the top of a lightly oiled steamer rack. Steam over hot water, for 20 minutes or until pork is cooked. Serve with plum sauce.

# CHEESE BALL _____

1 cup canned pitted ripe olives
2 packages (8 ounces each) cream cheese, room temperature
2 ounces blue cheese
8 ounces grated sharp Cheddar cheese
$1/2$ teaspoon Worcestershire sauce
$1/4$ cup chopped fresh parsley

Chop $3/4$ cup olives. Soften cream cheese. Add blue cheese, grated Cheddar and Worcestershire sauce; beat until smooth and well blended. Mix chopped olives with cheese. Line a small bowl with aluminum foil and pack cheese mixture into it. Cover and chill thoroughly. Lift cheese out of bowl and shape into a ball. Pat chopped parsley over cheese ball. Serve with crisp crackers.

# VEGETABLE CROUSTADES

- 2 tablespoons butter, room temperature
- 24 slices fresh thin-sliced white bread
- 4 tablespoons butter
- 3 tablespoons shallots, minced
- 1/2 pound mushrooms, finely chopped
- 2 tablespoons all-purpose flour
- 1 cup heavy cream
- 1/2 teaspoon salt
- 1 tablespoon fresh parsley, chopped
- 1 tablespoon chives, chopped
- 1/2 teaspoon freshly squeezed lemon juice
- 3 tablespoons freshly grated parmesan cheese
- 2 (12 cups each) mini muffin tins

Preheat oven to 400°F. Coat the inside of muffin tins generously with soft butter. Cut a 3-inch round from each slice of bread. Carefully fit it into muffin tins, pushing center of bread in well and gently molding so it fits securely. Bake 10 minutes, cool. Remove from tins.

**Filling**
Heat butter in skillet; sauté shallots until tender, about 3 minutes. Add mushrooms, cook until moisture has evaporated, about 8-10 minutes. Blend flour in heavy cream and stirring constantly, bring mixture to a boil. When thick, lower heat and simmer 1 minute. Remove from heat, season. Cool, cover and refrigerate. Fill croustades, mound filling slightly. Sprinkle with cheese, dot with butter, place on a cookie sheet. Bake at 350°F. for 10 minutes.

# POTATO PANCAKES _

**Makes 4 servings**

3 large potatoes
1 medium onion, grated
4 tablespoons all-purpose flour
1 teaspoon salt
3 eggs, slightly beaten
4-5 tablespoons butter

In a large mixing bowl grate potatoes. Mix in remaining ingredients except butter. Melt butter in a large heavy skillet over medium heat. Drop pancake batter from tablespoon onto skillet forming pancakes. Cook until firm and with spatula turn pancakes over and continue frying until cooked. Serve warm with applesauce or commercial sour cream.

# TOMATO TEASER ____

1 pint cherry tomatoes
1/2 pound bacon, cooked and crumbled
1/4 teaspoon tabasco

Cut out small hole in the top of each tomato. Combine crumbled bacon with tabasco. Spoon bacon mixture into tomatoes. Serve with food picks.

# ENGLISH MUFFIN PIZZA

**Makes 12 servings**

  6 **English muffins**
12 **slices Mozzarella cheese**
  1 **can (8 ounces) pizza sauce**
  2 **tablespoons vegetable oil**
    **Salt and pepper to taste**
    **Garlic powder**
    **Oregano**
1/4 **cup freshly grated Parmesan cheese**

Split and toast English muffins. Place a slice of Mozzarella cheese on each half; top with pizza sauce, spread with back of spoon. Drizzle lightly with oil. Sprinkle with salt, pepper, garlic powder and oregano. Top with generous helping of Parmesan cheese. Arrange on a cookie sheet. Bake at 375°F. for 10 minutes, until the cheese bubbles.

# PASTIES _____

**Makes 6 large or 12 small pasties**

**Pastry**
    3 cups flour
    1 teaspoon salt
    ³/₄ cup butter, cold, cut into small pieces
    ¹/₄ cup lard, cold, cut into small pieces
  6-7 tablespoons ice water

**Filling**
    2 cups each finely diced lean veal and peeled pota-
      toes
    1 cup each, coarsely chopped onions; white or yellow
      turnips
    1 teaspoon salt
    1 teaspoon each ground marjoram, thyme, minced
      fresh parsley
  ¹/₂ teaspoon ground pepper
    2 tablespoons butter
    1 egg, lightly beaten

**Pastry**

Mix flour and salt in a large bowl, cut in butter and lard until mixture resembles coarse crumbs. Stir in 6 tablespoons ice water, 1 at a time, until dough gathers easily into a ball; add remaining water only if necessary. Cover and chill 1 hour.

**Filling**

Mix all ingredients except butter and egg in a large bowl. Roll pastry on lightly floured surface to ⅛-inch thickness. Cut pastry into 6-inch rounds, using a bowl or cutter as a guide. Heap ½ cup of the filling in the center of each pastry round. Dot top of filling with ½ teaspoon butter. Brush edges of pastry with warm water, and fold pastry over filling to make a half-moon shape. Press seams by hand, then with fork tines to seal. Cut a small slit in the top of each pastry. Brust tops with beaten egg. Bake on ungreased baking sheet at 400°F. for 10 minutes. Reduce temperature to 350°F. and bake 20-30 minutes or until golden brown. Cool on a wire rack, 5 minutes.

# HAM DEVILED EGGS

6 **hard-boiled eggs**
1 **can (2¼ ounces deviled ham or ¼ cup finely chopped cooked ham**
3 **tablespoons mayonnaise**
1 **tablespoon prepared mustard**
⅛ **teaspoon onion powder**
 **Paprika**

Cut eggs in half; remove yolks and mash well. Add ham, mayonnaise, mustard and onion powder. Mix thoroughly. Spoon mixture into whites. Sprinkle with paprika.

# VEGETABLE STRUDEL

4 tablespoons bacon drippings
1 medium onion, sliced thin
1 small head cabbage, shredded
6 strips bacon, fried, crumbled, reserve drippings
4 tablespoons chopped fresh dill weed
4 tablespoons chopped fresh parsley
2 eggs, hard-boiled, peeled and chopped
$1/2$ teaspoon salt
$1/4$ teaspoon pepper
$1/2$ pound phyllo dough, available at gourmet food stores
6 tablespoons butter, melted
$3/4$ cup bread crumbs

In a deep large skillet heat bacon fat over medium heat. Sauté onion and cabbage over low heat stirring often until the cabbage and onions are soft and the liquid has evaporated, about 15 minutes. Place vegetables in a deep mixing bowl, mix with bacon, dill weed, parsley and eggs. Combine and season with salt and pepper; cool. Working quickly, butter and layer 6 sheets of phyllo, place on cookie sheet sprinkle with bread crumbs. Spread cabbage evenly down the middle of phyllo, roll up the dough, jelly roll style, seam side down. Bake at 350°F. for 45 minutes.

# QUICHE _____

**Makes 6-8 servings**

**Crust**
    6 **tablespoons shortening**
    1 **cup all-purpose flour**
  1/2 **teaspoon salt**
    3 **tablespoons ice water**

In a large deep bowl combine flour and salt. With a pastry knife cut in the shortening. Sprinkle with ice water, 1 tablespoon at a time until mixture gathers together. Form dough into a ball. Cover with plastic wrap, refrigerate thirty minutes. Roll dough on a lightly floured board until it is one inch larger than a nine-inch round pan. Line bottom and sides of pan with the pastry. Prick over bottom of pan. Bake pie crust at 350°F. for 10-12 minutes.

**Filling**

    4 **ounces Swiss cheese, grated**
    1 **jar (2 ounces) green pitted olives, sliced**
    4 **eggs**
    1 **cup half-and-half**
  1/2 **teaspoon salt**
  1/4 **teaspoon pepper**
    1 **9-inch unbaked pie crust**

Sprinkle bottom of pie crust with Swiss cheese and sliced olives. Beat eggs, mix in cream, salt and pepper. Pour over cheese. Bake 425°F. for 15 minutes. Reduce temperature to 375°F. and continue baking 25 minutes longer. Cool slightly, cut into wedges.

# CREAM CHEESE BONBONS

1 package (8 ounces) cream cheese, room temperature
2 tablespoons dry white wine
2 tablespoons crumbled blue cheese
$1/8$ teaspoon curry powder
$1/2$ cup chopped walnuts
$1/2$ cup toasted sesame seeds

In a large mixing bowl combine cream cheese, wine, blue cheese and curry powder. Shape mixture into 1-inch balls. Roll each ball in either the walnuts or sesame seeds. Serve with sliced fruit or crackers.

# SMOKY BEEF DIP

2 cups cottage cheese
1 $3^{1}/_{2}$-ounce package smoked sliced beef, finely chopped
1 tablespoon minced onion
1 tablespoon chopped parsley
  Freshly ground pepper to taste

Beat cottage cheese until fairly smooth. Add beef, onion, parsley and pepper. Blend well. Serve with crisp vegetables such as carrot, green pepper and celery sticks.

# HERBED DRUMSTICKS _____

1 cup crushed herb stuffing mix
2/3 cup grated Parmesan cheese
1/4 cup chopped parsley
1 clove garlic, minced
8 chicken drumsticks
1/3 cup melted butter

Wash and dry the drumsticks. Combine first 4 ingredients. Dip chicken in the melted butter, then roll in crumbs. Arrange chicken, skin side up, on greased baking pan. Sprinkle remaining butter and crumbs over chicken. Bake at 375° for about 1 hour. Do not turn chicken.

# FRENCH-STYLE APPETIZER _____

1 12 ounce can luncheon meat
8 tablespoons butter or margarine
1/2 teaspoon tabasco
1/4 cup minced parsley
    (or 1 teaspoon garlic powder)
1 package party rye bread

Cut luncheon meat into thin 2-inch squares. Mix softened butter with tabasco, parsley, garlic. Spread thickly on bread. Top with luncheon meat. Cover with foil. Refrigerate until butter hardens. Serves 12.

# SOUPS

# —Soups—

## SUGGESTED SOUP GARNISHES

Crumbled bacon

Chopped parsley

Minced chives

Hot dog coins, sliced hot dogs

Lemon slices

Lime slices

Orange slices, cut in half

Crumbled potato chips

Croutons

Garlic croutons

Toasted sliced almonds

Spoonful of commercial sour cream

Grated Cheddar cheese

Grated Parmesan cheese

Thinly sliced black olives

Thinly sliced pimento-stuffed olives

French Fried onions

Popcorn

Broad Leaf Parsley

Tortilla chips crumbled

Dumplings

# STOCKS AND BROTHS

# HOT SHERRY CONSOMMÉ

**Makes 6 servings**

- 2 11-ounce cans, consommé
- 1 cup water
- ¼ cup dry sherry

Combine all ingredients in a large bowl and transfer to a warm serving dish. Ladle consomme into glasses at the table. Serve with cheese straws and candied nuts.

# BASIC CHICKEN STOCK

**Makes 6 servings**

    4 pounds chicken necks and backs
    3 cloves
    1 large onion, sliced
    2 stalks celery, sliced
    2 carrots, sliced
    3 sprigs parsley
1¹/₂ teaspoons salt
  ¹/₄ teaspoon pepper

Wash necks and place in a stock pot. Place cloves in onion. Add vegetables, spices, and water to cover chicken pieces. Cover and simmer chicken stock for 2¹/₂ hours, or until chicken is cooked. Strain stock and return stock to pot. Remove fat. Continue to simmer 20 minutes. Check for seasoning.

# CHICKEN STOCK WITH PUREED VEGETABLES

**Makes 8 servings**

- 1 chicken, 3 pounds
- 1 large onion, sliced thinly
- 2 carrots, sliced
- ¼ cup chopped fresh parsley
- 4 stalks celery with leaves, chopped
- 2 teaspoons salt
- ½ teaspoon white pepper
- 1 small bell pepper, seeded and sliced
- 1 cup cooked rice

Clean and wash chicken thoroughly in cold running water. Place chicken in a stock pot, cover with cold water. Bring mixture to a boil. Skim soup if necessary. Add onion, carrots, parsley, celery, salt, pepper, and bell pepper; simmer for 1 hour. Occasionally stir soup. Remove chicken, reserve for chicken salad. Strain through cheesecloth. Puree carrots and onions and return to soup. Check soup for seasonings, simmer 15 minutes. Serve with cooked rice and extra shredded white chicken meat.

# BASIC DUCK STOCK

**Makes 6 cups stock**

**Cracked carcasses, necks and giblets from 2 ducks**
**1 onion, sliced**
**3 carrots, sliced**
**3 ribs celery, sliced**
**2 cloves garlic, crushed**
**3 bay leaves**
**1/2 teaspoon crushed thyme**
**3 stalks parsley**
**1 teaspoon black peppercorns, crushed**

In a large roasting pan, roast duck carcasses in 375° oven for 30 minutes. In a large stock pot combine all ingredients and 2 quarts water. Bring soup to a boil, reduce heat to simmer, continue cooking uncovered 3 hours. Skim soup as necessary. Strain soup through a double layer of cheesecloth. Place in a covered container and refrigerate or freeze until needed.

# BASIC FISH STOCK _____

**Makes 1 quart**

2 pounds fish (bones, heads, and skins)
1 large onion, sliced
2 carrots, sliced
3 stalks celery, sliced
2 bay leaves
1/2 teaspoon ground thyme
1/4 teaspoon peppercorns, cracked

Combine all ingredients in a large stock pot, cover with 2 quarts water and bring to a boil, reduce heat to simmer. Continue cooking uncovered for 1 hour. Skim occasionally. Strain stock through a double thickness of cheesecloth.

# CLAM BROTH _____

**Makes 2 servings**

1 1/2 dozen clams in shells
3 stalks celery with leaves, sliced
1/2 teaspoon salt
1/4 teaspoon pepper

Wash and scrub the clams. Place clams in a large saucepan. Cover clams with 2 1/2 cups water, celery, salt, and pepper. Cover and steam with high heat for 15 minutes. Strain broth through cheesecloth. Return to saucepan; season and serve.

# BASIC BEEF STOCK

**Makes 8 servings**

   3-4 **pounds beef bones**
   1 **pound beef shank, cut into 2-inch pieces**
   3 **stalks celery, sliced**
   2 **carrots, sliced**
   1 **onion, sliced**
   3 **sprigs parsley**
   1 **teaspoon salt**
   1/2 **teaspoon black peppercorns, cracked**

In a large stock pot, combine all ingredients and 3 quarts water. Bring soup to a boil, skim off any scum as it may rise to the surface. Reduce soup to a simmer, cover and continue cooking for 2 hours. Skim soup again, remove meat and bones. Strain soup through cheesecloth and discard vegetables and spices. Place in covered container and refrigerate or freeze until ready to use.

# BASIC VEAL STOCK

**Makes 8 servings**

4-5 pounds veal knuckles
  2 bay leaves
$1/2$ teaspoon thyme
  5 whole cloves
$1/2$ teaspoon salt
  1 teaspoon white peppercorns, crushed
  1 large onion, sliced
  4 ribs celery, coarsely chopped
  1 large carrot, sliced

Brown veal knuckles in a large roasting pan at 375° for 20 minutes. Place browned veal knuckles in a stock pot. Add remaining ingredients and 4 quarts water. Continue cooking, uncovered, for $2^1/2$ hours or until liquid is reduced in half. Strain stock, cool, refrigerate until ready to use.

# CHILLED SOUPS

## GAZPACHO

**Makes 10 servings**

- 2 **medium cucumbers**
- 2 **large green peppers**
- 3 **medium tomatoes**
- 2 **medium Spanish onions**
- 1 **green onion**
- 4 **cloves garlic**
- 3 **cups tomato juice**
- 3 **cups V-8 juice**
- 2 **tablespoons freshly squeezed lemon juice**
- ½ **teaspoon salt**
- ¼ **teaspoon freshly ground pepper**
- 1½ **teaspoons chopped dill weed**
- 4 **dashes Tabasco**
- 1½ **teaspoons olive oil**
- **Garlic croutons for garnish**

Peel cucumber, halve lengthwise, seed, mince. Halve and seed green peppers, chop. Peel tomatoes after dipping in boiling water to loosen skin, chop. Mince onions and garlic. Combine vegetables in a large deep mixing bowl. Add tomato juice, V-8 juice, lemon juice, salt, pepper, dill weed, Tabasco and olive oil. Mix well, cover and chill overnight. Stir and serve garnished with garlic croutons.

# GAZPACHO WITH OLIVES

**Makes 8 servings**

- 1 medium onion, minced
- 3 cloves garlic, peeled and minced
- 3 table tomatoes, peeled, seeded, and minced
- 1 cucumber, peeled, seeded, and minced
- 1 green bell pepper, seeded and chopped
- 1/2 teaspoon Worcestershire sauce
- 1 teaspoon freshly squeezed lemon juice
- 1 quart tomato juice
- 1/2 cup black olives, pitted and chopped
- 2 cups seasoned croutons

In a large deep bowl combine all ingredients except olives and seasoned croutons. Cover and refrigerate until ready to serve. Stir: pour soup into coffee mugs. Garnish with chopped black olives and seasoned croutons.

# ANDALUZ GAZPACHO

**Makes 8 servings**

- 4 large tomatoes, peeled and quartered
- 2 cucumbers, peeled and sliced
- 1/2 green pepper, seeded and sliced
- 1 small onion, peeled and quartered
- 2 cloves garlic
- 4 tablespoons olive oil
- 3 tablespoons wine vinegar
- 6 slices white bread, trimmed and cubed
- 1/2 teaspoon pepper
- 1 cup garlic croutons
- 1/2 cup green onion, chopped
- 1/2 green pepper, minced
- 1 large tomato, chopped

Puree first nine ingredients in food processor with steel blade or in a blender with 1 cup water. Puree until smooth. Place soup in deep bowl. Cover; chill. The soup will be thick but not solid. Serve in cups with croutons and vegetable garnish.

# CALIFORNIA AVOCADO SOUP

**Makes 8 servings**

- 6 large ripe avocados, peeled and boned
- 6 cups chicken bouillon
- 2 cups heavy cream
- 1/4 teaspoon salt
- 1/4 teaspoon freshly grated nutmeg
- Toasted slivered almonds for garnish

Puree the avocados in a food processor fitted with steel blade or in a blender with half of the chicken bouillon. Pour mixture into a deep mixing bowl, blend in remaining bouillon and cream. Season with salt and nutmeg. Cover and chill. When ready to serve, pour into individual bowls and garnish with slivered almonds.

# JELLIED MUSHROOM SOUP _

- 1 pound mushrooms
- 4 cups consommé
- 2 envelopes unflavored gelatin
- 1/2 teaspoon salt
- 1/4 teaspoon pepper
- 1/4 teaspoon crushed tarragon
- 1/4 cup sherry
- Watercress leaves

Trim and mince mushrooms. In a large saucepan, add consommé and mushrooms; simmer for 30 minutes. Place gelatin in 1/2 cup water, allow to stand 5 minutes to dissolve; stir into the hot soup. Stir in salt, pepper, crushed tarragon, and sherry; combine. Pour soup into individual small soup bowls, refrigerate until set. Garnish with watercress leaves.

# CHILLED CREAM OF ZUCCHINI SOUP

**Makes 8 servings**

- 3 tablespoons butter or margarine
- 1 large onion, sliced thin
- 3 medium zucchini, sliced
- 1/2 teaspoon garlic
- 1/2 teaspoon ginger
- 1/2 teaspoon salt
- 1/4 teaspoon pepper
- 3 tablespoons chopped fresh dill weed
- 4 large lettuce leaves, trimmed
- 2 cups milk
- 2 cups half-and-half
- 1 cup commercial sour cream
- Chopped fresh dill weed for garnish

In a large saucepan, melt butter. Sauté onion and zucchini for 2 minutes. Add 1 cup water, garlic, ginger, salt, pepper, dill weed, and lettuce leaves. Simmer 5 minutes. Pureé vegetables in a food processor fitted with a steel blade or a blender. Pour in milk and half-and-half; blend. Cover and chill until ready to serve. Garnish with a dollop of sour cream and fresh dill weed.

# CHILLED CARROT SOUP

**Makes 8 servings**

  4 **tablespoons butter**
  1 **pound carrots, sliced**
  1 **large onion, sliced thin**
  $1/2$ **teaspoon garlic powder**
  $1/2$ **teaspoon salt**
  $1/2$ **teaspoon pepper**
  1 **large potato, peeled and cubed**
  3 **cups cream or half-and-half**
    **Croutons for garnish**

In a large heavy saucepan, melt the butter. Sauté carrots and onion 1 minute over medium heat. Stir in garlic powder, salt, pepper, potato and 2 cups water. Continue cooking, covered, until the vegetables are tender; cool. Puree vegetables in a food processor fitted with a steel blade or in a blender. Add half-and-half; combine. Pour carrot soup into a deep bowl, cover and chill until ready to serve. Garnish with croutons.

# JELLIED MADRILENE

**Makes 8-10 servings**

- 1 small green pepper, seeded and sliced
- 1 medium onion, sliced
- 1 small carrot, sliced
- 2 stalks celery, sliced
- 1/2 teaspoon salt
- 1/4 teaspoon celery salt
- 1/4 teaspoon white pepper
- 1/8 teaspoon grated nutmeg
- 1/2 cup boiled ham, cubed
- 1/4 pound ground beef
- 3 egg whites
- 3 envelopes unflavored gelatin
- 3 cans tomatoes and liquid
- 3 cups chicken broth
- 1/2 lemon

In a stock pot place vegetables, seasonings, meat, and egg whites. Dissolve gelatin in 1/2 cup cold water, add to stock pot. Add tomatoes and chicken broth; bring mixture to a boil slowly. Reduce heat to a simmer and continue cooking for 1 1/2 hours. Remove from heat. Squeeze lemon juice over soup. Strain soup through cheesecloth into a large deep bowl. Adjust seasonings. When soup is cool, place in refrigerator until jellied and chilled. Serve cold.

# SORREL SOUP

**Makes 8-10 servings**

1 **pound fresh sorrel or spinach**
6 **green onions, chopped**
1 **teaspoon salt**
 **Sour salt to taste**
1 **egg, slightly beaten**
1 **cup commercial sour cream**

Wash and chop sorrel, place in a saucepan with 1 cup of water. Simmer 10 minutes. Place sorrel in a large saucepan. Add green onions, 2 quarts water, and salt; bring mixture to a boil. Reduce heat to a simmer, partially cover and continue cooking for 15 minutes. Taste; soup should be tart. If more tartness is desired add 2 crystals of sour salt. Simmer 10 minutes. Remove 1 cup of soup, combine it with the egg. Return egg to soup, stir to blend. Cover soup, chill. Stir in sour cream. Serve with hard-boiled eggs.

# CHILLED MINT PEA SOUP

**Makes 8 servings**

- 3 cans, 10½ ounces each, split pea soup
- ¼ teaspoon salt
- ¼ teaspoon fresh ground pepper
- ½ teaspoon chopped fresh mint leaves
- 3 cups unflavored yogurt
- Flavored croutons for garnish

In a blender, combine all ingredients except yogurt; blend until smooth. Place mint pea soup in a deep mixing bowl. Cover; refrigerate until ready to serve. Just before serving; stir in yogurt. Pour into coffee mugs, garnish with croutons.

# BLENDER WATERCRESS SOUP

**Makes 6 servings**

- 2 cups trimmed watercress, chopped
- 1 cup chicken or turkey stock
- 1 cup half-and-half
- ½ teaspoon curry powder
- 3 stalks celery, sliced
- Commercial sour cream for garnish

In a food processor fitted with a steel blade, or in blender, combine all ingredients and puree. Place in a covered container; chill until ready to serve. Stir; pour into small bowls. Garnish with sour cream.

# INSTANT BEET BORSCHT

**Makes 6 servings**

```
    4 eggs
    1 jar, 32 ounces, beet borscht
    1 can, 8¹/₄ ounces, sliced beets, include juice
    3 large potatoes, peeled, cubed, boiled, drained
1¹/₂ cups commercial sour cream
```

In a deep mixing bowl, beat eggs until light. Puree beet borscht and sliced beets, include juice. Mix with eggs, cover, chill until ready to serve. Serve instant beet borscht in a deep bowl, chilled, with hot potatoes and sour cream.

# OLD-FASHIONED SPINACH BORSCHT

**Makes 8 servings**

>  5  large beets, grated
>  1  can, 8 ounces, spinach or beet greens, chopped
>  1  can, 16 ounces, tomatoes and juice
>  1  medium onion, minced
>  1/4  cup superfine sugar
>  3  tablespoons freshly squeezed lemon juice
>  1/2  teaspoon salt
>  1/4  teaspoon pepper
>  1  cup commercial sour cream

In a large saucepan combine beets, spinach, tomatoes and onion. Stir in 5 cups water. Cover and cook until the beets are tender. Add remaining ingredients except sour cream; simmer 15 minutes. Check seasoning, add more lemon juice or sugar as desired. Place soup in a covered container and chill until ready to serve. Serve in a deep soup bowl with sour cream.

# TANGY CUCUMBER BEET SOUP

**Makes 6 servings**

- 2 cucumbers, peeled, seeded, and pureed
- 3 cups buttermilk
- 1 cup julienne sliced beets
- 1/2 cup beet juice
- 1/2 cup commercial sour cream
- 1/4 teaspoon salt
- 1/4 teaspoon pepper
- 6 celery stalks with leaves for garnish

In a food processor fitted with a steel blade, or a blender, puree and combine all ingredients. Place in a covered container. Chill 2 hours. Serve in a glass with a stalk of celery for garnish.

# POLISH BORSCHT

**Makes 8 servings**

- 6 cups beef bouillon
- 6 large cooked beets, pureed
- 1 tablespoon tarragon vinegar
- 3 dill gherkins, chopped
- 1/4 teaspoon salt
- 1/4 teaspoon pepper
- Commercial sour cream for garnish

In a large heavy saucepan add bouillon and pureed beets, simmer 10 minutes, uncovered. Blend in tarragon vinegar and gherkins. Season with salt and pepper. Pour soup into a covered container, chill until ready to serve. Garnish with sour cream.

# CREAMY CUCUMBER SOUP

**Makes 8 servings**

- ¼ cup butter
- 3 large cucumbers, peeled, seeded, chopped
- 2 large leeks, sliced
- 2 tablespoons cornstarch
- 3 cups chicken stock
- ½ teaspoon salt
- ¼ teaspoon pepper
- Grated nutmeg, to taste
- 2 cups half-and-half
- 1 tablespoon crushed chopped basil for garnish

In a large saucepan, melt butter; sauté cucumbers and leeks until tender. Gradually stir in cornstarch, mix until absorbed. Blend in chicken stock. Continue cooking over medium heat until soup is slightly thickened. Blend in salt, pepper, and nutmeg. Pour into a deep mixing bowl, cover, chill. When ready to serve blend in the half-and-half. Serve garnished with chopped basil.

# CHILLED SQUASH-APPLE SOUP

**Makes 8 servings**

- 5 tablespoons butter or margarine
- 1 large onion, sliced
- 2 pounds butternut squash, peeled, seeded, and cubed
- 3 tart cooking apples (Rome or Granny Smith) peeled, cored, and grated
- 4 cups chicken or turkey stock
- 1/2 teaspoon crushed marjoram
- 1/2 teaspoon salt
- 2 cups heavy cream, beat until peaks form
- 2 sweet apples, cored and sliced thin

Heat butter in a stock pot, sauté onion and squash until tender. Puree squash and return to stock pot. Mix in apples, chicken stock, marjoram and salt; simmer 30 minutes, stirring occasionally. Place in a covered container, chill until ready to serve. Fold in heavy cream; pour soup into tall glasses. Garnish with apple slices.

# EASY HARVEST FRUIT SOUP

**Makes 6 servings**

- 1 can, 29 ounces, peach slices
- 1 can, 8 ounces, crushed pineapple
- 1 cup combined juice from drained fruits
- 1 pint fresh strawberries
- 1 egg
- 3 tablespoons freshly squeezed lemon juice
- 1 teaspoon lemon zest
- 1/2 teaspoon cinnamon
- 1/4 teaspoon freshly grated nutmeg
- Strawberries for garnish
- Mint sprigs for garnish

Drain canned fruit, reserving 1 cup of the juice. Wash and hull the strawberries. Puree fruit and remaining ingredients in a food processor fitted with steel blade or a blender. Place fruit soup in a large deep bowl, cover, chill. Serve in cups or shallow soup bowls garnished with a fresh strawberry and a sprig of mint.

# ELEGANT STRAWBERRY RASPBERRY SOUP

**Makes 8 servings**

2 quarts strawberries
1 pint raspberries
1 cup freshly squeezed orange juice or water
1¼ cups superfine sugar
2 teaspoons orange zest
2 tablespoons freshly squeezed lemon juice
2 cups sweet red wine
1 cup sweetened whipped cream

Wash, hull and drain strawberries. Puree strawberries and raspberries; place in a deep mixing bowl. In a small saucepan, combine orange juice and sugar; cook over medium heat until the sugar dissolves. Continue cooking for 5 minutes, reducing the syrup. Add zest and lemon juice. Add syrup to pureed fruit, mix in wine; cover and chill until ready to serve. Stir, serve with a dollop of sweetened whipped cream.

# SPICED SOUR CHERRY SOUP

**Makes 6 servings**

- 1 cup superfine sugar
- 1/2 teaspoon cinnamon
- 3 1/2- 4 cups pitted sour cherries or drained, canned sour cherries
- 2 tablespoons cornstarch
- 1 cup heavy cream
- 1 cup dry red wine
- 6 cinnamon sticks

In a large saucepan, combine 3 cups water, sugar, and cinnamon; bring mixture to a boil. Mix in cherries. Reduce heat to simmer, cover and continue cooking for 45 minutes. Remove one-half cup of soup, whisk in cornstarch, return to soup. Stirring constantly, bring soup almost to a boil. Reduce heat to simmer and continue cooking 2 minutes or until soup is clear and slightly thickened. Pour soup into a covered container, chill. When ready to serve stir in heavy cream and red wine. Serve with cinnamon sticks.

# COOL DRIED FRUIT SOUP

**Makes 8 servings**

1 package, 16 ounces, pitted dried prunes
1 package, 8 ounces, dried apricots
1 can, 6 ounces, frozen orange juice concentrate
2 teaspoons lemon zest
2 tablespoons instant tapioca
1 3-inch cinnamon stick
½ cup superfine sugar
Commercial sour cream

In a large saucepan combine prunes, apricots, orange juice, and 5 cups water. Allow fruit to stand 1 hour. Add lemon zest, tapioca, cinnamon stick, and sugar. Cover and simmer fruit for 10 minutes. Remove and discard cinnamon stick; cool. Serve in glass bowls with sour cream.

# CLASSIC VICHYSSOISE

**Makes 10 servings**

    4 tablespoons butter
    6 leeks, white part only, cleaned and sliced
    1 large onion, sliced
    6 potatoes, peeled, diced
    4 cups chicken stock
    2 cups heavy cream
 1/2 teaspoon salt
 1/2 teaspoon white pepper
    Ground nutmeg
    Chopped chives

In a large heavy saucepan melt butter; sauté leeks and onion until tender, stirring occasionally. Add potatoes and chicken stock, simmer until potatoes are tender, about 20 minutes. Strain vegetables, puree and return to stock. Mix in cream, salt and pepper. Cover and refrigerate until ready to serve. Stir, pour into individual soup bowls. Garnish soup with ground nutmeg and chopped chives.

# VEGETABLE SOUPS

# ARTICHOKE SOUP

**Makes 8 servings**

- 6 tablespoons butter
- 2 large leeks, cleaned well, minced
- 3 stalks celery, chopped
- 1 can, 14 ounces, artichoke bottoms, minced
- 4-5 cups chicken stock
- 1/2 teaspoon salt
- 1/4 teaspoon white pepper
- 1/2 teaspoon ground thyme
- 2 cups heavy cream
- Croutons for garnish

In a large skillet heat butter, sauté leeks and celery until tender, over medium heat, stirring occasionally. Stir in artichokes, stock, salt, pepper and thyme; bring soup to a boil, reduce heat to simmer and continue cooking for 15 minutes. Puree vegetables, using a food processor fitted with a steel blade or a blender. Return pureed vegetables to soup. Stir in cream, simmer only until soup is heated. Garnish with croutons.

# ASPARAGUS SOUP

**Makes 8 servings**

- 2 cups chicken stock
- 1 large onion, thinly sliced
- 2 cups asparagus, cut into 1-inch pieces (including ends)
- 1 teaspoon freshly squeezed lemon juice
- 1/4 teaspoon ground mace
- 3 tablespoons butter
- 3 tablespoons all-purpose flour
- 1/2 teaspoon salt
- 1 cup milk
- 1 cup half-and-half

In a large saucepan, combine chicken stock, onion, asparagus pieces, lemon juice and mace; bring mixture to boiling point. Reduce heat to simmer, cover and continue cooking for 10 minutes or until the asparagus is tender. Puree asparagus in a food processor fitted with a steel blade or use a blender. Return asparagus to saucepan. In a separate small saucepan, add the butter and whisk in flour and salt and continue working until the flour is absorbed. Mix in milk, continue cooking until mixture thickens. Pour mixture into soup, combine. Mix in half-and-half, simmer until soup is heated. Serve garnished with extra asparagus tips.

# CREAM OF ASPARAGUS SOUP

**Makes 8 servings**

> 5 tablespoons butter or margarine
> 2 cans asparagus or $3/4$ pound cooked fresh aspara-
>   gus, cut into 1-inch pieces
> 1 medium onion, quartered
> $1/2$ teaspoon salt
> $1/4$ teaspoon white pepper
> 6 cups beef bouillon
> 2 cups light cream
>   Ground nutmeg for garnish

In a large saucepan, heat butter. Sauté asparagus and onion until tender. Season with salt and pepper. Blend in 1 cup of beef bouillon, puree mixture, return to saucepan. Blend in remaining bouillon. Simmer, uncovered, for 20 minutes. Mix in light cream, simmer only until soup is warm. Garnish with ground nutmeg.

# BLACK BEAN SOUP

**Makes 8 servings**

    4 tablespoons bacon drippings
    3 cloves garlic, peeled and minced
    1 onion, minced
    1 pound black beans, washed
    4 stalks celery, sliced
    1 quart beef stock
    1 teaspoon salt
    ½ teaspoon ground pepper
    ½ cup chopped onion for garnish
    4 hard-boiled eggs, peeled and chopped for garnish

In a stock pot, heat bacon drippings. Sauté garlic and onion until tender, stirring occasionally. Add beans, celery, 1 quart water and beef stock; bring soup to a boil. Reduce heat to simmer, cover and continue cooking for 2½ hours, stir occasionally. Mix in salt and pepper. Cool beans and puree. Return beans to liquid, combine. Heat soup, adjust seasonings. Serve with chopped onions and chopped eggs on the side.

# MIXED BEAN SOUP

**Makes 12 servings**

- 1 cup navy beans
- 6 cups beef stock
- 1 cup split peas
- 1 cup barley
- 3 carrots, sliced
- 1 large onion, sliced thin
- 1 large potato, peeled, diced
- 1 teaspoon salt
- 1/4 teaspoon ground pepper

Rinse beans, place in a deep mixing bowl covered with 8 cups water. Drain, rinse, place in a large saucepan. Mix in stock, peas, barley, carrots, onion, potato, salt and pepper. Bring soup to a boil, reduce heat to simmer. Cover and continue cooking for 1½ to 2 hours, stirring occasionally. Adjust seasonings. Serve with dark rye bread.

# NAVY BEAN SOUP

**Makes 12 servings**

- 1 pint dried navy beans
- 1½ pounds salt pork
- 1 onion, thinly sliced
- 4 stalks celery, chopped
- 1 teaspoon salt
- ½ teaspoon pepper
- ½ teaspoon cumin
- 1 lemon, sliced, for garnish

Wash and soak beans in a large mixing bowl overnight in 3 quarts cold water. Next day add 2 quarts water to stock pot. Add washed and drained beans and remaining ingredients; simmer until beans are soft, about 3 hours. Add more water if necessary. Remove salt pork, cut into small pieces, press through a sieve, return liquid to pot, simmer 10 minutes. Serve with sliced lemon.

# WASHINGTON SENATE BEAN SOUP

**Makes 8-10 servings**

  2 pounds dried navy beans, washed carefully
1¹/₂ pounds smoked ham hocks
  2 tablespoons butter
  1 medium onion, minced
  1 teaspoon salt
¹/₄ teaspoon ground pepper

Place beans in a large deep mixing bowl. Cover with water, soak overnight. Drain beans, place in a large saucepan covered with 4 quarts water; add ham hocks. Cook over medium heat to boiling point; skim if necessary, reduce heat to simmer, cover and continue cooking until beans are tender, about 3 hours, stirring occasionally. Remove ham hocks, remove any meat, chop, return to soup. In a medium skillet, heat butter. Sauté onion until tender over medium heat, stirring occasionally. Add onion, salt and pepper, to soup. Adjust seasonings. Soup will thicken on standing. Add water as necessary.

# VEGETABLE BEAN SOUP

**Makes 12 servings**

- 3 tablespoons vegetable oil
- 1 clove garlic, minced
- 1 large onion, sliced thin
- 3 stalks celery, sliced thin
- 3 cans, 10½ ounce each, condensed beef consommé or beef stock
- 1 can, 6 ounces, tomato paste
- 1 can, 16 ounces, kidney beans, drained
- 2 carrots, sliced thin
- 1 cup frozen peas
- 1½ cups string beans, trimmed
- 1 teaspoon salt
- ½ teaspoon pepper
- ½ teaspoon oregano
- ½ teaspoon chopped basil
- 1 parsley root, peeled, grated
- 2 cups cooked egg noodles

Heat oil in a large saucepan. Sauté garlic, onion and celery until tender. Stir in consommé, 4 cups water and tomato paste. Add remaining ingredients except noodles. Bring mixture to a boil; reduce heat to simmer and continue cooking for 1½ hours. Adjust seasonings. Serve with cooked egg noodles.

# CABBAGE AND TOMATO SOUP _

**Makes 8-10 servings**

- 1 small head cabbage
- 2 cans, tomato soup
- 1 can, 16 ounces, tomatoes, cut in quarters
- 1 large onion, sliced thin
- 2 tablespoons freshly squeezed lemon juice
- ½ cup firmly packed brown sugar
- ½ pound chuck steak, cubed
- ½ cup ground gingersnaps

Place cabbage in a stock pot; cover with hot water. Simmer over medium-low heat 30 minutes; stirring occasionally. Add remaining ingredients. Simmer uncovered 1½ hours, stirring occasionally.

# CARROT YOGURT SOUP

**Makes 8 servings**

- 3 tablespoons butter or margarine
- 2 large leeks, washed well and thinly sliced
- 2 cups carrots, sliced, cooked, and drained
- 1/2 teaspoon ground cinnamon
- 1/2 teaspoon freshly ground nutmeg
- 1/2 teaspoon salt
- 1/4 teaspoon white pepper
- 1 1/4 quart chicken stock
- 1 1/2 cups unflavored yogurt

In a large heavy saucepan, melt butter over medium heat; add leeks and sauté until soft, stirring occasionally. Mix in carrots, combine with leeks. Puree carrots and leeks in blender or in food processor fitted with steel blade. Return vegetables to saucepan. Blend in spices and stock, simmer 10 minutes. Slowly stir in yogurt, stirring constantly. Heat through but do not boil.

# CAULIFLOWER SOUP

**Makes 6 servings**

  3 tablespoons butter or margarine
  1 medium onion, sliced thin
  2 leeks, cleaned well, sliced
  2 cups cooked cauliflower, cut into small pieces
  2 cups milk
  1 cup half-and-half
  1/2 teaspoon dry mustard
  1/4 teaspoon white pepper
  1/4 cup Gruyere cheese, grated

In a large heavy saucepan, melt butter; sauté onion and leeks until soft, over medium heat. Add cauliflower, continue cooking 1 minute. Stir in milk and half-and-half; mix well, reduce heat to simmer. Add remaining ingredients, stir to combine. Heat uncovered until the cheese melts, stirring often. Serve garnished with extra grated Gruyere cheese.

# IOWA CORN SOUP

**Makes 8 servings**

    4 tablespoons butter
    1 large onion, sliced thin
    2 tablespoons all-purpose flour
    3 cans crushed corn
    3 cups milk
    2 cups half-and-half
  1/2 teaspoon salt and pepper

In large saucepan melt butter; sauté onion over medium heat until soft. Whisk in flour and continue cooking until it is absorbed. Add corn; continue simmering for 15 minutes. Add remaining ingredients, simmer until warm.

# VELVET CORN SOUP

**Makes 8 servings**

- 4 cups chicken stock
- 2 tablespoons cornstarch
- 1/2 teaspoon salt
- 1/2 teaspoon ground ginger
- 1 can, 8 ounces, creamed corn
- 4 tablespoons white wine
- 1/2 cup cooked ham, minced
- 2 egg whites, beat until foamy

Pour chicken stock into a large saucepan, bring soup to a boil, reduce heat to simmer. Transfer 1/2 cup chicken stock to a small bowl, whisk in cornstarch. Return mixture to soup, combine, simmer 10 minutes uncovered, stirring occasionally. Blend in salt, ginger, creamed corn, white wine and ham, simmer 5 minutes. Bring soup to a boil, stir in egg whites, simmer 2 minutes, serve in individual bowls.

# CORN CHOWDER

**Makes 8 servings**

  4  tablespoons diced salt pork
  3  large potatoes, peeled, diced
  3  cans, cut corn, drained
  2  cups milk
 ½  teaspoon salt
 ½  teaspoon white pepper
  2  cups half-and-half
  4  tablespoons chopped fresh parsley

Heat salt pork in a stock pot over medium heat. Stir in potatoes and 2 cups boiling water, continue cooking 10 minutes. Mix in corn, milk, salt and pepper, continue cooking 10 minutes. Reduce heat to a simmer, add half-and-half, continue cooking only until soup is warm. Serve garnished with chopped parsley and soda crackers.

# CREAM OF CAULIFLOWER SOUP

**Makes 8 servings**

- 4 tablespoons butter or margarine
- 4 large leeks, cleaned well and sliced
- 2 cups cauliflower pieces, cooked and pureed
- 5 cups chicken stock
- 1/2 teaspoon ground cinnamon
- 1/4 teaspoon salt
- 2 egg yolks
- 2 cups half-and-half
- Chopped fresh parsley for garnish

In a large heavy skillet, melt butter over medium heat. Sauté leeks until tender. Mix in cauliflower, chicken stock, cinnamon and salt. Simmer 20 minutes, stirring occasionally. In a small mixing bowl combine egg yolks and half-and-half. Blend in one-half cup of soup. Blend egg mixture into soup, stirring constantly. Continue cooking until soup is warm, about 1 minute. Garnish with chopped fresh parsley.

# LEEK AND PUMPKIN SOUP

**Makes 6 servings**

- 4 tablespoons butter
- 3 leeks, washed well, sliced thin
- 1 large potato, peeled, cubed
- 1 can, 16 ounces, pumpkin
- 3 cups chicken stock
- 1/2 teaspoon cinnamon
- 1/4 teaspoon allspice
- 1/4 teaspoon ground nutmeg
- 1 cup half-and-half

In a large saucepan melt butter, sauté leeks and potatoes until soft, stirring occasionally. Mix in pumpkin and chicken stock, simmer 15 minutes, uncovered, stirring occasionally. Blend in cinnamon, allspice, nutmeg and half-and-half. Simmer until soup is warm and vegetables are tender.

# CREAMY MUSHROOM SOUP

**Makes 8 servings**

- 3 tablespoons butter or margarine
- 1 large onion, thinly sliced
- 1 pound fresh mushrooms, trimmed and sliced
- 1 quart beef stock
- 4 tablespoons butter or margarine
- 3 tablespoons all-purpose flour
- 2 cups light cream
- 1/2 teaspoon salt
- 1/4 teaspoon pepper
- 1/2 teaspoon allspice

In a large saucepan, melt butter over medium heat. Add onion, sauté until tender. Add mushrooms, sauté 3 minutes, stirring occasionally. Stir in beef stock; cover and continue to simmer 12 minutes. Strain vegetables, puree and return to saucepan. In a small skillet, heat butter over medium heat. Whisk in flour and continue to cook until flour is absorbed. Add butter-flour mixture to soup. Mix in cream, salt, pepper and allspice. Simmer soup until hot. Sprinkle with chopped chives.

# MUSHROOM BARLEY SOUP

**Makes 8 servings**

- 1 pound oxtails
- 1/2 pound barley, washed, drained
- 1/2 cup lima beans
- 1 pound mushrooms, sliced
- 1 teaspoon salt
- 1/2 teaspoon pepper
- 2 carrots, sliced
- 5 stalks celery, sliced
- 1 large onion, sliced thin

In a stock pot combine oxtails, barley and lima beans, cover with 2 quarts water. Bring soup to a boil, reduce heat to a simmer. Continue cooking uncovered until meat is cooked, about 1 hour. Add remaining ingredients, continue simmering until the vegetables are tender. Serve hot with a dark rye bread.

# EASY SPLIT PEA SOUP

**Makes 8 servings**

   1 package, 6 ounces, split pea soup mix
   2 carrots, sliced
   1 large onion, sliced thin
   1 large potato, peeled, diced
  1/2 teaspoon salt
  1/2 teaspoon pepper

In a large saucepan combine all ingredients, mix well. Cover with 2 quarts water. Bring soup to a boil, reduce heat to a simmer. Cover and continue cooking 1 1/2 hours, stirring occasionally. Adjust seasonings. Serve with dark bread.

# PIMIENTO BISQUE

2 1/2 tablespoons butter or margarine, melted
2 1/2 tablespoons flour
   5 cups milk
  1/2 teaspoon grated onion
  3/4 cup pimiento
   Salt and pepper to taste

Add flour to melted butter. Mix well. Add milk and cook in a heavy saucepan, stirring constantly until thick. Add onion and coarsely sieved pimiento. Season to taste. Heat, stirring occasionally. Do not boil.

# YELLOW PEA SOUP

**Makes 8 servings**

  2 cups whole dried yellow peas
  1 pound pork shoulder, cubed
  1 large onion, sliced thin
  2 carrots, sliced
  1 teaspoon salt
  $1/2$ teaspoon white pepper
  $1/2$ teaspoon crumbled dried marjoram

Wash and drain yellow peas. Arrange peas in a stock pot. Add 2 quarts water; bring mixture to a boil, cook 2 minutes. Remove peas from heat, cover, soak 1 hour. Discard any pea husks that float to surface. Add pork, bring mixture to a boil, skim. Add remaining ingredients. Reduce heat to a simmer, cover and continue cooking 2 hours or until the yellow peas are tender, stirring occasionally. Add more water if soup is too thick.

# POTATO SOUP

**Makes 8 servings**

4 tablespoons butter or margarine
1 large onion, thinly sliced
4 large potatoes, peeled and diced
2 cloves garlic, peeled and minced
3 stalks celery, sliced
2 carrots, thinly sliced
1 teaspoon salt
¼ teaspoon white pepper
1 cup milk
1 cup half-and-half

In a large saucepan, melt butter. Sauté onion until tender over medium heat. Add potatoes, garlic, celery, carrots, salt, and pepper. Mix in 3 cups water; cook until tender, about 20 minutes. Stir in milk and half-and-half, simmer only until the soup is warm.

# CREAM OF POTATO SOUP

5 large potatoes
1/2 cup sliced carrots
6 slices bacon
1 cup chopped onion
1 cup sliced celery
1 1/2 teaspoon salt
1/4 teaspoon white pepper
2 cups milk
2 cups light cream or evaporated milk
   Cheddar cheese, shredded Parsley

Wash, pare and slice potatoes. Cook with the carrots in boiling water to cover until tender. Drain. Sauté bacon until crisp. Drain on absorbent paper and crumble. Sauté onion and celery in 2 tablespoons of the bacon fat. Combine all ingredients except cheese and parsley. Simmer 30 minutes. Garnish each serving with cheddar cheese and parsley.

# THANKSGIVING SOUP IN A PUMPKIN

**Makes 8 servings**

- 4 tablespoons butter
- 1 medium onion, sliced thin
- 1 can, 29 ounces, pumpkin puree
- 4 cans chicken bouillon
- 1/2 teaspoon salt
- 2 cups heavy cream
-   Ground nutmeg
- 1 medium pumpkin

In large saucepan melt butter over medium heat. Sauté onions until soft, stirring occasionally. Blend in pumpkin and bouillon. Mix in salt; simmer, uncovered 10 minutes. Stir in cream, continue cooking until warm. Cut top off pumpkin, clean inside, cut slice off bottom to help balance. When ready to serve, pour soup into pumpkin, grate nutmeg over soup. Bring pumpkin to the table and ladle soup from pumpkin.

# SPICED CREAM OF SPINACH SOUP

**Makes 8 servings**

- 1 quart milk
- 1 cup heavy cream
- 2 tablespoons all-purpose flour
- 4 tablespoons butter, melted
- 1 pound spinach, cooked and chopped
- 1/2 teaspoon salt
- 1/4 teaspoon nutmeg
- 1/2 teaspoon chopped fresh dill weed

Heat milk in a large saucepan over low heat. Add heavy cream, combine. In a cup, whisk together flour and butter. Mix into milk and cream. Add remaining ingredients, stir until mixture is desired thickness. Simmer 10 minutes. Serve at once.

# CLEAR MUSHROOM SOUP

**Makes 4 servings**

- 1 pound mushrooms
- 4 cups consommé
- 4 teaspoons sherry

Chop mushrooms. Add to consommé and simmer, tightly covered, for 30 minutes. Strain and reheat. Add sherry.

# FLORENTINE SOUP

**Makes 8 servings**

- 1 package frozen chopped spinach
- 4 cups chicken stock
- 1 cup white kidney beans (canned)
- ½ teaspoon crushed thyme
- 1 teaspoon chopped dill weed
- 1 cup cooked rice
- 2 egg yolks
- 2 tablespoons freshly squeezed lemon juice
- 4 tablespoons freshly grated Parmesan cheese

Cook spinach according to package directions, do not drain. Puree beans and ½ cup of chicken stock. Place beans in a large saucepan, add spinach, remaining chicken stock, spices and rice. Simmer 10 minutes. In a small bowl beat egg yolks with lemon juice and add to soup, stirring occasionally. Serve with Parmesan cheese.

# SQUASH SOUP

**Makes 8 servings**

- 4 tablespoons butter or margarine
- 1 large onion, thinly sliced
- 2 pounds squash, peeled, seeded, cubed, cooked until tender
- 2 cups chicken stock
- 2 cups half-and-half
- $1/2$ teaspoon salt
- $1/2$ teaspoon mace
- 1 cup cooked thin egg noodles

In a large saucepan heat butter over medium heat. Sauté onions until tender. Puree squash in a blender or in a food processor fitted with a steel blade. Add squash to saucepan over medium heat, blend in half-and-half and spices, simmer until soup is warm. Serve in deep bowls over noodles.

# CREAM OF TOMATO SOUP

**Makes 8 servings**

- 3 **tablespoons butter**
- 1 **tablespoon olive oil**
- 1 **large onion, sliced**
- 4 **tomatoes, peeled, chopped**
- 4 **tablespoons tomato paste**
- 3 **tablespoons all-purpose flour**
- 3 **cups chicken stock**
- 1 **teaspoon honey**
- 1/2 **teaspoon salt**
- 1/4 **teaspoon white pepper**
- 1 **cup heavy cream**
  **Fried onion rings for garnish**

Melt butter and olive oil in a large saucepan; sauté onion until tender, stirring occasionally. Mix in tomatoes and tomato paste, simmer 2 minutes. Sprinkle with flour and stir until absorbed. Blend in chicken stock, honey, salt, and pepper. Continue simmering for 10 minutes, puree. Return soup to saucepan. Blend in cream, simmer until warm. Serve garnished with crumbled fried onion rings.

# SPICY TOMATO SOUP

**Makes 8 servings**

- 2 tablespoons butter or margarine
- 1 large onion, sliced thin
- 6 large tomatoes, peeled, chopped, including juice
- 3 cups chicken stock
- 1 can, 16 ounces, tomato wedges, undrained
- 1/2 teaspoon celery salt
- 1 teaspoon honey
- 1 teaspoon chopped basil
- 1/2 teaspoon marjoram, thyme, salt
- 1/4 teaspoon pepper
- 1 cup commercial sour cream for garnish

In a large saucepan heat butter, sauté onion until tender, over medium heat. Mix in tomatoes, chicken stock, tomato wedges, and seasonings. Reduce heat to simmer, cover and continue cooking for 45 minutes. Puree vegetables and return puree to the tomato soup. Simmer until warm. Serve garnished with a dollop of sour cream.

# OLD-FASHIONED VEGETABLE SOUP

**Makes 12 servings**

- 3 beef bones, washed, loose pieces of bone removed
- 1 can, 10½ ounces, beef bouillon
- 1 green pepper, seeded, chopped
- 1 large onion, minced
- 3 stalks celery, chopped
- 3 carrots, sliced
- 1 turnip, diced
- 2 large potatoes, peeled, diced
- 2 tomatoes, peeled, quartered
- 3 cups tomato juice
- 2 teaspoons salt
- ¼ teaspoon pepper

In a stock pot, place beef bones. Cover with 2 quarts water, simmer 2 hours. Remove bones from stock, discard, strain stock, return to stock pot. Add bouillon, vegetables and seasonings. Simmer, uncovered, 1 hour.

# SOUTHERN PEANUT BUTTER SOUP

**Makes 8 servings**

     4 tablespoons butter
     3 stalks celery, sliced
     1 medium onion, sliced thin
     2 tablespoons all-purpose flour
     1 quart chicken stock
     1 cup chunky peanut butter
 1/2 teaspoon salt
     1 cup heavy cream
 1/4 cup chopped peanuts, for garnish

Melt butter in a large saucepan, sauté celery and onion until soft. Whisk in flour, stir until flour is absorbed. Blend in chicken stock and simmer uncovered 30 minutes. Remove from heat, blend in the peanut butter and salt. Mix in cream, simmer 5 minutes. Serve at once with chopped peanuts.

# SPRING WATERCRESS SOUP _

**Makes 8 servings**

- 4 tablespoons butter
- 1 medium onion, thinly sliced
- 1 cup chopped watercress
- 2 cups chicken stock
- ¹/₂ teaspoon salt
- ¹/₂ teaspoon ginger
- 1 cup milk
- 2 cups heavy cream

In a large saucepan heat butter; sauté onion until tender over medium heat. Add watercress, mix together with onion. Add chicken stock, simmer 15 minutes. Remove vegetables, puree, return to soup. Blend in salt, ginger, and milk. Cook until soup is warm. Reduce heat to simmer, stir in heavy cream and simmer only until soup is warm.

# INTERNATIONAL SOUPS

# CHINESE VELVET CORN SOUP

**Makes 8 servings**

- 6 cups chicken stock
- 1 can crushed corn, undrained
- 1 cup cooked shredded chicken
- 1/4 cup Chinese mushrooms, reconstituted in hot water, shredded and stems removed
- 2 eggs, slightly beaten

In a large saucepan, bring the chicken stock to a boil. Reduce heat to a simmer and add remaining ingredients, except eggs. Continue cooking for 5 minutes. In a slow steady stream, add eggs to the soup, forming egg drops. Turn heat off, leave saucepan over heat for 1 minute. Stir and serve at once.

# CHINESE EGG DROP SOUP

**Makes 6-8 servings**

- 6 cups chicken stock
- 1/2 teaspoon salt
- 1 cup cooked chicken, shredded
- 1 small onion
- 1/2 cup water chestnuts, sliced
- 1/2 cup Chinese mushrooms, reconstituted in hot water, shredded, discard stems
- 4 eggs, slightly beaten

In a large saucepan combine chicken stock, salt, chicken, onion, water chestnuts and mushrooms; bring to a boil. Reduce heat to a simmer, cover and continue cooking for 20 minutes. In a slow steady stream drizzle eggs into the hot soup. Turn heat off, leave saucepan over heat 1 minute, stir, serve in Oriental cups.

# CHINESE HOT AND SOUR SOUP

**Makes 12 servings**

- 5 cups chicken stock
- 1/3 cup dried lily buds, reconstituted in hot water, shredded
- 1/3 cup clouds ears, reconstituted in hot water, shredded
- 1/2 pound cooked chicken, chopped
- 1/2 cup fresh bean curd, cut into 1/2-inch strips
- 5-6 Chinese mushrooms, reconstituted in hot water, shredded, discard stems
- 2 teaspoons light soy sauce
- 1/2 teaspoon salt
- 2 tablespoons cornstarch
- 2 eggs, slightly beaten
- 3 tablespoons wine vinegar
- 1/2 teaspoon ground pepper
- 2 teaspoons sesame seed oil
- 1/4 cup chopped green onions for garnish

Place chicken stock in large saucepan, bring to a boil, reduce heat to simmer. Mix in lily buds and clouds ears. Mix in chopped chicken, bean curd and mushroom shreds. Continue cooking 5 minutes. Blend in soy sauce, salt and cornstarch whisked together with 4 tablespoons of chicken stock. In a slow steady stream drizzle in the slightly beaten eggs. Immediately turn off heat, do not stir. The eggs will set slightly making egg drops. Stir in vinegar, pepper and sesame seed oil. Serve soup hot, garnished with green onions.

Chinese ingredients are available at Oriental food stores.

# CHINESE WINTERMELON SOUP

**Makes 8 servings**

- 6 cups chicken stock
- 2 pounds wintermelon, seeded, pared, cubed; available in Oriental grocery stores
- 3/4 cup cooked ham, cubed
- 1/4 cup Chinese mushrooms, reconstituted in hot water, shredded, discard stems; available in Oriental grocery stores
- 1/4 teaspoon white pepper

In a large heavy saucepan combine chicken stock and wintermelon, simmer for 10 minutes. Add remaining ingredients; continue cooking 10 minutes. Soup can be served in a whole wintermelon, using the melon as a serving vessel.

# FRENCH ONION SOUP

**Makes 8 servings**

- 6 tablespoons butter
- 5 large onions, thinly sliced
- 4 tablespoons all-purpose flour
- 6 cups beef bouillon or beef stock
- $1/4$ cup vermouth, or to taste
- $1/2$ teaspoon salt
- $1/4$ teaspoon ground pepper
- $1/4$ teaspoon crushed thyme
- 8 slices French bread, toasted
- $3/4$ pound Swiss cheese, grated

Heat butter in a large saucepan, sauté onions until tender. Mix in flour, continue cooking until butter is absorbed. Mix in bouillon, vermouth, salt, pepper and thyme; simmer 20 minutes. Ladle soup into heatproof crocks, place a toasted bread slice on soup, cover with grated cheese. Arrange crocks on a roasting pan, bake at 375° for 10 minutes or until the cheese has melted. Serve hot.

# FRENCH VEGETABLE SOUP ___

**Makes 8-10 servings**

  4 tablespoons vegetable oil
  1 veal bone, with some meat
 1/4 teaspoon Worcestershire sauce
 1/2 teaspoon salt
 1/4 teaspoon pepper
 1/2 teaspoon garlic powder
  1 large potato, peeled, cubed
  3 carrots, sliced
  1 large leek, cleaned well, sliced
  1 medium turnip, cubed
  1 cup string beans, trimmed
 1/4 pound cooked thin spaghetti
 1/4 pound Gruyere cheese, grated

Heat vegetable oil in a large skillet over medium heat, brown veal bone. Cover bone with water. Add seasonings; simmer for 1 hour, discard bone, return any meat to soup. Add potato, carrots, leek, turnip and beans, simmer 1 1/2 hours. Add cooked spaghetti; simmer 5 minutes. Sprinkle with Gruyere cheese; serve.

# GREEK LEMON SOUP ____

**Makes 8 servings**

  6 cups chicken stock
  $1/2$ cup uncooked rice
  3 eggs, separated
  $1/4$ cup freshly squeezed lemon juice
  $1/2$ teaspoon salt
  $1/4$ teaspoon pepper
  1 teaspoon lemon zest

In a large saucepan, bring chicken stock to a boil. Stir in rice, cover, reduce heat to a simmer and continue cooking for 15 minutes or until the rice is tender, reserve. In a small mixing bowl combine the egg yolks, lemon juice, salt, pepper and grated lemon zest. Scoop out $1/2$ cup of the soup and combine with egg mixture. Beat egg whites until soft peaks form. Fold egg whites into the hot soup. Add egg yolk mixture to the soup. Turn heat off, let soup stand for 2 minutes before serving.

# HUNGARIAN GOULASH SOUP

**Makes 8 servings**

      4 tablespoons butter
      1 large onion, thinly sliced
      2 cloves garlic, peeled and minced
      1 tablespoon sweet paprika
      3 green peppers, cubed
    1/2 teaspoon caraway seeds, crushed
      3 tablespoons all-purpose flour
      2 potatoes, peeled, cubed
      2 tomatoes, peeled, chopped
      4 cups beef stock or veal stock
      2 cups cooked beef or veal, cubed
      1 cup commercial sour cream

Melt butter in a large saucepan; sauté onion and garlic until tender. Sprinkle with paprika, combine. Mix in peppers and caraway seeds; sauté until peppers are tender. Sprinkle with flour, incorporate evenly. Add potatoes and tomatoes, combine. Mix in stock and beef cubes, simmer uncovered 20 minutes. Serve warm with a dollop of sour cream.

# MINESTRONE

**Makes 8 servings**

 1 medium onion, thinly sliced
 4 stalks celery, sliced
 2 large carrots, sliced
 1 medium zucchini, sliced
 2 cloves garlic, peeled and minced
 1 can, 16 ounces, whole tomatoes, including liquid
 6 cups tomato juice
 1/2 teaspoon ground oregano
 1/2 teaspoon salt
 1/4 teaspoon ground pepper
 3 cups cooked navy beans

In a stock pot, combine all ingredients except the navy beans. Bring soup to a boil; reduce heat to a simmer and continue cooking for 1 hour, stirring occasionally. Stir in beans, simmer 10 minutes. Serve hot.

# ITALIAN BEAN SOUP

**Makes 8 servings**

- 4 tablespoons olive oil
- 1 small onion, chopped
- 2 cloves garlic, peeled, minced
- 2 cans, 6 ounces each, tomato paste
- 1 can, 15 ounces, kidney beans, drained
- 1/2 teaspoon salt
- 1/4 teaspoon freshly ground pepper
- 2 cups elbow macaroni, cooked according to package directions, drained
- 1/2 cup freshly grated Parmesan cheese

In a large saucepan, heat the oil. Sauté onion and garlic until onion is soft. Mix in tomato paste and 2 cups water; combine. Add beans, salt and pepper. Simmer 30 minutes. Add elbow macaroni, stir to combine, cover, let stand about 5 minutes. Place in bowl, sprinkle with cheese.

# JAPANESE SEAWEED SOUP

**Makes 8 servings**

- 4 cups chicken stock
- 1 cup cooked chicken, shredded
- $1/2$ sheet seaweed, shredded, available in Oriental food stores
- 2 teaspoons sesame seed oil
- 1 cup cooked shrimp, shelled, deveined
- $1/4$ cup chopped green onions for garnish

Pour chicken stock into a large saucepan, bring soup to a boil, reduce heat to a simmer. Mix in remaining ingredients except green onions. Continue simmering for 10 minutes. Place in individual bowls, sprinkle soup with chopped green onions.

# SCOTCH BROTH

**Makes 8 servings**

- 2 pounds lamb bones
- 2 medium onions, sliced thin
- 6 carrots, sliced
- 1/2 cup chopped fresh parsley
- 1/2 cup uncooked barley
- 3 stalks celery, sliced
- 3/4 teaspoon salt
- 1/2 teaspoon pepper
- 1 lemon, sliced thin for garnish

In a stock pot, add lamb bones, half of the onions, carrots, and parsley and 1 1/2 quarts water; simmer uncovered 1 1/2 hours. Strain broth and skim fat; discard bones and return stock to the pot. Add barley, cook, over medium heat for 20 minutes. Add remaining onion, carrot, parsley, celery, salt and pepper. Cook, uncovered, for 20 minutes over medium heat. Serve garnished with a slice of lemon.

# SPANISH GARLIC SOUP

**Makes 8 servings**

- 2 quarts chicken stock
- 10 large garlic cloves, peeled, crushed only slightly
- 3 tablespoons all-purpose flour
- 2 egg yolks
- 1/2 cup heavy cream
- 1 tablespoon chopped tarragon

In a stock pot combine 1 quart of the chicken stock and garlic cloves, simmer for 30 minutes or until the garlic is tender. Remove garlic and puree. Add remaining chicken stock, cook over medium heat until soup is reduced by half. Return garlic puree to soup. Remove 1/2 cup of the soup, place in a bowl. Whisk in flour, return mixture to soup. Continue cooking until soup thickens slightly, about 15 minutes. In a small bowl whisk egg yolks with cream, slowly stir into soup, add tarragon and simmer 5 minutes.

# SPANISH VEGETABLE SOUP

**Makes 8 servings**

- 3 tablespoons olive oil
- 1/2 cup shredded cabbage
- 1 large potato, peeled and cubed
- 1 onion, thinly sliced
- 1 can, 16 ounces, chopped tomatoes including juice
- 1 cup chopped ham
- 1/2 teaspoon salt
- 1/4 teaspoon freshly grated black pepper
- 4 cups beef stock
- 1/2 cup frozen peas

Heat oil in a stock pot; sauté cabbage, potato and onion until tender. Add tomatoes, ham, salt, pepper, beef stock, and peas. Simmer 30 minutes, uncovered, stirring occasionally.

# OTHER SOUPS

# SPICY APPLE SOUP _____

**Makes 8 servings**

- 4 tablespoons butter
- 3 Granny Smith apples, peeled, cored, and chopped
- 1 large onion, thinly sliced
- 4 stalks celery, sliced
- 1 tablespoon curry powder
- 1/2 teaspoon salt
- 1/4 teaspoon pepper
- 3 tablespoons all-purpose flour
- 6 cups chicken stock
- 1/2 teaspoon cinnamon
- 1 1/2 cups commercial sour cream

In a large saucepan, melt butter over medium heat. Sauté apples, onion, and celery until tender. Add curry, salt, pepper and whisk in flour. Sauté until flour is absorbed, about 3 minutes. Add chicken stock and cinnamon; reduce heat to simmer. Cover, cook 10 minutes. When ready to serve, stir sour cream into the soup and garnish with more chopped apples if desired. Serve at once.

# BONGO BONGO SOUP

**Makes 6 servings**

- 3 cups milk
- 1 cup half and half
- 8 fresh oysters, shucked, pureed
- 1/2 cup cooked spinach, pureed
- 1 clove garlic, pureed
- 1/4 teaspoon salt
- 1/4 teaspoon white pepper
- 2 tablespoons cornstarch

In a 3-quart saucepan heat milk and half-and-half over medium-low heat. Add remaining ingredients, except cornstarch; continue simmering 10 minutes. Remove 1/2 cup soup, whisk together with cornstarch, return to soup. Continue simmering until soup thickens slightly.

# BOSTON FISH CHOWDER

**Makes 8 servings**

- 4 slices bacon
- 2 medium onions, thinly sliced
- 4 stalks celery, sliced
- 4 potatoes, peeled and diced
- 2 pounds firm-fleshed fish (haddock or halibut), boned and cut into 1-inch pieces
- 1 teaspoon salt
- 1/2 teaspoon white pepper
- 3 cups milk
- 2 cups half-and-half
- 3 tablespoons butter
- 2 cups soda crackers for garnish

In a large saucepan, cook bacon. Remove bacon, crumble, reserve; leave drippings in pot. Sauté onions and celery until tender. Add potatoes, fish, and 2 cups hot water. Simmer 20 minutes, uncovered, stirring occasionally. Season with salt and pepper. Add milk, half-and-half and butter; simmer until chowder is heated and the butter melts. Serve hot with soda crackers and sprinkle with crumbled bacon. Serve in deep bowls.

# BOUILLABAISSE

**Makes 10-12 servings**

 4 tablespoons olive oil
 2 cloves garlic, peeled and minced
 2 stalks celery, sliced
 2 leeks, cleaned well and sliced
 1 large onion, sliced
 4 large tomatoes, peeled and chopped
 1/2 pound mushrooms, sliced
 2 cups clam juice
 1 cup clam broth
 4 cups tomato juice
 1 teaspoon salt
 1/2 teaspoon ground pepper
 1/2 teaspoon saffron, optional
 4 bay leaves
 2 1/2 pounds firm fish fillets (scrod, snapper, or bass)
 1 pound shrimp, peeled and deveined
 1 pound scallops, washed
 1 pound mussels in shells, scrubbed
 1/2 pound crab legs, split and cut into 3-inch pieces (optional)

Heat oil in a stock pot; sauté garlic, celery, leeks, and onion until tender, stirring occasionally. Mix in tomatoes, mushrooms, clam juice and broth, tomato juice, and spices; simmer 5 minutes. Add fish; simmer 15 minutes. Add shrimp, scallops, mussels and crab pieces. Simmer uncovered for 10 minutes or until the fish is tender. Adjust seasonings; discard bay leaves. Serve with French bread.

# FAST SHRIMP BISQUE

**Makes 10-12 servings**

- 2 cans, 10$\frac{1}{2}$ ounces each, tomato soup
- 2 cans, 10$\frac{1}{2}$ ounces each, green pea soup
- 1 cup milk
- 1 cup half-and-half
- $\frac{1}{2}$ cup dry white wine or sherry
- $\frac{3}{4}$ pound cooked shrimp, peeled and deveined
- Croutons for garnish

Combine soups, milk, and half-and-half in a large saucepan. Bring mixture to a boil over medium heat, stirring occasionally. Mix in white wine and shrimp; simmer until soup is warm. Garnish with croutons.

# OYSTER BISQUE

1 dozen shucked large raw oysters
1 cup oyster liquid
3 cups milk
1 cup heavy cream
1 slice onion
2 stalks celery
1 sprig parsley
1 bay leaf
1/3 cup butter or margarine, melted
1/3 cup flour
1 3/4 teaspoon salt
1/2 teaspoon tabasco
Chopped chives

Drain oysters, reserving 1 cup liquid. Dice oysters into a saucepan and add liquid. Slowly bring oysters to boiling point, remove. In the same saucepan scald milk and cream with onion, celery, parsley, bay leaf. Strain. Blend butter with flour, salt and tabasco. Slowly stir in scalded milk. Stir over low heat until thick. Add oysters and cooking liquid. Heat. Garnish with chopped chives.

# MANHATTAN CLAM CHOWDER

**Makes 6 servings**

- 5 slices bacon
- 1 large onion, sliced thin
- 3 stalks celery, sliced
- 2 potatoes, peeled, diced
- 2 cans, 16 ounces each, minced clams
- 1 can, 16 ounces, stewed tomatoes
- 2 bay leaves
- 1 teaspoon salt
- 1/4 teaspoon pepper
- 1 teaspoon crumbled dried thyme
- 2 tablespoons chopped fresh parsley

In a large saucepan cook bacon until crisp, drain. Crumble bacon, reserve 3 tablespoons drippings; set aside. Reserve bacon. Reheat bacon drippings, sauté onion and celery until soft, over medium heat. Add potatoes, clams including liquid, tomatoes including liquid, bay leaves, salt, pepper, thyme and parsley. Add 3 cups water, combine. Bring mixture to a boil, reduce heat to a simmer. Simmer, uncovered 10 minutes, stirring occasionally. Return crumbled bacon, combine. Serve hot.

# CREAMY MUSSEL SOUP

**Makes 8 servings**

- 3 pounds mussels in shells, scrubbed
- 3 bay leaves
- 5 slices bacon
- 1 large onion, thinly sliced
- 3 stalks celery, sliced
- 3 potatoes, peeled and diced
- 1 teaspoon salt
- 1/2 teaspoon white pepper
- 1 cup milk
- 1 cup cream
- 3 tablespoons butter
- 1/4 cup chopped fresh parsley for garnish

Arrange mussels in a large saucepan with 1/2 cup water and bay leaves. Cook over medium heat just until the shells open. Discard any unopened mussels. Strain; reserve stock, discard bay leaves. Remove mussels from shells, chop. In a separate skillet fry bacon over medium heat, crumble bacon, reserve. Place bacon drippings in large saucepan, heat. Sauté onions and celery until tender. Add potatoes and seasonings. Stir in 1 cup mussel stock, simmer until potatoes are tender, about 20 minutes. Mix in milk and mussels; heat. Stir in cream; simmer until warm. Add butter, simmer until butter melts. Garnish with parsley.

# RICH OYSTER STEW _

**Makes 6 servings**

- 5 tablespoons butter or margarine
- 1 pint oysters
- 1 pint heavy cream
- 1 pint half-and-half
- 1/2 teaspoon salt
- 1/4 teaspoon white pepper
- 4 tablespoons dry sherry or dry white wine
- 2 cups soda crackers for garnish

In a large heavy saucepan, heat butter. Add oysters and simmer until oyster edges curl. In a separate medium saucepan, heat heavy cream and half-and-half only until warm over a low heat, stirring constantly. Blend cream into oyster-butter mixture. Season to taste with salt and pepper. Stir in sherry. Garnish with soda crackers.

# RED SNAPPER SOUP

**Makes 8 servings**

- 4 tablespoons butter
- 1 onion, thinly sliced
- 1 green pepper, seeded and sliced
- 4 stalks celery, sliced
- 1½ cups red snapper, boned and cut into pieces
- 2 cups fish stock
- 2 cups tomato sauce
- ½ cup sherry
- ½ teaspoon ground thyme
- ½ teaspoon ground oregano
- ½ teaspoon salt
- ¼ teaspoon pepper
- ¼ cup chopped fresh parsley for garnish

In a large saucepan, melt butter over medium heat. Sauté onion, green pepper and celery until tender, stirring occasionally. Add the red snapper and simmer for 3 minutes. Blend in remaining ingredients, simmer for 5 minutes. Serve hot. Garnish with parsley.

# CHEESE SOUP _____

**Makes 8 servings**

   4 tablespoons butter
   1 large onion, sliced thin
   4 stalks celery, sliced
   4 tablespoons all-purpose flour
   2 cups milk
   3 cups chicken stock
 1/2 teaspoon sweet paprika
   1 cup Swiss cheese, grated
   1 cup half-and-half

In a large saucepan melt butter. Sauté onion and celery until tender, stirring occasionally. Stir in flour until it is absorbed. Blend in milk, chicken stock and paprika, simmer 10 minutes. Blend in Swiss cheese and half-and-half, simmer until cheese melts, stirring often.

# BEEF TINGLER _____

**Makes 5 1/2 cups**

   2 10 1/2-ounce cans condensed beef broth
   2 soup cans water
 1/4 cup brandy
 1/4 cup heavy cream
 1/8 teaspoon vanilla
     Dash of nutmeg
 1/8 teaspoon grated orange rind

In a saucepan, combine soup, water and brandy. Heat, stirring occasionally. Meanwhile, in a small bowl, combine cream, vanilla and nutmeg. Beat until cream just mounds. Fold in orange rind. Serve on soup.

# TWO CHEESE SOUP _

**Makes 8 servings**

- 2 cups chicken stock
- 1 onion, thinly sliced
- 4 stalks celery, sliced
- 5 tablespoons butter
- 3 tablespoons all-purpose flour
- 2 cups half-and-half
- 1/2 teaspoon salt
- 1/2 teaspoon tarragon
- 1/2 cup grated Swiss cheese
- 1/2 cup grated Cheddar cheese
- 1/2 cup chopped peanuts for garnish

Heat stock in a large saucepan. Add onion and celery, simmer over medium heat until vegetables are tender, about 6 minutes. In a separate small saucepan, heat butter. Whisk in all-purpose flour until absorbed. Blend in half-and-half and seasonings. Continue stirring until mixture thickens. Stir in cheeses; stir until melted. Add cheese mixture to soup mixture, combine. Heat soup, serve garnished with chopped nuts.

# CREAM OF CHICKEN SOUP

**Makes 8 servings**

- 1 3-pound chicken, cut into 8 pieces
- 1 tablespoon instant chicken stock
- 3 carrots, sliced thin
- 2 stalks celery, sliced thin
- 1 large onion, sliced thin
- 1/4 cup chopped fresh parsley
- 1 cup milk
- 4 tablespoons butter
- 3 tablespoons all-purpose flour
- 1 cup half-and-half
- 2 cups cooked rice

In a stock pot combine chicken, 5 cups water, instant chicken stock, carrots, celery, onion and parsley. Cover and bring soup to a boil, reduce heat to a simmer and continue cooking for 1 hour, stirring occasionally. Remove chicken, discard skin and bones, chop chicken, return to soup. Stir in milk, bring soup to a boil. In a small skillet combine melted butter and flour until flour is absorbed. Add to stock mixture. Reduce heat to simmer, mix in half-and-half, heat only until soup is warm. Serve with cooked rice.

# TURKEY NOODLE SOUP _____

**Makes 8-10 servings**

  3 tablespoons butter or margarine
  1 medium onion, thinly sliced
  2 carrots, sliced
  3 stalks celery, sliced
  5 cups chicken stock or turkey stock
  1 cup leftover turkey stuffing
$1/2$ teaspoon garlic powder
$1/2$ teaspoon salt
$1/4$ teaspoon ground pepper
  2 cups cooked and drained egg noodles

In a large saucepan heat butter over medium heat; sauté vegetables until soft, stirring occasionally. Mix in chicken stock and stuffing. Bring soup to a boil; reduce heat to a simmer and continue cooking, $1/2$ hour. Stir in seasonings. Ladle soup over noodles in soup bowl.

# CHICKEN GUMBO ___

**Makes 8 servings**

  5 tablespoons vegetable oil
  1 3½-pound chicken, cut into 8 pieces
¼ pound ham, cut into cubes
  1 medium onion, thinly sliced
  1 small green pepper, seeded and sliced
  6 large tomatoes, peeled and chopped
  2 cups sliced okra
  2 bay leaves
  2 teaspoons salt
½ teaspoon pepper
  2 cups cooked rice

Heat oil in large saucepan; sauté chicken pieces and ham until browned. Add remaining ingredients, except rice, and 1 quart water. Simmer until tender, about 1 hour. When ready to serve place spoonfuls of cooked rice in each soup bowl. Ladle the gumbo over rice. Remove bay leaves, discard.

# OXTAIL SOUP

    4 tablespoons butter
    2 cloves garlic, minced
    1 large onion, sliced thin
2½ pounds oxtails
    ¼ cup chopped fresh parsley
    4 medium tomatoes, peeled, quartered
    3 stalks celery, sliced
    2 carrots, sliced
5-6 cups beef stock
    ½ teaspoon salt
    ½ teaspoon crushed thyme
    ½ teaspoon crushed sweet basil
    3 bay leaves
    3 cups cooked rice

In a large saucepan melt butter. Over medium heat sauté garlic, onion and oxtails until oxtails are lightly browned. Add parsley, tomatoes, celery, carrots, beef stock, 2 cups water, salt, thyme, basil and bay leaves; mix well. Simmer, uncovered, for 50 minutes. Cool soup to room temperature. Refrigerate until thoroughly chilled. Skim off fat. Reheat soup. Adjust seasonings; remove and discard bay leaves. Serve in deep bowls over hot cooked rice.

# LIVER DUMPLING SOUP

**Makes 8 servings**

- ¹/₂ pound beef liver, membranes removed, pureed
- 2 eggs
- 3 tablespoons melted butter or margarine
- ³/₄ cup unflavored bread crumbs
- 1 onion, minced
- ¹/₂ teaspoon crushed marjoram
- ¹/₂ teaspoon salt
- ¹/₄ teaspoon pepper
- 6 cups beef stock

In a large mixing bowl, combine all ingredients except beef stock. Cover and chill 20 minutes. In a large saucepan bring beef stock to a boil over medium heat, reduce heat to simmer. Form liver mixture into 1¹/₂-inch balls. Simmer liver dumplings in simmering beef stock for 10 minutes. Serve soup and liver dumplings in a large soup bowl.

# POULTRY
# AND
# STUFFING

# POULTRY
## AND
# STUFFING

## POULTRY

The chicken as we know it seems to be a relative of a Southeast Asian variety domesticated as early as 1500 B.C. Chicken was originally domesticated to insure availability of its prized eggs. Not until much later was chicken improved and bred for the table. The Greeks and Romans first developed distinctive breeds. In the middle ages, chicken was considered food for nobility. Now the chicken is the cheapest of all dinner meats, and is the all American favorite.

### GUIDE

When serving chicken estimate 1/2 pound per serving for each guest.

**Broilers**   Average weight is 3-3 1/2 pounds (6 to 8 weeks old). They are a fine all-purpose chicken with good flavor.

**Roasting Chicken**   Average weight from 3 1/2 to 5 1/2 pounds.

They are slightly older than broilers; they are an all-purpose chicken with good flavor.

**Capons**   Capons weigh from 4 to 7½ pounds. They are castrated chickens; this improves their flavor and tenderness.

**Stewing Chickens**   They weigh from 4 to 7 pounds, and they are less tender but are flavorful. Use only for stewing.

# DUCK

Most ducks used for the table are Long Island Duckling. Ducks have a thick layer of fat beneath the skin so they are usually cooked on a low heat over a rack with a pan containing water underneath. The pan is to catch the drippings. Allow more duck per person than chicken.

# TURKEY

The original American bird, the holiday special, is a domesticated bird and bred to have a broad breast and an abundance of white meat. When preparing a frozen turkey be sure to read the directions on the label.

# GOOSE

They are readily available frozen at supermarkets, around Christmastime especially.

# STORAGE HINTS

Remove original packaging from chicken, recover and store in the coldest area of the refrigerator. Uncooked chicken can only stay for 2 days in the refrigerator. If the chicken is cooked and properly covered it can stay for 1 to 2 days in the refrigerator. Chicken properly wrapped can stay frozen for 6 months, the giblets can stay frozen for 2 months. Cooked chicken, properly wrapped and without gravy, can be frozen for 1 month. Fried chicken, properly wrapped, can be frozen for 3 months. If chicken has gravy and is properly prepared for the freezer a time limit of 6 months is appropriate. Important, once the chicken has been thawed, do not refreeze and use it within two days of the thawing. If thawing is on a refrigerator shelf, allow 3 to 4 hours thawing time per pound. To thaw more rapidly, place wrapped chicken in a pan under running water. For best results be sure that a chicken is completely defrosted before cooking.

## TRUSSING

Trussing is used to help the bird keep its shape, and for ease in handling during cooking. Tuck the first part of the wings under the chicken. Push the legs toward the breast, this helps to plump up the bird. Thread the trussing needle with a long piece of soft string, knot the end of the thread. Insert the needle under the drumstick at the soft spot in the lower part of the backbone. Bring the needle out where the thigh and the drumstick join together. Turning the chicken on its breast, insert needle through the wing area and loose skin. Arrange the bird on its back and push the needle in the middle joint. Lift up the skin of the tail end and push the needle through. This holds the drumstick in place. Pull the string tight. The bird is now ready for cooking.

## CUTTING A CHICKEN IN HALF

Hold the chicken on its side, cut through the backbone on one side of the neck with a sharp knife. Carefully pull the chicken open and separate the backbone by cutting on the other side of the neck bone, discard backbone. Remove shoulder bones and rib cage on each side.

## BONING A CHICKEN BREAST

Remove the skin from the breast, grasp the skin and grasp the flesh in the other hand, pull to separate the flesh from the bone. With a sharp boning knife split the thin membrane that covers the breastbone. Separate it from the collarbone by twisting it from the cartilage. Remove ribs. Remove wishbone with the knife. Cut breast in half.

## BONING A CHICKEN

With a sharp boning knife remove the wings at the second joint, set aside. Lift the skin at the neck, exposing the flesh, follow the contour of the wishbone with the knife, prying it loose. Pull out the wishbone. Arrange chicken on breast, cut down the backbone to expose the flesh. Follow the carcass with your knife, begin cutting the flesh from the bone. Cut the joint at the shoulder. Cut on top and around the breastbone and down the other side, separating the flesh from the bone as you move along the carcass, removing the carcass in one piece. Cut around the thigh bone, pushing the flesh from the bone. Separate the thigh bone at the joint between the thigh and the drumstick. Cut tip off drumstick, push flesh back exposing the bone. Remove the loose flesh on the breast.

## DISJOINT THE WHOLE CHICKEN

With a sharp boning knife cut the leg off at the thigh bone. Locate the knee joint by moving the leg back and forth, cut through the joint. Remove wings from body, remove as little of the breast flesh as you can. Cut down the breast on each side. Divide back into two pieces, cut. Cut breast in half.

## BONING A DUCK

The purpose of boning a duck is to remove the carcass and main bones from the fowl while leaving the skin and flesh whole and intact. It is not as difficult to do the boning as it is to describe it. Cut off neck 2 inches from base. Slit neck skin to base. With a sharp boning knife, working close to the bone, carefully separate the flesh from the bone so as not to pierce the skin. When you reach the wing, disjoint the main wing bone from the shoulder; cutting close to the main bone, remove it, leaving the wing intact. Keep the knife close to the bone and work down to the lower part of the body, leaving the carcass separated from the flesh and skin. When you reach the legs, in the same fashion as the wings, detach and remove the thigh bones, leaving the skin intact.

## NUTRITIVE FOOD VALUE

Chicken is an excellent source of good protein. Chicken is also a good source for niacin, and a fair source of iron. Good news for those who watch weight, chickens in general are lower in fat content and calories than most other meats. It is easy to digest because it is a short fibered meat and is usually tender.

## TO ROAST A CHICKEN

Truss the chicken, stuff the bird when ready to roast, pack the chicken cavity lightly with the stuffing. Tuck the wing tips into the back area, holding the neck skin in place. Rub the chicken with a soft butter, oil or vegetable shortening. Arrange the chicken on a rack, breast side down, in a shallow roasting pan. Roast in preheated 375° oven. Turn chicken right side up for the last 10-15 minutes of roasting. To tell if the chicken is ready, the juices flow clear and the drumstick will wiggle easily when moved rapidly.

## TO FRY A CHICKEN

Dust a cut fryer or broiler with flavored crumbs or flour. Arrange skin side down into a heavy skillet that has about 1/4 of an inch of heated oil, brown chicken quickly, uncovered, reduce heat and continue frying on both sides until golden brown and tender. Drain on paper toweling.

## TO BROIL A CHICKEN

Arrange a chicken piece or half that has been oiled or brushed with barbecue sauce on a lightly oiled broiler. Cook on lowest rack for 20 minutes on each side.

## CARVING A CHICKEN

Remove trussing threads, allow chicken to rest for 10 minutes before carving. Cut off wings and legs first, place on serving platter. Slice the breast meat in long thin slices, on the diagonal. Remove each slice to the serving platter. Continue until all the meat has been carved.

# CHICKEN WITH ALMONDS

**Makes 6 servings**

- 4 tablespoons vegetable oil
- 3 cloves garlic, peeled, minced
- 1 onion, minced
- 1/2 teaspoon salt
- 2 tablespoons freshly squeezed lemon juice
- 3 1/2 pound chicken, cut into pieces
- 3 tomatoes, peeled, chopped
- 1/2 cup golden raisins
- 1/2 cup blanched, slivered almonds
- 1/2 cup sliced black olives
- 2 cups chicken stock

In a Dutch oven heat oil over medium heat. Sauté garlic and onion until tender, stirring occasionally. Sprinkle salt and lemon juice over chicken. Brown chicken on all sides. Add tomatoes, raisins, almonds, olives and stock; mix well. Simmer, uncovered, 30 minutes over medium heat or until chicken is tender. Serve in a deep bowl with white rice and warm tortillas.

# CHICKEN WITH PEANUTS

**Makes 3-11 servings**

2 chicken breasts, boned, skin removed, diced

**Marinade**

2 egg whites
1 tablespoon cornstarch
1/4 teaspoon salt and pepper

**Sauce**

1 teaspoon sugar
1 tablespoon light soy sauce
2 tablespoons catsup
1 tablespoon cornstarch dissolved with
3 tablespoons water

**Stir-Fry**

1/2 cup peanut oil
3 cloves garlic, peeled, minced
1 green pepper, seeded, cut in squares
1/2 cup bamboo shoots, shred, available in Oriental food stores
1/2 teaspoon red pepper flakes
3/4 cup raw peanuts, deep-fried in hot oil until lightly browned, drained

In a shallow bowl, combine marinade ingredients. Add chicken breasts; marinate 20 minutes, drain.

Combine sauce ingredients in a small bowl. In a wok or medium skillet with deep sides heat oil to 375°. Deep-fry chicken a few pieces at a time, 30 seconds. Drain on paper toweling. Remove all but 3 tablespoons of the cooled oil. Reheat oil. Stir-fry garlic and pepper flakes, 5 seconds. Mix in green pepper and bamboo shoots; stir-fry 2 minutes. Return chicken and peanuts, stir-fry about 30 seconds, or until chicken is cooked. Add sauce; simmer 1 minute or until sauce thickens. Serve over hot fluffy rice.

# SMOKED TEA CHICKEN _____

**Makes 4 servings**

3½ pound chicken
2 tablespoons salt
½ cup firmly packed dark brown sugar
4 tablespoons loose black tea leaves
1 tablespoon sesame oil, optional

Rub chicken inside and out with salt, let stand 1 hour, wash and pat dry with paper toweling. Place chicken on steamer rack, over simmering water, cover, steam 45 minutes. Place a double layer of aluminum foil on the bottom of a wok. Sprinkle with dark brown sugar and tea leaves. Place chicken on a rack over sugar-tea mixture. Cover with tight fitting lid. Cook over high heat 15 minutes. Open a kitchen window, it may be smokey. Turn off heat, let wok remain covered for 30 minutes. Remove chicken and rub with sesame oil. Cut into small pieces, serve warm or cold.

# CHICKEN WITH PEANUT SAUCE

**Makes 6 servings**

2 cloves garlic, peeled, minced
1 onion, minced
3 tablespoons vegetable oil
1 cup peanut butter
1 cup coconut milk

In a medium saucepan over medium heat cook garlic and onion until tender, stirring occasionally. Add peanut butter and milk, combine, simmer for 1 minute.

2 chicken breasts, skinned, boned, cut into strips, 3/4 inch x 3 inches
1 1/2 tablespoons freshly squeezed lemon juice
1/3 cup soy sauce
6 skewers
Coriander or parsley sprigs for garnish

Twist chicken onto six skewers. Place in a shallow ovenproof dish. In a small bowl combine lemon juice and soy sauce. Drizzle marinade over chicken and allow to marinate for 1 hour at room temperature. Broil chicken for 6 minutes on each side.

Arrange chicken on individual serving dishes. Drizzle with warm sauce, serve with rice. Garnish with coriander sprigs.

# CHICKEN MORNAY _

**Makes 7-8 servings**

- 1 package (10 ounces) frozen broccoli spears, defrosted
- 4 chicken breasts, cut in half
- 1/4 cup mayonnaise
- 2 cups chicken stock
- 3 tablespoons freshly squeezed lemon juice
- 1/4 teaspoon salt
- 1/2 cup bread crumbs
- 1 cup grated Swiss cheese

In a saucepan slightly undercook broccoli according to package directions, drain. Arrange broccoli spears in the bottom of a greased casserole pan. Arrange chicken breasts over broccoli. In a small bowl combine mayonnaise and chicken stock. Mix in lemon juice and salt. Pour mixture over chicken and broccoli. Sprinkle bread crumbs and cheese over top.

Bake at 350° for 1 hour.

# CHICKEN WITH COUSCOUS __

**Make 8-10 servings**

    3  tablespoons olive oil
    4  tablespoons butter
    3  cloves garlic, peeled, minced
    2  onions, sliced thin
    2  3½-pound chickens, cut into pieces
    1  can (16 ounces) tomatoes, including juice
    ½  teaspoon ground coriander
    1  teaspoon ground cumin
    ½  teaspoon salt
    ¼  teaspoon ground pepper
    2  large carrots, sliced thin
    1  cup green olives
    3  turnips, peeled, sliced
    3  large potatoes, peeled, diced
    1  l-pound box pitted prunes
       Couscous

Heat olive oil and butter in a Dutch oven. Sauté garlic and onions until tender, stirring occasionally. Sauté chickens, brown on all sides. Remove chicken, reserve. Reserve pan drippings. Add tomatoes, coriander, cumin, salt and pepper to pan drippings, reheat in Dutch oven. Add carrots, olives, turnips, potatoes, and prunes. Add reserved tomato juice and enough water to cover vegetables. Simmer 25 minutes uncovered. Return chicken to pan; mix lightly. Simmer until vegetables and chicken are tender, about 20 minutes.

# COUSCOUS ——————

1 box (1 pound) precooked couscous (available at
  specialty food stores)
  Boiling water or liquid from above stew
1 teaspoon salt

Measure amount of couscous in the box. Place in a large mixing bowl. Add an equal amount of boiling water or stewing liquid along with the salt; toss lightly. Let stand for 5 minutes.
Mound couscous in the center of a deep serving bowl or platter. Arrange chicken and vegetables around the edge of the
couscous.

# BUTTERMILK BAKED CHICKEN _____

**Makes 5-6 servings**

3½ pound chicken, cut into pieces
1 cup buttermilk
1½ cups bread crumbs
½ teaspoon salt
¼ teaspoon freshly ground pepper, rosemary
¼ teaspoon crushed rosemary

Arrange chicken in a shallow dish; cover with buttermilk. Marinate for 1 hour, drain. Preheat oven to 350° F. In a shallow dish combine bread crumbs, salt, pepper and rosemary. Dust chicken completely in bread crumb mixture. Arrange chicken pieces skin side up in a baking pan with the remaining buttermilk. Bake 1 hour or until it tests done.

# INDIAN YOGURT CHICKEN

**Makes 6 servings**

- 2 tablespoons butter
- 1 onion, minced
- 2 tomatoes, peeled, chopped
- 2 teaspoons chili powder
- 1/2 teaspoon turmeric
- 1 tablespoon ground coriander
- 1 tablespoon fresh ginger, peeled and minced
- 2 cloves garlic, peeled and minced
- 3 1/2 pound chicken cut into pieces
- 1 cup unflavored yogurt
- 1/2 teaspoon salt
- 3 green onions, minced

In a large skillet heat butter over medium heat; sauté onion until tender. Add tomatoes, chili powder, turmeric, coriander, ginger and garlic, mix well. Arrange chicken pieces, skin side up in skillet, continue cooking over medium heat until the meat is tender, about 40 minutes. Remove chicken to serving platter. Reduce heat, stir in yogurt and salt, simmer for 2 minutes, stirring continuously. Spoon sauce over chicken, garnish with minced green onions. Serve over rice.

# CHICKEN JUBILEE __

**Makes 8 servings**

2  3$\frac{1}{2}$ pound chickens, quartered
$\frac{1}{2}$ teaspoon salt
$\frac{1}{2}$ cup melted butter

Arrange chicken pieces, skin side up in a roasting pan. Drizzle with butter, season with salt.

**Sauce**

$\frac{1}{4}$ teaspoon pepper
$\frac{1}{2}$ cup golden raisins
$\frac{1}{2}$ cup firmly packed light brown sugar
1 teaspoon garlic powder
1 cup juice from cherries
1 large onion, sliced
1 bottle, 12 ounces, chili sauce
$\frac{1}{2}$ teaspoon Worcestershire sauce

In a medium bowl combine sauce ingredients. Pour sauce over chicken. Bake chicken at 325° for 1 hour.

**1 can (16 ounces) Bing cherries, juice reserved for sauce.**

**1 cup dry sherry**

In a medium bowl combine cherries and sherry, pour over chicken. Continue baking for 15 minutes.

# GEORGIA FRIED CHICKEN ____

**Makes 4-5 servings**

3½ pound chicken, cut into 8 pieces
2 cups buttermilk
½ cup all-purpose flour
½ teaspoon salt, thyme, paprika
3 eggs, slightly beaten
1½ cups seasoned bread crumbs
Peanut oil for deep frying

Place chicken in a glass pie plate or other shallow bowl. Soak chicken in buttermilk for 1 hour at room temperature, drain. In a separate shallow bowl combine flour, salt, thyme and paprika. Dust chicken with flour mixture. Roll chicken in egg mixture and then into the flour and finally roll in bread crumbs. Heat 1 inch oil in a large heavy skillet to 375°F. Fry chicken until golden brown and tender on all sides. Drain on paper toweling, serve.

# CHICKEN BREASTS FLORENTINE

**Makes 8 servings**

    1 cup all-purpose flour
  1/2 teaspoon salt and white pepper
    4 chicken breasts, boned, leave skin intact
    3 eggs, slightly beaten
    4 tablespoons butter
    3 tablespoons vegetable oil
    4 tablespoons butter
    2 cups sliced mushrooms
    2 packages (10 ounces each) frozen chopped spin-
      ach, defrosted, cooked
  1/2 cup grated Parmesan cheese

Combine flour, salt and pepper in a small bowl. Dust chicken breasts with flour. Dip chicken into beaten eggs, dust again. Heat butter and oil in a large skillet over medium heat. Fry chicken until golden brown on both sides, or until tender. While chicken is cooking, heat remaining 4 tablespoons of butter in a medium skillet over medium heat. Sauté mushrooms until tender, stirring occasionally, set aside. Drain spinach, arrange on heated serving platter. Sprinkle cheese over spinach. Place chicken pieces over spinach, cover chicken with sautéed mushrooms.

# CHICKEN CASSOULET

**Makes 6 servings**

    3 tablespoons vegetable oil
  1/2 pound sweet Italian sausages, cut into 1-inch
       pieces
    1 onion, sliced thin
    3 tablespoons vegetable oil
3 1/2 pound chicken fryer, cut into 8 pieces
  1/2 teaspoon salt, tarragon
  1/4 teaspoon pepper
    1 can (14 1/2 ounces) tomatoes, including juice
    1 can (15 ounces) white beans, drained

In a large heavy skillet, heat oil over medium heat; sauté sausages and onion until sausage is cooked, stirring often. Brown chicken pieces, remove and reserve. Add seasonings, tomatoes, stir until ingredients are combined. Pour mixture into an ovenproof casserole. Mix in beans and chicken, cover. Bake at 350° F. for 45 minutes.

# CHICKEN PIE

**Make 6-8 servings**

  4 tablespoons butter
  4 tablespoons all-purpose flour
1½ cups chicken stock
1½ cups cooked, diced chicken
  ½ cup pearl onions
  1 cup peas and carrots
  ¼ teaspoon salt
  ¼ teaspoon thyme
  ¼ teaspoon garlic powder
  ¼ teaspoon pepper
  1 cup canned onion rings
    Pastry for 9-inch 2-crust pie

In a large heavy skillet heat butter over medium heat, whisk in flour and continue cooking until flour is absorbed. Stir in chicken stock and cook, stirring often until mixture thickens. Mix in chicken and vegetables. Pour into a 9-inch unbaked pie crust. Sprinkle onion rings over pie. Cover with top crust and flute edges. Prick top and make a ½-inch steam vent in the center of the pie. Bake at 450°F. for 30 minutes, or until crust is golden brown.

# CHICKEN WITH ARTICHOKE HEARTS

**Makes 8 servings**

  4 tablespoons butter
  2 chickens (2¹/₂ pounds each), cut into quarters
¹/₂ teaspoon salt
¹/₂ teaspoon pepper
¹/₂ teaspoon garlic powder
¹/₂ teaspoon rosemary
  4 tablespoons butter
  1 can (14 ounces) artichoke hearts, drained
  1 pound mushrooms, sliced
  1 large onion, sliced thin
  3 tablespoons all-purpose flour
  1 cup chicken stock
¹/₄ cup dry white wine

In a large skillet heat butter over medium heat, brown chicken. Sprinkle with spices. Arrange chicken in an ovenproof casserole. Melt remaining butter in a skillet. Sauté artichoke hearts, mushrooms and onion until tender, push to one side of pan. Sprinkle flour over skillet. Whisk until absorbed. Stir in stock and wine, cook until sauce thickens, stirring often. Pour sauce and vegetables over chicken. Bake at 375°F. for 40-45 minutes.

# CITRUS CHICKEN ___

**Makes 6 servings**

3¹/₂ pound chicken, cut into eighths
2 stalks celery, sliced
1 green pepper, seeded, sliced
2 onions, sliced thin
1 can (20 ounces) pineapple chunks, drained, juice reserved
¹/₄ teaspoon salt
¹/₄ teaspoon pepper
¹/₄ teaspoon oregano
¹/₄ teaspoon garlic salt

**Sauce**

¹/₂ cup orange marmalade
¹/₂ cup vinegar
1 cup catsup
3 tablespoons pineapple juice

Arrange chicken in a 9x13x1³/₄-inch casserole. Sprinkle celery, pepper and onion over chicken. Cover with aluminum foil, bake at 350°F. for 45 minutes. Add pineapple and seasonings to chicken. In a small bowl combine sauce ingredients and pour over chicken. Cover, bake for 20 minutes, uncover and bake 10 minutes.

# BARBECUED CHICKEN

**Makes 10 servings**
**Sauce:**

1 cup catsup
1/2 cup water
1 tablespoon vegetable oil
3 tablespoons light brown sugar
1/2 teaspoon salt
1 teaspoon Worcestershire sauce
1/4 teaspoon pepper
3 broiler fryers, quartered

Combine sauce ingredients in a 1-quart saucepan, simmer for 2 minutes or until all ingredients are well blended. Brush chicken with sauce. Place chicken skin side up on grate about 5 inches above medium heat. Broil slowly 10-15 minutes, then turn and broil skin side down until brown. Turn several times and begin to baste about 10 minutes before chicken is done; barbecue sauce burns easily. Allow about 45 minutes total time for chicken. The chicken is done when the drumstick can be twisted easily. Spoon the remaining barbecue sauce over chicken when serving.

# GARLIC CHICKEN __

**Makes 5-6 servings**

3¹/₂ **pound chicken, cut into pieces**
  ¹/₂ **teaspoon salt**
  ¹/₄ **teaspoooon pepper**
  ¹/₄ **teaspoon nutmeg**
38- **40 cloves garlic**
   3 **tablespoons olive oil**
   2 **tablespoons melted butter**
   3 **stalks celery, sliced**
   3 **tablespoons fresh, minced parsley**
  ¹/₄ **cup dry white wine**
  ¹/₂ **cup heavy cream**

Sprinkle chicken pieces with salt, pepper and nutmeg, set aside. In a small saucepan over medium heat, bring 1 cup water to a boil, par-boil chicken for 30 seconds, drain. Remove garlic skins. Combine olive oil and melted butter, brush chicken. Pour remaining oil-butter on bottom of 2-quart casserole. Layer ¹/₂ of the garlic, celery, parsley in casserole, place ¹/₂ of chicken in casserole. Layer remaining garlic, celery, parsley and chicken. Season with salt. Pour dry white wine and heavy cream over chicken, cover. Bake at 350°F. for 1 hour and 15 minutes, baste occasionally.

# CHEESE AND CHICKEN TAMALES _

**Makes 8 servings**

- 28 fresh corn husks, silk removed
- 1/3 cup lard or vegetable shortening
- 1 1/2 cups masa harina
- 1/4 teaspoon salt
- 3/4 cup warm water
- 1 1/2 cups cooked minced chicken
- 1/2 cup grated Monterey Jack cheese
- 1/2 teaspoon garlic powder

Trim edges of corn husks two inches from the top and two inches from the bottom. Wash. Place husks in a large mixing bowl and cover with hot water. Let stand for one-half hour before using. Beat lard until light and fluffy in a small mixing bowl. Combine masa harina, salt and warm water in a medium mixing bowl. Add lard; mix until light and smooth. Drain husks. Lay two corn husks side by side, one with the wide end down. Overlap edges and seal with masa harina. In center of husks, spread three tablespoons of masa harina to form a 3x5-inch rectangle. Combine chicken, cheese and garlic powder in a medium-size mixing bowl. Top masa harina with two tablespoons of filling. Roll up, jelly-roll fashion; fold one end under and seal with masa harina or tie with string. Leave top side of tamale open. Arrange in a steamer with the open end facing up. Steam for 50 minutes. Carefully uncover steamer. When dough comes away from the husks, the tamales should be done.

# CHICKEN MOLD

3 tablespoons butter
1/2 pound fresh mushrooms, chopped
3 cups cooked chicken, minced
2 cups soft bread crumbs
1/2 cup cooked rice
1/2 teaspoon salt
2 tablespoons, pimiento, minced
2 cups chicken stock
4 egg yolks or 3 whole eggs

Preheat oven to 350°F. In a skillet, melt butter. Sauté mushrooms until tender. Transfer to a deep bowl. Mix in remaining ingredients. Press lightly into a buttered ring mold. Bake for 1 hour. Unmold onto serving platter. Serve with creamy mushroom sauce.

**Creamy Mushroom Sauce**

1/4 cup butter
1/2 pound fresh mushrooms
1/4 pound all-purpose flour
   Paprika
1/4 cup heavy cream
1 tablespoon freshly squeezed lemon juice
2 cups chicken stock

In a large skillet, melt butter. Sauté mushrooms until tender. Sprinkle flour over mushrooms; toss until flour is absorbed. Sprinkle with paprika. Stir in cream, lemon juice, and chicken stock. Simmer, stirring constantly, until sauce thickens.

# CHICKEN CROQUETTES

**Makes 8 servings**

- 2 stalks celery, chopped
- 1 large onion, minced
- 2 cups cooked, minced chicken
- 1/2 teaspoon salt
- 1/2 teaspoon pepper
- 3 tablespoons butter
- 3 tablespoons all-purpose flour
- 1 3/4 cups cream
- 1 cup bread crumbs
- Peanut oil for deep frying
- 3 eggs, lightly beaten

In a large mixing bowl combine celery, onion, chicken, salt and pepper, reserve. Heat butter in a small saucepan over medium heat. Add flour and whisk until flour is absorbed. Add cream and whisk until it begins to thicken, stirring continuously. Add sauce to chicken mixture, blend together. Shape into 2 x 3-inch croquettes. In a deep fryer or deep medium saucepan heat oil to 375° F. Roll croquettes in the eggs and roll in crumbs. Lower croquettes into the hot oil, fry about 3 at a time, until golden brown. Drain on paper toweling. Place 2 on each individual plate.

# CHICKEN QUENELLES

**Makes 6-8 servings**

1 egg white, beaten to soft peaks
2 cups cooked chicken, ground
½ teaspoon salt and white pepper
¼ teaspoon nutmeg
1 cup heavy cream

In a large mixing bowl whisk together all ingredients. Dip 2 tablespoons into cold water. Barely fill one of the spoons with chicken mixture. Place the other spoon over the top. Gently mold chicken mixture between the spoons. Carefully slide quenelles onto a buttered skillet. Fill skillet with a single layer, allowing room for expansion. Slowly pour enough salted water in from the side of the pan to cover the quenelles halfway. Simmer, turning once with a slotted spoon, until quenelles are firm, about 6-8 minutes. Remove and drain on paper toweling. Cover quenelles with aluminum foil until ready to serve. Serve with sauce of your choice.

# SYRACUSE CHICKEN WINGS

**Makes 6-8 servings**
**Wings**

2 dozen chicken wings, about 3$\frac{1}{2}$-4 pounds
3 cups peanut oil
$\frac{1}{4}$ cup butter
2-3 tablespoons hot sauce
1 tablespoon white vinegar

**Blue-Cheese Dressing**

1 cup mayonnaise
2 teaspoons minced onion
1 teaspoon minced garlic
$\frac{1}{4}$ cup minced fresh parsley
$\frac{1}{2}$ cup commercial sour cream
1 tablespoon freshly squeezed lemon juice
1 tablespoon white vinegar
$\frac{1}{4}$ cup crumbled blue cheese
Salt, freshly ground black pepper, to taste
Celery sticks

Cut off and discard the tip of each wing. Cut the main wing at the joint to yield two pieces. Sprinkle with salt and pepper. Heat oil in a deep heavy skillet to 375°F. Deep-fry wings, 1 cupful at a time, until crisp. Drain on paper toweling. Keep wings warm. Melt butter in a medium saucepan over medium heat. Stir in hot sauce and vinegar. Remove from heat. Pour over wings. In a deep bowl, combine all dressing ingredients. Chill 30 minutes. Serve wings with blue cheese and celery sticks.

# CURRIED CHICKEN LIVERS

**Makes 4-6 servings**

1½ pound chicken livers
3 tablespoons peanut oil
1 onion, sliced
2 cloves garlic, minced
1½ teaspoons curry powder
½ teaspoon turmeric
½ teaspoon ground cumin, or to taste
¼ teaspoon pepper

Trim chicken livers, set aside. In a deep heavy skillet, heat oil over medium heat. Sauté onion and garlic until tender, about 2 minutes. Stir in chicken livers and sprinkle with spices. Stir to coat livers. Cook about 3-4 minutes or until browned but slightly pink inside. Serve hot with buttered noodles.

# CORNISH HENS WITH A TANG

**Makes 6 servings**

- 3 Rock Cornish hens
- 1 cup hazelnuts, chopped
- 1 onion, minced
- 4 tablespoons butter, room temperature
- 1/2 teaspoon salt
- 1/4 cup minced fresh parsley
- 1 teaspoon dry mustard
- 1/4 teaspoon Tabasco sauce
- 1/4 pound melted butter
- 1 teaspoon seasoned salt
- 1/2 teaspoon paprika

Preheat oven to 425°F. Combine hazelnuts, onion, butter, salt, parsley, mustard and Tabasco sauce. Loosen the skin of the hens and stuff the filling between skin and meat of hens. Combine the melted butter, salt, and paprika; brush mixture over the hens. Roast on a rack over drip pan about 45 minutes to 1 hour, basting several times with remaining butter mixture. Cut hens in half lengthwise.

# CHRISTMAS GOOSE

**Makes 8 servings**

- **1 goose**
- **2 tablespoons melted butter**
- **3 day-old rolls, crumbled, soaked in milk, squeezed dry**

- **2 eggs, slightly beaten**
- **1/2 teaspoon salt**
- **1/2 teaspoon pepper**
- **1/4 teaspoon nutmeg**
- **3 tablespoons freshly squeezed orange juice**
- **1 orange, sliced**

Arrange goose on its back, remove fat from under the skin, remove as much fat as possible. Place goose on a roasting rack in a roasting pan over 1/2 inch of water. In a medium bowl combine butter and crumble. Mix in salt, pepper, nutmeg and juice. Stuff goose. Salt outside of goose lightly. Place orange slice over top of goose, cover with aluminum foil, roast at 350°F. for 2 1/2 hours or until goose is cooked. In one-half hour remove foil. Baste every half hour.

# DUCK WITH COCONUT

**Makes 8 servings**

- 2 ducklings, 4$\frac{1}{2}$-5 pounds each, quartered
- 1 cup grated coconut
- $\frac{1}{2}$ cup all-purpose flour
- $\frac{1}{4}$ teaspoon salt and white pepper
- 1 egg, slightly beaten


**Orange Sauce**

- 3 tablespoons duck drippings
- 2 tablespoons cornstarch
- 2 cups freshly squeezed orange juice
- $\frac{3}{4}$ teaspoon ground ginger
- $\frac{1}{2}$ teaspoon salt
- $\frac{1}{4}$ teaspoon pepper
- $\frac{1}{2}$ teaspoon crushed rosemary

Prick skin on duck. Place duck quarters on a rack over drip pan and bake at 400°F. for 30 minutes. Pour off all but 3 tablespoons of the drippings. Combine coconut, flour, salt, and pepper. Brush duck with egg and sprinkle with coconut mixture. Return to oven, continue to roast 15-20 minutes, basting once until crust has browned. Serve with orange sauce. To prepare sauce, blend 3 tablespoons cooled drippings with 2 tablespoons cornstarch. Add remaining ingredients. Cook and stir until bubbly.

# DUCK PATÉ EN CROUTE

 3 cups all-purpose flour
 1 teaspoon salt
 6 tablespoons butter, cut into cubes
 4 tablespoons vegetable shortening
 1 tablespoon olive oil
 1 egg
5-8 tablespoons ice water
 5-pound duck
 3/4 pound lean, boneless pork, ground
 1/2 pound pork fat, ground
 5 chicken livers, ground
 1 egg
 4 tablespoons Cognac
 1 teaspoon salt
 1/2 teaspoon each ground allspice, dried thyme, freshly
    ground black pepper
 1/2 cup shelled, unsalted green pistachio nuts
 1 egg yolk mixed with 1 teaspoon water, for glaze

**Crust**
In the work bowl of a food processor fitted with a steel blade or
in a large mixing bowl using a pastry knife, combine flour and
salt; add butter, vegetable shortening and olive oil, process until it resembles coarse crumbs. Slowly add egg and enough
water to bind. Gather dough into a ball. Knead for 1 minute on
a lightly floured pastry cloth. Cover with plastic wrap and re-

frigerate 1 hour. Prepare filling for paté.

**Filling**
Debone duck. Cut breast meat into long thin strips, cover and refrigerate until ready to use. Roughly chop the remaining duck meat, place in a large mixing bowl. Mix in pork, pork fat and chicken livers, combine. Mix in all ingredients except egg yolk mixture.

**To Assemble**
Divide dough in half. Roll out half of crust on a lightly floured board to 1/4 inch thick. Fit crust into 9 1/2 x 5 1/2 x 4 1/2-inch paté mold or terrine, leave 1-inch overhang. Roll out remaining dough. Fill half of mold with prepared filling, being sure that the corners are filled. Press the strips of duck breast over filling. Add remaining filling, mounding it on top. Bring up the edges of the crust. Cut out a top piece to fit exactly in the mold. Place it over the paté. Seal edges with egg mixture. Brush the crust with egg mixture, press edges with a fork securing a tight seal. Cut 3 vent holes, inserting aluminum foil funnel cones. Preheat oven to 325°F. Bake paté for 1 1/2 hours or until the juices run clear. Cover top loosely with aluminum foil if it seems to brown too quickly. Allow paté to cool overnight. Remove mold. Place paté on serving dish; slice and serve with small pickles and crackers.

# BAKED TURKEY BREAST IN TONNATO SAUCE

1 4-5 pound turkey breast, bone in,
  completely defrosted
**Butter**
**Salt, pepper, garlic powder, onion powder, paprika**

Preheat oven to 350°F. Season turkey breast with seasonings. Roast on rack in roasting pan until internal temperature reaches 175°F. Remove from oven and let stand at least 10 minutes. Slice into thin slices. Serve with Tonnato Sauce and garnish with parsley, capers, and tomatoes.

**Tonnato Sauce**

1 cup mayonnaise
1 can (7 ounces) tuna, preferably Italian tuna
2 anchovies, chopped
1/2 cup chopped celery
1/2 teaspoon salt
1/4 teaspoon pepper
1 tablespoon freshly squeezed lemon juice

Combine all sauce ingredients in a blender or in a food processor fitted with a steel blade. Chill until serving time.

# ROAST TURKEY WITH CUMBERLAND SAUCE

**Makes 6-8 servings**

> 3 tablespoons butter, room temperature
> 10 -12 pound turkey
> 1/2 teaspoon each salt, pepper and garlic powder

**Cumberland Sauce**

> 1 jar, 12 ounces, red currant jelly
> 1 1/2 cups port or dry sherry
> 1/2 cup freshly squeezed orange juice
> 1 tablespoon freshly squeezed lemon juice
> 1 teaspoon orange zest

Rub butter over turkey. Sprinkle with salt, pepper and garlic powder. Place turkey on rack in large roasting pan. Cover turkey with aluminum foil. Roast at 325°F. for 15-20 minutes per pound. Uncover turkey 30 minutes before end of roasting, baste and continue roasting uncovered browning turkey.

Combine all sauce ingredients in medium saucepan. Simmer until jelly melts and all ingredients are combined. Place in covered container until ready to serve. Let turkey rest 10 minutes before slicing. Slice turkey at table and pass Cumberland sauce.

# LEFTOVER TURKEY STIR-FRY

**Makes 4-6 servings**

3 tablespoons vegetable oil
1 clove garlic, minced
1/2 teaspoon ground ginger
1 cup shredded cabbage
1/2 cup sliced bamboo shoots
1 cup sliced fresh mushrooms
1/2 cup water chestnuts, sliced
1/2 teaspoon salt
1/4 cup chicken stock
2 1/2 cups cooked turkey, cubed
1/4 pound snow peas, trimmed

**Sauce**

2 tablespoons soy sauce
2 tablespoons oyster sauce
1 tablepoon dry white wine
1/2 teaspoon sugar
1/4 teaspoon pepper
2 teaspoons cornstarch combined with
2 tablespoons water
1 teaspoon sesame oil

Heat heavy skillet or wok over high heat until hot; add oil. Heat oil for 10 seconds. Stir in garlic and ginger. Add cabbage and bamboo shoots; stir-fry 30 seconds. Add mushrooms and water chestnuts; continue to stir-fry. Sprinkle vegetables with salt. Pour in chicken stock; stir to mix. Stir in turkey cubes, cover, and cook 30 seconds. Add snow peas; cook another 30 seconds. Combine sauce ingredients. Add sauce to turkey; simmer and stir until mixture begins to thicken. Transfer to a heated serving platter. Serve with hot fluffy rice.

# MOCK CHICKEN LEGS (FRIED FROG LEGS)

**Makes 4-6 servings**

1½ pounds frog legs, washed, trimmed, separated
1 cup white wine
2 cloves garlic, minced
2 tablespoons freshly chopped parsley
½ teaspoon salt, freshly ground black pepper
¼ teaspoon ground nutmeg
   All-purpose flour
1 egg, slightly beaten
3 tablespoons milk
   Peanut oil for frying
1 lemon sliced for garnish

Combine white wine, garlic, parsley, salt, pepper and nutmeg. Arrange the frog legs in the marinade and let stand for 1½ hours. Drain legs, pat dry with paper toweling. Dust legs with flour. Combine egg and milk in a shallow bowl. Dip frog legs into the egg-milk mixture. Heat oil in a deep heavy skillet to 375°F. Fry frog legs, a few at a time until cooked, about 4-5 minutes. Drain on paper toweling, sprinkle with salt, and garnish with lemon slices.

# STUFFING

## WILD RICE STUFFING

**Makes 8 servings**

- 1 can (3 ounces) sliced mushrooms, drained
- 1½ cups beef stock or canned condensed beef broth
- 1 large onion, minced
- ½ cup wild rice, washed
- 1 cup long grain rice
- 3 tablespoons butter
- 3 tablespoons chopped fresh parsley

In a medium skillet heat butter, sauté mushrooms over medium heat, stir occasionally, set aside. In a saucepan combine beef stock, ½ cup water and onions and bring mixture to boiling point over medium heat. Add wild rice, reduce heat. Cover and simmer for 20 minutes. Add long grain rice; return mixture to boiling point. Cover and reduce heat to simmer, continue cooking 20 minutes or until the rice is cooked. Stir in mushrooms and parsley.

# WHOLE-WHEAT STUFFING

**Makes 8-10 cups stuffing**

  1 **loaf whole-wheat bread, trimmed**
 1/2 **pound fresh chestnuts; cut a slit in the top of each chestnut with a sharp knife**
 3/4 **pound butter**
  1 **large onion, minced**
  4 **stalks celery, chopped**
  1 **leek, chopped**
 1/2 **teaspoon crushed thyme**
 1/2 **teaspoon crushed sage**
    **Liver from turkey, chopped**
 1/2 **teaspoon salt, pepper**
 1/4 **cup chopped fresh parsley**

Cut bread into cubes, place in a bowl, let stand overnight. Arrange chestnuts on a cookie sheet. Bake at 475°F. for 10 minutes, or until shells will peel easily. Remove shells and skins; chop chestnuts. Melt butter in a saucepan over medium heat. Stir in onion, celery, and leek. Continue cooking until tender. Add spices and liver. Cook, stirring occasionally, about 2 minutes. Pour mixture over bread cubes and toss. Season with salt and pepper. Toss with parsley.

# CORNBREAD STUFFING FOR TURKEY

**Stuffing for an 18-pound turkey**

1½ pounds bulk sausage
  2 onions, minced
  1 stalk celery, chopped
  6 cups soft white bread crumbs
  1 teaspoon salt
  2 teaspoons poultry seasonings
  1 teaspoon herb seasonings
  2 eggs, slightly beaten
  1 cup chicken stock
  6 cups crumbled cornbread

In a large skillet over medium heat, cook sausage breaking it up as you stir, drain. Transfer sausage to a large mixing bowl, leave ½ cup drippings in skillet. Reheat drippings, sauté onions and celery until tender, stirring occasionally. Add to sausage, combine. Add remaining ingredients, toss until combined. Cool stuffing before adding to turkey cavity.

# THANKSGIVING OYSTER DRESSING _

**Stuffing for a 12-14 pound bird**

- 5 tablespoons butter
- 5 tablespoons peanut oil
- 2 onions, chopped
- 4 stalks celery, chopped
- 7 slices bread, crust removed, soaked in milk, squeezed dry
- 4 tablespoons chopped, fresh parsley
- 1/2 teaspoon salt and pepper
- 3/4 teaspoon thyme, sage, marjoram, oregano
- 1 1/2 cups oysters, chopped
- 2 eggs, slightly beaten

In a large skillet heat butter and oil over medium heat. Sauté onions and celery until tender, stirring occasionally. Add bread, mix well. Add remaining ingredients, blend, simmer 1 minute.

# FISH
# AND
# SEAFOOD

# Fish
## And
# Seafood

Fish has always been an important source of protein for man. Once early man found a way of preserving fish and of sailing a distance to catch them, his earnest harvesting of the seas began. There were no fundamental changes from classical times until the nineteenth century, when the introduction of trawling, railways, and canning produced a jump to a new dimension. Now in the twentieth century the technique of freezing and availability of air transport have developed fishing even further.

Freshness is judged by examining the eyes of the fish. The gills should be a bloody red, not brown, and the skin should not have a gray cast. And of course a fish that is not fresh will smell; a fresh fish will not have an odor.

When fish is brought home, it should be rinsed, salted, rinsed again, and dried with paper toweling. Wrap it in paper or pack in ice and place in the coldest area of the refrigerator. To freeze a fish, wrap it well and freeze it quickly. Use frozen fish as soon as possible. Defrosting fish should be done overnight in the refrigerator.

## METHODS OF PREPARATION

**Pan-fried** In a skillet, heat just enough fat to cover the bottom of the pan. Do not let fat smoke. Fry fish quickly over moderate heat, 2 to 3 minutes. Turn carefully with a spatula. Fry only until golden brown and easily flaked with a fork, about another 2 to 3 minutes.

**Shallow-fried** In a deep skillet heat fat 1½ inches deep to 375°F. Dip fish in bread crumbs or cornmeal. Gently slide into hot fat, fry 3 to 4 minutes . Drain on paper towels.

**Poached** For a pretty presentation use a whole gutted fish with head and tail intact. Whitefish, salmon or turbot are good for this purpose. The fish has to be small enough to fit into your pan. Use a fish poacher, wok or turkey roaster. Make poaching liquid: 1 large carrot, sliced, 1 onion, sliced, 2 stalks celery, sliced, 3 bay leaves, 2 cups dry white wine and 3 quarts water. Bring mixture to a boil, simmer 20 minutes; strain. Pour liquid into poaching pan. Heat to a boil and reduce to a simmer. Place fish on rack below surface of liquid. Continue simmering and cook 10 minutes. Check to see if the fish is cooked. To poach a 3-pound fish takes approximately 12-15 minutes.

**Broiling** Using a thick fish or pieces of fish, grill briefly, until cooked under the broiler. Fish can be coated, marinated and/or basted depending on the individual recipe. Fish is cooked when it flakes easily. Brush fish with melted butter. Season with salt and pepper. Place in a preheated, lightly greased broiler pan lined with aluminum foil.

**Baked** Whole fish, steaks or fillets may be baked. Fillets and steaks may be dipped and breaded and baked in a hot oven, 400°F to 450°F. They may also be baked in a hot oven, 400°F to 450°F. The fish may also be baked in a sauce. Then a lower temperature is used for this method, about 350°F to 375°F.

## GENERAL SEAFOOD INFORMATION

**DRAWN** Scaled and insides removed.

**DRESSED** Scaled and the head, tail and fins removed.

**FILLETS** The sides of small to medium fish cut lengthwise away from the backbone, usually boneless.

**STEAKS** Crosswise sections of large fish such as salmon. They are cut not less than 1 inch thick and contain a piece of backbone.

## SHELLFISH

**CLAMS** Clams are sold by the dozen or quart. When purchased, the shells must be tightly closed. There are soft-shelled and hard-shelled clams. To help remove sand, place live clams in cold water to cover. Sprinkle oatmeal over the top, and let stand 2 to 3 hours before opening and cooking. Use a knife or steam to open.

**CRAB** Crabs are sold by the dozen or pound. Soft-shelled crab are usually fried; hard-shelled ones are boiled, and the meat picked from them for use in various dishes.

**LOBSTER** Live, plunge in boiling salted water. Boil 10 minutes, then simmer 25 minutes. Plunge in cold water and chill. Break off 2 large claws and 4 pairs of small ones. Separate tail and body joint. Cut a slit lengthwise through the center of the tail. Remove the black vein running down the back of tail meat. Remove stomach. The green portions are liver and roe; both are edible. Break open the claws and remove meat. If the lobster is frozen and to be broiled or baked, clean according to the above directions and cook according to recipe directions. You do not have to boil ahead of time.

**OYSTERS** Oysters are sold by the dozen either in shells or shucked. Shells should be tightly closed when purchased. Shucked oysters should be plump, with no evidence of shrinkage. Examine oysters carefully and remove any pieces of shell that cling to them. Cook the oysters only long enough for the gills to curl.

**SHRIMP** Shrimp are bought by the pound with the heads removed. Raw shrimp are grayish-green in color and cooked shrimp are reddish. When purchased, shrimp should be firm-fleshed. The shell is parchment-like and easily removed. Shrimp is cooked in salted water. Bring water to a boil and cook 5 minutes. Cool, shell, and chill. With a sharp knife, remove the black vein down the back. Shrimp remain one of America's costliest seafoods.

In these recipes saltwater fish can be substituted for one another, as can freshwater fish.

**Fat** fish have oil running through all the flesh. They are generally best for broiling, baking and planking.

**Lean** fish have drier flesh; they are best for boiling and steaming. When baked, add strips of bacon and when broiling, baste often with butter.

## Freshwater Fish

| | |
|---|---|
| **Carp** | lean |
| **Catfish** | lean |
| **Lake Trout** | fat |
| **Pike** | lean |
| **Rainbow Trout** | fat |
| **Smelt** | lean |
| **Sturgeon** | fat |
| **Whitefish** | fat |
| **Yellow Perch** | lean |

## Saltwater Fish

| | |
|---|---|
| **Cod** | lean |
| **Flounder or Sole** | lean |
| **Haddock** | lean |
| **Halibut** | lean |
| **Mullet** | lean |
| **Pollock** | lean |
| **Red Salmon** | lean |
| **Red Snapper** | lean |
| **Salmon** | fat |
| **Sea Bass** | lean |
| **Swordfish** | lean |
| **Tuna** | fat |
| **Turbot** | lean |
| **Whiting** | lean |

# POACHED TROUT WITH CURRY SAUCE

**Makes 6 servings**

- 2 carrots, sliced
- 1 large onion, sliced
- 2 stalks celery, sliced
- 2 cups white wine
- 2 bay leaves
- 6 peppercorns, crushed
- 4 sprigs parsley
- 1 3-pound trout, gutted, head and tail intact

Using a fish poacher or roasting pan, combine carrots, onion, celery, white wine, bay leaves, peppercorns, parsley and enough water to cover fish. Heat mixture to boiling; reduce heat to simmer. Arrange fish on rack in poacher; if using a roasting pan, wrap fish in cheesecloth. Simmer 25 minutes or until fish is cooked; cool. Remove fish to serving platter. Remove skin, serve with curry sauce.

**Curry Sauce**

- 1 cup mayonnaise
- 3 tablespoons chili sauce
- 3 green onions, chopped
- 1/2 teaspoon curry powder (or to taste)

In a small bowl combine all ingredients and chill until ready to serve.

# TWO-TONED SEAFOOD MOUSSELINE WITH SAUCE VERT _

**Makes 8-10 servings**

  1 **walleyed pike (¹/₂ pound skinned) cut into 1¹/₂-inch pieces**
  2 **egg whites**
  1 **egg**
¹/₂ **teaspoon nutmeg**
    **Salt and white pepper to taste**
  2 **cups heavy cream**
¹/₄ **cup Sauce Vert**

Using a blender or a food processor fitted with a steel blade puree fish, egg whites, egg, nutmeg, salt and pepper. Place bowl, covered, in refrigerator 20 minutes. Return bowl to food processor. With the machine running, pour in cream in a slow steady stream through the feed tube; cover, refrigerate mixture 20 minutes. Place 1 cup of the mixture into a medium mixing bowl, combine with Sauce Vert, reserve. Preheat oven to 350°. Line bottom of a 4-cup pate mold with parchment paper cut to fit exactly. Spoon pate into prepared mold; gently layer the remaining puree over first layer. Cover with buttered aluminum foil. Place seafood mousseline in a baking pan. Pour hot water halfway up pan. Bake 1 hour or until the pate tests done. Cool on a wire rack to room temperature. Refrigerate overnight. When ready to serve invert seafood mousseline onto a chilled serving dish, slice. Arrange sauce on a plate, place a slice of mousseline over sauce. Serve chilled.

**Sauce Vert**

   1/2 **cup cooked lettuce, drained**
   1/2 **cup watercress, trimmed**
     2 **green onions, cut into 2-inch pieces**
     1 **cup mayonnaise**

In blender combine and puree all ingredients. Place in a covered bowl, chill until ready to use.

# STEAMED NEW POTATOES WITH YELLOW WHITEFISH CAVIAR

**Makes 8 servings**

- 30 small, 1-inch, well-shaped new potatoes
- 4 ounces yellow whitefish caviar
- 2 cups commercial sour cream

Scrub potatoes clean. Arrange potatoes in a steamer over simmering water. Steam potatoes until tender, about 15-20 minutes, adding more hot water as necessary. Potatoes can be served room temperature or hot. Scoop out a shallow hole in top of each potato with a melon ball scooper. Top with dollop of sour cream and garnish with caviar. Place on serving dish and serve immediately.

A steamer can be improvised by using a vegetable steamer and a 4 or 5- quart saucepan or a platter over an inverted soup bowl. Be sure to keep simmering water underneath the level of the plate.

# FINNAN HADDIE WITH MUSTARD SAUCE

**Makes 8 servings**

2½ pounds smoked haddock, cut into 1-inch pieces, bone removed
1 large onion, sliced
2 cups milk
3 bay leaves

**Mustard Sauce**

3 tablespoons butter
3 tablespoons all-purpose flour
2 teaspoons prepared Dijon mustard

Arrange haddock in a large saucepan, cover with onion, milk and bay leaves, simmer for 30 minutes or until fish is tender. Remove fish to a serving platter, drain liquid, discard onion and bay leaves, reserve liquid.

In a medium saucepan, heat butter, whisk in flour until it is absorbed. Add reserved cooking liquid and continue cooking until sauce thickens, stirring often. Blend in mustard. Serve finnan haddie with mustard sauce on the side.

# FISH AND CHIPS

**Makes 6 servings**

- 2 pounds flounder, skinned, boned
- 4 teaspoons freshly squeezed lemon juice
- 1/2 cup all-purpose flour

**Beer Batter**

- 1 cup all-purpose flour
- 1 egg
- 1 cup light beer
- 1/2 teaspoon salt

**Chips**

- 4 large potatoes, peeled, sliced thin
- Peanut oil for deep frying
- Coarse salt

Cut fish into 1-inch pieces, sprinkle with lemon juice, reserve. Combine batter ingredients in a mixing bowl. Arrange potato slices in a bowl of ice water for 10 minutes, drain, dry with paper toweling. Heat oil in a medium skillet to 375°F. Carefully slide potatoes, a few pieces at a time, into the hot oil, fry until golden brown, drain. Continue until all the potatoes are fried, reserve. Dredge fish pieces in the batter, fry fish until golden brown, a few pieces at a time, drain. Sprinkle chips with coarse salt, serve.

# TROUT WITH DARK BUTTER SAUCE

**Makes 6 servings**

> 6 trout, rinsed and patted dry
> All-purpose flour
> 6 tablespoons butter

**Dark Butter Sauce**

> 6 tablespoons butter
> 1/3 cup capers, drained
> 3 tablespoons wine vinegar

Coat the trout with flour. In a large skillet heat butter, fry fish, 3 at a time, turning once. Arrange fish on serving plate.

In a medium saucepan, melt butter over high heat until it turns a medium brown. Stir in capers and continue cooking until butter turns a darker brown. Stir in vinegar and immediately pour sauce over fish.

# SOLE WITH SPINACH

**Makes 8 servings**

2½ **pounds sole fillets, washed and patted dry**
  3 **tablespoons butter, cut into cubes**
 ½ **teaspoon salt**
  1 **pound spinach, cooked, drained, chopped**
  1 **can cream of mushroom soup**
  2 **tablespoons butter, melted**
 ¼ **cup unseasoned bread crumbs**
  1 **cup sliced mushrooms for garnish**

Arrange sole in a 11¾ x 7½ x 1¾-inch casserole dish. Sprinkle with butter and salt, cover casserole with aluminum foil, bake at 350°F for 15 minutes, remove and drain liquid. Arrange the cooked, drained spinach over the fish, pour mushroom soup over spinach. Combine melted butter and bread crumbs and sprinkle over top. Bake, uncovered at 350°F for 20 minutes.

Garnish with mushrooms.

# FISH TURBANS _____

**Makes 6 servings**

   5 tablespoons butter
   1 large onion, chopped
   3 stalks celery, sliced thin
   1 carrot, grated
 1/2 cup chopped mushrooms
   2 teaspoons freshly squeezed lemon juice
   1 cup bread crumbs
1 1/2 pounds sole fillets, washed and patted dry

In a large skillet melt butter over medium heat; saufe onion, celery, carrot and mushrooms until tender. Sprinkle with lemon juice. Stir in bread crumbs, reserve. Butter 6 custard cups. Curl slices of fish so that they line the sides and bottom of cups. Fill center with stuffing. Cover with aluminum foil, arrange on cookie sheet for easy handling. Bake at 350°F for 15 minutes or until fish flakes easily. Invert fish onto serving plates.

# SPICY SALMON LOAF

**Makes 8 servings**

- 1 can (16 ounces) salmon, drained
- 1 cup flavored bread crumbs
- 2 eggs, slightly beaten
- 1/2 cup milk
- 4 green onions, minced
- 2 stalks celery, chopped
- 1/2 teaspoon salt
- 1/4 teaspoon white pepper

Combine all ingredients in a large deep mixing bowl. Mound mixture into a greased 9x5x3-inch loaf pan. Bake in a 350°F oven for 45 minutes or until salmon loaf is firm and lightly browned. Cool, unmold and slice.

# BROILED SWORDFISH STEAKS

**Makes 6 servings**

- 2 pounds swordfish steaks, about 1 inch thick
- 3 tablespoons soy sauce
- 3 tablespoons butter or margarine, melted
- 1/4 cup chopped fresh broadleaf parsley for garnish
- 1 lemon, sliced for garnish

Arrange swordfish steaks on greased broiler rack. Sprinkle with soy sauce and melted butter, broil, 2 inches below heat for 5-6 minutes on each side or until cooked. Place on serving dish, garnish with parsley and lemon slices.

# FISH SOUFFLE _____

**Makes 8 servings**

2¹/₂ **pounds trout, boned, cut into cubes, pureed**
  2 **medium onions, minced**
  3 **eggs, separated**
  1 **cup heavy cream**
¹/₂ **teaspoon salt**
¹/₂ **teaspoon ground tarragon**
¹/₄ **teaspoon white pepper**

Puree trout again with the onions in a food processor fitted with a steel blade. Add egg yolks, cream, salt, tarragon and pepper, blend. In a separate bowl beat egg whites until stiff peaks, but not dry, form. Fold egg whites into trout mixture. Mound mixture into a lightly buttered 6-cup ring mold. Place mold in a pan, fill halfway with hot water. Bake souffle at 325°F for 1 hour.

# TUNA MOUSSE WITH CUCUMBER SAUCE

**Makes 6 servings**

- 8 ounces cream cheese, room temperature
- 1 can, 11 ounces, tomato soup
- 2 tablespoons unflavored gelatin, dissolved in 1/2 cup cold water
- 2 cans, 6 1/2 ounces each, tuna fish, drained
- 5 stalks celery, chopped
- 1 green pepper, seeded, chopped
- 1 cup mayonnaise
- 1/2 cup sliced black olives

In a large saucepan, stir together cream cheese and tomato soup over a low heat, until combined. Remove from heat, cool, stir in gelatin. Mix in remaining ingredients, blend. Pour into a lightly greased mold. Chill until firm. Unmold onto a serving platter with sliced lettuce and garnish with olives.

**Cucumber Sauce**

- 1/2 cup commercial sour cream
- 1/2 cup mayonnaise
- 1 large cucumber, peeled, seeded, pureed
- 3 green onions
- 1 teaspoon wine vinegar

In a large bowl combine all ingredients, chill for 1 hour.

# SWEET AND SOUR MACKEREL

**Makes 10-12 servings**

- 3 large onions, sliced thin
- 5 pounds mackerel, cut into 2-inch pieces
- 1¾ cup vinegar
- ¾ cup freshly squeezed lemon juice
- 1½ cups firmly packed light brown sugar
- 1 cup golden raisins
- ½ teaspoon ginger
- ½ cup gingersnap crumbs
- 1 lemon, sliced

Arrange sliced onions on bottom of large saucepan; lay fish over onions. Combine remaining ingredients, pour over fish. Bring mixture to a boil, reduce heat and simmer 45 minutes. Cool in pan. Carefully transfer to a glass mixing bowl, chill 3 days before serving.

# MUSHROOM-STUFFED TROUT

**Makes 5-6 servings**

- 3 pound trout, cleaned and patted dry
- 4 tablespoons butter
- 2 cloves garlic
- 6 shallots, minced
- 1 pound mushrooms, sliced
- 1/2 teaspoon ground thyme, salt
- 1 cup dry bread crumbs

Arrange trout in a greased, large casserole. Heat butter in a large skillet; sauté garlic, shallots and mushrooms until tender. Season with thyme and salt. Stir in bread crumbs. Spoon stuffing into trout cavity. Place any extra stuffing around fish. Brush fish with oil. Bake, uncovered at 350°F for 40 minutes or until the fish flakes easily. Let stand 5 minutes before serving.

# POACHED SALMON WITH WINE SAUCE _

**Makes 6 servings**

  3 cups dry white wine
  1 cup clam stock
  1/2 teaspoon salt
  3-inch piece lemon peel
  3 bay leaves
  2 carrots, sliced
  4 1-pound salmon, cleaned, head and tail intact
  3 tablespoons all-purpose flour
  1 cup dry white wine
  1/2 teaspoon ground basil
  1 cup light cream

Combine 1 quart water, dry white wine, clam stock, salt, lemon peel, bay leaves and carrots in a poaching or roasting pan. Bring mixture to boil, reduce heat and simmer for 5 minutes. Wrap individually in cheesecloth. Lower fish into broth, covering with liquid. Poach fish for 8 minutes or until fish flakes easily. Lift fish from pan, unwrap and arrange fish on a serving platter. Skin fish, chill. Drain any broth that may accumulate on platter.

**Wine Sauce**

In a medium saucepan heat butter. Whisk in flour until absorbed. Stir in wine, 1/2 cup strained poaching liquid and basil. Simmer until mixture thickens, stirring often.

# RUSSIAN KULEBIAC

**Crust**

    2 cups all-purpose flour
  1/4 teaspoon salt
    3 tablespoons butter, cut into cubes
    4 tablespoons vegetable shortening
    5 tablespoons ice water

In a deep bowl, with pastry knife incorporate flour, salt, butter and vegetable shortening. Mix in ice water, 1 tablespoon at a time, until a smooth ball forms. Cover with aluminum foil, chill for 30 minutes.

**Fish**

1 1/4 pounds trout or salmon fillet
    1 cup red wine
    3 bay leaves
    1 carrot

Poach fillet with red wine, bay leaves, carrot and 2 cups water, gently for 10 minutes, drain.

**Filling**

    1 cup bread crumbs
    3 tablespoons butter
    1 onion, minced
  1/2 pound mushrooms, minced
    4 eggs, hard-boiled, peeled, minced
1 1/2 cups cooked rice
    1 cup bread crumbs

**1 egg slightly beaten**
**1¹/₂ cups commercial sour cream**

Roll dough on a lightly floured surface into a rectangle, 2 times the size of the fillet. Sprinkle center of crust with bread crumbs. In a medium skillet heat butter; saufe onion, mushrooms until tender, mix in eggs and rice. Place fillet in the center of crust. Arrange the filling over fillet. Fold edges of pastry over top; press seams to seal. Arrange, seam side down, on a cookie sheet. Make ¹/₂-inch steam vent. Brush crust with slightly beaten egg. Bake at 350°F for 35-40 minutes or until cooked. Cool 5 minutes, slice, serve with sour cream.

# WHITEFISH WITH TOMATO SAUCE

3 tablespoons butter
2½ pounds whitefish fillets, washed and patted dry
1 can (28 ounces) whole tomatoes; puree tomatoes, include juice
3 cloves garlic, peeled, minced
½ teaspoon ground tarragon
1 medium onion, minced
3 tablespoons wine vinegar
¾ cup white wine
1 teaspoon honey
¼ pound butter, room temperature
¼ cup broadleaf parsley for garnish

Heat butter in a large heavy skillet, pan-fry whitefish fillets, reserve. In a large saucepan combine remaining ingredients, except butter, cook over medium heat, uncovered, reducing mixture by half, stirring occasionally; strain through cheesecloth. Beat butter, 1 tablespoon at a time incorporating. Drain fish. Spread sauce over fish. Garnish with broadleaf parsley.

# FISH WITH MUSHROOMS AND TOMATOES

**Makes 6 servings**

    2 pounds flounder or sole fillets
 1/2 teaspoon salt
 1/4 teaspoon white pepper
 1/2 teaspoon garlic powder
    2 cups sliced mushrooms
    2 teaspoons freshly squeezed lemon juice
    1 onion, sliced thin
    1 can, 16 ounces, tomatoes, drained, chopped
    4 tablespoons butter, melted
 1/2 cup seasoned bread crumbs
 1/4 cup freshly grated Parmesan cheese

Arrange flounder fillets in a greased 13x9x1¾-inch baking dish. Season with salt, white pepper and garlic powder. Toss mushrooms with lemon juice, arrange over fish. Add onions and tomatoes. Bake at 350°F for 15 minutes. In a separate bowl combine melted butter, bread crumbs and Parmesan cheese, sprinkle over fish. Broil fish until it begins to brown, about 10 minutes.

# TROUT AMANDINE _

**Makes 6 servings**

6½ pounds trout fillets
6 tablespoons butter or magarine, melted
3 tablespoons freshly squeezed lime juice
½ teaspoon salt
¼ teaspoon paprika
4 tablespoons butter
¾ cup blanched, slivered almonds
¼ cup chopped fresh parsley for garnish

Arrange trout fillets in a buttered 13x9x1¾-inch baking dish. Drizzle melted butter and lime juice over fillets. Season with salt and paprika. Bake at 450°F for 20 minutes or until fillets flake easily. Arrange on serving plates. In a small saucepan melt butter, stir in almonds, continue cooking over medium heat until almonds are lightly browned. Pour almond-butter mixture over fish, garnish with chopped parsley.

# FILLET OF FLOUNDER VERONIQUE

**Makes 8 servings**

- 3 tablespoons butter
- 2 pounds flounder fillets
- 3 tablespoons freshly squeezed orange juice
- 1 teaspoon ground tarragon
- 2 cloves garlic, peeled and minced
- 1 cup dry white wine
- 1/2 pound seedless green grapes
- 3 tablespoons butter
- 2 tablespoons all-purpose flour
- 4 tablespoons freshly squeezed orange juice

In a large skillet heat butter, add flounder fillets, drizzle with orange juice. Sprinkle with tarragon, garlic and white wine; simmer 5 minutes, add grapes, cook 7 minutes or until fish flakes easily. Arrange fish on heated platter. In the skillet, melt additional butter, whisk in flour and continue cooking until flour is absorbed. Whisk in orange juice and cook until sauce thickens. Serve sauce over fish and cooked egg noodles as a side dish.

# RED SNAPPER WITH VEGETABLES

**Makes 8 servings**

2½ pound red snapper, cleaved, scaled, leave head and
     tail intact
  4 tablespoons freshly squeezed lime juice
  ½ teaspoon salt
  ¼ teaspoon ground pepper
  3 cloves garlic, peeled and minced
  1 large onion, sliced
  4 tomatoes, peeled and quartered
  1 cup jumbo black olives
  3 potatoes, partially cooked, peeled and sliced
  1 lime, sliced for garnish

Arrange red snapper in a greased 13x9x1¾-inch baking dish,
sprinkle with lime juice, salt and pepper. Place garlic and vegetables over and around fish, sprinkle with olives and place
potatoes around snapper. Bake at 350°F for 45 minutes or until
fish flakes easily. Serve garnished with sliced lime.

# CEVICHE
# (Marinated Fish) ____

**Makes 4-6 servings**

- 1 pound very fresh sole or bay scallops
  Freshly squeezed lime juice to cover fish
- 1 large red onion, thinly sliced
- 1 large tomato, peeled, seeded, chopped
- 3 tablespoons vegetable oil
- 2 tablespoons wine vinegar
- 1/2 teaspoon salt
- 1 tablespoon chopped fresh cilantro or parsley

Cut fish into 1/2-inch strips, arrange in a 2-quart glass bowl. Cover with freshly squeezed lime juice. Add remaining ingredients; mix gently. Cover with plastic wrap. Refrigerate for two days. Turn fish three times while it is marinating. Serve chilled on a bed of lettuce.

# GLAZED SALMON ___

**3¹/₂-4 pound whole salmon, dressed, tail and head intact**
**Court Bouillon**
**Seasoned Aspic Glaze: Recipe follows**
**Decorations: Lemon slices, pimiento and olives**
**Clear Glaze: Recipe follows**
**Bibb lettuce**
**Mayonnaise**

Place salmon on a rack in a fish poaching pan, or wrap in cheesecloth and suspend from the handles of a kettle. Pour cool Court Bouillon over fish. Cover, simmer 20 to 30 minutes or until fish flakes easily when tested with a fork. Remove fish immediately. Skin fish, place on a large serving platter, chill. To glaze fish, pour slightly thickened Seasoned Aspic Glaze evenly over the entire fish, chill. Continue glazing and chilling until you have built up an even clear ¹/₈ inch of glaze, chill. Remove glaze from platter. To decorate fish, place a border of lemon slices around fish. Decorate the top of the fish using pimiento and olives, chill again. Pour slightly thickened Clear Glaze over the entire fish, chill thoroughly. Remove glaze from platter and garnish with lettuce. Chill until serving time. Serve with mayonnaise.

**Court Bouillon**
**Makes 1¹/₄ quarts bouillon**

2 **quarts water**
2 **cups sliced celery**

1½ **cups sliced onion**
1 **cup sliced carrot**
½ **cup vinegar**
2 **tablespoons salt**
8 **peppercorns**
4 **lemons, sliced**
3 **sprigs parsley**
2 **bay leaves**
½ **teaspoon whole thyme**

Combine all ingredients in a 4-quart saucepan. Simmer, uncovered, for 45 minutes. Strain, cool.

**Seasoned Aspic Glaze**

2 **envelopes unflavored gelatin**
½ **cup water**
2 **cups boiling condensed chicken broth**
2 **tablespoons freshly squeezed lemon juice**

Soften gelatin in cold water. Dissolve gelatin in boiling broth. Add lemon juice. Chill until slightly thickened.

**Clear Glaze**

1 **envelope unflavored gelatin**
¼ **cup water**
¾ **cup boiling water**

Soften gelatin in cold water. Dissolve gelatin in boiling water. Chill until slightly thickened.

# SPANISH PAELLA

**Makes 10-12 servings**

- 6 tablespoons bacon drippings
- 1 large onion, sliced
- 1 green bell pepper, seeded, sliced
- 6 sausages, thinly sliced
- 8 chicken drumsticks
- 1 pound shrimp, shelled, deveined
- 1/2 teaspoon tarragon, salt, cayenne
- 1/2 teaspoon saffron dissolved in 1/4 cup water, strained, discard saffron
- 2 dozen clams, washed
- 3 pounds mussels, washed and scrubbed, discard any mussels with open shells, soak in water for 30 minutes
- 2 1/2 cups uncooked rice
- 4 cups chicken stock
- 1 cup cooked peas

In a paella pan or 13x9x1 3/4-inch baking dish heat bacon drippings, sauté onion, bell pepper and sausages, over medium-high heat. Push mixture to one side, brown drumsticks. Mix in shrimp, spices and saffron liquid. Add clams, mussels, rice and chicken stock. Cover and bake at 375°F for 1 hour. Sprinkle paella with cooked peas. Serve with crusty bread.

# ELEGANT SEAFOOD NEWBURG

**Makes 6-8 servings**

- 5 tablespoons butter
- 3 tablespoons all-purpose flour
- 1/2 teaspoon salt
- 1/4 teaspoon cayenne
- 2 cups half-and-half
- 2 egg yolks, slightly beaten
- 1 pound cooked crab meat, gristle removed, flaked
- 1 pound cooked shrimp, shelled, deveined
- 1/4 cup dry sherry
- 6 slices toast, crust removed, sliced in half

In a medium saucepan heat butter, whisk in flour and continue cooking until flour is absorbed. Sprinkle with salt and cayenne, blend in half-and-half and cook until mixture thickens. Remove 1/2 cup of sauce in a small bowl, carefully mix in the egg yolks, return mixture to sauce, blend. Stir in seafood; blend in sherry. Arrange toast points on individual dishes, ladle seafood newburg over toast, serve.

# FRIED CLAMS AND TARTAR SAUCE

**Makes 8 servings**

    2 eggs, separated
    1 cup milk
    2 tablespoons butter or margarine, melted
  1/4 teaspoon salt
    1 cup all-purpose flour
    4 dozen clams, shucked, drained
      Peanut oil to deep fry

In a large deep mixing bowl beat the egg yolks with 1/2 cup of the milk. Stir in butter, salt and flour, combine. Stir in remaining milk. Beat egg whites in separate bowl until stiff peaks form. Fold into the batter. Heat oil in a deep fryer or deep skillet to 375°F. Dredge clams in the batter, carefully fry, a few at a time until golden brown. Drain on paper toweling. Serve with tartar sauce.

**Tartar Sauce**

    1 egg, beaten
  1/2 teaspoon crushed tarragon
    1 tablespoon capers, drained
    1 tablespoon chopped fresh parsley
    1 cup mayonnaise

In a small bowl, beat egg. Blend in remaining ingredients.

# SCALLOPS WITH CREAM SAUCE

**Makes 8 servings**

  4 tablespoons butter
  1 onion, sliced thin
  1 carrot, sliced thin
1½ pounds small scallops
  2 tablespoons all-purpose flour
 ¼ cup white wine
  1 cup heavy cream
 ¼ cup chopped green onion for garnish

In a large skillet heat butter; sauté onion and carrots until tender. Add scallops; sauté until opaque. Remove scallops with a slotted spoon, reserve. Whisk in flour and continue cooking until the liquid is absorbed. Stir in wine and cream; whisk until sauce thickens. Arrange scallops and vegetables on serving plates, drizzle with sauce and sprinkle with chopped green onions.

# SCALLOP MOUSSE _

**Makes 8 servings**

1½ pounds scallops, pureed
¼ cup all-purpose flour
½ teaspoon salt
½ teaspoon white pepper, nutmeg
4 eggs, beat until light
1½ cups heavy cream

Butter a 2-quart ovenproof casserole. Adjust casserole into a slightly larger pan filled halfway with water. Place scallops in the large bowl of electric mixer. Blend in flour, salt, pepper and nutmeg. Mix in eggs and cream. Mound mixture into casserole. Bake uncovered for 1 hour or until set. Cool for 5 minutes before serving. Serve warm or chilled.

# STEAMED MUSSELS IN WHITE WINE AND CREAM

**Makes 4 servings**

48 large mussels, washed
2 shallots, minced
1 cup dry white wine
1 cup heavy cream
3 carrots, julienned
3 leeks, cleaned well, julienned
1 cup hollandaise sauce

Arrange cleaned mussels, minced shallots and white wine in a large saucepan over medium heat. Steam until mussels open. Discard any unopened mussels. Remove from heat, drain liquid into medium skillet. Add heavy cream and vegetables, reduce liquid by one-half, medium heat, stirring often. While the liquid is reducing in skillet, arrange 12 mussels in 4 heated serving bowls. When the liquid is reduced by one-half, remove skillet from heat, blend with hollandaise sauce. Serve immediately.

# MUSSELS IN THE STYLE OF NORMANDY

**Makes 8 servings**

> 5 pounds mussels in shells, washed and scrubbed, discard any mussels with open shells, soak mussels in water for 30 minutes
> 1/2 cup dry white wine
> 1 onion, chopped
> 3 bay leaves
> 2 tablespoons butter
> 2 tablespoons all-purpose flour
> 1 cup half-and-half
> 1/2 teaspoon chopped basil
> 1/2 teaspoon salt
> 1/4 teaspoon ground pepper

Arrange mussels in a large saucepan, add 1 cup water, wine, onion and bay leaves; steam over high heat until the shells open, about 15 minutes, stir occasionally, cool. Strain the juice through cheesecloth, place in small saucepan and simmer until it is reduced to 1 cup, reserve. In a small saucepan heat butter. Whisk in flour until it is absorbed. Stir in half-and-half, basil, salt and pepper, continue cooking over medium heat until the sauce thickens. Stir in reserved liquid. Divide mussels into 8 dishes, drizzle with sauce.

# MARYLAND CRAB CAKES —————

**Makes 6 servings**

- 1/2 **pound fresh crab meat, cartilage removed, shredded**
- 3 **tablespoons mayonnaise**
- 1 **medium onion**
- 1 **egg, beaten**
- 1/2 **teaspoon prepared mustard**
- 1/4 **teaspoon crushed tarragon**
- 1/2 **teaspoon salt**
- 1/4 **teaspoon white pepper**
- 3/4 **cup bread crumbs**
  **Peanut oil**

In a large deep mixing bowl, combine all ingredients except oil. Mold mixture into 6 crab cakes. In a large heavy skillet heat 1/4-inch oil over medium heat. Carefully slide crab cakes into oil, fry on one side and turn over, continue frying until cakes are cooked and a golden brown. Drain on paper toweling. Serve with tartar sauce.

# CLAM SAUCE WITH SPAGHETTI

**Makes 6-8 servings**

- 1/4 **cup olive oil**
- 4 **cloves garlic, peeled, minced**
- 2 **onions, sliced thin**
- 1 **quart cherrystone clams, shucked, chopped, reserve liquid or use canned chopped clams**
- 1 **cup bottled clam juice**
- 1/4 **cup chopped fresh parsley**
- 1/2 **teaspoon salt**
- 1/4 **teaspoon pepper**
- 3/4 **teaspoon ground oregano**
- 1 **pound thin spaghetti, cooked according to package directions**

In a large heavy skillet heat oil, saute garlic and onions until tender with medium heat. Add chopped clams. Place reserved clam liquid in measuring cup, add enough clam juice to make 1 cup liquid, stir into clam mixture. Add remaining ingredients except spaghetti; bring mixture to a boil, reduce heat to a simmer and cook 2 minutes, stirring often. Arrange spaghetti on plates, serve with clam sauce.

# SEAFOOD PASTA ___

**Makes 8 servings**

- 4 tablespoons butter
- 1 pound scallops
- 1 pound whitefish fillets
- 1/4 cup dry white wine
- 1/2 cup sliced green stuffed olives
- 1 onion, chopped
- 1 cup heavy cream
- 1 pound spinach noodles, cooked according to package directions
- 1/2 teaspoon garlic powder, salt, pepper, chopped basil

In a large skillet heat butter, sauté scallops and whitefish until cooked, place fish in a serving bowl. Toss with remaining ingredients. Serve warm.

# MEAT

# —Meat—

## Cooking Methods

### DRY HEAT METHODS FOR TENDER CUTS OF MEAT

**PANBROILING** is used instead of oven broiling for small, tender beef cuts, 1 inch thick or less.

1. Arrange beef in a heavy skillet. Do not add fat or water. Do not cover. Covering creates moisture which braises the beef.

2. Cook slowly, turning occasionally. Pour off fat as it accumulates. Brown meat on both sides. Season and serve at once.

**PANFRYING** is useful for tender steaks at least one inch thick and ground beef patties.

1. Place beef on rack in broiler pan. Place one-inch steaks or patties 2 to 3 inches from heat; thicker cuts, 3 to 5 inches. Broil until top surface is brown.

2. Season meat after browning. Turn meat with tongs, cook until done. Do not use a fork as it will puncture the meat, releasing juices.

**BARBECUE** A charcoal, electric or gas grill can be used. Use the same cuts of beef and follow the same steps as in broiling.

Success depends largely on consistent low to moderate heat. Cooking time will vary with the beef cut, fire or heat, position on grill, degree of doneness desired, and wind, if outdoors.

**ROASTING** is appropriate for any large, tender cut of beef or veal.

1. Season if desired. Place beef, fat side up, on a rack in open, shallow pan. The fat on top of the roast bastes it; the rack holds it out of the drippings.

2. Insert meat thermometer. Bulb should be in the center of the largest muscle and not touching bone or resting in fat. Do not add water. Do not cover. Roast in a slow oven, 300° to 325°F. (150°-160°C).

3. Roast to 4° below desired degree of doneness. Allow roast to stand 15 minutes before carving. Internal temperature will usually increase 5° while the roast stands.

4. Rotisserie cooking is a form of roasting. Use large, symmetrical cuts. Insert rotisserie rod, lengthwise, through center of the roast; fasten beef securely. Place a drip pan under the turning beef to prevent flareups. Arrange coals around the pan. Be sure the bulb does not touch the rotisserie rod.

**STIR-FRYING** is a form of panfrying used in Oriental cooking. A wok, large skillet or electric skillet can be used.

1. Cut ingredients to uniform size, shape and thickness before beginning to cook.

2. Heat oil in pan. Add ingredients one at a time, the one that will take the longest to cook first, stirring continuously until cooked. Repeat until all the foods are cooked. Combine all foods in pan. Add sauce, if called for in the recipe; serve.

**DEEP-FAT FRYING** is yet another form of frying.

1. Cut or shape beef into uniform pieces. Coat with batter, eggs and crumbs or flour, if called for in the recipe. Use a deep pan or a deep sided pan, such as a kettle, electric deep fat fryer or fondue pot and when necessary a wire frying basket.

2. Heat the fat to frying temperature, 375°F. Always heat enough fat to cover the beef pieces. Size of the pieces and whether the beef is cooked or uncooked determines the suitable temperature, usually between 300° and 375°F.

3. Place beef in frying basket. Lower beef a few pieces at a time into the hot fat. Never drop anything into hot oil. Fry until browned and cooked through. When cooked, remove beef from the fat and drain on paper toweling.

## MOIST HEAT FOR LESS TENDER CUTS OF MEAT

**BRAISING** To braise, brown beef in its own fat or in a small amount of added fat in a heavy utensil.

1. Brown all sides slowly. The beef may be dredged in flour. Season; herbs and spices can be added to flour or cornstarch as directed.

2. Add small amount of liquid, usually no more than 1/2 of a cup. Use water, soup stock, vegetable juice or marinade. Cover tightly, it will hold in the steam needed for softening the connective tissue and therefore tenderize the beef.

3. Cook at low temperature until tender. Cook on top of range

or in a slow oven at 300° to 325°F. Remove beef to heated platter and make sauce or gravy from the liquid in the pan if desired.

**COOKING IN A SLOW ELECTRIC COOKER** A slow cooker gently simmers the foods in a liquid at low temperature over a long period of time, 4 to 12 hours. It is most suitable for less expensive, less tender beef cuts.

## PREPARING MEAT FOR COOKING

**TENDERIZING** You may choose to tenderize less tender cuts before cooking them. They can be cooked by a dry heat method. You can use marinades, pound or cube the meat or use commercial tenderizing mixtures.

**MARINADES** are liquids which traditionally contain some sort of acidic food such as vinegar, wine, citrus or tomato juice. The acid helps soften the meat fibers and connective tissue and adds flavor. Most marinades also contain a small amount of oil and are especially appropriate for beef cuts which usually have little natural fat. Beef is placed in the marinade under refrigeration for 2 to 24 hours.

**POUNDING** with a heavy object such as a meat mallet, or with the edge of a heavy saucer, tenderizes by breaking down the beef fibers, particularly the connective tissues.

**CUBING** is a more thorough process than pounding because it breaks down the fiber structure even more. Beef is cubed by the butcher at the meat counter.

**COMMERCIAL TENDERIZERS** come in various forms and contain active ingredients called enzymes. There are natural enzymes as papain from the papaya fruit that is used in commercial tenderizers.

# STORAGE

**REFRIGERATING** Most fresh beef is prepackaged and should be stored wrapped, as purchased. Fresh beef which is not prepackaged should be unwrapped and loosely rewrapped in plastic wrap or aluminum foil before it is placed in the refrigerator. It can be stored for two to four days after you purchase it. Store at refrigerator temperatures from 36° to 40°F. The special meat compartment in some refrigerators is designed to maintain ideal temperature.

**FREEZING**

1. Freeze beef as soon as possible after purchase while fresh and in top condition.

2. Select proper freezer wrapping material such as, specially coated freezer paper, aluminum foil, heavy-duty plastic bags. The wrap must seal out air and lock in moisture. If air penetrates the package, moisture is drawn from the surface of the meat causing a harmless condition known as freezer burn which affects the palatability of beef when cooked. Plastic sandwich bags and waxed paper are unsuitable wrapping materials for freezing.

# GRADING MEAT

In buying meat, look for the Meat Inspection Stamp, the Meat

Grade and Brand names stamp and observe the appearance of the meat. Many shops advertise beef, veal and lamb that are "U.S. Graded". This means that before the meat was shipped from the meat packing plant, an official of the U.S. Department of Agriculture (USDA) has examined and assigned it a grade as a sign of expected eating quality; that is tenderness, juiciness and flavor. Meat is always inspected to be sure it came from healthy livestock and is wholesome and safe to eat. In descending order, the grades apt to be available in a store counter are: Prime, Choice, Good, Standard, Commercial. Usually a store carries only one grade, but some sell two grades. More choice meat is sold.

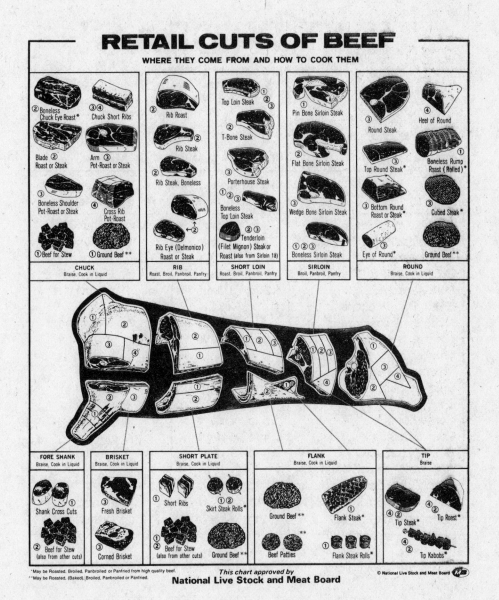

# RETAIL CUTS OF BEEF
### WHERE THEY COME FROM and HOW TO COOK THEM

**CHUCK**
Braise, Cook in Liquid

② Boneless Chuck Eye Roast*  ③④ Chuck Short Ribs
Blade ② Roast or Steak  Arm ③ Pot-Roast or Steak
Boneless Shoulder Pot-Roast or Steak  ④ Cross Rib Pot-Roast
① Beef for Stew  ① Ground Beef**

**RIB**
Roast, Broil, Panbroil, Panfry

Rib Roast
Rib Steak
Rib Steak, Boneless
Rib Eye (Delmonico) Roast or Steak

**SHORT LOIN**
Roast, Broil, Panbroil, Panfry

Top Loin Steak ①②③
T-Bone Steak ②
Porterhouse Steak ③
Boneless Top Loin Steak ①②③
Tenderloin (Filet Mignon) Steak or Roast (also from Sirloin 1a) ②③

**SIRLOIN**
Broil, Panbroil, Panfry

Pin Bone Sirloin Steak ①
Flat Bone Sirloin Steak
Wedge Bone Sirloin Steak ③
Boneless Sirloin Steak ①②③

**ROUND**
Braise, Cook in Liquid

Round Steak ③  Heel of Round
Top Round Steak* ③  Boneless Rump Roast (Rolled)* ①
Bottom Round Roast or Steak* ③  Cubed Steak*
Eye of Round* ③  Ground Beef**

**FORE SHANK**
Braise, Cook in Liquid

Shank Cross Cuts ①
② Beef for Stew (also from other cuts)

**BRISKET**
Braise, Cook in Liquid

Fresh Brisket
③ Corned Brisket

**SHORT PLATE**
Braise, Cook in Liquid

① Short Ribs  Skirt Steak Rolls* ①②
①② Beef for Stew (also from other cuts)  Ground Beef**

**FLANK**
Braise, Cook in Liquid

Ground Beef**  Flank Steak* ①
Beef Patties  Flank Steak Rolls* ①

**TIP**
Braise

Tip Steak* ④②  Tip Roast* ④②
Tip Kabobs* ④②

*May be Roasted, Broiled, Panbroiled or Panfried from high quality beef.
**May be Roasted, (Baked), Broiled, Panbroiled or Panfried.

*This chart approved by*
**National Live Stock and Meat Board**

© National Live Stock and Meat Board

# MEAT STORAGE CHART

### MEAT STORAGE TIME FOR MAXIMUM QUALITY

| Meat | Refrigerator (36° to 40°F.) | Freezer (at 0°F. or lower) |
|---|---|---|
| Beef | 3 to 5 days | 6 to 12 months |
| Pork, veal, lamb | 3 to 5 days | 6 to 9 months |
| Ground beef, veal, lamb | 1 to 2 days | 3 to 4 months |
| Ground pork | 1 to 2 days | 1 to 3 months |
| Pork sausage | 2 to 3 days | 2 months |
| Heart, liver, kidneys, brains, sweetbreads | 1 to 2 days | 3 to 4 months |
| Tongue | 6 to 7 days | 3 to 4 months |
| Smoked ham and picnics (whole or half) | 7 days | 2 months |
| Smoked ham slices | 3 to 4 days | 2 months |
| Bacon | 5 to 7 days | 2 months |
| Corned beef | 5 to 7 days | 1 month |
| Frankfurters | 4 to 5 days | 2 months |
| Smoked sausage | 14 to 21 days | 2 months |
| Sausage, dry and semi-dry (unsliced) | 14 to 21 days | 1 month |
| Luncheon meats (sliced) | 3 days | 2 months |
| Leftover cooked meat | 4 to 5 days | 3 to 4 months |

# ECONOMICAL MEAT

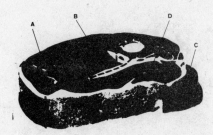

## ARM POT-ROAST
**(2 to 2¼ inches thick, about 6 pounds)**

**1.** Cut along natural seams to separate section A from the remaining meat. Chill, cut into four thin slices and braise. Or cut into two slices, pound and braise. Four servings.

**2.** Cut sections B and C from remaining meat. Remove arm bone. Cut meat into small pieces, cook in liquid (with bone if desired) for soup, chili or spaghetti sauce, or grind. Two to four servings.

**3.** Wrap long end of remaining meat (D) around to form small flat pot-roast, securing with skewers. Four to six servings.

Note: If section A is too small to make a meal (as it is in some cuts), separate section A from pot-roast by cutting at right angle to section D. Omit step 2 and form all remaining meat into a pot-roast

## 7-BONE POT-ROAST
**(2 to 2¼ inches thick, about 6 pounds)**

**1.** Cut around blade bone and remove sections A and B. Section A is the top blade and the most tender part of this cut. Remove membrane separating section A into two pieces; cut each into slices one-half inch thick. Panfry to rare or medium. Two to three servings.

**2.** Divide remaining meat by cutting along natural seam between sections C and D. Remove bone from D. Cut meat from D and B into cubes; cook in liquid for stew or soup or grind. Four servings.

**3.** Braise section C as pot-roast. Or chill and cut into thin strips to stir-fry or into four thin steaks to marinate and broil. Four servings.

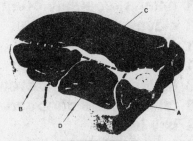

## ROUND STEAK
**(1¼ to 1½ inches thick, about 5 pounds)**

**1.** Cut across bone end of steak following natural seams, removing bone and small pieces of meat (A) attached. Remove eye section (B). Cut meat from (A) and (B) into small pieces and use for stew or soup (including bone if desired), or grind. Four servings.

**2.** Separate top round (C) from bottom round (D) by cutting along natural seams. The larger top round is the most tender part of the round steak. Score if desired, marinate and broil to rare or medium. Carve in thin slices across the grain. Four to six servings.

**3.** The bottom round (D) can be chilled and cut into thin strips for braising or marinating and stir-frying. Or it can be sliced into two thin steaks, pounded and braised as for Swiss steak. Four servings.

# BEEF

## SLOW COOKED BEEF STEW

**Makes 8 servings**

- 5 tablespoons butter
- 3 pounds stew meat or chuck, cut into 1-inch cubes
- 1/2 cup all-purpose flour
- 3 onions, coarsely chopped
- 3 cloves garlic
- 1 cup beef consommé
- 1 can, 12 ounces, beer
- 3 tablespoons dark brown sugar
- 3 tablespoons chopped fresh parsley
- 3 bay leaves
- 1 teaspoon ground thyme
  Salt and pepper to taste
- 3 potatoes, peeled and cubed
- 1 bag, 20 ounces, baby carrots, defrosted

Heat butter in a Dutch oven, over medium heat. Dust stew meat in flour; sauté meat until golden. Add onions and garlic, sauté until tender, stirring often. Add remaining ingredients except potatoes and carrots. Bake at 300°F covered, for 2½ hours or until meat is tender. Add potatoes and carrots during last hour of cooking. Remove and discard bay leaves. Serve in a deep dish with a dark rye bread.

# YANKEE BEEF STEW

**Makes 5-6 servings**

- 3 tablespoons butter
- 2½ pounds beef chuck, cubed in ¾-inch pieces
- 3 tablespoons all-purpose flour
- 4 tablespoons tomato paste
- 2 cloves garlic, peeled, minced
- ½ teaspoon thyme, salt
- ¼ teaspoon pepper
- 1 cup beef stock
- 3 carrots, sliced
- 2 onions, quartered
- 3 large potatoes, peeled, sliced

In a large, heavy saucepan heat butter. Dust meat with flour, brown quickly over medium-high heat, stirring often. Add remaining ingredients, combine. Cover and reduce heat to a simmer, continue cooking 1 hour, 15 minutes. Stir occasionally, adding more stock as necessary. Serve in deep bowls.

# BEEF STROGANOFF ——————

**Makes 5-6 servings**

- 1/4 cup all-purpose flour
- 1/2 teaspoon salt and pepper
- 1 1/2 pounds flank steak, cut into 1/2-inch strips, cut against the grain
- 3 tablespoons butter
- 1 cup sliced onions
- 3 cups sliced mushrooms
- 1/2 cup beef stock
- 3 tablespoons catsup
- 1/2 teaspoon Worcestershire sauce
- 2 cups commercial sour cream

Combine flour, salt, and pepper. Roll steak strips in seasoned flour. Melt butter in a large skillet over medium heat. Sauté onions and mushrooms until tender, stirring occasionally. Push vegetables to one side, sauté steak strips, stirring occasionally until cooked. Stir meat and vegetables together. Sprinkle beef stock, catsup and Worcestershire sauce over meat, mix well. Continue simmering until sauce begins to thicken. Remove from heat. Mix in 1 cup of the sour cream. Serve beef stroganoff over a bed of hot buttered noodles. Garnish with dollops of sour cream.

# STEAK WITH PEPPER

**Makes 4 servings**

  5 **tablespoons butter, room temperature**
  4 **shell steaks, cut ³/₄ inch thick**
 ¹/₂ **teaspoon salt**
  4 **tablespoons cracked black and green peppercorns**
  2 **tablespoons butter, room temperature**
  1 **onion, sliced thin**
  2 **tablespoons all-purpose flour**
  1 **cup cream**
 ¹/₄ **cup dry white wine**

Rub butter over steaks. Mix together the salt and cracked black and green peppercorns; press into steak. Place on broiler rack, and broil 4-5 minutes on each side. Place on serving dish. In a small saucepan melt butter over medium heat. Sauté onion, stirring occasionally. Whisk in flour, continue cooking until flour is absorbed. Remove pan from heat, stir in cream and wine, combine. Return to heat and simmer until sauce thickens. Drizzle sauce over steak. Serve hot.

# BEEF KABOBS

1 can, 20 ounces, pineapple chunks, drain, reserve

**Marinade**

- ¼ cup cider vinegar
- ¼ cup catsup
- ¼ cup firmly packed dark brown sugar
- ½ teaspoon ground ginger
- 2 tablespoons light soy sauce
- 2 pounds sirloin steak, cut into 1-inch cubes
- 3 green or red bell peppers, seeded, cut into 1-inch squares
- 2 large onions, cut into eighths
- 1 pint cherry tomatoes
- 8 skewers

Measure drained pineapple juice; add enough water to measure 1 cup of liquid. Add liquid to marinade in a glass pie plate. Add meat pieces and turn often. Marinate 4 hours or overnight. Drain meat. Thread skewers with meat, pineapple and vegetables. Place lengthwise on baking rack over drip pan. Broil until meat is cooked, turn as necessary.

# STEAK TERIYAKI ___

**Makes 8 servings**

**Marinade**

- ¼ **cup light soy sauce**
- ¼ **cup saki or dry sherry**
- 4 **tablespoons dark brown sugar**
- 1 **teaspoon ground ginger**
- ¼ **teaspoon salt**
- 2-3 **pound steak, cut 2 inches thick**

In a shallow glass pie plate combine marinade. Score the meat and arrange it in the marinade, turn meat. Marinate overnight, turn several times. Broil 5-7 minutes on each side or until cooked, or broil on an outside grill. Allow meat to rest 5 minutes; slice against the grain.

# SAUERBRATEN

**Makes 8-10 servings**

**Marinade**

1 onion, minced
4 cups red wine
1 cup water
3 tablespoons freshly squeezed lemon juice
3 bay leaves
4 whole cloves
½ teaspoon cracked peppercorns
½ teaspoon ground thyme
¼ teaspoon ground nutmeg

4 pounds, bottom round beef
5 tablespoons butter
2 onions, sliced
3 stalks celery, sliced
½ cup gingersnap crumbs
Salt, pepper and sugar
1 cup commercial sour cream

Combine marinade ingredients in a deep glass baking dish. Arrange meat in marinade, turn. Meat should be covered in marinade. Cover with plastic wrap, refrigerate, turn twice a day for 5-6 days.

**To cook**

Remove meat from marinade, strain, reserve. Pat meat dry with paper toweling. Heat butter in a Dutch oven, sauté vegetables over medium heat until tender, stirring occasionally. Push vegetables to one side, brown meat. In a separate saucepan heat strained marinade to boiling. Pour marinade over meat. Reduce heat to simmer, cover and continue cooking 3 hours or until meat is tender. Remove meat from sauce, allow to rest 10 minutes, slice. Place meat on serving dish. Strain juice and return to a saucepan. Heat sauce, stir in gingersnap crumbs. Season to taste with salt, pepper and sugar. Remove from heat, stir in sour cream. Pour sauce over meat.

# BEEF WELLINGTON WITH TRUFFLE SAUCE

**Makes 10-12 servings**

3¹/₂  4 pound beef tenderloin
    6 tablespoons dry sherry
    1 tablespoon Worcestershire sauce
2¹/₄ cups all-purpose flour
    1 teaspoon salt, divided
  ¹/₄ cup butter, cut into ¹/₂-inch pieces
  ¹/₄ cup vegetable shortening
  5-7 tablespoons ice water
    4 ounces fresh mushrooms
  ¹/₄ cup minced fresh parsley
  ¹/₂ cup chopped onions
    1 cup chopped celery
    3 tablespoons butter

**Preparing the tenderloin**

Trim fat from tenderloin and place in a large, shallow baking dish. Sprinkle sherry and Worcestershire sauce evenly over beef. Cover dish with plastic wrap and let stand to marinate for at least one hour. Preheat oven to 350°F. Remove plastic wrap from baking dish and place in oven. Bake for 20 minutes. Remove from oven and set aside while preparing crust.

### Crust

Combine flour and ¹/₂ teaspoon of salt in a large mixing bowl. Cut in butter and shortening with pastry knife, two knives, or food processor fitted with steel blade until consistency of coarse crumbs. Sprinkle ice water over flour mixture, 1 tablespoon at a time, tossing lightly with a fork until the dough clings together. Gather dough into a ball. Knead for 1 minute on a lightly floured pastry cloth. Cover with plastic wrap and refrigerate at least 1 hour. Prepare vegetable filling.

### Filling

Wipe mushrooms clean with damp towel. Place in food processor fitted with steel blade and chop coarsely, squeeze dry. Chop parsley, onions and celery. Combine all vegetables in a medium bowl. Melt butter in a large skillet over medium heat. Sauté vegetables until tender, stirring often, reserve.

### To Assemble

Generously brush baking sheet with vegetable oil. Remove dough from refrigerator and divide into two portions. Roll out each portion on a lightly floured surface into a ¹/₄-inch-thick rectangle. Place one rectangle on prepared baking sheet. Place tenderloin in center of rectangle. Spread vegetable filling evenly over top of tenderloin. Carefully place remaining rectangle over top of tenderloin. Bring upper and lower edges together; remove excess dough. Press edges together to seal. Re-roll remaining dough. Cut out decoratively-shaped designs as leaves, using designs on top of crust.* Preheat oven to 400°F. Bake beef for 45 minutes before slicing.

*Can be prepared ahead to this point and refrigerated or frozen. Bring to room temperature before baking.

# GROUND BEEF

Ground beef is a good source of many of the nutrients that our bodies need to keep running smoothly.

## STORAGE

The shorter the time from meat case to your refrigerator, the fresher the ground beef will stay. So try to make the meat case one of your last stops before checkout and make sure that the package that you buy feels cold. If you can use the whole package in a day or two, store it in the refrigerator. You won't need to rewrap the ground beef if it comes wrapped in a clear film or moistureproof meat wrap. For longer storage, rewrap or overwrap ground beef in wrappings designed for the freezer. If you bought the big economy size, divide it into smaller packages, the size that you typically use, before freezing. Large packages of ground beef freeze slowly and take longer to defrost when needed. When it is time to defrost frozen ground beef, transfer it to the refrigerator. When meat is left out at room temperature, bacteria can grow and possibly create a health hazard. Ground beef moved out of the freezer and into the refrigerator the night before you intend to use it will be defrosted in time to cook the next evening.

Never refreeze defrosted ground beef and be sure to use it as soon as possible after defrosting. Cooked combination dishes, such as casseroles and meat loaves, can be frozen. Whether you are freezing patties or cooked dishes, be sure to label and date the package. Uncoded ground beef can be frozen for three to four months, cooked combination dishes should be used within two or three months.

ROASTING Combine all ingredients, shape into a loaf. Place on a rack in an open roasting pan or lightly packed meat loaf mixture into a loaf pan; do not cover. Bake in a moderate oven, 350°F., until done. Let stand 10 minutes before slicing.

BROILING Place beef patties on rack in a broiler pan, or on grill over ash-covered coals, so surface of meat is 3 inches to 4 inches from heat. Broil until meat is brown on one side. Turn and broil second side until done. A 1-inch patty takes about 15 minutes for rare, and about 25 minutes for medium. Season each side after browning.

PANBROILING Place beef patties in heavy frying pan. Do not add fat or water, and don't cover. Cook over low heat, turning occasionally. Pour fat from pan as it accumulates. Brown meat on all sides. Cook to desired doneness and season to taste.

PANFRYING Brown beef patties or meatballs on all sides in a small amount of fat, if necessary. Season as desired. Do not cover. Cook at moderate temperature until done, turning occasionally.

## GROUND BEEF AND HAMBURGER

Whatever the meat-to-fat ratio, the name ground beef indicates that only beef skeletal meat, that attached to bone, can be used; no cuts from veal, pork or lamb can be added. When you see the words meat loaf or hamburger it means that other ingredients have been added. Although you may hear the word hamburger used interchangeably with ground beef, beware. It is important for you to know that hamburger on a label means ground beef with additions of fat and/or seasonings. If soy protein is added to ground beef, it must be shown on the label.

# MEATBALLS WITH SOUR CREAM

**Makes 6-8 servings**

     1 pound chuck steak, ground
    3/4 pound veal, ground
     2 slices dry rye bread, torn into pieces
     1 cup milk
     1 large onion, minced
     3 tablespoons chopped fresh parsley
     2 eggs, slightly beaten
    1/2 teaspoon paprika, salt, pepper, nutmeg
     5 tablespoons butter
     3 tablespoons all-purpose flour
     1 cup beef bouillon
     1 cup commercial sour cream

In a large deep mixing bowl combine all ingredients except butter, flour, bouillon and cream. Shape mixture into one-inch balls. Heat butter in a large skillet, over medium heat; fry meatballs until golden brown on all sides. Remove to a platter. Add flour to skillet, whisk until flour is absorbed. Add bouillon and whisk until mixture thickens. Remove from heat, slowly stir in sour cream. Return meatballs, heat, serve.

# RUSSIAN MEAT TURNOVERS

**Makes 3 dozen**

    2 cups all-purpose flour
    1/2 teaspoon salt, baking powder
    1/4 cup butter, cut into chunks
    1 egg, slightly beaten
    1/2 cup commercial sour cream
    1 egg yolk, slightly beaten with 1 tablespoon water

**Prepare pastry**

Combine flour, salt, baking powder and butter in a large bowl of electric mixer, until the mixture resembles rough cornmeal. Add egg and sour cream, mix until blended. Gather dough together, wrap in aluminum foil, chill for 1 hour. Roll out dough on lightly floured cloth to 1/4 inch thickness. Cut into 3-inch circles. Place 1 teaspoon of filling in center, fold in half and pinch edges together. Glaze with egg yolk mixture, arrange on buttered and floured cookie sheet. Bake at 375°F. for 30 minutes.

**Filling**

    1/2 pound ground meat
    3 green onions, minced
    1/2 teaspoon salt
    1/2 teaspoon pepper

**2 tablespoons butter**
**2 teaspoons all-purpose flour**
**1 cup commercial sour cream**
**1 bunch fresh dill for garnish**

In a large bowl combine ground meat, onions, salt and pepper. Heat butter in a medium skillet. Sauté meat until it loses color, stirring occasionally over medium heat. Sprinkle in flour, stir to combine, cook 1 minute. Remove from heat, cool.

**To serve**

Arrange meat turnovers on serving plate, serve hot with sour cream and garnish with fresh dill sprigs.

# TANGY SHALLOT-TARRAGON MEATBALLS

**Makes 6 servings**

> 3 tablespoons butter
> 5 shallots, minced
> 1 large onion, sliced thin
> 3 cups tomato juice
> 6 ground gingersnaps
> 1/2 teaspoon Worcestershire sauce
> 1 tablespoon freshly squeezed lemon juice
> 1/2 teaspoon salt, pepper
> 1 teaspoon chopped tarragon
> 1/2 cup firmly packed brown sugar

> 2 1/2 pounds ground beef
> 3/4 cup seasoned bread crumbs
> 2 eggs, lightly beaten
> 1/2 teaspoon chopped tarragon
> 3 tablespoons vegetable oil

**Sauce**

In a medium saucepan melt butter, over medium heat. Sauté shallots and onion until tender, stirring occasionally. Mix in remaining sauce ingredients, stir to combine. Simmer 5 minutes, reserve.

### Meatballs

In a large mixing bowl, combine ground beef, bread crumbs, eggs and tarragon. Roll meat mixture into ³/₄-inch meatballs. Heat oil in large skillet, brown meatballs over medium heat. Stir in sauce, cover and simmer 10 minutes. Serve over rice or noodles.

# BREAKFAST HASH _

**Makes 8 servings**

 4 tablespoons butter
 ¼ cup chopped chives
 1 large onion, sliced thin
 4 potatoes, cooked, peeled, diced
3-4 cups cooked corned beef or roast beef leftovers, diced
 ½ teaspoon salt, pepper, garlic powder

Heat butter in a large heavy skillet over medium heat; sauté chives and onion until tender. Add remaining ingredients, sauté stirring occasionally until all ingredients are heated and the mixture pulls together slightly. Serve hot with eggs and/or hash brown potatoes.

# RED CHILI WITH CORNMEAL

**Makes 8 servings**

  4 **strips bacon**
1½ **pounds ground round steak**
  1 **pound pork shoulder, cut into ½-inch pieces or roughly ground**
  1 **large onion, chopped**
  3 **tablespoons chili powder**
½ **teaspoon hot red pepper flakes**
  1 **teaspoon oregano**
  1 **teaspoon salt**
  1 **teaspoon cayenne pepper**
  2 **cups beef stock or canned beef broth**
¼ **cup cornmeal or masa harina, available in Mexican food stores**
  2 **cups sour cream for garnish**
  1 **package, 13⅓ ounces, tortillas**

Cut bacon into 1-inch pieces, fry until crisp in a large saucepan. Add ground round steak and pork cubes, fry until lightly browned, stirring often. When meat has lost its color add onion, chili powder, hot red pepper flakes, oregano, salt, cayenne pepper and beef stock, mix well. Bring chili to a boil, reduce heat to simmer. Cover saucepan and simmer chili for 1 hour, stirring occasionally. Skim off any excess fat. In a small bowl combine cornmeal and ½ cup water. Stir mixture into chili. Simmer uncovered 10 minutes. Serve chili hot, from a serving dish. Garnish with dollops of sour cream and serve with warm tortillas.

# PECOS CHILI WITH A TOUCH OF HONEY

**Makes 8 servings**

1½ cups uncooked dried pinto beans
 1 tablespoon salt
 3 tablespoons bacon drippings
 3 cloves garlic, peeled, minced
 2 large onions, chopped
 2 pounds chuck steak, coarsely ground
 1 can (28 ounces) tomatoes, include juice
 1 teaspoon salt
 ½ teaspoon pepper
 2 tablespoons chili powder
 1 tablespoon ground cumin powder
 2 teaspoons honey

Wash beans and remove any foreign matter. Combine beans with 5 cups cold water in a large saucepan. Bring to a boil, reduce heat to simmer, cover pan. Continue simmering 2 hours, stirring occasionally, until beans are tender. Add salt last 10 minutes of cooking. Drain beans, set aside. Heat bacon drippings in a large saucepan. Sauté garlic and onions until tender, stirring occasionally. Add ground chuck steak, fry until beef loses its color, stirring often. Quarter tomatoes, add tomatoes, juice, salt, pepper, chili powder, cumin and honey to saucepan, combine. Mix in beans. Simmer chili uncovered 45 minutes, stirring occasionally. Adjust seasonings. Ladle hot chili into deep bowls.

# EASY MEATBALLS IN BARBECUE SAUCE

**Makes 5-6 servings**

1½ pounds round steak, ground
 1 large onion, minced
1½ cups rye bread crumbs
 1 tablespoon prepared mustard
 ½ teaspoon oregano, salt, pepper
 4 tablespoons vegetable oil
 ½ cup prepared barbecue sauce
 1 can (8 ounces) tomato sauce
 3 tablespoons all-purpose flour
 1 tablespoon sugar
 ¼ cup water

In a large deep mixing bowl combine ground round steak, onion, bread crumbs, mustard and spices. Shape mixture into 1-inch balls. Heat oil in a large skillet over medium heat. Sauté meatballs until golden brown on all sides. Drain excess oil from skillet. Combine remaining ingredients, pour over meatballs. Heat to a boil, reduce heat to a simmer, continue cooking 10 minutes. Serve over rice.

# MEATLOAF

**Makes 6 servings**

1¹/₂ pounds ground chuck
  1 onion, minced
  2 eggs, slightly beaten
¹/₂ teaspoon salt, sage
¹/₄ teaspoon pepper, garlic powder
³/₄ cup bread crumbs
  1 cup milk

**Sauce**

¹/₂ cup catsup
  3 tablespoons dark brown sugar
¹/₄ teaspoon ground nutmeg
  1 teaspoon dry mustard

In a large mixing bowl combine ground chuck, onion, eggs, salt, sage, pepper and garlic powder. In a separate small bowl combine bread crumbs and milk for ten minutes. Add bread mixture to meat, combine. Lightly pack meatloaf into a greased 9 x 3-inch loaf pan. Bake at 350°F for 1 hour; drain off excess fat, unmold, slice. Combine sauce ingredients in a saucepan, heat 1 minute, stirring continuously. Drizzle sauce over meatloaf.

# LASAGNA _____

**Makes 10-12 servings**

1¼ pounds ground chuck
  2 cloves garlic, peeled, minced
  4 teaspoons ground basil
  1 teaspoon salt
  1 can (1 pound) tomatoes, include juice
  2 cans, 6 ounces each, tomato paste
  1 package lasagna noodles, cooked according to package directions, rinse
  4 cups creamed cottage cheese or combine with ricotta cheese
  2 eggs, slightly beaten
  1 teaspoon salt
 ½ teaspoon white pepper
 ½ cup freshly grated Parmesan cheese
  1 pound mozzarella cheese, sliced thin

In a large heavy skillet brown ground chuck over medium heat. Add garlic, basil, salt, tomatoes and juice and tomato paste, combine and simmer 15 minutes, stirring occasionally. In a large bowl combine cottage cheese or ricotta cheese, eggs, salt, pepper and freshly grated Parmesan cheese. Arrange one-third of the lasagna noodles in 13 x 9 x 1¾-inch baking dish. Spread half of the cheese mixture, half of the mozzarella and half of the meat sauce over the lasagna noodles. Repeat until all ingredients have been used, ending with meat sauce. Bake at 375°F for 25-30 minutes. Let stand 5 minutes before cutting. Serve with salad.

# STUFFED SWEET RED PEPPERS

**Makes 8 servings**

8 sweet red bell peppers, remove stem ends, seeds
3 tablespoons butter
2 cloves garlic, peeled, minced
1 large onion, minced
1/2 pound ground chuck
3/4 cup cooked rice
1/2 teaspoon salt, pepper, garlic powder, thyme
2 cans, 8 ounces each, tomato sauce
1/4 cup dry white wine
1 cup commercial sour cream

In a large heavy skillet, heat butter over medium heat; sauté garlic and onion until tender, stirring occasionally. Mix in ground chuck, brown, stirring often. Mix in rice, seasonings and 1 can of the tomato sauce. Stir until ingredients are combined. Fill peppers and arrange in a baking pan. In a bowl combine remaining tomato sauce, white wine and sour cream. Drizzle sauce over peppers. Bake at 350°F for 55-60 minutes, or until cooked.

# SAUSAGE

Sausages and ready-to-serve meats are generally grouped according to the processing method used. The following classifications will aid in the selection and care of these products.

**Fresh Sausages** are made from selected cuts of fresh meats; neither cooked nor cured. Keep refrigerated. Use within 2 to 3 days. Cook thoroughly before serving. Pork sausage, bulk, links, patties, country-style; fresh Kielbasa, Italian, Bratwurst, Knockwurst, Chorizos, link or bulk, fresh Theuringer.

**Uncooked, Smoked Sausage** sometimes includes cured meat. Has been smoked but not cooked. Keep refrigerated. Use within 1 week. Cook thoroughly before serving. Smoked pork sausage, Kielbasa, Mettwurst, smoked country-style.

**Cooked Sausages** usually made from fresh meats which are cured during processing and fully cooked. Keep refrigerated. Use within 4 to 6 days. Ready to eat, some may be served hot. Blood sausage, blood and tongue sausage, Knockwurst, precooked, Bratwurst, precooked, Kiszka, liver loaf, Yachwurst, Braunschweiger, liver sausage.

**Cooked, Smoked Sausages** are made from fresh meats which are cured during processing, and fully cooked. Keep refrigerated. Use within 1 week, longer if in unopened vacuum package, Bierwurst, beef salami, bologna, Mettwurst, Cotto salami, frankfurters, German-style Mortadella, Kielbasa, Knackwurst, Kakow, New England sausage, Berliner, Prasky, Smoked Theuringer links, Teawurst, Vienna sausage.

**Dry and/or Semi-Dry Sausages** are made from fresh meats

which are cured during processing, that are either smoked or unsmoked. Prepared by carefully controlled bacterial fermentation which acts as preservative as well as developing flavor. Most dry sausages are salami, most semi-dry are of the summer sausage type. Cool storage recommended for dry sausage; keep semi-dry refrigerated. Use unsliced and semi-dry sausages within 3 to 6 weeks. Ready to eat. Summer sausage, Cervelat, farmer, Theuringer, salami, Genoa, German, hard, Kosher, Milano, Chorizos, Fizzes, Levanon bologna, Lyons, Medwurst, Metz, Mortadella, Pepperoni.

**Speciality Meats** as luncheon meats are made from fresh meats which are cured during processing and are fully cooked; sometimes baked. Keep refrigerated. Use sliced meats within 3 days, unopened vacuum packages can be kept longer. Loaves, Dutch, ham and cheeses, honey, jellied tongue, minced ham, old-fashioned, olive, pepper, pickled and pimiento, chopped ham, head cheese, minced roll, scrapple, sylta, vienna sausage.

Sausage fits conveniently into modern lifestyles, yet its roots are planted firmly in the past. It is one of the oldest forms of processed food and history tells us that virtually all primitive people preserved meat for times when their food supplies were scarce. Our word sausage is derived from the Latin word salsus, meaning preserved or literally, salted. It has been reported that sausage was made and eaten by the Babylonians some 3,500 years ago and that the ancient Chinese also made sausage. The first recorded reference to sausage was in Homer's Odyssey written in the 19th century. By the middle ages sausage making was an art practiced commercially. Climate played an important role in the creation of certain sausages. The warmer climates of Italy, Spain and southern France encouraged the development of dry and semi-dry sausages while the cooler climates of Germany and Austria led to the making of fresh and cooked sausages. Available ingredients also influenced the development of specific sausages. Sausages were frequently known by the name of the town where they originated. Examples include bologna from Bologna, Italy; Genoa salami from Genoa, Italy; frankfurter from Frankfurt am Main, Germany; braunschweiger from Braunschweig, Germany; goteborg for Goteborg, Sweden and arles from Arles, France. Sausage making today is a unique blend of old and new. It has become a scientific, highly mechanized industry that represents centuries of progress and a world of variety and flavors.

## Consumer Hints

Consumers should look for a tightly filled package with a perfect seal. Consumers should not remove packaged meats, like cold cuts and hot dogs, from the original vacuum-sealed wrap until ready to use. The unused portion should be stored in the same package and refrigerated immediately.

Most processed meats should be used within seven days of the freshness control date or within seven days of opening the package, whichever comes first. In other words, the date should be ignored after the package is opened, and contents should be used within seven days.

Wieners and franks in vacuum-sealed "twin-packs" are packaged with freshness in mind. One unit can be opened and the other stored, in the refrigerator, unopened, for future use.

Vacuum-packaged products can be frozen for as long as a

month without a noticeable change in flavor or texture, as long as the seal is not broken. Freezing causes the package film to become brittle, however, so special care must be taken not to damage the package.

Processed meat products can be refrozen with safety as long as they still contain ice crystals or are cold to the touch. Meat should be thawed in the refrigerator, not at room temperature.

Freezing is not recommended for canned hams, however, because texture and flavor are lost. Properly sealed and refrigerated, canned hams will keep a minimum of one year from date of manufacture. Once the can is opened, unused portions can be wrapped and refrigerated for a week.

In general, consumers need to know that bacteria flourish at temperatures over 40°F. For optimal freshness, they should follow these storage guidelines: keep it cold, keep it clean and keep it covered. Finally, before eating, consumers should use sight, smell and touch as common-sense guidelines for freshness. In other words, when in doubt, throw it out.

# SAUSAGES

### NUTRITIVE VALUE OF SELECTED READY-TO-SERVE SAUSAGES

| | Typical Portion | | Calories Per Typical Portion | % of U.S. Recommended Daily Allowance Per Typical Portion | | | | | | |
|---|---|---|---|---|---|---|---|---|---|---|
| | | | | Protein | Iron | Zinc | Thiamin | Riboflavin | Niacin | Vitamin B-12 |
| Bologna | 57g | 2½ slices[1] | 181 | 15 | 5 | 7 | 7 | 5 | 7 | 13 |
| Braunschweiger | 54g | 3 slices[2] | 194 | 16 | 28 | 10 | 9 | 48 | 23 | 181 |
| Dutch Loaf | 57g | 2 slices[3] | 137 | 17 | 4 | 6 | 11 | 9 | 7 | 12 |
| Frankfurter | 57g | 1 link[4] | 182 | 14 | 4 | 7 | 8 | 4 | 7 | 12 |
| Head Cheese | 57g | 2 slices[3] | 121 | 20 | 4 | 5 | 1 | 6 | 3 | 10 |
| Liver Sausage | 54g | 3 slices[2] | 176 | 17 | 19 | * | 10 | 33 | * | 770 |
| Pork Sausage | 54g | 2 patties[5] | 199 | 24 | 4 | 9 | 27 | 8 | 12 | 16 |
| Thuringer | 57g | 2½ slices[1] | 198 | 20 | 6 | 8 | 6 | 10 | 12 | 44 |
| Dry Salami | 40g | 4 slices[6] | 167 | 20 | 3 | 9 | 16 | 7 | 10 | 13 |
| Bratwurst | 85g | 1 link[7] | 256 | 27 | 6 | 13 | 29 | 9 | 14 | 13 |
| Kielbasa | 85g | 1 link[7] | 264 | 25 | 7 | 11 | 13 | 11 | 12 | 23 |
| Smoked Sausage | 85g | 1 link[7] | 286 | 25 | 7 | 12 | 15 | 9 | 14 | 21 |

1) 20 slices/lb.
2) 25 slices/lb.
3) 16 slices/lb.
4) 8 links per pound
5) Raw patties approximately 2¾" dia. and ¼" thick
6) Approximately 11 slices/4 oz.
7) Approximately 1" diam. x 4¼" long

*Data not available

# SAUSAGE JAMBALAYA

**Makes 8 servings**

- 2 tablespoons vegetable oil
- 2 cloves garlic, peeled, minced
- 1 cup sliced onions
- 1 cup sliced green bell peppers
- 1/4 cup chopped fresh parsley
- 1 pound spicy sausage, cut into 1/2-inch pieces
- 1 can, 16 ounces, tomatoes, include juice
- 4 bay leaves
- 1/2 teaspoon thyme, salt and pepper
- 2 cups uncooked rice
- 1 cup water
- 1 pound medium-large shrimp, peeled, deveined, leave tails intact
- 1 cup coarsely chopped, cooked ham

Heat oil in a large saucepan over medium heat. Sauté garlic and onions until tender, stirring occasionally. Mix in peppers, parsley and sausage. Sauté until sausage is cooked, drain excess drippings. Mix in tomatoes, juice, bay leaves, spices. Add rice, water, shrimp and ham, combine, cover. Simmer for 20 minutes or until rice is cooked. Remove and discard bay leaves. Serve hot in a deep bowl.

# CHOUCROUTE ALSACIENNE

**Makes 6-8 servings**

- 2 pounds sauerkraut
- 12 slices lean bacon
- 1 large onion, chopped
- 3 large carrots, grated
- 3 apples, peeled, sliced
- 1/2 teaspoon salt, pepper
- 1/4 pound prosciutto
- 1 1/2 pounds sweet sausage, cut into 1-inch pieces
- 3 tablespoons butter
- 1 cup beef stock
- 2 cups dry white wine

Wash sauerkraut in several changes of water and drain well. In a 13 x 9 x 1 3/4-inch ovenproof pan arrange bacon slices, one-half of the sauerkraut. Layer onions, carrots and apples. Sprinkle with salt and pepper. Add a layer of prosciutto cubes and sausage, dot with butter. Cover with remaining sauerkraut, beef stock and wine. If casserole becomes dry during baking moisten with additional beef stock or wine. Stir occasionally. Bake at 275°F. for 4 hours.

# SAUSAGE IN CRUST

**Makes 8-10 servings**

  1 package, $1/4$ ounce, active dry yeast
$1/2$ cup lukewarm water, 105° to 110°F.
$2^1/2$ cups all-purpose flour
  1 teaspoon salt
  1 tablespoon honey
  2 eggs, slightly beaten
$1/4$ cup vegetable oil
$1/4$ cup warm water
  1 pound French sausage, herb seasoned or garlic
  1 egg yolk beaten with 1 teaspoon water
  1 tablespoon sesame seeds

**Crust**

Combine yeast and warm water in a measuring cup; let stand in a draft-free place for 5 minutes, or until foamy. Measure flour into a large mixing bowl. Add dissolved yeast. Mix in salt, honey, eggs, oil and water. Stir with a large wooden spoon until liquids are absorbed. Place dough on a lightly floured surface. Knead until smooth, about 5 minutes. Place dough in a greased bowl. Cover and let rise in a draft-free place until double in bulk, about $1^1/2$ hours. Punch dough down; press out any bubbles. Gather dough into a ball.

**To Assemble**

Remove casing from sausage, pierce well with a fork. Roll dough out on a lightly floured board 2 inches larger than sausage on all sides. Place sausage in the center of the dough. Pull dough up around sausage; seal tightly at sides and top. Place in prepared loaf pan or on a large baking sheet, seam-side down. Cover and let rise in a draft-free place for 25 minutes. Brush with egg wash, sprinkle with sesame seeds. Bake at 400°F. for 30 minutes or until the bread crust is golden brown. Remove from oven wire rack to cool slightly. Slice, serve with French mustard.

# COUNTRY SAUSAGE AND VEAL PATÉ

**Makes 8-10 servings**

- ½ pound sliced bacon
- 1¼ pounds veal, ground
- ¾ pound pork, ground
- 1¼ pounds mildly spiced, coarsely ground pork sausage
- ½ cup seasoned bread crumbs
- ½ cup milk
- 2 eggs, slightly beaten
- ⅓ cup Cognac
- ¼ cup chopped fresh parsley
- 3 cloves garlic, peeled, minced
- 5 shallots or green onions, minced
- ½ teaspoon crushed thyme
- 4 large bay leaves

**Preparing the terrine**

Blanch bacon in boiling water. Drain bacon on paper toweling. Line terrine, 8-cup terrine or a loaf pan, with bacon strips, overlapping as necessary and bringing ends of bacon up over sides of terrine. Reserve 2 strips bacon for top of paté.

**Paté**

Combine veal, pork and pork sausage in a large mixing bowl; blend well. In a separate bowl, combine bread crumbs and milk; let stand 10 minutes, or until liquid is absorbed. Add bread crumb mixture to ground meats; blend thoroughly. Add eggs and Cognac; blend well. Add parsley, garlic, shallots and thyme; stir until thoroughly blended. Turn meat mixture into prepared terrine. Pack firmly being certain that mixture fills all corners. Bring ends of bacon strips up and over top of paté. Using reserved bacon strips, arrange over top. Cover terrine tightly with aluminum foil and place in a pan large enough to accommodate it. Fill the outer pan with 2 inches of very hot water. Bake at 325°F., for 1½ hours or until paté is cooked. If juices are clear, paté is cooked. If juices are pink, return to oven. Cool overnight, unmold, slice.

# PORK

## DRY HEAT COOKING

For more juicy, tender results and less shrinkage, the cooking temperature should be low to moderate. With all cookery methods, fresh pork should be cooked to an internal temperature of 170°F.

**Roasting** Use for large pork cuts.

1. Place pork fat side up on a rack in an open roasting pan.

2. Insert meat thermometer so bulb is centered in roast. Do not add water. Do not cover. Roast in a slow 300-350°F. oven.

**Broiling** Use for pork chops cut at least one inch thick, steaks, 1/2 to 3/4 inch thick, back ribs, country-style ribs, spareribs, and ground pork patties. Termperature should be such that cuts are done in the center by the time they are browned on the outside.

1. Set oven regulator for broiling or start outdoor grill and wait until coals are covered with ash.

2. Place pork 3 to 5 inches from heat. Broil until pork is brown on one side. Turn and broil second side until done. Season each after browning if desired.

**Panbroiling** is used for small pork cuts, 1 inch thick or less. Convenient method when cooking a few chops or steaks. Also use for ham slices, bacon and ground pork patties.

1. Place pork in heavy skillet. Do not add fat or water. Grease pan for lean cuts. Do not cover. Cook slowly, turning occasionally. Pour fat from pan as it accumulates. Brown on both sides.

**Panfrying** is used for thin pork cuts and cuts that have been pounded, cubed or ground. Also use for cuts coated with flour, meal or egg and crumbs.

1. Brown pork on both sides in small amount of fat.

2. Season with salt and pepper if desired. Do not cover.

3. Cook at moderate temperature, turning occasionally until done.

**Stir-frying** is quick panfrying.

1. Cut ingredients to uniform size. Slice pork against the grain. Heat oil in skillet or wok. Stir continuously until cooked.

**Deep-fat Frying** is another form of frying. Cut pork into uniform pieces, coat if desired.

1. Use a deep pan. Heat fat to frying temperature, fry a few pieces of pork at a time, drain on paper toweling.

## MOIST HEAT COOKING

**Braising** is used for pork chops 1/2 to 1 1/2 inches thick, and for cuts such as cubes and blade and arm steaks.

1. Coat if desired, brown pork on all sides in heavy skillet, use a small amount of fat if necessary. Cover tightly, cook at low temperature until done.

**Cooking in Liquid** for cuts such as smoked shoulder roll, hocks, neck bones and cubes. Method used for making soup and stew. Dredge pork in seasoned flour if desired. Brown pork in small amount of fat, if desired. Cover with liquid, cover pot and cook at simmer until done. Add vegetables, if desired, just long enough before serving to be cooked.

## Storage

Handle with care is the first rule of meat storage. Proper storage in the refrigerator and freezer will protect the quality of pork and maintain maximum flavor. These products do not keep their high quality long in the freezer. The seasonings in these products speed up changes in flavor and texture during freezing. For best quality, smoked pork such as hams, arm picnics, loins and shoulder rolls and bacon should not be frozen for longer than 2 months. Frankfurters should not be frozen for longer than 1 month. Canned hams and canned picnics should not be frozen.

# RETAIL CUTS OF PORK
### WHERE THEY COME FROM AND HOW TO COOK THEM

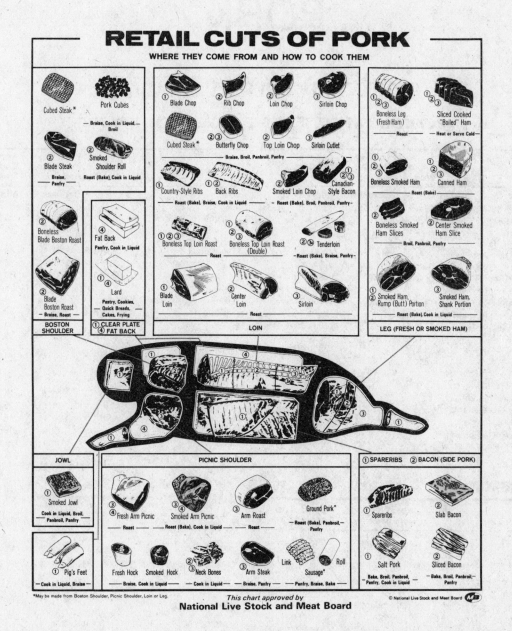

**BOSTON SHOULDER**

Cubed Steak*

Pork Cubes
— Braise, Cook in Liquid, Broil

② Blade Steak
Braise, Panfry

Smoked Shoulder Roll
Roast (Bake), Cook in Liquid

② Boneless Blade Boston Roast

② Blade Boston Roast
Braise, Roast

**① CLEAR PLATE ④ FAT BACK**

④ Fat Back
Panfry, Cook in Liquid

① ④ Lard
Pastry, Cookies, Quick Breads, Cakes, Frying

**LOIN**

① Blade Chop
② Rib Chop
③ Loin Chop
③ Sirloin Chop

Cubed Steak*
②③ Butterfly Chop
④ Top Loin Chop
Sirloin Cutlet
— Braise, Broil, Panbroil, Panfry —

① Country-Style Ribs
①② Back Ribs
③ Smoked Loin Chop
②③① Canadian-Style Bacon
— Roast (Bake), Braise, Cook in Liquid —   — Roast (Bake), Broil, Panbroil, Panfry —

①②③ Boneless Top Loin Roast
①②③ Boneless Top Loin Roast (Double)
②③ Tenderloin
— Roast —   —Roast (Bake), Braise, Panfry—

① Blade Loin
② Center Loin
③ Sirloin
— Roast —

**LEG (FRESH OR SMOKED HAM)**

①②③ Boneless Leg (Fresh Ham)
— Roast —
①②③ Sliced Cooked "Boiled" Ham
— Heat or Serve Cold —

①② Boneless Smoked Ham
①②③ Canned Ham
— Roast (Bake) —

② Boneless Smoked Ham Slices
③ Center Smoked Ham Slice
— Broil, Panbroil, Panfry —

①② Smoked Ham, Rump (Butt) Portion
①③ Smoked Ham, Shank Portion
— Roast (Bake), Cook in Liquid —

**JOWL**

① Smoked Jowl
Cook in Liquid, Broil, Panbroil, Panfry

① Pig's Feet
— Cook in Liquid, Braise —

**PICNIC SHOULDER**

③④ Fresh Arm Picnic
— Roast —
③④ Smoked Arm Picnic
— Roast (Bake), Cook in Liquid —
③ Arm Roast
— Roast —
Ground Pork*
— Roast (Bake), Panbroil, Panfry —

Fresh Hock   Smoked Hock
— Braise, Cook in Liquid —
③② Neck Bones
— Cook in Liquid —
③ Arm Steak
— Braise, Panfry —
Link   Roll Sausage*
— Panfry, Braise, Bake —

**① SPARERIBS ② BACON (SIDE PORK)**

① Spareribs
② Slab Bacon

① Salt Pork
② Sliced Bacon
— Bake, Broil, Panbroil, Panfry, Cook in Liquid —   — Bake, Broil, Panbroil, Panfry —

*May be made from Boston Shoulder, Picnic Shoulder, Loin or Leg.

© National Live Stock and Meat Board

*This chart approved by*
**National Live Stock and Meat Board**

# PORK

## TIME AND TEMPERATURE TABLES

### ROASTING AT 300°F.-350°F.* OVEN TEMPERATURE

| Cut | Approx. Weight | Final Thermometer Reading | Approx.[1] Cooking Time |
|---|---|---|---|
| **Smoked** | Lbs. | Degrees F. | Min. Per Lb. |
| Ham (fully-cooked) | | 130°F. to | |
| Whole (boneless) | 8 to 12 | 140°F. | 15 to 18 |
| Half (boneless) | 4 to 6 | | 18 to 25 |
| Portion (boneless) | 3 to 4 | | 27 to 33 |
| Ham (fully cooked) | | | |
| Whole (bone-in) | 14 to 16 | 130°F. to | 15 to 18 |
| Half (bone-in) | 7 to 8 | 140°F. | 18 to 25 |
| Ham (cook-before-eating) | | | |
| Whole (boneless) | 8 to 12 | 160°F. | 17 to 21 |
| Ham (cook-before-eating) | | | |
| Whole (bone-in) | 14 to 16 | 160°F. | 18 to 20 |
| Half (bone-in) | 7 to 8 | 160°F. | 22 to 25 |
| Portion (bone-in) | 3 to 5 | 160°F. | 35 to 40 |
| Loin | 3 to 5 | 140°F. | 20 to 25 |
| Arm Picnic Shoulder (fully cooked) | 5 to 8 | 140°F. | 25 to 30 |
| Arm Picnic Shoulder (cook-before-eating) | 5 to 8 | 170°F. | 30 to 35 |
| Shoulder Roll (butt) | 2 to 3 | 170°F. | 35 to 40 |
| Canadian-style Bacon (fully cooked) | 2 to 4 | 140°F. | 20 to 30 |
| Ground Ham Loaf | 2 | 160°F. | 1 ½ hrs. |

| Cut | Approx. Weight | Final Thermometer Reading | Approx.[1] Cooking Time |
|---|---|---|---|
| **Fresh** | Lbs. | Degrees F. | Min. Per Lb. |
| Loin | | | |
| Center | 3 to 5 | 170°F. | 30 to 35 |
| Half | 5 to 7 | 170°F. | 35 to 40 |
| Blade loin or Sirloin | 3 to 4 | 170°F. | 40 to 45 |
| Top (double) | 3 to 5 | 170°F. | 35 to 40 |
| Top | 2 to 4 | 170°F. | 30 to 35 |
| Crown | 6 to 10 | 170°F. | 25 to 30 |
| Arm Picnic Shoulder | | | |
| Bone-in | 5 to 8 | 170°F. | 30 to 35 |
| Boneless | 3 to 5 | 170°F. | 35 to 40 |
| Arm Roast | 3 to 5 | 170°F. | 30 to 35 |
| Blade Boston Shoulder | 4 to 6 | 170°F. | 40 to 45 |
| Leg (fresh ham) | | | |
| Whole (bone-in) | 14 to 16 | 170°F. | 22 to 24 |
| Whole (boneless) | 10 to 14 | 170°F. | 24 to 28 |
| Half (bone-in) | 7 to 8 | 170°F. | 35 to 40 |
| Tenderloin | ½ to 1 | 170°F. | 45 to 60 |
| | | | **Hours** |
| Back Ribs | | Cooked | 1 ½ to 2 |
| Country-style Ribs | | well | 1 ½ to 2 |
| Spareribs | | done | 1 ½ to 2 |
| Ground Pork Loaf | 2 | 170°F. | 1 ½ |

325°F. to 350°F. oven temperature is recommended for fresh pork and 300°F. to 325°F. oven temperature for smoked pork.
Based on meat taken directly from the refrigerator.

## BRAISING

| Cut | Approx. Weight or Thickness | Approx. Total Cooking Time |
|---|---|---|
| Chops, fresh | ¾ to 1 ½ inches | 45 to 60 min. |
| Spareribs | | 1 ½ hrs. |
| Backribs | | 1 ½ hrs. |
| Country-style Ribs | | 1 ½ to 2 hrs. |
| Tenderloin | | |
| Whole | ½ to 1 pound | 45 to 60 min. |
| Slices | ½ inch | 30 min. |
| Shoulder Steaks | ¾ inch | 45 to 60 min. |
| Cubes | 1 to 1 ¼ inches | 45 to 60 min. |

# PORK

## BROILING AT MODERATE TEMPERATURE

| Cut | Approx. Thickness | Approx. Total Cooking Time |
|---|---|---|
| **Fresh** | | |
| Rib, Loin, Blade or Sirloin Chops | ¾ to 1½ inches | 30 to 45 |
| Shoulder Steaks | ½ to ¾ inch | 30 to 45 |
| Spareribs | | 1-1½ hrs. |
| Backribs | | 1-1½ hrs. |
| Country-style Ribs | | 1-1½ hrs. |
| Ground Pork Patties | ½ inch | 12 to 15 |
| Pork Kabobs | 1 to 1¼-inch cubes | 26 to 32 |
| **Smoked** | | **Min.** |
| Ham Slice | ½ inch | 10 to 12 |
| Ham Slice | 1 inch | 16 to 20 |
| Loin Chops | ½ to 1 inch | 15 to 20 |
| Ham Kabobs | 1 to 1½-inch cubes | 16 to 20 |
| Canadian-style Bacon (sliced) | ½ inch | 6 to 8 |
| Ground Ham Patties | ½ inch | 10 to 12 |

## COOKING IN LIQUID

| Cut | Approx. Weight | Approx. Total Cooking Time |
|---|---|---|
| **Fresh** | | |
| Spareribs | | 2 to 2½ |
| Country-style Ribs | | 2 to 2½ |
| Hocks | | 2 to 2½ |
| **Smoked** | **Pounds** | **Hours** |
| Ham, Country or Country-style | 10 to 16 | 4½ to 5 |
| Half | 5 to 8 | 3 to 4 |
| Arm Picnic Shoulder | 5 to 8 | 3½ to 4 |
| Shoulder Roll | 2 to 4 | 1½ to 2 |
| Hocks | | 2 to 2½ |

# PORK CHOPS WITH PESTO STUFFING

8 pork rib chops, cut 1¼ to 1½ inches thick
1 cup firmly packed fresh basil leaves
½ cup minced fresh parsley
½ cup freshly grated Parmesan cheese
4 tablespoons pine nuts
2 cloves garlic, peeled and quartered
6 tablespoons olive oil, divided
7 slices white bread, lightly toasted and torn into ¼-inch pieces
4 tablespoons water
Salt and pepper to taste

Preheat oven to 350°F. Trim fat from pork chops. With a sharp knife, make a pocket in each chop by cutting into their side without cutting through the other side of chop. Set chops aside. In a blender container or food processor, place basil, parsley, Parmesan cheese, pine nuts, and garlic. Blend or process about 30 seconds or until finely chopped. With blender or food processor running, add 2 tablespoons olive oil. Transfer mixture to a small bowl; stir in bread pieces. Sprinkle water over bread mixture; toss lightly to mix. Spoon about ½ cup stuffing mixture into each chop. In large skillet, heat remaining oil; brown chops on each side. Place chops in a large baking dish, sprinkle with salt and pepper. Bake, covered, for 1 hour.

# SWEET AND SOUR PORK

**Makes 3-4 servings**

**Batter**

   1/2 cup all-purpose flour
   1 egg, slightly beaten
   1/4 cup water
   1 teaspoon baking powder

In a small, shallow bowl combine batter ingredients, set aside.

   1 pound pork, sliced into 1 inch x 1/2 inch-pieces
   Peanut oil to deep-fry

**Sauce**

   1/2 cup firmly packed light brown sugar
   2 teaspoons light soy sauce
   1/2 cup pineapple juice
   4 tablespoons catsup

Combine sauce ingredients in a small bowl, reserve.

   1 green bell pepper, seeded, sliced
   1 cup pineapple chunks, drained

**1 tomato, sliced**
**1 tablespoon cornstarch dissolved in**
**3 tablespoons water**

Coat pork pieces with batter. Heat oil to 375°F. in a wok or medium skillet with deep sides. Deep-fry pork, fry pieces one at a time until cooked and golden brown on all sides. Drain on paper toweling. Remove all but 4 tablespoons of cooled oil. Reheat remaining oil, stir-fry peppers, 30 seconds. Add pineapple and tomatoes, stir-fry 20 seconds. Return pork and sauce, heat until mixture thickens. Serve over rice.

# CHINESE ROAST PORK

**Makes 6 servings**

- ½ teaspoon ground ginger
- ½ teaspoon garlic powder
- 4 tablespoons dry sherry
- 2 tablespoons light soy sauce
- 5 tablespoons Hoisin sauce, available in Oriental food stores

Combine sauce ingredients in a small bowl. Cover pork roast with sauce, marinate in sauce for 2 hours in a shallow bowl, turn pork twice. Place roast on a rack over pan. Roast at 450°F. for 15 minutes, reduce heat to 350°F. and continue cooking for 35 minutes or until pork is cooked. Cool pork 10 minutes, slice. Drizzle with any remaining sauce. Serve over Oriental noodles.

# ORANGE-GLAZED PORK CHOPS

**Makes 6 servings**

6 pork chops, 3/4 inch thick
4 tablespoons light brown sugar
4 tablespoons orange marmalade
2 tablespoons wine vinegar
3/4 cup freshly squeezed orange juice
1/4 teaspoon salt, pepper, and garlic powder

In a large heavy skillet brown chops at medium-low heat. Drain off excess fat. In a medium bowl combine remaining ingredients. Pour sauce over chops. Cover and continue simmering 35 minutes or until chops are cooked. Serve with extra sauce and orange slices.

# PORK CHOPS WITH BLACK OLIVES

**Makes 6 servings**

- 1 **cup all-purpose flour**
- 1/2 **teaspoon salt, rosemary**
- 1/4 **teaspoon pepper**
- 6 **pork chops, cut 3/4 inch thick**
- 4 **tablespoons vegetable oil**
- 1/2 **pound mushrooms, sliced**
- 1/2 **cup black olives**
- 1 1/2 **cups commercial sour cream**

Season flour with salt, rosemary and pepper. Dust pork chops with flour. Heat oil in a large skillet; brown chops on both sides and transfer to an ovenproof baking pan. Add mushrooms, black olives and 1/2 cup sour cream. Cover and bake at 325°F. for 45 minutes. Arrange on serving plates and top with a dollop of sour cream.

# BARBECUED SPARERIBS

**Makes 6 servings**

4 pounds meaty spareribs
All-purpose flour
1/2 cup vegetable oil

**Sauce**

1 1/2 cups ketchup
1 tablespoon Worcestershire sauce
3 tablespoons wine vinegar
3 tablespoons melted butter
1 onion, minced
1/2 teaspoon honey
1/2 teaspoon salt
1/4 teaspoon pepper

Dust spareribs with flour. Heat oil in a large heavy skillet. Brown spareribs quickly, arrange ribs in a large roasting pan. Combine all sauce ingredients in a medium bowl. Brush ribs with sauce. Preheat oven to 450°F. Reduce heat to 350°F., bake ribs 1 1/2 hours, or until done, turn once. Cut into 4-rib sections. Serve with additional sauce.

# STUFFED PORK CHOPS

**Makes 6 servings**

- 3 tablespoons butter
- 3 shallots, minced
- 3 stalks celery, chopped
- 1/2 pound mushrooms, sliced
- 1 cup seasoned bread crumbs
- 1/2 cup slivered almonds
- 6 loin pork chops with pocket

In a large skillet heat butter over medium heat; sauté shallots, celery and mushrooms until tender, stirring occasionally. Stir in bread crumbs and almonds, stir until mixture is combined. Stuff pork chops with mixture, close openings with skewers or toothpicks. Brown pork chops on both sides. Place chops in a shallow baking dish. Bake at 350°F. for 35-40 minutes or until cooked.

# LAMB

Because lamb is naturally tender, most cuts can be prepared conventionally using dry heat methods. Rib, loin, shoulder, sirloin and leg cuts are excellent when roasted, broiled or panbroiled. Chops cut 1 inch thick are usually best panbroiled. Ground lamb may be roasted as loaves, broiled or panbroiled as patties or browned and included in casseroles or other combination dishes. To insure maximum tenderness, cuts from the neck, shank and breast are usually cooked by moist heat methods, such as braising or cooking in liquid, although riblets from the breast can be broiled. With all cooking methods, it is important that lamb be cooked at low to moderate temperature and that overcooking be avoided.

The fell, the thin paper-like covering on the outer fat, should not be removed from roasts and legs, because it helps these cuts retain their shape and juiciness during cooking. The fell has usually been removed from small cuts at the market.

At one time, lamb was only served well done, now more people are enjoying lamb cooked to rare, 140°F., medium 160°F., or well done 170°F.

To determine doneness in roasts and legs, a roast meat thermometer should be used. Since the lamb will continue to cook after it has been removed from the oven, the thermometer should register about 5° lower than the desired doneness. For easier carving, allow the lamb to rest 10-20 minutes.

# RETAIL CUTS OF LAMB

### WHERE THEY COME FROM AND HOW TO COOK THEM

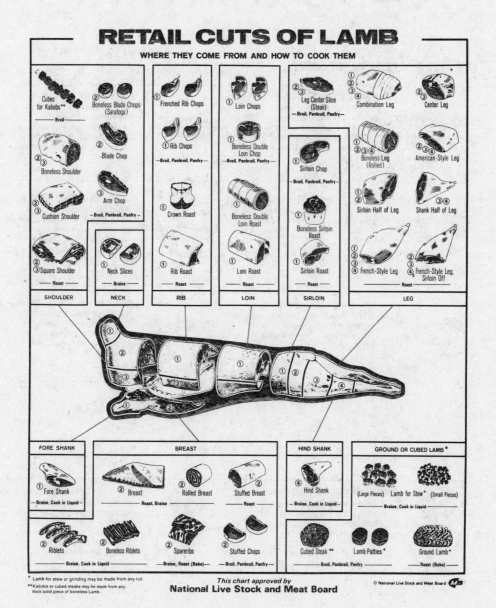

This chart approved by
**National Live Stock and Meat Board**

\* Lamb for stew or grinding may be made from any cut.

\*\*Kabobs or cubed steaks may be made from any thick solid piece of boneless Lamb.

© National Live Stock and Meat Board

# LAMB CARVING

## Carving Instructions

**ROAST LEG OF LAMB**
Place the roast on the platter with the shank to the carver's right and the tip section on the near side. From this, remove two or three slices lengthwise to form a base.

**LAMB LOIN ROAST**
Have retailer saw backbone free from ribs for easier carving. Backbone should not be removed nor should the saw cut into the meaty center.

Turn the roast up on the base and starting at the shank end, make slices perpendicular to the leg bone as shown in the illustration.

Before the roast is brought to the table, remove the backbone, cutting close along the bone and leaving as much meat on roast as possible. Place roast with bone side facing carver.

After reaching the aitch bone, loosen the slices by cutting under them, following the top of the leg bone. Remove slices to platter and then serve.

Insert the fork in the top of the roast. Make slices by cutting close along each side of the rib bone. One slice will contain the rib, the next will be boneless.

**CROWN ROAST OF LAMB**
Remove any garnish in the center of the roast that might interfere with carving. Steady roast by placing fork firmly between the ribs. Start carving at one of the two ends where the ribs are tied together.

Cut down between the ribs, allowing one or more ribs for each serving. Using the fork to steady it, lift the slice on the knife blade to the platter. Dressing can be cut and served with the slices.

# COOKING LAMB

### TO ROAST
1. Place lamb fat side up on rack in open roasting pan.
2. Insert meat thermometer so bulb is centered in roast and not touching bone.
3. Do not add water. Do not cover.
4. Roast in slow oven (300-325°F.) to desired degree of doneness.
5. Season with salt and pepper if desired.

### TO BROIL
1. Set oven regulator for broiling (preheat if desired) or start outdoor grill and wait until coals are covered with ash.
2. Place lamb 3 to 5 inches from heat.
3. Broil until lamb is brown on one side.
4. Turn and broil second side until done.
5. Season each side after browning if desired.

### TO PANBROIL
1. Place lamb in heavy frying pan.
2. Do not add fat or water. Grease pan if necessary. Do not cover.
3. Cook slowly, turning occasionally.
4. Pour fat from pan as it accumulates.
5. Brown lamb on both sides.
6. Cook until done. Season if desired.

### TO COOK IN LIQUID
1. Dredge lamb in seasoned flour if desired.
2. Brown lamb on all sides in small amount of fat if desired.
3. Cover with liquid, cover utensil and cook below boiling (simmer) until done.
4. Add vegetables if desired just long enough before serving to be cooked.

### TO PANFRY
1. Brown lamb on both sides in small amount of fat.
2. Season with salt and pepper if desired.
3. Do not cover.
4. Cook over moderate temperature, turning occasionally until done.

### TO BRAISE
1. Dredge lamb in seasoned flour if desired.
2. Brown lamb on all sides in heavy utensil, using a small amount of fat.
3. Add small amount of liquid.
4. Cover tightly.
5. Cook at low temperature until done.

# LAMB
## *Time and Temperature Tables*

### BROILING AT MODERATE TEMPERATURE

| Cut | Approx. Thickness | Approx. Weight | Distance from heat | Approx. Total Cooking Time |
|---|---|---|---|---|
| | Inches | Ounces | Inches | Minutes |
| Shoulder Chops | ¾ to 1 | 5 to 9 | 3 to 4 | 7 to 11 |
| Rib Chops | 1 | 3 to 5 | 3 to 4 | 7 to 11 |
| | 1½ | 4.5-7.5 | 4 to 5 | 15 to 19 |
| Loin Chops | 1 | 3 to 5 | 3 to 4 | 7 to 11 |
| | 1½ | 4.5-7.5 | 4 to 5 | 15 to 19 |
| Sirloin Chops | ¾ to 1 | 6 to 10 | 3 to 4 | 12 to 15 |
| Leg Steaks | ¾ to 1 | 11 to 18 | 3 to 4 | 14 to 18 |
| Cubes for Kabobs | 1 to 1½ | | 4 to 5 | 8 to 12 |
| Ground Lamb Patties | ½ x 4 | 4 | 3 | 5 to 8 |

### COOKING IN LIQUID

| Cut | Average Size | Approx. Total Cooking Time |
|---|---|---|
| Lamb for Stew | 1 to 1½-inch pieces | 1½ to 2 hours |

### BRAISING

| Cut | Avg. Wt. or Thickness | Approx. Total Cooking Time |
|---|---|---|
| Neck slices | ¾ inch | 1 hour |
| Shoulder chops | ¾ to 1 inch | 45 to 60 minutes |
| Breast, stuffed | 2 to 3 pounds | 1½ to 2 hours |
| Breast, rolled | 1½ to 2 pounds | 1½ to 2 hours |
| Riblets | ¾ to 1 pound each | 1½ to 2 hours |
| Shanks | ¾ to 1 pound each | 1 to 1½ hours |
| Lamb for Stew | 1½-inch pieces | 1½ to 2 hours |

### ROASTING AT 325°F. OVEN TEMPERATURE (NOT PREHEATED)

| Cut | Approx. Weight | Final Thermom. Reading | Approx.[1] Cooking Time |
|---|---|---|---|
| | Lbs. | Degrees F. | Min. per Lb. |
| Leg | 7 to 9 | 140°F. (rare) | 15 to 20 |
| | | 160°F. (medium) | 20 to 25 |
| | | 170°F. (well) | 25 to 30 |
| Leg | 5 to 7 | 140°F. (rare) | 20 to 25 |
| | | 160°F. (medium) | 25 to 30 |
| | | 170°F. (well) | 30 to 35 |
| Leg, Boneless | 4 to 7 | 140°F. (rare) | 25 to 30 |
| | | 160°F. (medium) | 30 to 35 |
| | | 170°F. (well) | 35 to 40 |
| Leg, Shank Half | 3 to 4 | 140°F. (rare) | 30 to 35 |
| | | 160°F. (medium) | 40 to 45 |
| | | 170°F. (well) | 45 to 50 |
| Leg, Sirloin Half | 3 to 4 | 140°F. (rare) | 25 to 30 |
| | | 160°F. (medium) | 35 to 40 |
| | | 170°F. (well) | 45 to 50 |
| Shoulder,[2] Boneless | 3½ to 5 | 140°F. (rare) | 30 to 35 |
| | | 160°F. (medium) | 35 to 40 |
| | | 170°F. (well) | 40 to 45 |

[1] Based on meat taken directly from the refrigerator.

[2] For pre-sliced, bone-in shoulder, add 5 minutes per pound to times recommended for boneless shoulder.

---

## TIMETABLE FOR ROASTING
### 325°F. Oven Temperature (not preheated)

| | Min. per pound | | | Min. per pound |
|---|---|---|---|---|
| **Leg (7 to 9 Pounds)** | | | **Leg, Shank Half (3 to 4 Pounds)** | |
| 140°F. (rare) | 15 to 20 | | 140°F. (rare) | 30 to 35 |
| 160°F. (medium) | 20 to 25 | | 160°F. (medium) | 40 to 45 |
| 170°F. (well) | 25 to 30 | | 170°F. (well) | 45 to 50 |
| **Leg (5 to 7 Pounds)** | | | **Leg, Sirloin Half (3 to 4 Pounds)** | |
| 140°F. (rare) | 20 to 25 | | 140°F. (rare) | 25 to 30 |
| 160°F. (medium) | 25 to 30 | | 160°F. (medium) | 35 to 40 |
| 170°F. (well) | 30 to 35 | | 170°F. (well) | 45 to 50 |
| **Leg, Boneless (4 to 7 Pounds)** | | | **Shoulder,* Boneless (3½ to 5 Pounds)** | |
| 140°F. (rare) | 25 to 30 | | 140°F. (rare) | 30 to 35 |
| 160°F. (medium) | 30 to 35 | | 160°F. (medium) | 35 to 40 |
| 170°F. (well) | 35 to 40 | | 170°F. (well) | 40 to 45 |

*For pre-sliced, bone-in shoulder, add 5 minutes per pound.

# BUTTERFLIED LEG OF LAMB WITH MINT SAUCE _

**Makes 8 servings**

 4-5 pound leg of lamb, have butcher butterfly lamb
  4 tablespoons vegetable oil
 1/2 teaspoon garlic powder
  2 teaspoons dried mint, crushed

**Sauce**

 1 1/2 cups beef stock or bouillon
  2 tablespoons all-purpose flour
  2 teaspoons dried mint, crushed
 1/2 teaspoon salt
 1/4 teaspoon pepper

Rub butterflied leg of lamb with oil, sprinkle with garlic powder and dried mint. Place lamb flat on a broiler rack over pan. Roast at 325°F. until lamb is cooked according to meat thermometer. Place on serving platter, let meat rest 10 minutes, slice. Serve with mint sauce.

**Sauce**

Drain 1/2 cup of drippings from roasting pan; pour into a small saucepan. Cook over medium heat until warm. Whisk in flour, continue whisking until flour is absorbed. Stir in bouillon and continue until sauce thickens. Season with mint, salt and pepper. Serve warm.

# LEG OF LAMB WITH PARSLEY-SPICE CRUST

4 cloves garlic, peeled, cut in half
5-6 pound leg of lamb, trimmed of fat
1 teaspoon salt
1/2 teaspoon black pepper
2 tablespoons prepared mustard

Insert garlic slivers into 8 slits on lamb leg. Sprinkle salt and pepper over the lamb. Rub the mustard over the lamb. Arrange lamb on a roasting rack in pan. Roast at 325°F. for 1 1/2 hours, remove lamb from oven. Press crumb crust onto lamb, return lamb to oven; bake for 30 minutes or until cooked. Place lamb on heated serving platter. Slice lamb at the dinner table. Spoon crumbled crust over sliced lamb.

**Parsley-Spice Crust**

1 1/2 cups flavored crumbs
1/4 cup minced fresh parsley
1 teaspoon crushed basil
6 tablespoons melted butter

Combine all Parsley-Spice Crust ingredients in a small bowl.

# LAMB PATTIES

**Makes 4-5 servings**

1¼ pounds lamb shoulder, ground
½ teaspoon white pepper, crushed oregano, ground basil
1 onion, minced
½ cup bread crumbs
2 eggs, slightly beaten
3 tablespoons butter
2 tablespoons vegetable oil

In a large deep mixing bowl combine all ingredients except butter and oil. Heat butter and oil in a large heavy skillet over medium heat; form lamb mixture into patties, fry on both sides until cooked, drain.

# EASTER ROAST LEG OF LAMB

**5-7 pounds leg of lamb**
**3 tablespoons prepared mustard**
**¼ cup soy sauce**
**6 cloves garlic**

Place leg of lamb, fat side up on a rack in a roasting pan. Rub lamb with prepared mustard. Sprinkle lamb with soy sauce. Cut 6½-inch slits in lamb, insert garlic cloves. Insert meat thermometer so that the bulb is centered into the thick part of the leg. Roast at 325°F. until lamb is cooked. Do not cover. Remove from oven when thermometer registers 135°F. for rare; 160°F. for medium and 170°F. for well done. Let lamb stand on the counter for 10 minutes; slice. Serve with sauce if desired.

# BROILED LAMB CHOPS

**Makes 6 servings**

- 6 blade lamb chops, cut 3/4 inch thick
- 1/4 teaspoon salt, pepper, garlic powder
- 3 tablespoons butter
- 1 tablespoon vegetable oil
- 2 green bell peppers, seeded, sliced
- 2 onions, sliced thin
- 1 teaspoon chopped basil

Arrange lamb chops on a broiler rack in a pan so that the surface of the meat is 3-4 inches from the heat. Broil 5 minutes, season chops with salt, pepper and garlic powder, turn over. Broil 4 minutes or until cooked. While chops are cooking prepare vegetables. In a large skillet heat butter and oil over medium heat. Sauté peppers and onions until tender, stirring occasionally. Season with basil. Arrange chops on serving dish, top with sautéed vegetables.

# GROUND LAMB IN PITA POCKETS

**Makes 6 servings**

- 1 pound ground lamb
- 1/2 teaspoon garlic powder
- 1/2 teaspoon chopped basil, rosemary, salt
- 1/4 teaspoon pepper
- 6 pita pockets
- 2 cups commercial sour cream
- 1 large onion, chopped

In a large deep bowl combine lamb and seasonings. Sauté lamb in large skillet over medium heat, stirring often, drain except drippings. Spoon into pita pockets. Spoon sour cream over lamb, top with chopped onions.

# MOUSSAKA _____

**Makes 10-12 servings**

  2 **large eggplants, 1 pound each, peeled, sliced ¼ inch, salt, weigh down for 30 minutes**
  4 **tablespoons olive oil**
  2 **tablespoons olive oil**
1½ **pounds ground lamb**
  1 **large onion, chopped**
  2 **cloves garlic, peeled, minced**
  1 **can tomatoes, 16 ounces, drained, chopped**
  1 **teaspoon ground thyme, oregano**
  ½ **teaspoon nutmeg, pepper**
  ½ **cup bread crumbs**
  2 **eggs, separated**
  3 **tablespoons butter**
  3 **tablespoons all-purpose flour**
1½ **cups half-and-half**
  1 **cup grated Gruyere cheese**

Rinse eggplant with cold water, press out excess moisture with paper toweling. Heat 4 tablespoons olive oil in a large skillet, sauté eggplant until lightly browned on both sides. Use just enough oil to keep eggplant from sticking. Drain eggplant on paper toweling, reserve. Prepare meat sauce; in a large skillet heat 2 tablespoons olive oil, sauté lamb, onion and garlic over medium heat stirring often. Drain excess liquid. Stir in tomatoes, spices, simmer until lamb is cooked, about 5 minutes; cool. Stir in bread crumbs and egg whites, combine, reserve.

Prepare white sauce: melt butter in a heavy saucepan over medium heat. Whisk in flour and stir until absorbed. Remove from heat and add half-and-half in a slow steady stream while whisking to make a smooth sauce. Whisk in lightly beaten egg yolks. Heat, over low heat, until sauce thickens, stirring constantly, do not boil.

In a 3-quart, deep ovenproof casserole, alternate layers of eggplant, white sauce and grated cheese beginning with eggplant. Pour white sauce over. Bake at 350°F. for 45 minutes.

# LAMB SATÉ

**Makes 6 servings**

2½ pounds lamb, cut into bite-sized cubes
  2 tablespoons vegetable oil
  ¼ teaspoon ground pepper
  2 cloves garlic, peeled, minced
  1 cup soy sauce
  ¼ cup firmly packed dark brown sugar
  1 large onion, sliced thin
  2 limes, sliced thin
  2 tablespoons deep-fried onion rings

In a mixing bowl place lamb and cover with a mixture of vegetable oil, black pepper and garlic. Combine soy sauce with brown sugar, add half to lamb mixture and reserve remaining sauce. Allow lamb to marinate 20 minutes, drain. Thread meat on skewers. Grill over charcoal, broil or bake in a preheated 500°F. oven until cooked, turn once. Serve with sliced onion, limes and onion rings.

# LAMB CURRY ————

**Makes 8 servings**

5 tablespoons butter
2 tablespoons vegetable oil
3 pounds lamb shoulder, cut into ³/₄-inch cubes
¹/₄ cup all-purpose flour
2 cloves garlic, peeled, minced
1 large onion, sliced thin
1 cup sliced celery
3 large firm apples, peeled, cured, sliced
¹/₂ cup golden raisins
1 tablespoon curry powder or to taste
¹/₄ cup water
3 eggs, slightly beaten
¹/₂ cup half-and-half
¹/₄ cup all-purpose flour

Heat butter and oil in a large heavy saucepan, over medium heat. Dust lamb with flour, discard excess flour. Sauté lamb until lightly brown on all sides. Remove lamb, reserve. Sauté garlic, onion and celery until tender, stirring occasionally. Add apples and raisins, return lamb to saucepan; simmer 15 minutes. Stir in curry powder and water, combine. Cover, simmer 15 minutes. Stir together eggs, half-and-half and flour. Stir egg mixture into lamb curry. Continue cooking 2 minutes, or until sauce thickens. Serve with rice.

# VEAL

## ROLLED VEAL SCALLOPS WITH MUSHROOMS

**Makes 8 servings**

- 4 tablespoons butter
- 2 cloves garlic, peeled, minced
- 1 onion, sliced thin
- 1 pound mushrooms, sliced
- 8 slices veal scallops, pound thin, trim off fat and membranes
- 1/2 teaspoon salt and pepper
- 4 tablespoons butter
- 1 cup dry white wine
- 1 cup chicken stock

Melt butter in a large heavy skillet; sauté garlic and onion until tender over medium heat, stirring occasionally. Sauté mushrooms until tender, remove vegetables from heat. Sprinkle veal with salt and pepper. Divide vegetables among scallops, roll. Tie scallops with kitchen string. Melt butter in a larger skillet over medium heat. Sauté veal until golden brown on all sides, do not overcook. Pour wine and stock into skillet, cover. Simmer for 15 minutes or until veal is tender. Place one rolled bird on each plate, serve hot.

# VEAL WITH MUSHROOMS AND CREAM

**Makes 6 servings**

 1/2 **teaspoon salt**
 1/4 **teaspoon pepper and ground nutmeg**
1 1/2 **pounds veal cutlets, thinly sliced**
 4 **tablespoons butter**
 2 **cups sliced mushrooms**
 1 **onion, sliced**
 1 **cup heavy cream**

Sprinkle spices over veal cutlets, reserve. Heat butter in a large skillet. Sauté onion and mushrooms until tender over medium heat, stirring occasionally. Add veal, brown quickly on both sides, do not overcook. Remove veal to a warm serving tray. Drizzle cream over vegetables, combine. Pour vegetables and sauce over veal. Serve with buttered noodles.

# VEAL WITH LEMON

**Makes 6 servings**

- ¼ cup butter
- 1 tablespoon vegetable oil
- 2 pounds veal scallops, flattened, fat and membranes removed
- ½ cup all-purpose flour
- 2 tablespoons freshly squeezed lemon juice
- 1 tablespoon lemon zest
- 4 tablespoons Cognac
- 2 large lemons, cut into wedges for garnish
- ½ cup parsley sprigs

Melt butter and oil in a large skillet over medium heat. Dust veal scallops in flour. Brown scallops lightly on both sides, do not overcook. Remove veal and place on a heated serving dish. Add lemon juice, zest and Cognac to the remaining butter in the skillet. Simmer 1 minute over medium heat. Drizzle sauce over veal. Garnish with lemon wedges and trim with parsley.

# VEAL PARMAGIANA

**Makes 6 servings**

2$\frac{1}{2}$ pounds veal cutlets
  3 eggs, slightly beaten
  $\frac{1}{2}$ teaspoon salt and pepper
  1 cup seasoned bread crumbs
  $\frac{1}{4}$ cup vegetable oil
  3 tablespoons butter
  3 cloves garlic, peeled, minced
  $\frac{1}{2}$ cup sliced onions
  3 cans, 8 ounces each, tomato paste
  1 teaspoon crushed basil and oregano
  1 cup water
  6 slices, about $\frac{1}{2}$ pound Mozzarella cheese

Trim fat and membrane from sides of cutlets. Pound to $\frac{1}{4}$ inch thick. Beat together eggs, salt and pepper, place in a shallow dish. Dip cutlets into egg mixture; roll in bread crumbs. Heat oil and butter in a large skillet over medium-high heat. Fry cutlets quickly on both sides, reserve and arrange in a 13 x 9 x 1$\frac{3}{4}$-inch pan. Preheat oven to 350°F. Reduce heat to medium in skillet. Sauté garlic and onions until tender, stirring occasionally. Stir in remaining ingredients except Mozzarella cheese. Simmer 5 minutes. Pour sauce over cutlets. Cover and bake for 10 minutes. Uncover, arrange a slice of Mozzarella cheese over each cutlet. Increase heat to 450°F. Bake veal until cheese has melted, about 5-7 minutes. Serve with salad and pasta.

# BREADED VEAL

**Makes 6 servings**

- ¹/₄ cup minced fresh parsley
- 3 cloves garlic, peeled, minced
- 1 cup bread crumbs
- 4 ounces Parmesan cheese, grated
- ¹/₂ teaspoon salt and pepper
- ¹/₂ cup all-purpose flour
- 2 eggs, slightly beaten
- 4 tablespoons milk
- 5 tablespoons vegetable oil
- 3 tablespoons butter
- 6 veal cutlets, pound thin
- 2 lemons, sliced for garnish

Combine parsley, garlic, bread crumbs, Parmesan cheese, salt and pepper in a shallow dish. Place flour on a sheet of waxed paper. Combine eggs and milk in a shallow dish. Heat oil and butter in a large heavy skillet over medium heat. Dip each veal piece in flour, dip into egg mixture and dip into the bread crumb mixture. Fry on both sides until cooked, do not overcook as veal tends to get tough. Arrange on serving plate, garnish with lemon slices.

# ROAST LOIN OF VEAL _____

**Makes 6 servings**

   2 **tablespoons vegetable oil**
   2 **pounds veal loin**
     **Salt and pepper to taste**
   1 **cup pear poaching liquid**
   1 **cup veal stock**
   4 **ounces Pear Williams brandy**
   1 **pound mushrooms, sliced**
   2 **poached pears, sliced**
   2 **green onions, chopped**
 ¹/₂ **pound asparagus spears, blanched**

Pour oil into a roasting pan large enough to accommodate the veal loin. Place roasting pan over medium heat until oil becomes clear. Season veal loin with salt and pepper; sauté in roasting pan until golden brown on all sides. Place roast in oven, bake at 350°F. for 15 minutes or until the roast reaches 120°F. on meat thermometer or it is medium rare. Remove roast from oven and let rest. While veal is resting reduce the pear poaching liquid, the veal stock and the Pear Williams Brandy by two-thirds, in a small saucepan over medium heat.

Slice veal loin into 24 thin slices. Arrange 6 slices of veal on each dinner plate in half moon design. Arrange sliced mushrooms over veal, add sliced pears and asparagus spears. Drizzle the reduced sauce over the veal and the pear.

# VITELLO TONNATO _

**Makes 8 servings**

- 1 large onion, sliced
- 3 large carrots, sliced
- 4 stalks celery, sliced
- 2½ pounds veal roast
- 1 cup water
- ½ cup white wine
- 3 bay leaves
- ¾ teaspoon salt
- ½ teaspoon pepper

Arrange onion, carrots and celery in the bottom of a Dutch oven. Place veal over vegetables. Add water, wine, bay leaves, salt and pepper. Bring mixture to a boil. Reduce heat to a simmer. Cover and continue simmering for 1½ hours or until veal is tender. Cool, slice veal. Prepare sauce.

**Sauce**

- 1 can, 2 ounces, Italian anchovies
- 1 can, 6½ ounces, tuna fish, packed in olive oil; drain, add additional vegetable oil to measure ¼ cup
- 2 tablespoons freshly squeezed lemon juice
- 4 tablespoons capers, drained
- 1 lemon, sliced for garnish
- 6 parsley sprigs for garnish

Combine anchovies, tuna and olive oil. Add lemon juice, mix well. Pour sauce over veal. Sprinkle capers over and around veal. Garnish with lemon slices and parsley.

# STUFFED BREAST OF VEAL

Makes 8-10 servings

- 2 cloves garlic, peeled, minced
- 1/2 cup chopped onions
- 4 tablespoons butter
- 2 carrots, grated
- 1 tomato, peeled, seeded, chopped
- 1 cup sliced mushrooms
- 2 cups seasoned bread crumbs
- 1/2 teaspoon crushed tarragon, salt and pepper
- 1 cup sliced onions
- 2 carrots, sliced
- 1/2 cup veal stock or water
- 5-6 pounds breast of veal, with a pocket
- 1 teaspoon pepper
- 1/2 teaspoon garlic powder

Heat butter in a skillet over medium heat. Sauté garlic and onions until tender, stirring occasionally. Stir in carrots, tomato and mushrooms, combine, sauté until tender. Add bread crumbs, spices, combine. Sauté 1 minute. Preheat oven to 350°F. Sprinkle onions and carrots over bottom of a large roasting pan. Add stock. Place veal over vegetables. Stuff pocket, truss or sew pocket together. Sprinkle veal with spices. Roast covered for 1 1/2 hours. Uncover and continue roasting for 30 minutes or until tender. Cool 5 minutes, slice, serve.

# SAUCES, GRAVIES AND MARINADES

# Sauces, Gravies and Marinades

When you have a freezer filled with soup stocks (see soup chapter) the world of sauces and gravies opens up. The makings of many creative sauces are at your fingertips. With the addition of drippings and a small amount of flour or cornstarch, the gravy can be prepared. You can add a small amount of wine or sautéed vegetables and season to taste. Be creative by adding chervil, onions, nutmeg, curry, garlic, leeks, Madeira, or sherry. Just open your cabinet doors and create.

The French have contributed the wonderful egg-based sauces. These sauces can be created easily and quickly. They are an elegant addition to an everyday dinner as well as to a V.I.P. gala. Mayonnaise, although available commercially, is more tasty when made at home. A dash of mustard or pepper makes it your very own creation.

Now that you have cooked a wonderful sauce be sure not to drown the food in it. Treat it delicately, adding a small amount around the food or drizzled lightly over it. Most sauces will keep for a week in a covered container, refrigerated. Do not keep them too long.

# SOUBISE SAUCE ____

**Makes 2½ cups**

 2 large onions, minced
 1 cup milk
 3 tablespoons butter
 2 tablespoons all-purpose flour
 ½ teaspoon salt
 ½ cup heavy cream

Place onions and milk in a heavy saucepan, simmer until onions are tender, stirring occasionally. Puree onions, reserve. In a medium saucepan melt butter over medium heat. Whisk in flour, continue whisking until flour is absorbed, do not brown. Return puree and milk, cook until sauce thickens. Season with salt. Stir in cream, simmer 1 minute.

# RED BUTTER SAUCE _____

**Makes 2 cups**

1³/₄ cups red wine
  1 tablespoon wine vinegar or tarragon vinegar
  3 shallots, minced
³/₄ pound butter, room temperature, cut into pieces
¹/₄ teaspoon salt, pepper, tarragon

In a small saucepan add red wine, vinegar and shallots; cook over medium heat until mixture is reduced to ¹/₄ cup liquid. Remove pan from heat; whisk in butter, one piece at a time. Season with salt, pepper and tarragon. Keep warm until ready to serve.

# MORNAY SAUCE ____

**Makes 2¹/₂ cups**

  5 tablespoons butter
  4 tablespoons all-purpose flour
¹/₂ teaspoon dry mustard, salt
1¹/₂ cups milk
¹/₂ cup grated Swiss cheese
¹/₂ cup cream

In a medium saucepan melt butter over medium heat. Whisk in flour, continue cooking until flour is absorbed, do not brown. Stir in mustard, salt and milk, continue cooking until sauce thickens. Stir in Swiss cheese and cream, simmer 3 minutes, stirring continuously.

# BÉARNAISE SAUCE

**Makes 1 cup**

    3  tablespoons butter
    3  shallots, minced
    ½  cup dry red wine
    1  cup Espanol sauce; recipe follows

In a small saucepan heat butter over medium heat; sauté shallots until tender, stirring often. Stir in wine and simmer until mixture is reduced to ¼ cup liquid. Stir in Espanol sauce and simmer 5 minutes, serve.

# HOLLANDAISE SAUCE

**Makes ½ cup**

    ½  cup butter, room temperature, cut into pieces
    4  egg yolks
    1  tablespoon freshly squeezed lemon juice
       Salt to taste
    2  tablespoons boiling water

In the top of a double boiler over simmering water blend butter into the egg yolks. Mix in lemon juice and salt. Whisk in the boiling water, stirring constantly until sauce thickens.

# ESPANOL SAUCE

**Makes 1¹/₂ cups**

- 3 tablespoons butter
- 2 teaspoons olive oil
- 1 medium onion, minced
- 1 carrot, sliced
- 2 stalks celery, sliced
- ¹/₂ cup mushrooms
- 2 tablespoons all-purpose flour
- 2 tomatoes, peeled, chopped
- 2 tablespoons tomato paste
- 1¹/₂ cups chicken stock
- 4 tablespoons dry white wine
- ¹/₄ teaspoon salt and pepper
- 1 bay leaf

In a medium saucepan heat butter and oil, over medium heat; sauté onion, carrot and celery until tender, stirring often. Add mushrooms, cook until tender. Sprinkle flour over vegetables and continue cooking until flour is absorbed. Mix in remaining ingredients, bringing mixture to a boil, reduce to a simmer and continue cooking 30 minutes, stirring occasionally; strain.

# BORDELAISE SAUCE

**Makes 1¼ cups**

2 tablespoons minced shallots
¾ cup dry red wine
1 bay leaf
¼ teaspoon crushed thyme
3 tablespoons butter
1 cup mushrooms, sliced
2 tablespoons all-purpose flour
1 cup beef stock
Salt and pepper to taste

In a small saucepan combine shallots, wine, bay leaf and thyme. Simmer, until wine is reduced to about ¼ cup. Strain liquid, reserve. In a separate pan heat butter over medium heat, sauté mushrooms until tender. Whisk in flour and continue stirring until flour is absorbed. Add beef broth and cook, stirring constantly until mixture thickens. Season to taste with salt and pepper. Add wine mixture and simmer 4-5 minutes.

# BASIC WHITE SAUCE

**Makes 3 cups**

- 6 tablespoons butter
- 4 tablespoons all-purpose flour
- 3 cups milk
- 1/4 teaspoon salt and white pepper

In a medium saucepan melt butter over medium heat. Whisk in flour, continue stirring until flour is absorbed. Remove pan from heat; stir in milk in a slow steady stream. Stir in seasoning. Return to heat, cook over medium-low heat until sauce thickens, about 3 minutes, stirring constantly. Cover.

# BECHAMEL SAUCE

**Makes 1 1/2 cups**

- 4 tablespoons butter
- 4 tablespoons all-purpose flour
- 1/2 teaspoon salt
- 1 cup milk
- 4 tablespoons heavy cream

In a small heavy saucepan heat butter; whisk in flour until flour is absorbed, do not brown. Slowly stir in salt and milk. Simmer until sauce thickens, stir in heavy cream. Simmer until sauce is warm, about 1 minute.

# SCANDINAVIAN SAUCE

**Makes 3¹/₂ cups**

    1 quart lingonberries, wash
    1 tablespoon white wine
1¹/₄ cups sugar

In a medium saucepan simmer lingonberries with wine until berries are tender. Stir in sugar and simmer until sugar has dissolved. Serve sauce warm over crepes and/or pancakes.

# MEXICAN HOT SAUCE

**Makes 1¹/₄ cups**

    3 tomatoes, peeled, chopped
    4 green onions, chopped
    1 can, 4 ounces, green chilies, chopped
    1 teaspoon vegetable oil
 ¹/₂ teaspoon salt, pepper, oregano, garlic powder

In a medium bowl combine tomatoes, onions and green chilies. Blend in oil. Season to taste with salt, pepper, oregano and garlic powder. Mix well, place in a covered container.

# MARINARA SAUCE _

**Makes 3 cups**

- 2 tablespoons olive oil
- 3 cloves garlic, peeled, minced
- 8 ripe tomatoes, peeled, pureed
- 2 tablespoons dark brown sugar
- 3/4 teaspoon crushed oregano
- 1/2 teaspoon chopped fresh parsley
- 1/2 teaspoon crushed basil
- 1/4 teaspoon salt, pepper

Heat olive oil in a large skillet; sauté garlic until tender, stirring often. Stir in pureed tomatoes, bringing mixture to a boil over medium heat. Stir in brown sugar, oregano and basil. Simmer for 15 minutes. Season with salt and pepper. Serve warm or place in a covered container and refrigerate until ready to use.

# TERIYAKI SAUCE ____

**Makes 1 cup**

- ½ cup light soy sauce
- ½ cup sake, or dry white wine
- ½ teaspoon ground ginger
- ¼ cup catsup
- 1 teaspoon prepared mustard
- 1 teaspoon Worcestershire sauce
- 4 tablespoons brown sugar

In a small bowl combine all ingredients. Use for a marinade or brush on steaks or chicken as a sauce.

# CHERRY SAUCE ____

**Makes 1½ cups**

- 1 can, 1 pound, pitted red tart cherries
- 1 tablespoon cornstarch
- ¼ teaspoon ground cinnamon, nutmeg

Drain juice from cherries into a cup, reserve cherries. Blend cornstarch into juice. Stir in cinnamon and nutmeg. In a small saucepan cook cherry juice mixture, over medium heat until mixture begins to thicken; about 2 minutes. Stir in reserved cherries. Serve warm.

# ORIENTAL HOT SAUCE

**Makes ½ cup**

- 1 tablespoon chili paste with garlic
- 2 tablespoons white rice vinegar
- 1 tablespoon light soy sauce
- 1 teaspoon sesame oil, or to taste

Combine all ingredients in a small bowl, mix well until all ingredients are blended. Taste and adjust seasonings.

# HORSERADISH SAUCE

**Makes 2 cups**

- 1 cup heavy cream
- 4 tablespoons prepared white creamy horseradish
- 1 teaspoon sugar

In a large bowl or electric mixer whip cream until stiff peaks form. Fold in remaining ingredients. Cover and chill until ready to serve. Good with beef.

# PARSLEY SOUR CREAM SAUCE _____

**Makes 1¹/₂ cups sauce**

1¹/₂ **cups commercial sour cream**
³/₄ **cup fresh chopped dill**
¹/₂ **cup fresh chopped parsley**

In a small bowl combine all ingredients. Cover and chill until ready to serve.

# NEW ENGLAND TARTAR SAUCE _____

**Makes 2¹/₄ cups**

2 **cups mayonnaise**
1 **jar, 3 ounces, chopped capers, drained**
1 **teaspoon freshly squeezed lemon juice**
1 **small onion, minced**
¹/₄ **cup dill pickles, minced**

In a small bowl combine all ingredients. Cover and chill until ready to serve. Serve with seafood.

# ROUILLE SAUCE

**Makes 1 cup**

- 1 egg yolk
- 4 teaspoons minced garlic
- 1/4 teaspoon pepper
- 2 teaspoons freshly squeezed lemon juice
- 3/4 cup pure olive oil

Combine egg yolk, minced garlic, pepper and lemon juice in a medium mixing bowl. In a slow steady stream, beat in the olive oil.

# LIGHT BEER SAUCE

**Makes 1 1/2 cups**

- 1 cup mayonnaise
- 1/4 cup catsup
- 1/4 cup light beer
- 1 tablespoon prepared mustard
- 2 teaspoons freshly squeezed lemon juice
- 1/2 teaspoon prepared horseradish

Combine all ingredients in a small bowl; mix well. Place in a covered container, chill.

# COCKTAIL SAUCE __

**Makes ¹/₂ cup**

    4 tablespoons tarragon vinegar
    ¹/₂ teaspoon paprika
    2 teaspoons prepared cream-style horseradish
    ¹/₂ teaspoon Worcestershire sauce
    ¹/₂ cup chili sauce

In a small bowl combine all sauce ingredients together until well blended. Cover and chill until ready to serve.

# COCKTAIL SAUCE II _

**Makes 1¹/₄ cups**

    1 cup chili sauce
    3 tablespoons freshly squeezed lime juice
    1 tablespoon prepared horseradish
    2 green onions, chopped
    ¹/₄ teaspoon salt

In a small mixing bowl combine all sauce ingredients; chill. Serve with seafood.

# WHITE CLAM SAUCE

**Makes 1½ cups**

- 3 tablespoons olive oil
- 3 tablespoons butter
- 1 medium onion, minced
- 2 cloves garlic, peeled, minced
- ¼ teaspoon salt
- ¼ teaspoon pepper, crushed oregano
- 2 cans, 8 ounces each, minced clams, drain, reserve liquid

In a medium saucepan heat olive oil and butter; sauté onion and garlic until tender, stirring occasionally. Season with salt, pepper and oregano. Stir in minced clams and ½ cup of reserved liquid. Simmer until warm. Serve over cooked pasta.

# PESTO SAUCE _____

**Makes 4 cups**

- 1/2 cup Romano cheese, grated
- 4 cups fresh basil leaves, washed, drained and tightly packed
- 1/4 cup chopped fresh parsley
- 3/4 cup olive oil
- 4 cloves garlic, peeled, minced
- 1/2 cup pignoli nuts (pine nuts)
- 1/2 teaspoon salt

Use a blender or a food processor fitted with a steel blade. If using a food processor, process in two batches. Process cheese until minced. Add remaining ingredients except olive oil; puree. Add half of the oil, combine. In a slow steady stream add remaining oil through the feed tube until combined. Place in a covered container and refrigerate until ready to use.

# PESTO PARSLEY SAUCE

**Makes 2½ cups**

- 4 ounces Romano cheese, grated
- 2 cloves garlic, peeled
- 2½ cups parsley sprigs, trimmed
- 1 cup fresh spinach, stems removed
- 3 tablespoons pignoli nuts (pine nuts)
- ½ cup olive oil

Use a blender or a food processor fitted with a steel blade. Process cheese until minced. Add remaining ingredients except oil, combine. In a slow steady stream add oil through the feed tube until combined. Place in a covered container and refrigerate until ready to use.

# ITALIAN TOMATO SAUCE _____

**Makes 2¹/₂ cups**

- ¹/₄ **cup olive oil**
- 4 **green onions, minced**
- 2 **cloves garlic, peeled, minced**
- 1 **can, 28 ounces, Italian-style plum tomatoes, crushed**
- 1 **can, 12 ounces, tomato paste**
- 1 **cup water**
- 1 **teaspoon crushed basil**
- ¹/₂ **teaspoon salt and pepper**
- 1 **teaspoon honey**

In a large saucepan heat oil; sauté onions and garlic until tender, over medium heat, stirring occasionally. Stir in tomatoes, tomato paste and water. Bring sauce to a boil, season with spices and honey. Reduce heat to simmer. Continue cooking 30 minutes, stirring occasionally.

# CAPER SAUCE _____

**Makes 1¹/₄ cups**

    3 tablespoons butter
    1 small onion, minced
    3 tablespoons all-purpose flour
    ¹/₄ cup dry white wine
 1¹/₂ cups beef stock
    2 tablespoons capers, drained
    ¹/₂ teaspoon freshly squeezed lemon juice
    ¹/₄ teaspoon ground nutmeg

Heat butter in a medium saucepan over medium heat. Sauté onion until tender, stirring occasionally. Whisk in flour to make a roux, continue cooking until flour is absorbed. Stir in wine and stock. Continue simmering until sauce thickens. Stir in remaining ingredients. Continue cooking until thickened, stirring often.

# MIDDLE EAST SESAME SEED SAUCE

**Makes 1¹/₂ cups**

    1 cup Tahini, available at gourmet food stores
    ¹/₂ cup freshly squeezed lemon juice
    ¹/₂ teaspoon salt
    2 cloves garlic, peeled, minced
    ¹/₂ teaspoon ground cumin
    2 teaspoons olive oil

Place in bowl of blender or food processor fitted with a steel blade. Blend with lemon juice. Add remaining ingredients except olive oil. Place mixture into serving bowl. Top with olive oil. Use as a sauce when baking fish, a salad dressing or spread on warm pita bread.

# RAISIN SAUCE _____

**Makes 1 cup**

1/2 **cup firmly packed dark brown sugar**
1/4 **teaspoon dry mustard**
1 1/4 **tablespoons cornstarch**
1/4 **teaspoon salt, ground cinnamon, allspice**
1/4 **cup vinegar**
1 **cup water**
1/2 **cup dark raisins**

In a small saucepan combine all dry ingredients. Stir in vinegar, water and raisins. Cook over medium heat until sauce thickens, stirring constantly. Serve warm.

# CUMBERLAND SAUCE _____

**Makes 1 cup**

1 **orange, sliced thin**
4 **tablespoons freshly squeezed orange juice**
1/2 **cup port**
1/2 **cup red currant jelly**
1 **tablespoon cornstarch**
2 **tablespoons water**

In a small saucepan combine orange slices, orange juice, port and currant jelly; simmer over low heat 5 minutes, stirring occasionally. Combine cornstarch and water in a cup. Whisk into cumberland sauce, continue cooking until sauce thickens, about 2 minutes; cool.

# ORIENTAL HOT MUSTARD

**Makes ½ cup**

> 1 tablespoon dry mustard
> 3 tablespoons water
> 1 tablespoon white rice vinegar
> ½ teaspoon salt
> ½ teaspoon chili sauce

In a small bowl whisk together all ingredients. Allow to stand 10 minutes, stir again. Cover until ready to serve.

# FOOD PROCESSOR MAYONNAISE

**Makes 1 cup**

> 1 egg
> 1 teaspoon freshly squeezed lemon juice
> 1 teaspoon Dijon mustard
> 1 cup vegetable oil

Place all ingredients except vegetable oil in processor bowl fitted with steel blade. With the machine running, pour mixture through feed tube in a slow steady stream, until mixture is combined.

# CHUTNEY _____

**Makes 3 cups**

  2 cups dried apricots
1½ tablespoons candied ginger, chopped
  1 cup dark raisins
 ½ lime, sliced thin
  1 large onion, sliced thin
1½ cups firmly packed dark brown sugar
 ½ cup wine vinegar
  3 cloves garlic, peeled, minced
  1 teaspoon dry mustard
 ½ cup tomato sauce
 ½ teaspoon ground cinnamon
 ½ teaspoon ground allspice
 ½ teaspoon ground cloves

Wash and chop apricots. In a medium-heavy saucepan combine all ingredients, simmer for 25 minutes, stirring often, until mixture blends together and is thick in consistency. Place cooled chutney in a covered container.

# GREEN PEPPERCORN GRAVY

**Makes 1¹/₂ cups**

> 3 tablespoons drippings
> 2 tablespoons all-purpose flour
> ¹/₄ cup dry white wine
> 1 cup beef stock
> 3 tablespoons green peppercorns, drained, crushed
> ¹/₂ cup heavy cream or half-and-half

Heat drippings in a small skillet, over medium heat. Whisk in flour, continue cooking until flour begins to brown. Stir in wine and stock, continue cooking until gravy thickens. Stir in peppercorns. Mix in cream and simmer until gravy is warm, about 2 minutes.

# BROWN SAUCE GRAVY BASE _____

**Makes 1¹/₄ cups**

- 3 **tablespoons drippings**
- 3 **shallots, minced**
- 2 **tablespoons all-purpose flour**
- ¹/₂ **teaspoon salt, crushed tarragon**
- 1 **cup beef stock**

Heat drippings in a small skillet; sauté shallots until tender, over medium heat, stirring often. Whisk in flour, continue cooking until flour is brown. Season with salt and tarragon. Continue cooking until sauce thickens.

# BROWN GRAVY _____

**Makes 1¹/₄ cups**

- 3 **tablespoons drippings from the roast**
- 2 **tablespoons all-purpose flour**
- 1 **cup soup stock**

Pour 3 tablespoons drippings from the roast into a small saucepan; cook over medium heat until warm. Stir in flour and continue stirring until flour is absorbed and brown. Gradually stir in soup stock. Season to taste; strain, serve.

# ITALIAN MARINADE

**Makes 1¹/₂ cups**

1 can (6 ounces) tomato paste
²/₃ cup Italian or your favorite salad dressing
¹/₄ cup water
1 tablespoon Worcestershire Sauce

Combine all ingredients in a medium bowl. Marinate meat or fish according to recipe directions. Baste several times during cooking.

# CRANBERRY MARINADE

**Makes 1³/₄ cups**

1 clove garlic, minced
2 tablespoons vegetable oil
1 cup jellied cranberry sauce
¹/₄ cup light soy sauce
¹/₂ cup freshly squeezed orange juice
2 tablespoons freshly squeezed lemon juice

Combine ingredients in a medium bowl until smooth. Pour over skewers filled with lamb, orange slices, and drained canned onions. Let stand at room temperature 1 hour. Baste before and after broiling with the marinade. Heat remaining sauce and serve with kabobs.

# TARRAGON MARINADE _____

**Makes 1¹⁄₄ cups**

    1 large onion, minced
    2 tablespoons freshly squeezed lemon juice
    1 teaspoon lemon zest
    3 cloves garlic, crushed
    ¹⁄₂ teaspoon dry mustard
    ¹⁄₂ teaspoon salt, pepper
    1 cup vegetable oil
    3 tablespoons tarragon vinegar
    ¹⁄₂ cup dry red wine

In a medium bowl combine all ingredients. Use as a marinade for flank steak and other meats.

# TOMATO BEER MARINADE _____

    1¹⁄₂ cups tomato sauce
    ¹⁄₂ cup beef bouillon
    2 cloves garlic, minced
    1 teaspoon Worcestershire Sauce

Combine marinade ingredients and spoon evenly over meat and/or vegetables. Marinate 2 hours at room temperature. Broil, basting several times.

# PLUM MARINADE __

**Makes 2 cups**

    1 jar (16 ounces) plums
    2 tablespoons freshly squeezed lemon juice
    1 tablespoon light soy sauce
  1/2 teaspoon Worcestershire sauce
    1 small clove garlic, crushed
  1/2 teaspoon salt
  1/4 teaspoon pepper

Drain plums. Reserve syrup. Remove pits, puree plums. Add 1/2 cup of the syrup and the remaining ingredients to the pureed plums. Pour marinade over meat and marinate overnight. Thread onto skewers and broil, basting occasionally.

# TERIYAKI MARINADE ___

**Makes 3/4 cup**

  1/3 cup light soy sauce
  1/3 cup saki or dry white wine
 3-4 tablespoons light brown sugar
    1 tablespoon ground ginger
  1/4 teaspoon salt

Combine ingredients. Score the meat and place in a low pan. Pour sauce over meat and marinate for several hours or overnight, turning several times. Broil, according to the broiling charts.

# SALADS AND SALAD DRESSINGS

# Salads
# and
# Salad
# Dressings

Revive slightly wilted salad vegetables and greens in a bath of cold water and ice cubes. Drain; spin dry.

Occasionally use salad greens other than lettuce. Try chicory, escarole, endive, kale, spinach, dandelion greens, romaine, watercress, Chinese cabbage, or a combination of these greens.

Remember to sprinkle either orange, lemon, lime or pineapple juice on fruits that may turn dark, such as apples, bananas, or peaches.

Preventing wilting and sogginess by drying the greens used in salads, by draining canned foods well before adding to the salad, and by using just enough salad dressing to moisten.

For raw vegetable salads, add dressing at the last minute.

Store most greens unwashed for a week in the crisper section of your refrigerator or in plastic bags.

Wash and dry greens well: spin dry in a salad spinner, whirl wire basket, or layer leaves between paper towels or a clean tea towel.

Possible fruit combinations for salads:
Sliced pineapple, apricot halves, sweet red cherries
Watermelon balls, peach slices, and orange slices
Grapefruit sections, banana slices, berries, cherries
Grapefruit sections, unpared apple slices
Peach slices, pear slices, red plums
Pineapple wedges, banana slices, strawberries
Cooked dry fruit, cherries, red raspberries, raisins.

Possible fruit and vegetable combinations:
Shredded raw carrots, diced apples, raisins
Sliced cucumber, pineapple cubes
Avocado sections, grapefruit sections, and orange slices

Possible vegetable combinations:
Grated carrots, diced celery, cucumber slices
Spinach, endive, or lettuce with tomato wedges
Sliced raw cauliflower flowerets, chopped green pepper, celery, pimiento
Shredded cabbage, cucumber slices, sliced celery
Cubed cooked beets, sliced celery, onion slices

Gelatin desserts will unmold easily if the mold is lightly greased with a small amount of salad oil.

For molded salads the gelatin is chilled to the consistency of unbeaten egg whites. At this stage, gently fold in vegetables, seafoods, meat, or fruit so that the food will remain suspended in the gelatin.

When the mold is completely set and firm to the touch, it is ready to be unmolded. To unmold a salad, loosen the edges of the mold with a spatula. Place serving plate upside down on top of the mold. Invert plate with the mold and shake gently until the gelatin falls out onto plate. Lift off the mold and garnish as desired or as directed in the recipe. If the gelatin does not drop out easily, dip the mold in warm water up to the rim for 5 seconds, and proceed as above.

# MUSHROOM SALAD

**Makes 6 servings**

- 6 heads bib lettuce, separated, wash and dry
- 1 pound large mushrooms, sliced
- 1 large red onion, minced

**Dressing:**

- 1 onion, minced
- 1/2 cup vegetable oil
- 1/4 cup red wine vinegar
- 2 teaspoons sugar
- 1 teaspoon dry mustard
- 1/4 teaspoon salt, ground black pepper

Arrange lettuce on 6 chilled salad plates. Sprinkle sliced mushrooms over lettuce. Top with sliced onions. In a small bowl combine all dressing ingredients, blend well. Place in a covered container and refrigerate until ready to serve. Drizzle dressing over mushroom salad.

# HEARTS OF PALM SALAD

**Makes 6 servings**

- 1 head red-leaf lettuce, torn into bite-size pieces
- 3 tomatoes, sliced
- 1 onion, sliced
- 1 can, 14 ounces, hearts of palm, drained
- 1/2 cup black olives, sliced
- 2 tablespoons olive oil
- 4 tablespoons vegetable oil
- 4 tablespoons tarragon vinegar
- 1/4 teaspoon crushed tarragon
- 1/2 teaspoon salt
- 1/4 teaspoon freshly ground black pepper

Arrange lettuce on 6 individual salad plates. Place tomatoes, onions and olives over lettuce. Slice hearts of palm into 1/4-inch pieces, sprinkle over salad. In a small bowl combine remaining ingredients. Drizzle dressing over salad. Chill until ready to serve.

# AVOCADO SALAD __

**Makes 6 servings**

    Bib lettuce for 6, trimmed
1 tablespoon freshly squeezed lime juice
3 ripe avocados, pared, pitted, cut into slices
2 tomatoes, sliced
2 cloves garlic, peeled, minced
1/4 cup vegetable oil
1/4 cup tarragon vinegar
1/4 teaspoon salt, fresh ground pepper
3 green onions, minced

Tastefully arrange the bib lettuce on 6 chilled plates. Sprinkle lime juice over avocados. Place avocados and tomatoes in a fan-like arrangement over lettuce. Combine remaining ingredients except green onions in a small mixing bowl. Drizzle dressing over salad. Sprinkle with green onions, serve.

# ONION SALAD _____

**Makes 6 servings**

- 1/2 cup olive oil
- 2 tablespoons freshly squeezed lemon juice
- 1/2 teaspoon salt
- 1/4 teaspoon ground pepper
- 1/2 teaspoon sugar
- 1/2 cup blue cheese, crumbled
- 4 large red onions, sliced

In a small bowl, combine olive oil, lemon juice, salt, pepper and sugar. Stir in blue cheese. Arrange onion slices in a glass bowl. Cover with dressing, cover, chill overnight.

# JICAMA SALAD _____

**Makes 6 servings**

- 2 1/2 cups jicama, peeled, diced
- 2 red bell peppers, seeded, diced
- 1 onion, chopped
- 1 cucumber, sliced
- 5 tablespoons olive oil
- 3 tablespoons wine vinegar
- 1/2 teaspoon salt, white pepper

In a large bowl combine jicama, pepper, onion and cucumber. In a separate bowl mix together olive oil, vinegar, salt and pepper, toss with salad. Cover and chill until ready to serve.

# MARINATED VEGETABLES ____

    1 large cucumber, sliced
    1 can, 16 ounces, French-style green beans, drained
    1 can, 17 ounces, peas
    1 large onion, sliced thin
    4 stalks celery, sliced
    1 red bell pepper, seeded, sliced
    1 jar, 2 ounces, pimiento, chopped
    2 cans, 8½ ounces each, artichoke hearts, drained,
      quartered
 ½ cup corn oil
 ¼ cup vinegar
    1 teaspoon sugar
 ½ teaspoon salt

In a large glass salad bowl combine and toss all vegetables. In a separate small bowl combine oil, vinegar, sugar and salt. Drizzle dressing over vegetables, toss. Drain before serving.

# BEAN SALAD _____

**Makes 8 servings**

    1 can, 16 ounces, kidney beans, drained, rinsed
    1 can or jar, 4½ ounces, sliced mushrooms, drained
    1 can, 16 ounces, green beans, drained
    1 can, 16 ounces, waxed beans, drained
    1 large onion, sliced

In a large glass bowl combine all ingredients. Toss with dressing and mix together. Cover, chill until ready to serve.

**Dressing:**

    ¾ cup salad oil
    ¼ cup tarragon vinegar
    ½ teaspoon sugar, salt, dry mustard, thyme
    ¼ teaspoon ground pepper
    2 cloves garlic, minced

Combine all ingredients in a screw-top jar, mix well. Chill until ready to use, shake well before using.

# POTATO SALAD I ___

**Makes 6-8 servings**

- 6 large potatoes, unpeeled
- 1 tablespoon dry white wine
- 2 tablespoons white wine vinegar
- 6 tablespoons olive oil
- 1/2 teaspoon dry mustard
- Salt and pepper to taste
- 2 green onions, chopped
- 4 tablespoons chopped fresh parsley

Place potatoes in a large saucepan, cover with boiling water, cook 20 minutes or until fork tender. Drain potatoes, peel, and slice while still warm. Sprinkle with wine. In a small bowl, whisk together vinegar and oil. Blend in mustard and salt and pepper to taste. Drizzle sauce over potatoes. Sprinkle potatoes with onions and parsley; toss lightly. Refrigerate until ready to serve, about 4 hours.

# POTATO SALAD II

**Makes 8-10 servings**

4 pounds potatoes
2¼ cups mayonnaise
¼ cup freshly squeezed lime juice
1 teaspoon salt
½ teaspoon freshly ground pepper
1 teaspoon dry mustard
1 cup chopped celery
1 red bell pepper, seeded and chopped
6 green onions, chopped

Place unpeeled potatoes in a large saucepan. Cover with water; boil for 20 minutes or until fork tender. Peel and slice in a large salad bowl, combine remaining ingredients. Add potatoes; toss to mix. Cover and chill 3 hours before serving.

# HOT POTATO SALAD

**Makes 6 servings**

    4 large potatoes, cooked, peeled, sliced
    6 slices bacon, cut into 1-inch pieces
    1 onion, chopped
    4 stalks celery, chopped
  1/2 cup fresh chopped dill
    2 dill pickles
3 1/2-4 cups dill pickle liquid
    1 tablespoon sugar
  1/2 teaspoon caraway seeds
  1/2 teaspoon dry mustard, salt

In a large heavy skillet sauté bacon pieces until partially cooked over medium heat. Stir in onion, celery and pickles, sauté for 2 minutes or until tender, stirring occasionally. Add potatoes and remaining ingredients. Cover and simmer 8-10 minutes; lift cover occasionally and stir with a spatula. Serve hot, good with smoked sausage or ham.

# POTATO SALAD WITH AN ITALIAN FLAIR

**Makes 8-10 servings**

- 3 pounds potatoes
- 6 hard-boiled eggs, chopped
- 1 cup sliced celery
- 1/4 cup chopped onion
- 1 red bell pepper, seeded and sliced
  Salt and pepper to taste
- 1 can (2 ounces) anchovies, drained and chopped
- 3-4 ounces freshly grated Parmesan cheese
- 1/2 cup mayonnaise
- 1/2 teaspoon ground oregano

Place unpeeled potatoes in a large pan. Cover with water; cook for 20 minutes over medium heat or until potatoes are fork tender. Drain potatoes, peel, and cube. In a large salad bowl, combine remaining ingredients. Add potatoes. Toss to mix. Chill for 3 hours before serving.

# GERMAN POTATO SALAD

**Makes 8 servings**

6 slices bacon, cooked, crumbled; reserve all drippings
Salad oil
1/3 cup granulated sugar
3 tablespoons all-purpose flour
1 teaspoon salt
1/2 teaspoon freshly ground black pepper
1 cup cider vinegar
1 cup water
4 pounds salad potatoes, cooked, sliced while warm
1 red onion, sliced thin

Combine enough oil with bacon drippings to make 1/2 cup. Stir in sugar, flour, salt, and pepper. Gradually mix vinegar and water; cook 3 minutes over medium heat, stirring constantly. Pour mixture over potatoes and toss with onion. Let stand at room temperature for 2 hours. Sprinkle potato salad with bacon.

# APPLESAUCE _____

**Makes about 6 cups**

> 1 **cup water**
> 2 **cups apple juice**
> ³/₄ **cup sugar**
> ³/₄ **cup firmly packed dark brown sugar**
> 3 **tablespoons cinnamon**
> ¹/₂ **teaspoon nutmeg**
> ¹/₂ **teaspoon vanilla**

Combine water, apple juice and sugars in a large saucepan. Bring liquids to a boil over medium heat. Add apples to liquid. Bring mixture to a boil again, reduce heat to a simmer. Continue cooking until the apples are soft and tender, stirring occasionally. If applesauce seems too dry during cooking add water by the tablespoonful. Mix in seasonings and vanilla. Cook until applesauce is reduced to a puree. Remove applesauce to a large deep bowl. Serve hot or cold. Good with cream.

# FROZEN FRUIT SALAD _____

**Makes 12 servings**

> 2 cups commercial sour cream
> 2 tablespoons freshly squeezed orange juice
> 1/2 cup sugar
> 1 cup crushed pineapple, drained
> 1/2 cup maraschino cherries
> 2 bananas, diced
> 3/4 cup slivered almonds

Combine all ingredients in a large mixing bowl. Pour into 12 muffin tins lined with baking cups. Freeze for several hours. Serve on salad greens. Garnish with miniature marshmallows.

# CRANBERRY RELISH _____

**Makes 2 cups**

> 1 medium orange, sliced thin
> 1/2 small lemon, sliced thin
> 1/2 teaspoon cinnamon
> 3 cups cranberries, washed
> 1 1/4 cups water

Combine all ingredients in a heavy saucepan, simmer, medium heat, stirring occasionally, for 5 minutes. Cool. Refrigerate until ready to serve.

# WALDORF SALAD __

**Makes 6 servings**

   6 **large lettuce leaves, washed, dried**
1½ **cups cottage cheese**
  ¾ **cup chopped walnuts**
   3 **large apples, peeled, cored, chopped**
   1 **tablespoon freshly squeezed lemon juice**
   1 **cup mayonnaise**
   1 **cup raisins**

Arrange lettuce on 6 individual chilled salad plates. Place ¼ cup cottage cheese in the center of each. Combine walnuts, apples, celery and mayonnaise in a small bowl. Spoon mixture over cheese. Sprinkle with raisins.

# THANKSGIVING MOLD

**Makes 6-8 servings**

- 2 packages raspberry gelatin
- 2 cups boiling water
- 1/2 cup crushed pineapple, drained, reserve juice
- 1 can, 16 ounces, jellied cranberry sauce
- 1 cup chopped walnuts
- 1 cup diced celery

In a large mixing bowl combine and dissolve raspberry gelatin and boiling water. Place in a medium saucepan with 1/4 cup of reserved pineapple juice; bring mixture to a boil, continue boiling 1 minute. Remove from heat. Mix in remaining ingredients. Lightly grease a 6-cup ring mold; mound prepared gelatin mixture into mold. Cover with aluminum foil, chill until set. Loosen edges with a spatula, unmold onto a bed of chopped lettuce and garnish with mandarin oranges.

# APRICOT MOLD ____

**Makes 8-10 servings**

- 2 **packages orange-flavored gelatin**
- 1 **cup boiling water**
- 1 **can, 1 pound, apricots, bone**
- 1 **cup commercial sour cream**
- 2 **large bananas**

In a medium bowl dissolve gelatin in boiling water. Place apricots and juice in blender, puree; mix into gelatin. Pour half of apricot mixture into 6-cup mold. Chill until firm, about 2 hours. Beat remaining gelatin mixture with ½ cup sour cream. Arrange banana slices on gelatin in mold. Spread with remaining sour cream. Pour remaining gelatin mixture carefully over top. Chill in refrigerator until firm. Unmold onto serving plate.

# BLUEBERRY MOLD __

**Makes 12 servings**

- 2 packages, 3 ounces each, raspberry or black cherry gelatin
- 1 package, 8 ounces, cream cheese, room temperature, whipped
- 1 teaspoon vanilla
- 2 cups heavy cream, whipped
- 2 cans, 1 pound, ½ ounce each, blueberries, include juice

Place gelatin in a large bowl, measure blueberry juice, add enough water to measure 2 cups. Heat to boiling point. Add cream cheese and vanilla in a separate bowl. Mix into cooled gelatin. Mix in blueberries and whipped cream. Pour into lightly oiled 8-cup mold. Refrigerate until set. Loosen mold; unmold onto serving platter.

# CRAB-SHRIMP MOLD

**Makes 8 servings**

- 1 **package unflavored gelatin**
- ¼ **cup cold water**
- ¼ **cup boiling water**
- ¾ **cup cooked shrimp, shelled, deveined, chopped**
- ¾ **cup crab meat, shred**
- 1 **cup mayonnaise**
- ¾ **cup chopped celery**
- ½ **cup chopped stuffed green olives**
- 3 **green onions, chopped**
- ½ **cup chili sauce**
- 2 **teaspoons freshly squeezed lemon juice**
- ¼ **teaspoon Worcestershire sauce**
- ¼ **cup sliced black olives for garnish**
- 1 **cucumber sliced for garnish**

In a small bowl dissolve gelatin in cold water, stir. Add boiling water, combine. Place remaining ingredients in a large deep bowl, toss. Stir in dissolved gelatin. Mound mixture into a lightly greased fish mold. Cover with aluminum foil, chill until firm. Loosen sides with a spatula, unmold onto a salad platter. Garnish with olives and cucumber.

# SHRIMP MOUSSE __

**Makes 8 servings**

  1 package unflavored gelatin
½ cup cold water
  1 can, 10½ ounces, tomato soup
  2 packages, 8 ounces each, cream cheese, room temperature whipped
  1 cup mayonnaise
  1 onion, minced
  4 stalks celery, chopped
  2 cans, 4½ ounces each, shrimp, drained
½ teaspoon garlic powder

Combine gelatin and cold water in a small bowl. Heat soup in a small saucepan, stir in gelatin and cook until gelatin is dissolved. In a large bowl combine soup, whipped cream cheese and mayonnaise, blend well. Stir in remaining ingredients. Pour into a 6-cup, slightly greased ring mold. Cover with aluminum foil, chill until set. Loosen edges with a spatula, unmold onto serving platter.

# SALMON SALAD ___

**Makes 8-10 servings**

  4 **cups cold, cooked macaroni**
1¹/₂ **cups shredded Cheddar cheese**
  1 **onion, minced**
¹/₂ **cup black olives, sliced**
  4 **tablespoons fresh parsley, chopped**
  1 **cup flaked canned salmon, drained**

In a large bowl or salad bowl combine all ingredients. Drizzle dressing over salad, toss lightly. Chill until ready to serve.

**Dressing:**

  3 **cloves garlic, minced**
  1 **teaspoon sugar**
¹/₄ **teaspoon ground pepper**
  1 **teaspoon prepared mustard**
¹/₄ **cup red wine vinegar**
³/₄ **cup salad oil**

In a screw-top jar combine all ingredients except oil. Add oil and shake vigorously. Store in refrigerator until ready to use. Shake well before using.

# CORNED BEEF SALAD

**Makes 8 servings**

- 1 cup boiling water
- 1 package lemon-flavored gelatin
- 1 tablespoon vinegar
- 3/4 pound cooked corn beef, diced
- 3 stalks celery, chopped
- 1/2 teaspoon salt
- 1 green bell pepper, seeded, chopped
- 1 onion, minced
- 4 eggs, hard-boiled, shell removed
- 1 cup mayonnaise
- 2 teaspoons prepared horseradish

In a large bowl pour boiling water over gelatin; stir until dissolved. Stir in vinegar; refrigerate until slightly thickened, about 45 minutes. Stir in corn beef, all fat removed. Add remaining ingredients, combine. Mound mixture into a lightly greased 6-7 cup ring mold. Refrigerate until set. Unmold onto lettuce and arrange on serving platter.

# PARTY EGG SALAD _

**Makes 8 servings**

 2 envelopes unflavored gelatin
1/2 cup cold water
1/2 teaspoon salt, garlic powder, crushed basil
 3 tablespoons freshly squeezed lemon juice
 1 cup mayonnaise
 1 onion, minced
 5 stalks celery, diced
 1 green bell pepper, seeded, chopped
 8 eggs, hard-boiled, shell removed, minced
 6 sprigs parsley for garnish
 3 tomatoes, sliced for garnish

In a small bowl sprinkle gelatin over cold water, stir, soften. Place gelatin in a small saucepan, cook over medium heat until dissolved. Stir in salt, garlic powder, basil, and lemon juice. Chill. Stir in mayonnaise; add remaining ingredients. Mound into a lightly greased loaf pan, chill until firm. Loosen with a spatula, unmold onto a serving platter. Garnish with parsley and sliced tomatoes.

# CHICKEN OR TURKEY SALAD ____

**Makes 6 servings**

3$\frac{1}{2}$ cups diced, cooked chicken
  6 stalks celery, diced
  3 tablespoons freshly squeezed lime juice
  1 small onion, minced
2-2$\frac{1}{2}$ teaspoons curry powder
$\frac{1}{2}$ teaspoon salt
$\frac{1}{4}$ teaspoon white pepper
  2 apples, peeled, cored, chopped
$\frac{1}{2}$ cup golden raisins
$\frac{3}{4}$ cup mayonnaise

In a large deep bowl toss chicken, celery, lime juice and onion. Add spices and remaining ingredients. Cover, chill until ready to serve.

# LARGE LAYERED SALAD

**Makes 18-20 servings**

- 1 pound fresh spinach, trimmed, wash, dry
- 8 eggs, hard-boiled, shell removed, sliced
- 1 medium head lettuce, wash, dry, tear into bite-sized pieces
- 2 large onions, sliced
- 1 pound bacon, cook, crumble
- 1 can, 16 ounces, sliced beets
- 1 package, 8 ounces, cream cheese, room temperature
- 1½ cups mayonnaise
- 4 ounces shredded cheddar cheese

Tear spinach into bite-sized pieces; line bottom of a 9 x 13 x 1¾-inch pan with spinach. Layer egg slices over spinach. Sprinkle lettuce over eggs. Place onion rings in salad. Arrange crumbled bacon over salad. Add sliced beets. In a small bowl combine cream cheese and mayonnaise. Spread over top of salad. Sprinkle with cheddar cheese.

# TOMATO, ROQUEFORT AND PISTACHIO SALAD

**Makes 4 servings**

- 4 large ripe tomatoes
- 2 ounces cream cheese
- 2 ounces commercial sour cream
- 4 ounces shelled pistachios
- 4 ounces Roquefort cheese, crumbled
  Salt and pepper to taste
- 12 Romaine lettuce leaves

Core tomatoes and place in boiling water for 10 seconds. Remove tomatoes and place in ice water. With paring knife, peel skin away from each tomato. Using a melon scoop, remove two-thirds of the inside of the tomato, being careful to remove all the seeds. Mix cream cheese and sour cream together until smooth. Add pistachios and Roquefort cheese. Do not overmix. Season with salt and pepper to taste. Place stuffing mixture in a pastry bag without a tube. Pipe mixture into each tomato, being careful to keep outside of tomato perfectly clean. Line four salad plates with three Romaine leaves each. Place each tomato over Romaine leaves in center of plate. Pour sauce over each salad. Garnish with pistachio nuts. Serve immediately.

# SALAD NICOISE ___

**Makes 6-8 servings**

- 1 medium head iceberg lettuce, wash, dry, tear into bite-size pieces
- 3 large tomatoes, sliced
- 1 cucumber, peeled, sliced
- 1 onion, sliced thin
- 3 large potatoes, peeled, boiled, cooled, sliced
- 2 red bell peppers, seeded, sliced
- 1 cup whole, pitted ripe olives
- 2 cans, 2 ounces each, anchovies, drained
- 2 cans, 6½ ounces each, tuna, drained, flaked
- 1 lemon, sliced

**Dressing:**

- 3 cloves garlic
- 3 tablespoons wine vinegar
- ½ teaspoon dry mustard, salt, ground black pepper
- 3 tablespoons vegetable oil
- 3 tablespoons olive oil

Arrange lettuce on a serving platter. Place tomatoes decoratively around lettuce. Place remaining vegetables and olives on serving platter. Spread anchovies, tuna and lemon slices on salad.

Combine all dressing ingredients in a small bowl. Drizzle salad dressing over salad.

# CHEF'S SALAD

**Makes 8 servings**

- 1 head lettuce, tear into bite-size pieces
- 1 cup cooked ham, cut into thin strips
- 1½ cups cooked turkey or chicken, cut into thin strips
- 4 ounces Swiss cheese, cut into thin strips
- 2 tomatoes, cut in wedges
- 4 hard-boiled eggs, shelled, sliced
- 1 cup garlic croutons

Arrange lettuce in a salad bowl or serving platter. Arrange remaining ingredients over lettuce. Sprinkle with croutons and drizzle with dressing.

**Dressing:**

- ¾ cup salad oil
- 3 tablespoons wine vinegar
- 3 cloves garlic, minced
- ¼ teaspoon ground pepper
- ¼ cup Gorgonzola cheese, crumbled
- 1 small onion, minced
- 3 tablespoons cream

Combine oil, vinegar, garlic and pepper in a bowl. In a separate bowl mash cheese, onion and cream. Blend cheese with oil mixture until combined. Place in a covered container until ready to use, chilled.

# CAESAR SALAD ___

**Makes 6 servings**

   2 **tablespoons anchovy paste**
   1 **clove garlic, peeled, minced**
 1/4 **teaspoon salt and pepper**
   2 **whole raw eggs**
   7 **tablespoons olive oil**
   4 **tablespoons wine vinegar**
   2 **tablespoons freshly squeezed lemon juice**
   1 **large head Romaine lettuce, washed and dried**
11/2 **cups croutons**
 1/2 **cup Parmesan cheese, grated**

In a small bowl combine anchovy paste, garlic, salt, pepper, and eggs. Stir in oil, vinegar and lemon juice, adjust seasonings.

Arrange lettuce leaves in a salad bowl. Before serving, toss lettuce with dressing. Add croutons and toss again. Serve on individual plates.

# GREEN GODDESS SALAD DRESSING __

**Makes 1 1/2 cups**

- 3/4 cup mayonnaise
- 1/4 cup commercial sour cream
- 1/4 cup wine vinegar
- 1 teaspoon anchovy paste
- 1/2 cup minced fresh parsley
- 3 green onions, minced
- 1/2 teaspoon prepared mustard

In a small bowl combine all dressing ingredients. Place in a covered container and refrigerate until ready to serve.

# POPPY SEED DRESSING I _____

   ³/₄ **cup mayonnaise**
    3 **tablespoons sugar**
1¹/₂ **tablespoons freshly squeezed lemon juice**
    1 **tablespoon poppy seeds**

In a small bowl combine all ingredients until well blended. Place in a covered container, refrigerate until ready to use.

# POPPY SEED DRESSING II _____

¹/₄ **cup honey**
¹/₄ **cup cider vinegar**
 2 **tablespoons prepared mustard**
 3 **tablespoons poppy seeds**
 1 **small onion, minced**
¹/₄ **teaspoon salt**
³/₄ **cup salad oil**

Combine all ingredients except oil in screw-top jar. Add oil and shake vigorously until dressing is of correct consistency. Chill in refrigerator until ready to serve. Shake well before using.

# WALNUT OIL DRESSING

**Makes 1 cup**

6 sprigs chopped fresh parsley
3 shallots, minced
1 teaspoon dry mustard
2 tablespoons wine vinegar
6 tablespoons walnut oil
3 tablespoons salad oil
1/2 teaspoon salt, ground black pepper

Combine all ingredients in a small bowl, mix well. Refrigerate in a covered container until ready to serve. Serve over mixed green salad.

# CREAMY ROQUEFORT DRESSING

**Makes 3¹/₂ cups**

- 2 cups mayonnaise
- 1 cup commercial sour cream
- ¹/₂ cup wine vinegar
- 3 tablespoons anchovy paste
- 2 tablespoons freshly squeezed lemon juice
- 2 cloves garlic, peeled, minced
- ¹/₄ pound Roquefort cheese

In a medium mixing bowl combine mayonnaise, sour cream, vinegar, anchovy paste, lemon juice and garlic, combine. Crumble cheese into dressing, mix lightly. Cover and chill.

# BOILED DRESSING __

**Makes 2 cups**

  2 eggs
1/4 cup vinegar
  2 tablespoons water
1/2 cup sugar
  1 teaspoon dry mustard
1/2 teaspoon salt
  1 cup commercial sour cream

Combine eggs, vinegar, water, sugar, mustard and salt in top of double boiler over simmering water, stirring constantly until mixture boils and thickens. Cool. Beat in sour cream. Place in covered container. Chill.

# VEGETABLES AND LEGUMES

# Vegetables and Legumes

## General Selection Hints

**ASPARAGUS** stalks should be tender and firm, tops should be close and compact. Choose the stalks with very little white, for they are the more tender stalks. Use asparagus soon as it toughens rapidly.

**BEANS, SNAPS** with wet small seeds inside the pods are best. Avoid beans with dry-looking pods.

**BROCCOLI, CAULIFLOWER** should have tight flower clusters and be close together.

**BRUSSELS SPROUTS** should be firm and compact. Smudgy

spots may indicate insects.

**CABBAGE AND HEAD LETTUCE** should be heavy in size. Avoid cabbage with worm holes, lettuce with discoloration or soft rot.

**CUCUMBERS** should be long and slender for the best quality. May be dark or medium green but yellowed ones are undesirable. Oversized radishes may be pithy, oversized turnips, beets and parsnips may be woody. Fresh carrot tops usually mean fresh carrots, but condition of leaves on most other root vegetables does not indicate degree of freshness.

# POTATOES

Avoid potatoes that are wrinkled or have wilted skins, or soft dark areas, cut surface or with a green appearance. Choose potatoes of uniform size for even cooking.

### STORING

Store potatoes in a cool, humid (but not wet), dark place that's well ventilated. The ideal temperatures are 45 to 50 degrees F.

At 45 to 50 degrees F. potatoes will keep well for several weeks. At temperatures much over that, potatoes should not be stored for more than one week. Warmer temperatures encourage sprouting and shriveling. (Sprouting potatoes can still be used but there will be some waste. Just break off sprouts and you may want to peel them before cooking.)

Avoid prolonged exposure to light which causes potatoes to turn green. This greening causes a bitter flavor so it should be pared off before the potato is used.

Don't refrigerate potatoes. Below 40 degrees F. potatoes will develop a sweet taste, the result of an accumulation of sugars in the tubers. This increased sugar will cause the potato to darken when cooked.

## TO MASH

Prepare boiled or steamed potatoes; drain, peel. Using a potato masher, electric mixer or ricer, mash potatoes. Gradually add milk, salt and pepper to taste, and a bit of butter or margarine. Beat until potatoes are light and fluffy. The texture of potatoes will depend on the amount of milk used. The more milk, the creamier and thinner the potatoes will be.

## TO PAN ROAST

Prepare boiled or steamed potatoes but cook only 10 minutes; drain, peel. Arrange potatoes in a shallow pan. Brush with melted butter or margarine or salad oil. Bake uncovered at 400 degrees F. for 45 minutes or until fork-tender, turning occasionally and basting with more fat.

If roasting with meat, arrange peeled, raw, halved or quartered potatoes around meat in roasting pan about 1½ hours before serving. Baste with pan drippings. Turn and baste frequently to brown.

## TO STEAM

This is an excellent way to preserve nutrients.

Place wire rack on bottom of a kettle or large saucepan and add water to just below the level of the rack. Bring the water to a boil, add potatoes and cook, tightly covered, until fork-tender, whole, 30-45 minutes; cut-up, 20-30 minutes. (Check occasionally to see if water should be added, if lid is not tight fitting.)

NOTE: If rack isn't available, invert custard cups or crumple aluminum foil to make an elevated platform.

## TO FRENCH FRY

Peel and cut raw potatoes into strips about 1/4 inch thick. Toss strips into a bowl of ice and water to keep crisp and white while cutting the remainder. Don't soak. This lets the potato absorb water and prolongs the cooking time which makes the potatoes oily and soggy.

Pat the strips dry with paper towels. Heat about 4 inches of salad oil to 390 degrees F. in a deep fat fryer or large heavy saucepan. Place a layer of potato strips in a wire basket and immerse basket into the hot oil. Cool well on paper towels; salt lightly and keep warm in 300 degrees F. oven until ready to serve.

**TO BAKE**

A medium-size potato (about 3 per pound) will bake in 40 to 45 minutes at 400 degrees F. However, oven temperatures can range from 325 to 450 degrees F. so you can bake them along with whatever you have in the oven. Adjust the time according to the temperature. Pierce the skin of each potato to prevent bursting. Foil baking gives a softer skin and helps retain heat, but some feel it steams rather than bakes the potato. Bake them directly on oven rack or a cookie sheet. Potatoes are done when they are soft when pinched with mitted hands, or tested with a slim skewer or fork. If soft skins are desired, rub each potato with a little salad oil before baking.

# Types of Potatoes

U.S. potatoes may be categorized into 4 groups:

1. **Round White**
2. **Russet**
3. **Round Red**
4. **Long White**

This categorization is from appearance only. Internal qualities and eating appeal vary from group to group and within groups.

It is impossible to recommend any one potato for any one use. The user must decide on his preference through usage and experience. Storing ability, solids content, texture and other characteristics have an influence on usage and preference.

A breakdown of the common potato varieties that fit into each group are as follows:

**1. Round White Group—**
   a. Kennebec
   b. Katahdin
   c. Superior
   d. Norchip
   e. Irish Cobbler
   f. Monona
   g. Sebago
   h. Ontario
   i. Chippewa

**2. Russet (mostly long) Group—**
   a. Russet Burbank
   b. Norgold Russet
   c. Centennial Russet

**3. Round Red Group**
   a. Norland
   b. Red Pontiac
   c. Red La Soda
   d. La Rouge
   e. Red McClure

**4. Long White Group—**
   a. White Rose

The Potato Board

## DRY PEAS—HANDY TO COOK

**TO MEASURE** Since Dry Peas are usually sold in 1-pound packages (2$^1/_3$ cups or 2 cups rounded), use the package as a measure. One pound will give around 6 servings of $^3/_4$ cup each or 5 rounded cups.

**TO PREPARE** Put Dry Peas in colander in sink of cold water or under cold running water. Wash well. Drain and place in heavy kettle or Dutch oven with tight-fitting cover. Add measured amount of cold or hot water. The usual amount is 2 cups of water for 1 cup Dry Split Peas. When using a 1-pound package (2$^1/_3$ cups) Dry Peas, allow $^2/_3$ cup water extra or 4$^2/_3$ cups for the pound measure, unless approximately $^2/_3$ cup of other liquid is to be added later. If heavy utensil is tightly covered and range surface cookery has carefully controlled temperature, the 4 cups of water is sufficient.

**TO COOK SPLIT PEAS FOR SOUP, PUREE, MASHING** Since Split Peas are dry whole peas with skins removed, soaking is unnecessary. After combining washed peas with water, rapidly bring water to boiling point. Reduce heat to simmer. Cover tightly. Cook gently 45 to 50 minutes. Hardness of water and high altitudes influence cooking time. Pressure cooking is not advised.

**TO COOK SPLIT PEAS FOR RETAINING SHAPE (SHORT SOAK METHOD)** Add 1 pound washed Split Peas to 4$^2/_3$ cups boiling water. Bring water to boiling point again and boil 2 minutes. Remove from heat. Cover and let soak ¹/₂ hour.

(1) Surface Cooking: After soaking, bring peas and soaking water to boiling point. Reduce to low heat. Cover tightly. Simmer 20 minutes. Do not stir during cooking.

(2) Oven Cooking: After soaking, place Split Peas and soaking water in casserole. Add seasonings. Cover tightly. Bake at 350 degrees F. (moderate oven) for 35 minutes, longer if desired, depending upon additions of meat, seasonings, etc. Follow recipe directions. Note: Always an exception: when Split Peas are lightly browned, as in a Pilaf, the short soak method is not used.

**TO COOK DRY WHOLE PEAS** Soaking is necessary. Allow 5²/₃ cups water to 1 pound peas. Soak 12 hours or overnight in the measured amount of cold water. Or add peas to the boiling water. Boil 2 minutes. Cover. Let soak 1 hour. For surface cooking, bring soaked peas and soaking water to boiling point. Reduce heat; cover. Simmer until tender, about 1 hour. If to be used in baked dishes, parboil peas until almost tender. The pressure cooker may be used for soaked Dry Whole Peas, following cooker directions.

**TO SEASON DRY WHOLE AND SPLIT PEAS** Salt is usually added to the cooking water. Allow 1 teaspoon salt to 1 rounded cup of peas unless other ingredients are salty. Dry Peas have a delicate but distinctive flavor, to be accented lightly with melting butter, a sprinkling of herbs; in cooking, the addition of smoked and cured meats—ham, salt pork, bacon, sausage of all kinds. As partners to main course dishes, dry pea dishes go well with lamb, ham, chicken, veal, pork. You don't have to do much dressing-up to enjoy them.

**GREEN AND YELLOW SPLIT PEAS** May be used to match your table's color scheme. The reds of tomatoes, pimientos, scarlet peppers; the greens of parsley and chives; the distinctive colors of ripe and green stuffed olives serve well as accents.

For full natural flavor and to save valuable vitamins and minerals, use the soaking water for Dry Whole Peas for cooking. If par-boiled peas are drained for baking, keep liquid for soups or for adding to peas if dry or leftover.

# PEAS

**DRY SPLIT PEAS CONTAIN:**

| | 100 (g) Grams | | 1 lb. as purchased | |
|---|---|---|---|---|
| Water content | 10 | % | 10 | % |
| Calories (food energy) | 344. | | 1564. | |
| Protein | 24.5 | g | 111.2 | g |
| Fat | 1.0 | g | 4.5 | g |
| Phosphorous | 268. | mg | 1217. | mg |
| Carbohydrates (total) | 61.7 | g | 280.1 | g |
| Calcium | 33. | mg | 150. | mg |
| Iron | 5.1 | mg | 23.2 | mg |
| Vitamin A (International units) | 370. | | 1680. | |
| Thiamine | .77 | mg | 3.48 | mg |
| Riboflavin | .28 | mg | 1.28 | mg |
| Niacin | 3.1 | mg | 14.2 | mg |
| Ascorbic acid | 2. | mg | 9. | mg |
| Ash | 2.8 | g | 12.6 | g |
| Fiber | 1.2 | g | 5.4 | g |

(g)   Grams
(mg) Milligrams

# BEANS

**REFRIGERATING AND FREEZING COOKED BEANS** Cooked beans should be covered, and they can be refrigerated up to four or five days. Cooked beans and bean dishes can be frozen in covered containers up to six months.

**STORAGE** Dry beans can virtually be kept indefinitely if stored in a tightly covered container in a dry place. Store canned beans like other canned foods; in a cool to moderate (below 70 degrees F.) dry place.

**SOAKING DRY BEANS AND COOKING CONVENTIONALLY** Dry beans need to be soaked, then cooked, before being used as an ingredient in recipes. There are two methods of soaking.

Overnight salt-soak: Wash and sort beans; place in a large saucepan with 6 cups of water and 1 teaspoon salt per pound of beans. Cover and let stand overnight. Quick-soak: Wash and sort beans; place in large saucepan with 6 cups of water per pound of beans. Bring to a boil and cook 2 minutes. Remove from heat, cover, and let stand 1 hour.

After either method of soaking, simmer beans about 2 hours, or until tender, adding additional water if necessary. Seasonings may be added during this cooking time if you wish.

Beans soaked overnight keep their shape and have a more uniform texture than quick-soak beans.

Increase both the soaking time and cooking time in hard water or high altitude areas.

**COOKING DRY BEANS IN A PRESSURE COOKER** Soak the washed and sorted beans by either the overnight or quick method. Place in pressure cooker; cooker should be no more than 1/3 filled to allow for expansion. Add water to cover and 1 tablespoon of oil to reduce foaming. Cover; cook at 10 pounds pressure about 20 minutes.

**COOKING DRY BEANS IN A CROCKERY COOKER** Place beans in boiling water (enough to cover) and simmer for 10 minutes. Then place beans in crockery cooker and add 6 cups water per pound of beans. Cook on low for 12 hours. This takes care of both the soaking and initial cooking steps.

As wattage and cooking temperatures of microwaves may vary, always be sure to consult the recipes and temperature directions developed for your microwave by the maufacturer.

**COOKING TIPS**

•A tablespoon of oil or butter added during cooking reduces foaming and boil-overs.

•Simmer beans gently to prevent skins from bursting. Stir occasionally to prevent sticking.

•Cook a double batch of bean soup and freeze the extra.

•Add any acid substances, such as lemon juice, vinegar, to-matoes or wine at the end of cooking time since acid makes beans firm.

•Give baked beans or other bean dishes a flavor change by using other varieties of beans or substituting maple syrup or orange marmalade for molasses of brown sugar in baked beans.

**BEAN ARITHMETIC**

•A pound of beans measures about 2 cups.

•Beans triple in volume when soaked and cooked.

•A cup of dry beans yields 3 cups cooked.

•A pound of dry beans yields 6 cups cooked.

•A pound of dry beans makes about 9 servings of baked beans.

•A pound of dry beans makes about 12 servings of bean soup.

•A one-pound can of cooked beans measures about 2 cups.

**LOCATING DRY BEAN VARIETIES** Navy, Kidney, and Pinto beans are normally merchandised in the dry bean sections of grocery stores, but other varieties of dry beans may not be as available.

To locate those other types, check the health foods section of your grocery store, health food or ethnic stores.

Your grocery manager may be able to secure these other varieties of dry beans also.

## CANNY IDEAS FOR CANNED BEANS

- Make a delicious base for casseroles, sandwiches, dips and side dishes with canned beans.

- Add chunks of frankfurters and pineapple to a can of pork and beans for a quick-easy casserole. Or spoon beans over hot dogs, then top with shredded Swiss cheese, mustard and pickle relish.

- Mash canned beans into tomato sauce with relish, onions and crumbled bacon and serve as a dip with chips or crackers. Or spread the dip on thin rounds of Boston brown bread, sprinkle with cheese and broil.

- Doctor up a can of molasses baked beans with ketchup, brown sugar, onions, crumbled bacon and crushed gingersnaps.

# Food Composition of Cooked Beans

| | 1 cup cooked Navy Beans (wg.= 190 g) | 1 cup beans with pork and tomato sauce (wg.= 225 g) | 1 cup beans in tomato sauce (wg= 255 g) |
|---|---|---|---|
| CALORIES | 224 | 311 | 306 |
| PROTEIN (g) | 14.8 | 15.6 | 16.1 |
| FAT (g) | 1.1 | 6.6 | 1.3 |
| CARBOHYDRATE (g) | 40.3 | 48.5 | 58.7 |
| CALCIUM (mg) | 95 | 138 | 173 |
| PHOSPHORUS (mg) | 281 | 235 | 309 |
| IRON (mg) | 5.1 | 4.6 | 5.1 |
| SODIUM (mg) | 13 | 1,181 | 862 |
| POTASSIUM (mg) | 790 | 536 | 683 |
| VITAMIN A (IU) | 0 | 330 | 150 |
| THIAMIN (mg) | .27 | .20 | .18 |
| RIBOFLAVIN (mg) | .13 | .08 | .10 |
| NIACIN (mg) | 1.3 | 1.5 | 1.5 |
| ASCORBIC ACID (mg) (Vitamin C) | 0 | 5.0 | 5.0 |
| ZINC (mg) | 1.9 | * | * |
| COPPER (mg) | * | .43 | * |
| FIBER (mg) | 2.85 | 3.57 | 3.57 |

# BAKED ARTICHOKES

**Makes 6 to 8 servings**

   4 tablespoons butter
   2 packages, 9 ounces each, artichokes, drained
   3 slices bacon, cut into 1-inch pieces
   3 tablespoons Parmesan cheese
   1 onion, sliced thin
   1 can, 6 ounces, tomato paste
 ½ cup dry white wine
   1 teaspoon oregano
 ½ teaspoon salt
 ¼ teaspoon pepper
   1 teaspoon sugar

Heat butter in a large skillet; sauté artichoke hearts, until tender, over medium heat, stirring occasionally. Arrange artichoke hearts in a greased pie plate. Sprinkle with Parmesan cheese. In same skillet sauté bacon and onion until tender. Stir in remaining ingredients. Combine and pour sauce over artichokes. Bake at 400° F. for 20 minutes.

# CHEESY STUFFED ARTICHOKES

**Makes 8 servings**

   8 **artichokes**
   4 **tablespoons butter**
   2 **tablespoons all-purpose flour**
  $1/2$ **cup milk**
  $1/2$ **teaspoon crushed tarragon**
  $3/4$ **cup grated Cheddar cheese**
   3 **egg yolks**
   3 **egg whites, stiffly beaten**

Wash artichokes; cut tips off artichoke leaves, remove thistle with teaspoon, reserve artichokes. Melt butter in a medium saucepan, whisk in the flour. Continue whisking until flour is absorbed. Stir in milk and whisk in tarragon and cheese. Blend in egg yolks. Fold in stiffly beaten egg whites. Spoon mixture into artichokes and mound on tip. Place the artichokes in a buttered baking dish; bake at 375° F. for 20-25 minutes or until puffed and baked. Serve at once.

# DEEP-FRIED ASPARAGUS

**Makes 6-8 servings**

> 1 pound asparagus, trimmed
> All-purpose flour
> 1 egg, slightly beaten
> Parmesan cheese, grated
> 2 cups vegetable oil for frying

Boil asparagus in salted water for 8 minutes or until fork tender. Drain. When asparagus are cool, take each individual piece of asparagus and dip in flour, then dip it in beaten egg and into Parmesan cheese and back into the flour. Place oil in a heavy skillet, heat to 375° F. over medium-high heat. Fry asparagus, a few pieces at a time until golden brown, drain on paper toweling. Serve hot.

# BEANS MEXICAN STYLE

**Makes 8 servings**

2 cups dried red, black or pinto beans
6 cups water
2 cloves garlic, crushed
1 large onion, chopped
1/2 teaspoon crushed basil
1 teaspoon salt
3 tablespoons bacon drippings

Wash beans carefully to remove any foreign particles. Place beans in a heavy large saucepan. Pour water over beans. Add garlic, onion and basil. Simmer, covered, for 2 hours. Check beans periodically to see if they are still covered with water. If not, add water to cover. Add salt and bacon drippings; mix well. Cover and simmer for 30 minutes, or until beans are tender. Serve hot.

# REFRIED BEANS ___

**Makes 8-10 servings**

 3 strips bacon
 2 cups red or pinto beans
 6 cups water
 3 cloves garlic, crushed
 1 large tomato, peeled, seeded, chopped
 4 tablespoons bacon drippings
 1/2 teaspoon salt

Fry bacon in a medium skillet; drain. Crumble bacon and reserve drippings. Set bacon aside. Wash beans carefully to remove any foreign particles. Place beans in a heavy large saucepan. Cover with water. Add garlic and tomato; cover, simmer 2 hours. Stir in bacon drippings and salt. Cover, simmer 30 minutes, or until beans are tender. Drain beans; puree with masher or in a food processor. Return remaining bacon drippings to skillet. Add bacon and beans, fry over medium heat until beans are dry, stirring often. Taste, adjust seasonings. Place beans in a covered container and refrigerate until ready to use. When reheating beans, add water as needed to make beans a pasty consistency.

# EASY
# BAKED BEANS ____

**Makes 8 servings**

    2 cans, 1 pound each, pork and beans
    ½ cup diced bacon
    ½ cup brown sugar
    2 tablespoons catsup
    1 teaspoon prepared mustard
    3 tablespoons dark molasses
    1 onion, minced

Combine all ingredients in a casserole or in a bean pot. Bake at 325° F. for 40 minutes. After baking garnish with extra cooked, crumbled bacon.

# HARVARD BEETS ____

**Makes 8 servings**

  6  **large beets, peeled, cooked, sliced thin**
  2  **medium onions, sliced thin**
  ¼  **cup sugar**
  ¼  **cup cornstarch**
  2  **tablespoons butter**
  ¼  **cup wine vinegar**

Combine beets and onions, toss, reserve. In a small bowl combine remaining ingredients and ¾ cup water. Place vegetables and sauce in a medium saucepan, blend together. Bring mixture to a boil over medium heat, reduce heat to a simmer and cook until the mixture thickens, stirring often. Place beets in a serving dish.

# BROCCOLI WITH STUFFING _____

2 packages (10 ounces each) frozen broccoli
2 eggs, beaten
1 onion, chopped fine
1 can mushroom soup
1/2 cup mayonnaise
1 cup grated Cheddar cheese
1/4 cup melted butter or margarine
1 package herbed stuffing mix

Cook broccoli. Combine eggs, onion, soup and mayonnaise. Place layer of broccoli in a 2-quart casserole. Add layer of cheese. Pour small amount of sauce on top. Repeat layers until all are used. Top with stuffing mix. Sprinkle butter or margarine on top. Bake for 30 minutes at 350° F.

# SWEET AND SOUR RED CABBAGE

**Makes 8 servings**

    1 medium red cabbage, shredded
 1/4 cup red wine vinegar
    2 tablespoons sugar
    2 tablespoons light brown sugar
    1 teaspoon salt
 4-5 tablespoons bacon drippings
    3 tart apples, peeled, cored, diced
    1 large onion, sliced thin
    3 bay leaves
 1/4 teaspoon pepper
 1/4 teaspoon allspice
 1/4 teaspoon cloves
 1/2 cup raisins
    1 cup boiling water
 1/4 cup dry red wine
 1/4 cup red currant jelly

In a large deep bowl toss red cabbage with wine vinegar and half of the sugars, reserve. In a heavy saucepan heat bacon drippings; add remaining sugars, when foaming subsides, add apples and onions. Cook until tender over medium heat, stirring occasionally. Add cabbage and remaining ingredients except wine and jelly, mix well. Bring mixture to a boil over heat. Stir, cover and reduce heat to simmer. Simmer until cabbage is tender, about 2 hours, stirring occasionally. If necessary add more boiling water, 1/2 cup at a time. When cabbage is cooked there should be only a small amount of liquid remaining in pan. Remove bay leaves. Stir in wine and jelly, stir until melted.

# CABBAGE IN A WOK

**Makes 8 servings**

    4  tablespoons peanut oil
    2  cloves garlic, minced
  1/2  teaspoon ground ginger
    1  onion, sliced thin
    1  cup sliced mushrooms
  1/2  pound snow peas, trimmed
  1/2  head small Chinese cabbage, shredded
    3  tablespoons light soy sauce
  1/2  cup chicken stock
  1/2  teaspoon salt and pepper

Heat oil in a wok or in a large heavy saucepan. Stir-fry garlic and ginger about 10 seconds. Add onion, mushrooms and snow peas, stir fry about 1 minute. Add cabbage, soy sauce, chicken stock and salt and pepper; stir-fry until cabbage is tender. Check for seasoning.

# CARROT MOLD WITH LEMON ZEST _

**Makes 10-12 servings**

    2 cups vegetable shortening
    1 cup firmly packed light brown sugar
    2 eggs
    3 cups grated raw carrots
    4 tablespoons freshly squeezed lemon juice
    1 tablespoon lemon zest
    1 tablespoon orange zest
2 1/2 cups all-purpose flour
    2 teaspoons baking powder
    1 teaspoon baking soda
    1/2 teaspoon cinnamon
    1/2 teaspoon nutmeg

In a large bowl cream shortening and brown sugar until light. Mix in eggs, beat until light. Mix in carrots, blend well. Mix in remaining ingredients. Pour mixture into a well greased 6-cup ring mold. Bake at 350° F. for 1 hour or until it tests done. Cool 5 minutes, unmold onto serving platter.

# CARROT PUFFS ____

**Makes 6 servings**

- 2 **eggs, well beaten**
- 2 **tablespoons milk or cream**
- 1 **teaspoon baking powder**
- 1 **cup cooked carrots, drained and pureed**
- 1 **cup mashed potatoes**
- 1/4-1/2 **cup all-purpose flour**
- 1/2 **teaspoon salt**
  - **Vegetable oil for deep frying**

In a large deep bowl, combine all ingredients except oil, until well blended. Heat 1 inch of oil in a medium skillet with high sides or use a wok, until 375° F. With 2 teaspoons shape carrot puffs into a 1-inch puff. Carefully slide puffs, one at a time, into oil. Cook about 4-5 at a time. Cook until golden brown on all sides. Drain on paper toweling.

# GLAZED CARROTS _

**Makes 8-10 servings**

1½ pounds carrots, julienned
½ cup firmly packed light brown sugar
4 tablespoons butter

Cook carrots in a small amount of boiling salted water until just tender, drain, about 7-8 minutes. In a medium skillet melt the sugar over medium heat, until lightly caramelized, stirring often. Mix in butter, cook until butter melts; stir in carrots, toss until glazed, about 2 minutes.

# CAULIFLOWER AND BROCCOLI _____

**Makes 6 servings**

½ head cauliflower, separated into flowerets
½ head broccoli, separated into flowerets
¼ cup flavored bread crumbs
3 tablespoons freshly grated Parmesan cheese

Cook cauliflower and broccoli in small amount of boiling salted water until just tender, about 8 minutes; drain. In a heavy skillet, brown butter over medium heat until the butter is just a delicate brown. Toss vegetables with butter. Add bread crumbs, combine. Place vegetables in a serving bowl; sprinkle cheese over top.

# CELERY IN CREAM SAUCE WITH HAZELNUTS __

1/4 cup butter or margarine
 1 quart celery (sliced diagonally into 1/8-inch cres-
    cents)
1/2 teaspoon salt
 1 tablespoon minced onion
 2 tablespoons minced chives
 1 tablespoon all-purpose flour
1/2 cup chicken stock
1/2 cup light cream
1/4 teaspoon white pepper
1/4 cup blanched hazelnuts, chopped

In a medium, wide-bottom saucepan, melt the butter; add the celery and salt. Cover tightly and cook over low heat about 3 minutes or until celery is tender yet still crisp; shake the pan several times to prevent scorching. Add onions and chives and cook 2 minutes longer. Stir in flour and combine; mix in chicken stock. Continue cooking and stir constantly until the sauce thickens. Add cream and pepper, stirring while the cream heats. Serve sprinkled with chopped hazelnuts.

# CELERY ROOT

**Makes 6 servings.**

- 3-3½ cups celery root, celeriac, cut into julienne strips
- 1 clove garlic, minced
- 4 tablespoons butter, room temperature
- 1 medium onion, sliced
- ½ teaspoon salt
- ½ teaspoon white pepper
- ½ cup grated Cheddar cheese
- ½ cup seasoned bread crumbs

Place the julienne strips in a large saucepan of salted boiling water; cook over medium heat 8-10 minutes. Place drained celery root in a large mixing bowl. Mix in garlic, butter, and onion. Sprinkle with salt and pepper. Toss with grated Cheddar cheese. Mound into 9x9-inch baking dish. Sprinkle with bread crumbs. Bake at 425° F. for 10-12 minutes.

# CORN FRITTERS ___

**Makes 6-8 servings**

1¹/₂ **cups all-purpose flour**
 ³/₄ **teaspoon baking powder**
  1 **teaspoon baking soda**
 ¹/₂ **teaspoon salt**
 ³/₄ **cup milk**
  1 **can (8.5 ounces) cream-style corn**
  1 **can (16 ounces) whole kernel corn, drained**
  1 **egg, well beaten**
  2 **tablespoons sugar**
    **Corn oil for deep frying**

In a large bowl combine dry ingredients. Blend together egg and milk in a small bowl; mix in the two cans corn, egg and sugar. Heat 1 inch of oil in a medium skillet with high sides or use a deep fryer. Slide 1 tablespoon of mixture into oil at a time. Fry about 5 corn fritters at a time, until golden brown, turning once. Drain on paper toweling. Serve hot.

# CORN BAKE _____

**Makes 7 servings**

 3 cans (16 ounces each) whole kernel corn, drained
 1 cup milk
 2 eggs
 1/2 cup ground ham
 1/4 cup ground cheese
 1 slice ground bread
 2 tablespoons onion, finely chopped (optional)
   Salt and pepper to taste

Mix above ingredients together and pour into a greased 10x6x1 1/2-inch baking pan. Mix 1 1/2 cups bread (cubed) with 2 or 3 tablespoons melted butter and place on top of corn mixture. Sprinkle with 1 tablespoon grated parmesan cheese. Place pan on a cookie sheet and bake at 350° F. for 25 minutes.

Chopped peppers may also be used for added color and flavor if desired.

# GREEN BEANS WITH ALMOND BUTTER SAUCE

**Makes 8-10 servings**

1½ **pounds green beans, trimmed**
   **Salt**
 ½ **cup butter**
 6 **ounces chopped almonds**
 2 **teaspoons tarragon wine vinegar**

Steam the green beans until fork tender, reserve and keep warm. Melt the butter in a small saucepan and when it is hot but not yet brown, add the chopped almonds. Continue cooking and stir just until the nuts are a light brown, about 30 seconds. Add vinegar. Stir once more and drizzle sauce over warm green beans.

# MARINATED GREEN BEANS _____

**Makes 6 servings**

    1 pound fresh green beans, trimmed
    3 tablespoons peanut oil
    3 tablespoons wine vinegar
    1/2 teaspoon ground cumin
    1/2 teaspoon salt
    1/2 teaspoon pepper
    1/4 teaspoon dry mustard
    1 large onion, sliced thin

Place green beans in a large saucepan, cover with boiling, salted water. Cook over medium heat about 5 minutes or until beans are cooked but still firm. Drain beans, reserve. In a small bowl combine remaining ingredients. Place beans in a large salad bowl; toss with dressing. Chill 3 hours before serving.

# EGGPLANT PARMIGIANA

**Makes 6 servings**

- 1 medium eggplant, peeled
  Salt
- 1 egg, slightly beaten
- 1/2 cup milk
- 1 cup all-purpose flour
- 1/2 teaspoon salt and pepper
- 4 tablespoons vegetable oil for frying
- 1 can (8 ounces) tomato sauce
- 1 onion, minced
- 1 cup shredded Mozzarella cheese
- 1/3 cup freshly grated Parmesan cheese

Cut eggplant into 1/2-inch slices, sprinkle with salt. Let stand 15 minutes. Wash eggplant, dry with paper toweling removing moisture, reserve. Combine egg and milk. Dip eggplant slice in egg mixture and then dust with flour. Combine with salt and pepper. Heat oil in a large heavy skillet; fry eggplant slices until golden brown on both sides. Drain on paper toweling. In a 1 1/2-quart casserole alternate layers of eggplant with sauce combined with onions and cheese. Sprinkle top with Parmesan cheese. Bake at 325° F. for 40 minutes or until the cheese has melted.

# LENTIL SPROUTS __

**¹/₄ cup lentils**
**2 cups lukewarm water**
**1 1-quart wide mouth jar**
**Cheesecloth**

Wash and drain the lentils, place them in the jar. Add 2 cups lukewarm water. Fasten the cheesecloth over the top with a rubber band. Let stand overnight. Drain off water, turn jar upside down until all of the water is drained out. Hold jar on its side. Shake it so that the lentils are scattered along one side of the jar. Place the jar, on its side, in a dark area as a closet. Each morning run luke warm water into the jar, leave the cloth on it. Drain the jar until all of the water is drained out. Shake the jar so that the lentils lay on their side. The sprouts are ready to use when ¹/₄ inch long, about 4 days. Store in the refrigerator. The sprouts taste better when eaten within a week.

# STUFFED MUSHROOMS ___

**½ pound large fresh mushrooms, chop stems
1 tablespoon corn oil
1 shallot, minced
1 clove of garlic, minced
½ cup unseasoned bread crumbs
2 dashes cayenne pepper
½ teaspoon tarragon leaves
2 teaspoons freshly chopped dill
2 teaspoons freshly chopped parsley
1 tablespoon vermouth or dry white wine**

Heat ½ tablespoon oil in skillet until hot. Add chopped mushroom stems, garlic, shallot and sauté until wilted. Add tarragon and cayenne. Pour in wine and cook for about 1 minute. Add bread crumbs and herbs. Reserve. Sauté mushroom caps for 30 seconds on each side. Stuff mushrooms, sprinkle with balance of parsley and dill. Bake at 350° F. until heated through, about 5 minutes.

# MUSHROOM TURNOVERS

**Makes 8 servings**
**Pastry**

- 1/4 pound butter
- 1 package, 3 ounces cream cheese
- 1 cup all-purpose flour

**Filling**

- 1/2 pound mushrooms
- 1/4 cup butter
- 3 tablespoons all-purpose flour
- 1/2 teaspoon salt
- 1 cup light cream
- 2 teaspoons minced chives
- 1 teaspoon freshly squeezed lemon juice

With fingers work butter and cream cheese into the flour in a deep bowl. When well blended form pastry into a ball. (Can be formed in a food processor using a steel blade). Cover and chill for 1 hour. Roll pastry thin on a lightly floured board. Cut pastry into 2-inch circles. Place 1 teaspoon of filling on each round. Fold and seal securely. Arrange on a lightly buttered cookie sheet. Bake in a preheated 400° F. oven for 10 minutes or until golden brown.

Clean and chop mushrooms. Heat butter in a skillet over medium heat. Sprinkle mushrooms with flour and salt. Stir in cream and chives, cook until mixture thickens. Mix in lemon juice, cool.

# FRENCH FRIED ONION RINGS ____

**Makes 6 to 8 servings**

   1 **pound large yellow onions**
   2 **egg whites, slightly beaten**
  ½ **cup milk**
  ½ **teaspoon salt**
  ½ **teaspoon white pepper**
   1 **cup flavored bread crumbs**
     **Peanut oil for deep fat frying**

Slice onions into ⅓-inch-thick rings, separate. Combine egg whites and milk; dip onions into mixture. Dust with salt and pepper. Roll onion rings in bread crumbs. Heat oil in medium skillet with high sides to 1-inch depth to 375° F. Carefully slide 1 cup onion rings into batter, fry until golden brown on both sides. Remove with slotted spoon; drain on paper toweling.

# ENGLISH PEA AND CHESTNUT CASSEROLE

1/2 cup butter
1 small onion, minced
2 tablespoons chopped green pepper
1 cup sliced celery
2 cans English peas, drained
1 can water chestnuts, sliced
2 diced pimientos
1 can cream of mushroom soup, undiluted
Butter cracker crumbs

Melt butter in a heavy skillet. Add onion, green pepper and celery. Sauté over medium heat, stirring often until soft. Remove from heat and add peas and chestnuts. Fold in pimientos. Arrange a layer of the vegetable mixture in bottom of a 2-quart buttered casserole. Top with undiluted soup. Repeat layer. Sprinkle with buttered cracker crumbs. Bake at 350° F. for 30 minutes.

# POTATO PANCAKES _

**Makes 8 servings**

2¹/₂ cups grated raw potatoes
  1 small onion, grated
  1 teaspoon salt
  2 eggs, well beaten
  2-3 tablespoons flour
  ¹/₂ teaspoon baking powder
  4 tablespoons vegetable oil

Drain any accumulated liquid from potatoes. In a large deep bowl combine potatoes, onion, salt, eggs, baking powder and flour. In a large heavy skillet heat oil. Drop potato mixture by tablespoonful, patting down the center with the back of the spoon making a pancake shape. Brown well on both sides, turning with a spatula. Drain on paper toweling; serve with commercial sour cream and applesauce.

# HOLIDAY SWEET POTATOES

**Makes 8 servings**

    4 medium oranges, cut in half
    6 large sweet potatoes, cooked and skinned
  1/4 cup butter
  1/2 teaspoon salt
  1/2 cup freshly squeezed orange juice
    2 tablespoons grated orange peel
  1/2 cup firmly packed light brown sugar
  1/2 cup chopped walnuts
  1/4 cup dry white wine
  1/2 cup miniature marshmallows

Cut oranges in half, extract juice. Reserve 1/2 cup juice for potato mixture. Carefully scoop out pulp, keep shell intact, reserve. Mash potatoes until smooth and fluffy. Mix in butter, salt, orange juice, orange peel and sugar; beat until combined. Stir in walnuts and wine. Arrange orange shells on a cookie sheet; mound, or use a pastry bag with a wide opening, mixture into orange shells. Dot with marshmallows. Bake at 350° F. for 20 minutes or until heated.

# SOUTHERN
# SWEET POTATO PIE _

**Makes 6-8 servings**

     4 tablespoons butter, room temperature
   ¹/₄ cup granulated sugar
   ¹/₄ cup firmly packed light brown sugar
     2 tablespoons freshly squeezed lemon juice
     3 egg yolks
   ¹/₄ teaspoon cinnamon
   ¹/₄ teaspoon allspice
   ¹/₄ teaspoon ground nutmeg
2¹/₄ cups mashed, cooked sweet potatoes
     1 cup milk or cream
     3 egg whites, stiffly beaten
     1 unbaked 9¹/₂-inch pie shell

In a large deep bowl cream butter, mix in sugars until well blended. Stir in lemon juice, egg yolks, spices, potatoes and milk, combine. Fold in stiffly beaten egg whites. Mound into unbaked pie shell, smooth top of pie with a spatula. Bake at 425° F. for 10 minutes; reduce temperature to 350° F. and continue baking for 40 minutes or until a knife inserted in the center comes out clean.

# PUREE OF PEAS ____

**Makes 6 servings**

- 2 cups cooked green peas, pureed
- 4 eggs, well beaten
- 6 tablespoons heavy cream
- 1/2 teaspoon curry powder
- 3 tablespoons butter
- 1/2 teaspoon salt
- 1/4 teaspoon ground nutmeg
- 1 tablespoon minced fresh parsley

Combine all ingredients in a mixing bowl. Mound mixture into greased 9-inch square baking pan. Bake at 400° F. for 10 minutes. Spoon onto individual dishes.

# SLICED POTATOES __

**Makes 8 servings**

- 4 large raw potatoes
- 5 tablespoons butter, melted
- 1/2 teaspoon salt
- 1/2 teaspoon white pepper

Peel potatoes, slice crosswise into 1/8-inch pieces. Place in cold water. Drain and pat dry with paper toweling. Dip each slice into the melted butter. Arrange potato slices into a 1 1/2-quart casserole, overlapping. Season and drizzle with remaining butter. Bake at 450° F. for 10 minutes, reduce heat to 350° F. and bake until tender, about 25-30 minutes. Unmold onto serving platter. Serve hot.

# CRISP POTATO SKINS

**Makes 6 servings**

    6 medium potatoes, about 2 pounds
 1/4 cup melted butter
    1 teaspoon soy sauce
      Coarse salt

Scrub potatoes thoroughly and pierce each with a fork. Bake at 400° F. until potatoes are tender, about 45 minutes to 1 hour. Cool, then cut in quarters lengthwise and in half crosswise to form 8 sections. Scoop flesh from skins leaving 1/8-inch shell. Reserve flesh for use in other recipe. Increase oven temperature to 500° F. Mix together melted butter and soy sauce and brush on both sides of skins. Place skins on cookie sheet and bake until crisp, about 10-12 minutes. These can be made ahead and reheated in a 400° F. oven. Sprinkle with coarse salt and top as desired, melted cheese is good.

NOTE: To use scooped potato pulp, either mash and season, or use in potato salad with your favorite dressing.

# POTATO PUFFS ____

**Makes 8 servings**

- 2 pounds sweet potatoes, cooked and mashed
- 3/4 cup milk or light cream
- 3 tablespoons butter, melted
- 2 eggs, separated
- 1/4 teaspoon ground nutmeg
- 1/2 teaspoon ground cinnamon
- 1/2 teaspoon salt
- 1/2 teaspoon pepper

Mash and whip together all ingredients except egg whites. Beat egg whites until stiff but not dry. Fold egg whites into sweet potato. Arrange mixture into a buttered 1 1/2-quart casserole. Bake in a preheated 375° F. oven for 30 minutes or until mixture is puffed and lightly browned.

# PARSLEY POTATOES .

**Makes 6 servings**

- 8 to 12 small "new" red-skinned potatoes or
- 3 to 4 Idaho potatoes
- 3 tablespoons finely chopped parsley

Peel potatoes. If the potatoes are large, cut them in half or quarters. Place potatoes in water, boil and simmer until tender. Drain and sprinkle with parsley.

# SPINACH RING MOLD _____

**Makes 6-8 servings**

- 2 packages (10 ounces) frozen chopped spinach, defrosted
- 6 tablespoons butter
- 1 large onion, minced
- ¼ teaspoon nutmeg
- ¼ teaspoon pepper
- ½ teaspoon salt
- 3 tablespoons all-purpose flour
- 1 cup half-and-half
- 1 can (16 ounces) artichoke hearts, drained on paper toweling
  Butter

In a medium saucepan cook the spinach according to package directions. Drain, set aside. In a small saucepan heat butter and sauté onion until tender, stirring occasionally, over medium heat. Whisk in flour; stir in half-and-half and whisk until combined and beginning to thicken. Mix in spinach. Arrange the drained artichoke hearts in the bottom of a well buttered 9-inch ring mold. Bake at 350° F. for 35 minutes or until done. Cool 5 minutes, unmold onto a serving platter.

# SPINACH TIMBALES

**Makes 6 servings**

- 4 **tablespoons butter**
- 2 **cloves garlic, peeled and minced**
- 3 **shallots, minced**
- 1 1/2 **pounds fresh spinach, trimmed, cooked, drained, and minced**
- 3 **tablespoons all-purpose flour**
- 1 **cup milk**
- 4 **eggs, lightly beaten**
- 1/2 **teaspoon salt**
- 1/2 **teaspoon ground nutmeg**

Heat butter in a medium saucepan; sauté garlic and shallots until tender, stirring often. Whisk in flour and continue cooking until flour is absorbed, whisking continuously. Stir in milk and eggs; stir until the mixture thickens. Blend in spinach, salt and nutmeg. Pour spinach mixture into 6 buttered timbale molds or custard cups. Place mold in a baking pan. Add 1 1/2 inches water, bake at 375° F. for 20 minutes or until timbales are firm. Let stand at room temperature for 5 minutes. Loosen with a spatula, unmold onto serving platter. Serve cold or hot.

# SPINACH WITH ALMONDS

**Makes 6 servings**

- 1 **pound fresh spinach, trimmed**
- 3 **tablespoons cream**
- 2 **teaspoons freshly squeezed lemon juice**
- 2 **tablespoons butter**
- ³/₄ **cup chopped almonds**

Wash spinach, do not shake off excess water. Place spinach in a saucepan, over medium heat and cook for 7-8 minutes, or until spinach is wilted. Squeeze out excess moisture and puree. Mix cream, lemon juice and butter, combine. Arrange spinach into a mound in the center of the serving dish. Sprinkle with almonds.

# ITALIAN-STYLE CHERRY TOMATOES

**Makes 6 servings**

- 2 pints cherry tomatoes, remove skins with hot water
- 2 tablespoons olive oil
- 1/2 teaspoon salt
- 1/2 teaspoon oregano
- 1/2 teaspoon sugar
- 1/4 teaspoon ground pepper
- 3 tablespoons minced fresh parsley, for garnish

Heat olive oil in a large skillet over medium heat. Add remaining ingredients except parsley. Sauté until tomatoes are warm, stirring often. Garnish with parsley, serve.

# PUREED TURNIPS AND PEARS

**Makes 6-8 servings**

2½ pounds turnips, peeled, quartered
  6 tablespoons butter, room temperature, cut into
    pieces
  1 can (16 ounces) pears, drained, pureed
 ½ teaspoon salt
 ¼ teaspoon ground nutmeg

Place turnips in a 2-quart saucepan. Cover with water and cook over medium heat until turnips are tender. Drain, cool and puree turnips. In a large deep mixing bowl combine all ingredients until well blended. Mound mixture into a well buttered 9-inch square baking dish. Bake at 375° F. for 20 minutes. Serve warm.

# FRIED ZUCCHINI ___

**Makes 6 servings**

1³/₄ **cups all-purpose flour**
 ¹/₂ **teaspoon salt**
 ¹/₄ **teaspoon ground nutmeg**
  4 **tablespoons olive oil**
  2 **eggs, separated**
 ¹/₃ **cup dry white wine**
  1 **cup cold water**
  2 **cups vegetable oil**
 3-4 **medium-small zucchini, quartered and cut into**
    **2-inch pieces**

Combine flour, salt and nutmeg in a deep bowl. Stir in olive oil and combine. Mix in egg yolks, wine and water; batter should be smooth. Let batter rest at room temperature for 30 minutes. Heat oil in a medium saucepan until 375° F. Beat egg whites until stiff. Fold whites into the batter. Dip each piece of zucchini into batter, turning to coat; slide, carefully into the oil, cook until golden brown; cooking a few pieces at a time. Remove with slotted spoon and drain on paper toweling. Serve immediately.

# EGGS

# Eggs

Since chickens honor neither the metric nor the standard systems, an egg is an egg is an egg. Most recipes are designed for large eggs. Eggs fit easily into metric or standard recipes. Because recipes call for whole eggs, whole yolks, or whites, the egg requires no metric measuring.

When it comes to measuring up as a good food buy, eggs fill the bill with any system. Eggs are such high quality protein that they are often used as a standard for other protein foods. Eggs also provide all vitamins, except C, along with thirteen important minerals, including iron, phosphorus and magnesium. Only 80 calories each.

Eggs are incredibly versatile. You can fry, poach, bake, or scramble them, or cook them in their shells. Eggs can leaven, as in souffles, or thicken, as in sauces and custards. Eggs also bind ingredients, as in meat loaves; coat foods for frying, emulsify, and clarify. It is no wonder that one French chef called eggs, "the cement that holds the castle of cuisine."

Always look for shells that are clean and whole. Cracked eggs are always removed from production lines but some may be broken in handling. If one cracks between market and home, use it as soon as possible in a fully cooked dish such as baked custard, souffle or in other baked goods.

Important factors in maintaining egg quality are proper handling and refrigeration. Eggs lose quality very rapidly at room temperature so buy them quickly and refrigerate them immediately. At temperatures of 35°F. to 45°F. eggs will maintain high quality for several weeks.

Eggs are marketed according to grade and size standards established by the U.S. Department of Agriculture or by state departments of agriculture. The USDA shield on the egg carton means that the eggs have been federally inspected. Some egg packers, particularly smaller or on-farm plants, may follow state standards which are the equivalent of USDA standards. Some states may have state seal programs which indicate that the eggs are produced within that state and are subject to continuing state quality checks.

Size and grade are two entirely different factors bearing no relationship to each other. Grade is determined by the interior and exterior quality of the egg. Size is determined by the average weight per dozen. Eggs are marketed according to grade and size standards established by the U.S. Department of Agriculture. Grades are AA, A, B and C. Grades B and C are most often processed into dried or other egg products.

Grade AA egg will stand up tall. The yolk is firm and the area covered by the whites is small. There is a large proportion of thick white to thin white. In some areas, these are called "Fresh Fancy." Grade A egg covers a relatively small area. The yolk is round and upstanding. The thick white is large in proportion to the thin white and stands fairly well around the yolk. Grade B spread out more. The yolk is flattened and there is about as much or more thin white as thick white. If not properly refrigerated, or if refrigerated for lengthy periods of time, eggs will lose carbon dioxide and water which causes them to spread out more when broken into a pan. This natural aging process does not affect the nutritional quality of the eggs but may cause them to be classified as a lower grade. These eggs still perform well in scrambled or baked dishes. Size is based on minimum net weight per dozen. Although any size egg may be used for frying, scrambling, cooking in the shell or poaching, most recipes for baked dishes are based on large eggs.

Refrigeration, drying or freezing are the best ways of preserving egg quality. Fresh eggs are so readily available that long storage periods are rarely necessary. Fresh shell eggs can be stored in their carton in the refrigerator for at least 4 to 5 weeks. Grade quality losses should be insignificant if the eggs are refrigerated as soon as possible after purchase from a refrigerated case. For most purposes, it is best not to let eggs sit out—they will age more in one day at room temperature than in one week in the refrigerator. It is best to store eggs in their cartons because eggs can absorb refrigerator odors. Hard-cooked eggs should be stored in the refrigerator as soon as they are cooled and should be used within a week. Raw whites will keep a week to 10 days if refrigerated in a tightly covered container. Store unbroken raw yolks, covered with water, in a tightly covered container in the refrigerator and use within 2 to 3 days.

Yes, eggs can be frozen; whole eggs, whites and yolks and hard-cooked yolks can be frozen successfully. Hard-cooked whole eggs or hard-cooked whites will become tough if frozen. Eggs cannot be frozen in their shells. To freeze egg whites, pour them into freezer containers, seal tightly, label with the number of whites and date and freeze. If you like, first freeze each white in an ice cube tray and then transfer the frozen cubes to a freezer container.

Yolks or whole eggs require special treatment before freezing. When frozen the gelatin property of the yolk causes it to thicken or gel. To help retard this, add either $1/8$ teaspoon salt or $1^1/2$ teaspoons sugar or corn syrup for each 4 yolks or 2 whole eggs. Label containers with the number of yolks or whole eggs, the date and whether you have added salt (for use with main dishes) or sweetener (for baking or desserts). You may find that the finished product is somewhat thicker than it would be if made with fresh eggs.

Thaw frozen eggs overnight in the refrigerator or under running cold water. Use yolks or whole eggs as soon as they have thawed. Once thawed, whites will beat to better volume if allowed to sit at room temperature for about 30 minutes.

Hard-cooked yolks can be frozen to be used later for toppings or garnishes. To cook them, carefully place the unbroken raw yolks in a saucepan and cover with tap water to come a least l inch above the yolks. Cover the pan and bring just to boiling. Remove the pan from the heat and let the yolks stand covered in the hot water for 15 minutes. Remove the yolks with a slotted spoon and drain them well before bagging or wrapping and freezing.

Eggs are one of today's best food buys. They supply high-quality protein and a variety of important vitamins and minerals at a very low price. A dozen large eggs weighs $1\frac{1}{2}$ pounds. So, the price for a pound of large eggs is $\frac{2}{3}$ of the price per dozen. Or, when they are 90 cents a dozen, they are 60 cents a pound.

# EGGS

# FRIED EGGS _____

**Makes 2 servings**

   2  **tablespoons butter or margarine**
   4  **eggs**
  1/4 **teaspoon salt, white pepper**

In a medium skillet over medium high heat, melt butter until just hot enough to sizzle a drop of water. Break and slip eggs into skillet. Reduce heat to low, continue cooking until desired consistency. Season with salt and pepper, remove with a spatula. Try serving with a Mexican tomato sauce.

# SCRAMBLED EGGS _

**Makes 2-3 servings**

   4  **eggs**
   4  **tablespoons milk**
  1/4 **teaspoon salt, white pepper**
   2  **tablespoons butter or margarine**

In a medium bowl whisk together eggs, milk, salt and pepper. In a medium skillet over medium heat, melt butter. Pour in egg mixture. As eggs begin to scramble turn so they will cook on all sides and scramble. As eggs become thick and begin to dry, remove to a serving platter. Good with fried bacon.

# SHIRRED EGGS _____

**Makes 2 servings**

   4 eggs
 1/2 teaspoon salt
 1/4 teaspoon white pepper
   4 tablespoons light cream

Butter 2 ramekins or custard cups. Break and slip eggs into ramekins. Season with salt and pepper. Spoon cream over eggs. Bake at 325°F., 15 minutes or until the whites are set and the yolks are soft and creamy.

# BAKED CUSTARD ___

**Makes 6 servings**

   4 eggs, slightly beaten
 1/2 cup sugar
   1 teaspoon vanilla
 1/4 teaspoon salt
   3 cups milk, scalded
 1/2 teaspoon ground cinnamon

In a medium mixing bowl beat together eggs, sugar, vanilla and salt. Stir in milk. Arrange 6 custard cups in a large baking pan. Pour egg mixture into custard cups. Sprinkle with ground cinnamon. Pour hot water, half way around custard cups. Bake at 350°F. for 25 minutes or until done.

# HARD-BOILED EGGS

**Makes 2 servings**

4 eggs

Arrange eggs in a single layer in a medium saucepan, cover with water. Bring water to a boil; turn heat off. Cover, allow to stand for 18-20 minutes. Run cold water over eggs to cool. Crackle egg shells by tapping gently all over. Roll egg between hands to loosen shell, peel, starting at large end. Hold egg under running cold water to help ease off shell.

# POACHED EGGS

**Makes 2 servings**

4 eggs
1/2 teaspoon vinegar

Fill medium saucepan halfway with water and vinegar, bring to a boil over medium heat. Reduce heat, keep water simmering. Break eggs, one at a time, into a saucer, slip each egg into the water. With a spoon make a swirling motion around each egg. Simmer 3 minutes or until eggs are poached. Remove eggs with slotted spoon.

# JELLY OMELET

**Makes 1 serving**

   2 eggs
   3 tablespoons water
1/4 teaspoon salt, white pepper
   1 tablespoon butter
   3 tablespoons strawberry jelly or jam
      Confectioners' sugar

In a small mixing bowl, mix eggs, water, salt and pepper, until well blended. Melt butter in a 7-8 inch omelet pan or skillet over medium heat. When the butter is hot pour in egg mixture. With a spatula, push edges toward center, tilting the pan. When the top is still moist place jelly on one-half of the omelet. With the spatula, fold omelet in half and invert it onto a plate sliding it on the plate. Sprinkle with Confectioners' sugar.

# EGGS BENEDICT

**Makes 8 servings**

- 8 English muffins, split, toasted and buttered
- 1 pound Canadian-style bacon, broiled or pan-fried, drained
- 16 eggs, poached
- 1½ cups Hollandaise Sauce

For each serving, top 2 English muffin halves with bacon, a poached egg and drizzle Hollandaise Sauce over eggs. Serve warm.

**HOLLANDAISE SAUCE**
**Makes 1½ cups**

- 6 egg yolks
- 2 tablespoons lemon juice
- ¼ teaspoon salt
- ¼ teaspoon white pepper
- 1 cup melted butter

Arrange all ingredients except butter in a blender or food processor fitted with steel blade. Cover, blend until mixture is combined. Add butter. Blend on low speed until combined and thickened. Place in a covered container, refrigerate.

# SAUSAGE WRAPPED IN A PANCAKE

**Makes 6 servings**

**Pancakes**
2 **eggs**
1/2 **cup milk**
1/2 **cup all-purpose flour**
1/4 **teaspoon salt**
1 **tablespoon butter**
2 **apples, peeled, grated**
1/4 **cup butter, melted**
2 **packages  heat and serve sausages**
**Toothpicks**

In a medium bowl combine eggs, milk, flour, 1 tablespoon butter, apples and salt. Whisk until eggs are light and fluffy. Heat 1/4 cup butter in a heavy large skillet over medium-high heat. Drop batter from tablespoon, forming a 4-inch pancake. When bubbles form, turn pancakes over with a spatula. Continue cooking until pancakes are cooked. Arrange on platter. In a large skillet sauté sausages, turning several times. Drain on paper toweling. Roll each sausage inside a pancake; secure with toothpicks. Serve warm.

# FRENCH TOAST

**Makes 6 servings**

6 eggs, separated
1 teaspoon cinnamon, mixed with
4 tablespoons sugar
1 cup milk
6 slices French bread, cut into 1-inch thick slices
3-4 tablespoons butter

In a large, deep mixing bowl beat egg whites until soft peaks form. Sprinkle with cinnamon-sugar, incorporate. In a medium bowl beat egg yolks until combined; mix in milk. Fold egg whites into egg yolks; pour half of egg mixture into a glass 9-inch pie plate. Arrange bread slices, in a single layer in the pie plate. Pour remaining egg mixture over top of the French bread. Allow mixture to stand I hour, or chill overnight. Heat butter in a large, heavy skillet; sauté bread slices slowly over medium-low heat. Turn once, fry until golden brown on each side. Arrange on serving platter. Serve with maple syrup and additional cinnamon-sugar.

# MERINGUES

No one knows which clever cook first discovered the wonderful results of whipping egg whites and then sweetening and stabilizing the airy mixture with sugar. We do know that the name, meringue, probably comes from the European town of Mehrinyghen, where a 16th century pastry chef created memorable desserts from those simple ingredients.

A meringue can do many things: top a pie, pudding or cake; swirl with nuts, dried fruits or coconut to become cookies or candies; lighten elegant fillings; smooth frozen desserts; even insulate ice cream, in Baked Alaska. Meringue begins with egg whites, which are liquid. As you beat the clear, almost opalescent liquid, you incorporate air, first in large bubbles, then in countless tiny air cells. The liquid becomes a white foam increasing seven or eight times in volume.

The foam is a delicate mixture, though, and begins to return to the liquid state quickly unless stabilized. This is why acid ingredients, such as cream of tartar, vinegar or lemon juice are added before beating. Sugar also stabilizes the foam and turns it into a meringue.

When heated the air cells expand and the protein coagulates around them giving permanence to the foam. This leavening property of egg white is responsible for the airy structure of angel food, sponge and chiffon cakes, souffles, puffy omelets and meringues.

For perfect meringues:

Be sure beaters and bowls are sparkling clean and free from any fat. Use only metal or glass bowls; plastic bowls, even clean ones, can have a greasy film that can prevent foaming.

Separate the eggs carefully. Be sure not even a bit of yolk gets in with the whites because fat in the yolk can keep the foam from forming. Separate the eggs while they are cold.

Let egg whites stand at room temperature for about half an hour after separating . They will whip to greater volume than if beaten when cold.

Add ¹/₈ teaspoon cream of tartar, or other acid ingredients as recipe directs, for each egg white before beating.

Beat with rotary beater, whisk or electric mixer at high speed just until foamy. Then gradually begin adding sugar, about 1 tablespoon at a time, beating as you slowly sprinkle the sugar over meringue. Adding sugar too quickly can keep the foam from forming. Be sure to move the beaters or the bowl so all of the egg/sugar mixture reaches the beaters. Continue to beat at high speed until the sugar is dissolved and whites stand in soft or stiff peaks, depending on recipe directions.

Check to be sure the sugar is dissolved by rubbing a bit of meringue between your thumb and forefinger. If you can still feel sugar crystals, beat some more.

Soft peaks are mountains of meringue that come up as you lift the beaters and then fold over at the tips.

Stiff peaks are mountains whose peaks remain upright after you lift the beaters away.

Choose a dry, not humid, day to make meringue. Because of the high sugar content it can absorb moisture from the air and become limp and sticky.

The difference between hard meringues and soft meringues in addition to texture is in the amount of sugar added and the cooking. Soft meringues top pies, puddings and Baked Alaska. A soft meringue uses 2 tablespoons of sugar for each egg white and is beaten to soft peaks. Soft meringues can be baked on pies, or poached in milk to top custard for Floating Island. Pie meringues should go on hot fillings and be swirled to seal the pastry all around. Bake as recipe directs.

Hard meringues require ¼ cup, 4 tablespoons sugar for each egg white. Hard meringues are baked or, more accurately, dried in a low oven. The meringue mixture for hard meringues is beaten to stiff peaks and then formed with the back of a spoon into large or small nests or shells on baking sheets, or piped onto baking sheets through a pastry tube. The mixture can also be swirled into a greased pie plate, cake pan or spring form pan for baking. Prepare baking sheets for hard meringues by greasing with unsalted shortening or lining sheets with waxed paper, brown paper or aluminum foil. Hard meringue can be stored in an air-tight container for several weeks. If it does lose its crispness, reheat it in a preheated 250°F. oven for 15 to 20 minutes.

You can microwave soft meringues on top of pies or puddings. Microcook about one minute on Full Power for each egg white. Meringue is done when point of a knife inserted horizontally into the side comes out clean. Hard meringues do not work in a microwave because they will not dry and become crisp as in a conventional oven.

# MERINGUE

### STEP BY STEP TO A DOZEN PERFECT MERINGUE SHELLS

*Follow these directions for individual hard meringue shells. For large shells follow directions under Italian Meringue. For soft meringue see recipe for Lemon Meringue Pie.*

1) Add ½ teaspoon cream of tartar to 4 room temperature whites.

2) Beat whites till foamy, then very gradually add 1 cup sugar.

3) Beat at high speed until stiff peaks form.

4) Rub a bit of meringue between thumb and forefinger to be sure sugar is dissolved.

5) Using about ⅓ cup for each meringue, shape into shells on paper-lined baking sheets. Bake in preheated 250°F. oven until firm and delicately browned, about 50 minutes.

6) Turn oven off. Leave meringues in oven for 1 hour. Fill shells with fresh fruit, custard or pudding.

# LEMON ANGEL PIE

**Makes 8 servings**

**Crust**
5 eggs, separated
1/4 teaspoon cream of tartar
1/2 cup sugar
**Filling**
4 tablespoons all-purpose flour
1/2 cup sugar
1/2 cup warm water
2 tablespoons freshly squeezed lemon juice
2 tablespoons lemon zest
1 cup heavy cream, whipped

**Crust**

Butter a 9-inch pie plate. Preheat oven to 300°F. Beat egg whites and cream of tartar until peaks form. Sprinkle 4 tablespoons of sugar over egg whites, incorporate. Continue until all the sugar has been used and stiff peaks form. Spread meringue over pie plate, make a 2-inch edge around pie plate. Bake 1 hour, cool in oven with door open until meringue is dry.

**Filling**

Combine flour and sugar in a medium saucepan. Add water and lemon juice. With medium heat cook to just below the boiling point. Add slightly beaten egg yolks in a slow steady stream, whisking constantly. Pour mixture into the top of a double boiler over simmering water. Simmer until mixture thickens, stirring often. Add lemon zest. Remove from heat, cool. Fold in whippped cream. Pour mixture into meringue crust. Leave pie at room temperature until ready to serve.

# AUSTRALIAN PAVLOVA

**Makes 12 servings**

- 6 egg whites
- ³/₄ teaspoon cream of tartar
- 1¹/₂ cups sugar
- 1 teaspoon vanilla
- 2 cups peeled, sliced kiwi fruit
- 1 cup sweetened whipped cream

In a large mixing bowl, beat egg whites and cream of tartar until soft peaks form. Gradually add sugar, 1 tablespoon at a time, beating constantly until sugar is absorbed and whites stand in firm, stiff, but not dry peaks. Beat in vanilla. On waxed paper-covered baking sheet, spread about ¹/₃ of meringue in 2 circles, each about 8 inches in diameter. Using remaining meringue, form nests around each circle with back of a spoon or pastry tube, building a rim on each circle about 1¹/₂ inches high. Bake in preheated 250°F. oven for 1 hour 15 minutes. Turn off oven. Leave meringues in oven with door closed for 1 hour. Remove from oven and cool completely. Fill each shell with 2 cups sliced kiwis and top with sweetened whipped cream.

# WHIPPED CREAM ANGEL FOOD CAKE

**Makes 12 servings**

    12 egg whites
     1 teaspoon cream of tartar
    ³/₄ cup granulated sugar
     1 teaspoon vanilla
    1¹/₂ teaspoons almond extract
     1 cup cake flour
    1¹/₄ cups Confectioners' sugar
    ¹/₄ teaspoon salt

In a large mixing bowl beat egg whites and cream of tartar until soft peaks form . Gradually add sugar, 1 tablespoon at a time, beating constantly until sugar is absorbed and egg whites stand in stiff, but not dry, peaks. Beat in vanilla and almond extract. Sift flour, Confectioners' sugar and salt together twice. Sift about ¹/₂ cup flour mixture over egg whites and gently fold in just until flour disappears. Repeat folding in remaining flour mixture ¹/₂ cup at a time. Turn into ungreased 10-inch tube pan. Gently cut through batter with metal spatula. Bake at 375°F. until top springs back when touched lightly with finger, 30-40 minutes. Invert cake, still in pan on funnel or bottle neck, to cool.

# LEMON MERINGUE PIE

**Makes 6-8 servings**

2 cups sugar, divided
1/3 cup cornstarch
1/4 teaspoon salt
1 1/4 cups cold water
1/2 cup freshly squeezed lemon juice
5 eggs, separated
2 tablespoons butter
2 teaspoons lemon zest
1 deep 9 1/2-inch pie shell, baked
1/2 teaspoon cream of tartar
1 teaspoon vanilla

In a large saucepan combine 1 1/2 cups of the sugar, cornstarch and salt. Gradually stir in water and lemon juice until smooth. Beat egg yolks and blend into sugar mixture. Add butter. Cook, stirring constantly, over medium heat until mixture thickens and boils, continue cooking, stirring constantly, 1 minute. Remove from heat and stir in lemon zest. Pour hot filling into baked pie shell. In a large mixing bowl beat egg whites and cream of tartar at high speed of electric mixer or with a whisk, until soft peaks form. Add remaining sugar, sprinkle 1 tablespoon at a time, beat constantly until sugar is absorbed and whites form stiff, but not dry, peaks. Beat in vanilla. Spread meringue over hot filling, starting with small amounts at edges and sealing to crust all around.

Cover pie with remaining meringue, spreading evenly in attractive swirls. Bake in preheated 350°F. oven until peaks are lightly browned, about 12 minutes. Cool to room temperature.

# ITALIAN MERINGUE _

**1 cup sugar**
**1/3 cup water**
**3 egg whites**
**1/4 teaspoon cream of tartar**

In a small saucepan combine sugar and water, boil to 238°-240°F. or until syrup forms a soft ball when dropped into cold water. Meanwhile, beat egg whites and cream of tartar until stiff but not dry or until whites no longer slip when the bowl is tilted. Very slowly pour the hot syrup in a very thin stream over the beaten whites, beating constantly until cool. Spread meringue on 2 8-inch cake layers or 1 10-inch tube cake.

or

Use to top puddings or other desserts.

or

Form 2 9-inch or 12 3-inch shells on greased or paper-lined baking sheets.

or

Spread mixture over bottom and up sides of 2 greased 9-inch pie plates and bake in preheated 225°F. oven until wooden pick inserted in center comes out clean, about 1 hour.

# MARSHMALLOW MERINGUE

**3 egg whites**
**1/8 teaspoon salt**
**1 cup, 1/2 of 7-ounce jar, marshmallow creme**

Beat egg whites with salt until soft peaks form. Gradually beat in marshmallow creme just until completely blended and whites no longer slip when bowl is tilted. Spread meringue over hot filling, starting with small amounts at edges and sealing to crust all around. Cover pie with remaining meringue, spreading evenly in attractive swirls. Bake in preheated 350°F. oven until peaks are lightly browned, 12 to 15 minutes.

# POACHED MERINGUES

Either a soft, hard or Italian meringue mixture can be used to make poached meringues, or Snow Eggs as they are sometimes called. This confection is used to top custard, a fruit sauce or as the islands on a Floating Island custard dessert.

To poach, drop the meringue mixture by tablespoonfuls onto simmering milk or water and simmer, uncovered, until firm about 3-5 minutes, turning once. Lift from liquid with slotted spoon and drain on absorbent paper. Islands will expand some as they poach so allow an inch or so of space between them.

# BAKED ALASKA ____

**Makes 8 servings**

- 3 pints chocolate ice cream, partially softened
- 6 egg whites
- 1/2 teaspoon cream of tartar
- 3/4 cup sugar
- 1 teaspoon vanilla
- 1 9-inch round brownie cake layer or round sponge layer

Line a 1 1/2-quart round mixing bowl, 7 or 8 inches in diameter with aluminum foil. Press ice cream firmly into bowl and freeze until firm, 3 hours. Preheat oven to 450°F. Beat egg whites and cream of tartar in a large deep bowl or with an electric mixer, until soft peaks form. Sprinkle with sugar, continue beating until sugar is incorporated and stiff peaks, not dry, form. Mix in vanilla . Place cake on oven-proof serving plate. Remove ice cream from bowl and place on cake, flat side down. Remove foil. Working quickly, cover all of ice cream and sides of cake completely and evenly with meringue. Spread meringue in attractive swirls. Bake on lowest rack in preheated oven until peaks are lightly browned, 3-5 minutes. Serve immediately.

# KEY LIME PIE

**Makes 6 servings**

- **4 eggs, separated**
- **1 can, condensed milk**
- **¹/₂ cup freshly squeezed lime juice**
- **9-inch baked pie shell**
- **¹/₂ cup sugar**
- **¹/₂ teaspoon cream of tartar**
- **1 teaspoon vanilla**

In a medium bowl, beat egg yolks until light. Mix in condensed milk and lime juice, beat until light and fluffy. Pour mixture into baked pie shell. In a large mixing bowl beat egg whites and cream of tartar at high speed until soft peaks form. Sprinkle sugar, beat until sugar is absorbed and egg whites stand in firm, not dry, peaks. Mix in vanilla. Spread meringue over filling, starting with small amounts at edges and sealing to crust all around. Cover pie with remaining meringue, spreading evenly in attractive swirls. Bake in 350°F. oven until peaks are lightly browned, 12 minutes. Cool to room temperature.

# CREPES

Crepe pronounced either krep like step, or krap like shape, is a thin, tender pancake that can enfold anything from eggs, fish and fruit to meats, poultry and vegetables. A crepe can be an appetizer, a main dish, a vegetable or a dessert.

Crepe-making is a skill, but not difficult to acquire. All it takes are some directions and a little practice on your part. First of all, get acquainted with your crepe pan. Read any directions that came with it, then study our directions, mix up the crepe batter and you are ready to go.

**TRADITIONAL PAN** (6½- to 10-inch slope-sided omelet or crepe pan with or without non-stick interior)

**To season pan** follow manufacturer's directions OR wash pan with hot suds, rinse and dry thoroughly. Place dry pan over medium-high heat until you can no longer hold your hand on the surface. Pour in just enough salad oil to cover the bottom of the pan. Brush oil up sides of pan, generously coating the entire surface . Remove pan from heat. Let pan stand several hours at least, preferably overnight. Wipe with paper towel to remove excess oil.

**To bake crepes** on medium-high heat, heat seasoned pan until just hot enough to sizzle a drop of water. Brush lightly with melted butter. For each crepe, pour in just enough batter to cover bottom of pan, tipping and tilting pan to move batter quickly over bottom. Smaller pans will take about 2 to 3 table-spoons batter, larger pans about ¼ cup. Pour off any excess batter. If crepe has holes add just a drop or two of batter to patch. Cook until lightly browned on bottom and dry on top. Remove from pan or, if desired, turn and brown other side . If your pan doesn't have a non-stick finish you may need to brush it with melted butter after each 2 or 3 crepes.

### DIP PAN

**To season pan** follow manufacturer's directions OR wash pan with hot suds, rinse and dry thoroughly. Lightly coat with salad oil using paper towel or brush. Heat over low heat about 5 min-utes. Remove from heat. Cool. Wipe off excess oil with paper towel.

**To bake crepes** pour batter into a deep heatproof dinner plate, pie plate or other similar container. Place pan over me-dium-high heat until hot enough to sizzle a drop of water. Re-move from heat. Dip pan in batter for just a second or two , tilting pan all around so entire surface of pan is coated. Gently but quickly lift up, invert and return to heat. Pan should be coated with a thin layer of batter. If crepe has holes, add a drop or two of batter to patch. Cook until edges are lightly browned and top is dry. Remove from heat. Invert pan over plate or waxed paper, loosen edges with spatula and let crepe peel off. If necessary, loosen center of crepe with spatula to help ease it off the pan.

## ELECTRIC DIP PAN

**To season pan** follow manufacturer's directions OR wash surface of pan with hot suds, rinse and dry thoroughly. Lightly coat with salad oil using paper towel or brush. Preheat pan for about 3 minutes. Cool. Wipe off excess oil with paper towel.

**To bake crepes** pour batter into a deep heatproof dinner plate, pie plate or other similar container. Heat pan until hot enough to sizzle a drop of water. Dip preheated pan in batter for just a second or two, tilting pan all around so entire surface is coated. Gently but quickly lift up, invert and set pan on legs or base. Pan should be coated with a thin layer of batter. If crepe has holes, add a drop or two of batter to patch. Cook until edges are lightly browned and top is dry. Invert pan over plate or waxed paper, loosen edges with spatula and let crepe peel off. If necessary, loosen center of crepe with spatula to help ease if off the pan.

## HANDLING BAKED CREPES

**For immediate use** simply stack crepes, as they are baked, on a deep dinner plate, pie plate or other similar container. Keep crepes covered with foil, plastic wrap or a large pan or pot cover and store at room temperature. To keep crepes hot or to reheat, stack crepes on a deep dinner plate, pie plate or other similar container, cover tightly with foil to prevent drying and place in 250°F. oven about 5 to 10 minutes or until warm.

**To refrigerate crepes for a day or two** place a sheet of foil, waxed paper or plastic wrap between each crepe. Cover tightly with plastic wrap or foil or seal in a plastic bag. Store flat in the refrigerator.

**To freeze crepes** layer with waxed paper, foil or plastic wrap, as above. Put stack of crepes on paper plate, in pie plate or deep dinner plate or in round freezer container to protect them. (Crepes become brittle when frozen and could break.) Cover tightly with plastic wrap or seal in a heavy-duty plastic bag or freezer container. Store flat in your freezer. Crepes will keep for several weeks.

**To thaw crepes** remove them from freezer and let stand at room temperature for several hours or in refrigerator overnight. For faster thawing, unwrap crepes and heat in 250°F. oven, carefully peeling crepes apart as they thaw and become flexible. You can also thaw crepes in the microwave oven for a minute or two.

## VARIATIONS FOR CREPE BATTER

**Parmesan Cheese Crepes:** Add ¼ cup grated Parmesan cheese to batter. Stir batter frequently to keep cheese distributed.

**Herbed Crepes:** Add ½ teaspoon dried dill weed to batter. Stir batter frequently to keep dill distributed.

**Whole Wheat Crepes:** Substitute whole wheat flour for all-purpose flour. Stir batter frequently to keep flour distributed.

**Cornmeal Crepes:** Reduce flour to ¹/₄ cup and add ¹/₂ cup cornmeal. Add ¹/₄ teaspoon cayenne pepper. Stir batter frequently to keep cornmeal distributed.

**Note:** The exact number of crepes you can bake from this or any other batter depends on a variety of things—the batter itself, the size and type of crepe pan you use, and your skill in pouring or dipping the batter.

# BASIC DESSERT CREPE BATTER

**Makes 18 crepes**

  3/4 cup all-purpose flour
  4 tablespoons sugar
  1/4 teaspoon salt
  2 eggs
  2 egg yolks
  1 3/4 cups milk
  1 tablespoon flavoring, as orange juice
  4 tablespoons melted butter

In a large mixing bowl combine all ingredients. Cover and chill for 1 hour. After the crepe pan is lightly greased for the first crepe it should not be necessary to grease the crepe pan again. A tablespoon and a half of batter is used for each crepe in a 5 or 6-inch pan.

# REGULAR BASIC CREPE BATTER

**Makes 12 crepes**

  3 eggs
  1/2 cup milk
  1/2 cup water
  3 tablespoons butter, melted
  3/4 cup all-purpose flour
  1/4 teaspoon salt

In a large mixing bowl combine all ingredients, whisk until blended. Cover and chill for 1 hour.

# FLAT MUSHROOM CREPES

**Makes 8 servings**

- 5 tablespoons butter
- 2 pounds mushrooms, sliced
- 4 tablespoons all-purpose flour
- 1/2 teaspoon salt, oregano
- 1/4 teaspoon pepper
- 2 cups half-and-half
- 1 1/2 cups grated Swiss cheese
- 10 crepes

Heat butter in a large saucepan over medium heat; sauté mushrooms until tender. Whisk in flour, continue stirring until flour is absorbed. Season with salt, oregano and pepper. Whisk in half-and-half, stirring until mixture thickens. Mix in cheese, combine. Assemble crepes on a buttered, heatproof serving dish. Arrange one crepe on dish. Spread with 5 tablespoons filling. Arrange a crepe over filling and continue stacking crepes and filling until all crepes and filling have been used ending with sauce. Cover lightly with aluminum foil. Bake at 350°F. for 15 minutes. Cut into pie-shaped wedges.

# SEAFOOD CREPES __

**Makes 12 servings**

- 4 **tablespoons butter**
- 1 **tablespoon oil**
- 1 **onion, chopped**
- 2 **tablespoons all-purpose flour**
- 1 **cup bay scallops**
- 1 **cup filet of sole**
- $^1/_2$ **teaspoon salt, ground tarragon**
- $^1/_4$ **teaspoon white pepper**
- 1$^1/_4$ **cups half-and-half**
- $^3/_4$ **cup grated Cheddar cheese**
- 24 **crepes**

**Seafood filling**

Heat butter and oil in medium skillet; sauté onion until tender. Whisk in flour, cook until flour is absorbed. Add scallops, sole and seasonings, cook over medium heat, stirring constantly until fish is cooked, sole will flake. Blend in half-and-half, simmer until mixture thickens; cool. Fill and roll crepes. Place seam side down in a buttered 13 x 9 x 1$^3/_4$-casserole dish. Drizzle any remaining sauce over crepes, sprinkle with cheese. Bake at 350°F. for 20 minutes.

# SPINACH CREPES

**Makes 12 servings**

 4 **tablespoons butter**
 1 **onion, minced**
 1 **cup sliced mushrooms**
 4 **packages, 10 ounces each, chopped spinach, defrosted, drained**
 1 **cup commercial sour cream**
 1/2 **teaspoon salt, basil**
24 **crepes**
 2 **cups commercial sour cream**
 1 **cup grated Swiss cheese**

Heat butter in medium saucepan, sauté onion and mushrooms until tender. Mix in spinach, sauté until liquid is absorbed. Remove from heat; mix in sour cream, salt and basil, combine. Cool. Fill and roll crepes. Place seam side down in a buttered 13 x 9 x 1¾-inch casserole dish. Combine sour cream and cheese in a small bowl, drizzle over crepes. Bake at 350°F. for 20 minutes.

# CHICKEN CREPES

**Makes 6 servings**

- 3 tablespoons butter
- 1 onion, sliced
- 2 tablespoons all-purpose flour
- 1 cup chicken stock
- 1/2 teaspoon salt, chopped basil
- 1 cup sliced mushrooms
- 1/2 cup heavy cream
- 1 1/2 cups cooked cubed chicken
- 12 crepes
- 1/2 cup shredded Cheddar cheese
- 1 cup commercial sour cream for garnish
- 1/4 cup chopped fresh parsley

In a medium saucepan heat butter; sauté onion until tender. Whisk in flour, continue mixing until flour is absorbed. Blend in stock, season with salt and basil. Stir in mushrooms, heavy cream and chicken. Simmer until warm, about 1 minute. In a caserole pan, 11³/₄ x 7¹/₂ x 1³/₄-inches, fill crepes with chicken filling; fold over. Cover and bake at 350°F. for 15 minutes. Garnish with cheese, sour cream and fresh parsley.

# APPLE CREPES

**Makes 6 servings**

    4 tablespoons butter
    6 firm apples, peeled, cored and sliced
 1/4 teaspoon almond extract
    I cup blanched, slivered almonds
 1/2 cup firmly packed light brown sugar
    4 tablespoons granulated sugar

In a medium saucepan heat butter; saute apple slices until tender, stirring often. Mix in almond extract and blanched almonds. Blend in sugar, continue cooking over medium heat, stirring often until the sugar melts, reserve. In a casserole, 11³/₄ x 7¹/₂ x 1³/₄-inches, fill crepes with 5 tablespoons of apple mixture, roll up jelly-roll style. Sprinkle with granulated sugar. Bake at 350°F. for 20 minutes. Serve warm with sweetened whipped cream if desired.

# CREPES SUZETTE

**Makes 12 servings**

  1  **cup Confectioners' sugar**
  3  **tablespoons orange zest**
$1/2$  **cup freshly squeezed orange juice**
  3  **tablespoons Grand Marnier (optional)**
36  **crepes**
     **Butter**
     **Confectioners' sugar**

**Orange Topping**

In a small bowl combine all ingredients until well blended. Butter each crepe with the mixture and fold crepes into quarters. Heat crepes in a buttered large skillet or crepe suzette pan. Sprinkle with Confectioners' sugar. Arrange 3 crepes on each serving plate, drizzle with sauce.

# BREAKFAST CREPES

**Makes 6 servings**

- 6 hard-boiled eggs, peeled, chopped
- 2 cups minced cooked ham or other breakfast meat
- 1½ cups commercial sour cream
- 3 green onions, minced
- ½ teaspoon dry mustard
- ½ teaspoon salt
- 12 crepes
- 1 cup shredded Cheddar cheese

In a mixing bowl combine all ingredients except crepes and cheese. Place 5 tablespoons of filling on each crepe. Roll up jelly-roll style. Arrange crepes in shallow casserole pan, sprinkle with Cheddar cheese. Bake at 350°F. for 15-20 minutes.

# LEMON CREPE SOUFFLE

**Makes 8 servings**

- 16-18 crepes
- 2 tablespoons butter
- 3 tablespoons all-purpose flour
- ¾ cup freshly squeezed lemon juice
- 1 tablespoon lemon zest
- 4 eggs, separated
- ¼ teaspoon salt
- ½ teaspoon cream of tartar

Heat butter in medium saucepan. Whisk in flour, cook over medium heat, stirring constantly until flour is absorbed. Stir in juice, whisk until smooth, and begins to thicken, remove from heat. Mix in zest and egg yolks, one at a time, reserve. In a separate bowl, beat egg whites with salt and cream of tartar until they stand in soft peaks. Fold in lemon mixture. Serve with a lemon sauce or raspberry sauce if desired.

**To assemble**

Place 4-5 tablespoons lemon souffle mixture in each crepe, fold over, arrange crepes in a buttered 9 x 13 x 1¾-inch casserole, in a single layer. Bake at 375°F. for 15 minutes.

# SOUFFLES

Souffle is the French word for puff, a dish which puffs up dramatically while baking in the oven. A classic souffle consists of a thick white sauce blended with egg yolks and leavened by stiffly beaten egg whites. Other pureed, shredded or finely chopped foods are often added for flavor. Savory or sweet, a souffle can be sensationally impressive as a main dish, side dish or dessert. It is not as difficult to make as you might think. The following recipes use easy steps for simplified souffle-making.

A traditional souffle dish is nice, but not necessary. Any oven-proof, straight-sided casserole, baking dish, soup cups or mugs will do. The dish should not be buttered or greased unless it is also dusted with fine dry bread crumbs, cornmeal or grated Parmesan cheese. A buttered dish is slippery and won't allow a souffle to climb the sides reaching its maximum height.

Size is important. If the dish is too small, the mixture may run over in the oven; too large, and the mixture will not rise above the rim to produce the lofty puff that is part of a souffle's charm. As a general guide, if, when you pour the souffle mixture into the dish, there is less than about 1/2 inch of space left in the dish, put a "collar" on the dish or use a larger dish. For a collar, make a 4-inch wide band of triple or double thickness aluminum foil long enough to go around the dish and overlap 2 inches. For easy removal later, butter the band and then dust it lightly either with fine dry bread crumbs, grated Parmesan cheese or cornmeal. For a sweet souffle, granulated sugar can be used for dusting. Wrap the band around the dish wih the dusted side in and attach it with scotch tape, paper clips or string. Be sure the collar stands at least 2 inches above the rim of the dish. After baking, quickly, but gently, remove the collar before serving.

In souffle-making, egg yolks and egg whites are separated to take advantage of the thickening property of the yolks and the leavening property of the whites. It is easiest to separate the eggs when they are cold, straight from the refrigerator. However, whites will beat up to their highest volume when allowed to sit at room temperature for about 30 minutes. When making a souffle, first separate the eggs. Then prepare the souffle dish and remaining ingredients and proceed with the recipe. This will allow time for the whites to warm up. An expensive copper bowl and balloon whisk are not necessary for souffle making. The same chemical reaction which stabilizes the foam when you beat egg whites in a copper bowl is produced by cream of tartar in these recipes. But do use clean beaters and either a glass or metal bowl for beating the whites. Plastic may retain fat which inhibits the egg white foam. Be sure, too, that not a speck of egg yolk gets into the whites.

Beating the egg whites to the proper degree is probably the only true secret to successful souffle making. Underbeaten egg whites won't leaven properly. Overbeaten egg whites will form dry puffs that don't hold air well and are difficult to fold into yolk mixture. Tilt the bowl to test the stiffness of the whites. If they slip and slide in the bowl, beat just a little more. When they no longer slip, they're ready.

Although a classic souffle is made with a thick white sauce, you can substitute a can of condensed cream of "anything" soup. For a sweet dessert souffle, you use sugar in the sauce.

Use your imagination. Although a souffle is often considered the ultimate in gourmet cuisine, it is also a good way to use the leftovers you have on hand. Unless the recipe directs otherwise, cook the additional ingredients first and drain them well. It is better to use pureed, shredded or finely chopped foods in a souffle, since large chunks of food can sink and weigh a souffle down.

Gently folding, not stirring the egg yolk mixture into the whites in also very important. Some cooks like to lighten very heavy yolk mixtures by folding in a dollop of beaten whites before folding. To fold, first pour the yolk mixture onto the whites. Then use a rubber spatula or whisk to cut down gently through the mixture, across the bottom of the bowl, then up and over the mixture. Come up through the center of the mixture every few strokes while rotating the bowl frequently. Fold only until no streaks remain and the mixture has a uniform texture throughout. The basic idea is to blend the yolk mixture thoroughly with the whites without breaking the air bubbles you've beaten into the whites.

When the center of a souffle rises higher than its sides, the souffle has a crown or a top hat. To create this effect, take a spoon, table knife or narrow spatula and simply cut through the unbaked souffle mixture in a circle. Make a ring about 1 inch from side of dish and 1 inch deep. Sweet souffles seldom top hat, but may crack on top. Sifting confectioners' sugar over a baked sweet souffle before serving will cover any cracks.

The French like to serve their souffles when the center is still rather runny and can be ladled over the souffle as a sauce. Most Americans seem to prefer their souffles more evenly done. Test for doneness by gently moving the oven rack back and forth so that you can see whether the souffle is still quite shakey or more firmly set. Once you have made a souffle or two you will develop a feel for when it is done enough for you.

When you have decided that your souffle is done, hurry it from the oven to the table, where the guests should be waiting. The most pretty puffed souffle in the world won't stay puffed forever. If the souffle must wait for the guests, leave it in the oven with the heat off for no more than 5 to 10 minutes. To serve the souffle, gently break the top crust of the souffle into portions with two forks held back to back. Then, lightly spoon out portions. Be sure to include some of the top and side crusts with each servings. Last, but not least, sit back and enjoy your culinary creation. No one needs to know how easy it was to create.

## SAVORY VARIATIONS

After the sauce has thickened, stir in;

1 can, 14 ounces, asparagus, drained, pureed, use liquid in place of some of the milk, and 1 small minced onion.

1½ cups shredded cheese, any soft cheese will do; as Cheddar, mozzarella, Monterey Jack or Swiss.

1 box, 10 ounces, frozen spinach, drained, pureed, use liquid in place of some of the milk and 1 cup artichoke bottoms arranged on bottom of souffle mold.

# TURKEY SOUFFLE __

**Makes 8 servings**

- 1/2 **cup grated Cheddar cheese**
- 3 **tablespoons butter**
- 3 **tablespoons all-purpose flour**
- 1/2 **cup milk**
- 1/2 **cup turkey stock**
- 3 **egg yolks, beaten until light**
- 1 1/4 **cups minced, cooked turkey**
- 1/4 **teaspoon salt, pepper, nutmeg**
- 3 **egg whites**
- 1/2 **teaspoon cream of tartar**

Butter a 1-quart souffle dish, dust with grated cheddar cheese. Tie a buttered dusted aluminum foil collar around mold. In a medium saucepan over medium heat melt butter, whisk in flour, milk and turkey stock, continue cooking until mixture thickens stirring constantly, remove from heat. Slowly blend in egg yolks. Mix in turkey and seasonings, cool. In a separate deep bowl, beat egg whites until soft peaks form, sprinkle with cream of tartar, beat until stiff but not dry. Fold egg whites into turkey mixture. Mound into souffle mold. Bake at 350°F. for 50 minutes. Serve immediately. Serve with a tomato sauce if desired.

# CHEESE SOUFFLE __

**Makes 6 servings**

  1/3  **cup butter**
  1/3  **cup all-purpose flour**
  1/2  **teaspoon salt, dry mustard**
1 1/2  **cups milk**
   6  **egg yolks, beat until light**
   1  **cup shredded Cheddar cheese**
   6  **egg whites**
  1/2  **teaspoon cream of tartar**
      **Bread crumbs**

In a medium saucepan over medium-high heat, melt butter. Whisk in flour, season with salt and dry mustard. Cook, stirring constantly, until flour is absorbed. Blend in milk. Continue cooking until mixture thickens, reserve, cool. Mix in egg yolks. Blend in Cheddar cheese. In a large separate bowl, beat egg whites, sprinkle with cream of tartar, beat until stiff but not dry. Fold in stiffly beaten egg whites. Spoon mixture into a buttered, dusted with bread crumbs, 2-quart souffle dish. Bake at 350°F. for 45-50 minutes. Serve immediately.

# SOUFFLE ROLL WITH SPINACH FILLING

**Makes 8-10 servings**
**Souffle Roll**

- 4 **tablespoons butter**
- 1/2 **cup all-purpose flour**
- 1/4 **teaspoon salt and pepper**
- 2 **cups milk**
- 5 **eggs, separated**

Melt butter in a medium saucepan; whisk in flour, continue whisking until flour is absorbed, over medium heat. Season with salt and pepper. Blend in milk, continue cooking for 1 minute, stirring constantly. Beat yolks until light, in a separate bowl. In a slow steady stream blend eggs into milk mixture, being sure not to allow eggs to curdle by being too warm, cool mixture. In a separate bowl, beat egg whites until stiff peaks form. Fold egg whites into cooled sauce. Spread mixture into a greased and floured jelly-roll pan, 15 1/2 x 10 1/2 x 1 inches; line with greased wax paper, dust with flour. Bake at 400°F. for 20 minutes. Turn onto a clean towel, roll in jelly-roll style with towel.

**Filling**

- 4 **tablespoons butter**
- 4 **green onions, minced**

**2** cups cooked chopped spinach, drained well
**1/2** cup cooked bacon, crumbled
**1/2** teaspoon cinnamon, salt
**1/4** teaspoon ground nutmeg, pepper
**1** package, 8 ounces, cream cheese, room temperature, in chunks

**Souffle Roll**

Heat butter in medium saucepan; sauté green onions until tender over medium heat. Stir in spinach, sauté until dry, 1 minute. Season with crumbled bacon, cinnamon, salt, nutmeg and pepper. Blend in cream cheese; cool to room temperature.

Unroll souffle; spread filling over souffle, gently. Reroll souffle using the towel as a rolling aid. Slide souffle onto the serving platter, seam side down. Serve with tomato sauce or a mushroom sauce if desired.

# CHOCOLATE SOUFFLE WITH VANILLA SAUCE

**Makes 8 servings**

- ¹/₂ cup sugar
- 2 tablespoons cornstarch
- ¹/₄ teaspoon salt
- ³/₄ cup milk
- 3 ounces semi-sweet chocolate, melted
- 2 tablespoons butter
- 4 egg yolks, beat until light
- 4 egg whites
- ¹/₂ teaspoon cream of tartar
- 1 teaspoon vanilla

Butter a 1-quart souffle mold, dust with sugar; tie a buttered and sugared aluminum foil collar around mold. In a medium saucepan over medium heat combine sugar, cornstarch, salt and milk, cook until thickened, stirring constantly. Remove from heat, mix in chocolate and butter, stir until combined. Mix in egg yolks, cool. Beat egg whites, sprinkle with cream of tartar and vanilla, beat until stiff but not dry. Fold gently into chocolate mixture. Mound into souffle dish. Bake at 350°F. for 50 minutes. Serve immediately with vanilla sauce.

**Vanilla Sauce**

- **1 cup half-and-half**
- **1 egg**
- **1 egg yolk**
- **4 tablespoons sugar**
- **2 teaspoons vanilla**
- **1 cup heavy cream, beat until soft peaks form**

Scald half-and-half in a small saucepan over medium heat, cool. In a separate bowl combine egg, egg yolk and sugar. Blend in cream. Heat mixture in top of double boiler over simmering water until sauce coats a spoon and has thickened. Remove from heat, mix in vanilla, cool, fold in whipped cream.

# INDIVIDUAL ORANGE SOUFFLES

**Makes 12 servings**

    12 firm oranges
     1 cup freshly squeezed orange juice
     1 envelope unflavored gelatin, softened in
    1/4 cup cold water
     2 eggs
    1/2 cup sugar
     1 cup heavy cream, whipped

Cut tops off oranges. Scoop out pulp, reserve. Cut tips off bottoms of oranges for balance. Place oranges on a cookie sheet, for easy handling. Place in freezer until ready to use. Place orange juice in top of a double boiler over simmering water. Sprinkle gelatin/water mixture over juice, combine. In a separate medium mixing bowl, beat egg and sugar until light and fluffy. Mix into orange juice. Simmer 5 minutes, stirring constantly. Chill until mixture begins to set. Fold whipped cream and 1 cup of the reserved orange pulp into orange mixture. Mound into frozen orange shells. Freeze. Remove individual orange souffles 10 minutes before serving.

# LIME SOUFFLE WITH RUM SAUCE

**Makes 8 servings**

- 5 tablespoons butter
- 4 tablespoons all-purpose flour
- 1 cup milk
- 6 eggs, separated
- 1/2 cup sugar
- 6 tablespoons freshly squeezed lime juice
- 2 tablespoons lime zest
- 1/2 teaspoon cream of tartar
- 1/4 teaspoon salt

Butter a 2-quart souffle mold, dust with sugar; tie a buttered and sugared aluminum foil collar around mold. In a medium saucepan over medium heat melt butter; whisk in flour, cook until flour is absorbed, stirring constantly. Whisk in milk, continue cooking until mixture thickens. In a separate bowl, beat egg yolks and sugar until light and fluffy. Mix in lime juice and lime zest. Mix with milk. In a separate bowl, beat egg whites, sprinkle with cream of tartar and salt, beat until stiff but not dry. Fold gently into lime mixture. Add 2-3 drops of green food coloring if desired. Mound into souffle dish. Bake at 350°F. for 50 minutes. Serve immediately with rum sauce.

**RUM SAUCE**

- 2 egg yolks
- 1/2 cup superfine sugar

1 **teaspoon vanilla**
2 **tablespoons light rum or 1 teaspoon rum flavoring**
1/2 **cup heavy cream, whipped**

In a medium bowl beat egg yolks until light and fluffy. Add sugar gradually, incorporate. Stir in vanilla and rum. Fold in whipped cream. Chill until ready to serve.

# COLD RASPBERRY SOUFFLE

**Makes 10-12 servings**

1 **package unflavored gelatin**
1/4 **cup cold water**
1 **cup milk, scald**
4 **egg yolks**
1/2 **cup sugar**
1 **package, 10 ounces, raspberries, defrosted, include juice**
1 **cup heavy cream, whipped**
2 **egg whites beat until stiff with**
1/2 **teaspoon cream of tartar**

Clip a lightly oiled and sugared aluminum foil collar, folded in half lengthwise, around a 1 1/2 cup souffle mold. Dissolve gelatin in cold water, stir to soften. Pour cooled milk in the top of a double boiler over simmering water. In a separate bowl, beat egg yolks and sugar until light and fluffy. Slowly add egg yolk mixture and gelatin mixture to milk, combine. Simmer until mixture thickens, stirring constantly. Blend in raspberries and juice. Chill until mixture begins to set. Fold in whipped cream and stiffly beaten egg whites. Mound into prepared souffle dish. Chill until souffle is set, about 2 hours. Carefully remove collar.

# COLD WHITE CHOCOLATE MOUSSE

**Makes 6 servings**

- 4 ounces white chocolate, break into pieces
- 2 eggs, separated
- 1/4 cup sugar
- 1 ounce white Creme de Cacao
- 1/4 teaspoon cream of tartar
- 1 cup heavy cream

Melt white chocolate slowly in the top of a double boiler over warm water, remove from heat. In a separate bowl beat egg yolks with half of the sugar until light and fluffy. Fold egg yolk mixture into the melted white chocolate. Blend in liquor, mix until smooth. In a separate mixing bowl, beat egg whites, sprinkle with cream of tartar and remaining sugar until stiff, but not dry, peaks form. Fold egg white mixture into chocolate mixture. Whip cream until stiff peaks form, fold into cooled chocolate mixture. Mound mousse into individual serving dishes and refrigerate for 2 hours. Garnish with shaved dark chocolate if desired .

# STIRRED CUSTARD

Stirred custard is so smooth and creamy, so delicious that it has been a favorite treat for centuries. This thick, but pourable mixture is a combination of eggs and milk, usually sweetened with sugar, that is cooked and stirred over low heat to produce a light golden sauce or soft custard. Preparing a perfect stirred custard is not difficult, if you treat the egg/milk mixture with the loving care it deserves.

Use a heavy saucepan for even heat.

Mix the ingredients together in the saucepan and gradually add cold milk until well blended. Scalding the milk is not necessary.

Cook custard over low heat. At high heat egg protein coagulates and the mixture may curdle. Low heat, heavy saucepan and caution eliminate the need for a double boiler.

Stir constantly to heat the custard evenly, prevent sticking and overcooking and to keep the custard smooth.

Never boil custard. Stirred custard is done at a temperature 20 to 30 degrees below boiling. Overcooking causes limpy custard.

Test for doneness by dipping the bowl of a metal spoon part way into the custard. When custard coats the spoon, leaving a thin layer on the surface, it is done.

Cool the custard immediately by placing the pan in a bowl of ice or cold water to stop the cooking process. Stir to help the cooling process and keep the custard smooth. Cover the custard with plastic wrap placed directly on top of the custard so a "skin" does not form. Refrigerate or serve warm.

Serve stirred custard as a sauce over cake, fruit or pudding. It is also the basis for many other enticing treats.

# STIRRED CUSTARD

**STEP-BY-STEP FOR
PERFECT STIRRED CUSTARD**

1) In large saucepan blend together 4 eggs (or 6 egg yolks), 1/2 cup sugar and 1/4 teaspoon salt.

2) Gradually stir in 2½ cups milk.

3) Cook over low heat, stirring constantly, until mixture thickens and just coats a metal spoon, 15 to 20 minutes. Stir in 1½ teaspoons vanilla.

4) Cool quickly by setting pan in bowl of ice or cold water and stirring for a few minutes.

5) Cover by placing plastic wrap directly on custard. Chill thoroughly.

6) Serve over fresh fruit for a fanciful dessert that's simplicity itself. Makes about 3½ cups.

# BAKED CUSTARD

Eggs, milk, a dash of salt and some sugar and vanilla are all you need. The usual proportion is one egg and two table-spoons sugar to one cup of milk. Or you can substitute two egg yolks for one whole egg. The preparation could not be simpler. Just follow the step-by-step directions. Bake the custard in cups or a baking dish. You can sprinkle it with nutmeg, top with a simple sauce or create an elegant dessert with a Floating Island. Custard isn't just for dessert. Stir vegetables, chopped meat or cheese into the egg-milk mixture for a main dish. You can even bake custard in your covered electric skillet or pressure cooker. Just follow manufacturers' directions. There are few calories in custard, about 197 per serving. When you serve custard you are supplying high quality protein, vitamins and many important minerals. And because custards are so easy to eat and digest they are often recommended for infants and convalescents.

For a perfect custard, heat the milk before blending with the beaten eggs for a shorter cooking time and evenly baked custard.

Add the hot milk gradually to the beaten eggs, so they won't overcook.

Use a 1-quart liquid measuring cup or other container with a pouring spout to portion custard mixture into baking cups.

Test for doneness by inserting a knife near but not at the center of the custard. If the knife comes out clean, the custard is done. The very center may not be quite done but the heat retained in the mixture will continue to cook it after you take it from the oven.

Set cups in the baking pan before pouring in the custard. Then put the pan with cups on the rack in the oven and pour in the hot water.

Pour hot water into the pan around the custard to within 1/2 inch of the top of the custard. The hot water bath may seem a bother but it is important for evenly baked custard with satiny smooth texture.

Use the proper oven temperature. Too high a temperature will make the custard weep; at too low a temperature the custard will not cook.

Time baking carefully. Too long and the custard will be rubbery and watery. Too short a time and the custard will not set.

Take the custard out of the water bath as soon as it tests done; otherwise the hot water will continue to cook it even after removal from the oven.

Serve custard warm or chill to serve cold. Be sure to cover and refrigerate any leftovers.

# FLOATING ISLAND __

**Makes 8 servings**

     2 eggs, separated
 1/4 teaspoon cream of tartar
     4 tablespoons sugar
3 1/2 cups milk
     6 eggs
 1/2 cup sugar
 1/4 teaspoon salt
     1 teaspoon vanilla

In a mixing bowl beat egg whites and cream of tartar until foamy. Add sugar, beating constantly until sugar is absorbed and stiff peaks form. In a large skillet heat milk over low heat until simmering. Poach meringues, by forming a meringue ball with a tablespoon and lowering it into the simmering milk, continue until all the meringue has been used, cook 2 minutes on each side or until cooked. With a slotted spoon transfer meringue balls to paper toweling, drain, reserve. Reserve milk for custard. In a large saucepan beat egg yolks and egg with remaining sugar and salt until light. Slowly pour reserved warm milk into egg mixture, stirring until blended. Cook and stir constantly over low heat until mixture thickens slightly and just coats a metal spoon. Remove from heat. Stir in vanilla. Pour into a 2-quart shallow serving dish. Top custard with meringues. Serve warm or chilled.

# SMALL FLANS

**Makes 4 servings**

- 4 eggs, lightly beaten
- 1 cup evaporated milk
- 2/3 cup water
- 1/3 cup granulated sugar
- 1 1/2 teaspoons vanilla
- 1/4 teaspoon salt
- 4 tablespoons dark brown sugar

In a large mixing bowl combine eggs, evaporated milk, water, granulated sugar, vanilla and salt, combine. Lightly press one tablespoon of the brown sugar into each of 4 custard cups. Pour custard carefully into cups. Arrange custard cups in a shallow baking pan; add one inch of water to pan. Bake at 350°F. for 50 minutes or until custard tests done. Loosen edges with a spatula and unmold onto individual serving plates. Garnish with fresh fruit.

# CREME BRULEE

**Makes 4 servings**

- 5 **egg yolks**
- 8 **tablespoons sugar**
- 2 **cups heavy cream**
- 2 **teaspoons vanilla**
- 5 **tablespoons brown sugar, sifted**

In a large mixing bowl beat egg yolks and sugar until light and fluffy. In a small heavy saucepan over low heat, warm cream. Mix in egg yolks. Stir in vanilla, pour mixture into 4 souffle ramekins. Place ramekins in a roasting pan. Pour boiling water halfway around ramekins. Bake at 325°F. for 45 minutes or until tests done. Remove from the water bath, cool, refrigerate. Set ramekins in a roasting pan filled with crushed ice. Sprinkle tops of custard with brown sugar. Place custard under broiler, about 6 inches from heat. Broil until the sugar caramelizes, about 30 seconds. Serve immediately.

# FLAN

**Makes 8 servings**

- ¹/₂ cup sugar
  Custard
- 8 eggs, beat until light
- ¹/₂ cup sugar
- ¹/₄ teaspoon salt
- 1 teaspoon vanilla
- 3¹/₂ cups milk

In a small saucepan combine sugar and 2 tablespoons water; cook over medium heat, stirring until the sugar melts and forms a light brown syrup. Pour carefully into a 6-cup mold; tip from side to side to coat the pan; refrigerate until needed.

**Custard**

In a large mixing bowl combine eggs, sugar and salt, beat until light and fluffy. Mix vanilla and milk into egg mixture. Pour into prepared mold. Place mold in larger pan, fill halfway with hot water. Bake at 350°F. for 50 minutes or until custard tests done.

# ENGLISH TRIFLE

**Makes 8-10 servings**

8 slices pound cake, 1/2 inch thick
4 tablespoons raspberry jam
  Custard
4 tablespoons sherry
1 cup fresh raspberries or frozen raspberries, drained

Spread cake slices with preserves, cut into strips. Pour 1/2 of the custard into a 2-quart serving bowl. Arrange half of the cake strips over custard in a layer. Sprinkle with 2 tablespoons sherry. Top with 1/2 cup raspberries. Pour 1/2 or remaining custard over fruit. Top with remaining cake, sherrry, raspberries and ending with remaining custard. Garnish with raspberries or sweetened whipped cream. Chill until ready to serve.

**Custard**

3/4 cup sugar
3 tablespoons all-purpose flour
1/4 teaspoon salt
4 cups milk
6 egg yolks, slightly beaten
2 teaspoons vanilla

In a large saucepan combine sugar, flour and salt. Blend together milk and egg yolks. Stir small amount of milk mixture into dry ingredients, making a smooth paste. Gradually blend in remaining milk mixture. Cook over medium heat, stirring constantly, until mixture thickens. Remove from heat, stir in vanilla. Cool, chill until ready to use.

# ITALIAN ORANGE RUM TRIFLE

**Makes one 10-inch round angel cake or sponge cake or two 9-inch loaf angel cakes; 8-10 servings**

> 1/4 **cup dark rum**
> **Custard**
> 8 **egg yolks**
> 1/4 **cup sugar**
> 1/4 **teaspoon salt**
> 3 **tablesponns orange zest**
> 4 **tablespoons all-purpose flour**
> 2 1/2 **cups milk, scald, cool**
> 1 **teaspoon vanilla**
> **Topping**
> 1 **cup heavy cream**
> 1/4 **cup sugar**
> 4 **tablespoons chopped candied orange peel**

Cut angel cake into 3 horizontal layers using a serrated knife. Place 1 layer on a serving plate. Sprinkle with half of the rum.

**Custard**

In a large mixing bowl beat egg yolks until light and fluffy. Add sugar, mix well. Place mixture in the top of a double boiler over simmering water. Stir in salt, orange zest, flour and milk. Cook over medium heat, whisking constantly until mixture thickens. Mix in vanilla. Remove from heat, cool. Sprinkle half of the cooled custard over bottom layer of cake. Set second layer of cake on top. Sprinkle with remaining rum. Cover with custard. Set third layer of cake on top.

**Topping**

Beat heavy cream until it begins to thicken. Sprinkle sugar over cream, continue beating until soft peaks form. Cover sides and top of cake with whipped cream. Sprinkle candied orange peel over top of cake. Refrigerate until ready to serve.

# CUSTARD RICE PUDDING

**Makes 8 servings**

    3 cups milk
    ½ cup sugar
    ½ teaspoon salt
  1½ cups cooked rice
    4 eggs, beat until light
    2 teaspoons vanilla
    ½ cup golden raisins

In a medium saucepan combine milk, sugar and salt. Bring mixture to boiling; stir in rice. Remove from heat, let stand 5 minutes, stir. In a separate bowl combine eggs, vanilla and raisins; in a slow steady stream add milk to rice mixture. Pour rice mixture into 3-quart baking dish or milk. Place mold into a larger pan, fill halfway with hot water. Bake at 350°F. for 30 minutes or until it tests done. Serve warm with sweetened whipped cream.

# QUICHE

Quiche is an unsweetened, open-faced custard pie that is superb either hot or cold as an entree, appetizer or snack. A quiche can be equally at home at a formal dinner or a casual family lunch or supper.

Contrary to what some people think, quiche is incredibly simple to prepare. It requires only a few ingredients, eggs, half-and-half or milk, cheese, seasonings and whatever else you might wish to add. The only dishes you will need to prepare it are a mixing bowl, a whisk, a few measuring utensils, and maybe a knife if you are adding a chopped ingredient.

Most quiches require a pastry crust and that may intimidate some cooks. If so the solution is as close as the supermarket freezer case—a deep-dish style frozen pie shell. For the recipes that follow, you must use the deep-dish variety if you are opting for a frozen shell.

Quiche possibilities are virtually limitless. You can stick to the recipes here or make up your own combination, be creative.

# QUICHE LORRAINE _

**Makes 6 servings**

> 9-inch baked pie shell
> 8 slices bacon, cooked, drained, crumbled
> 1 cup shredded Swiss cheese
> 6 eggs
> 1¼ cups half-and-half
> ½ teaspoon salt
> ⅛ teaspoon ground nutmeg, white pepper

Sprinkle bacon and cheese into pie shell. Beat together remaining ingredients in a large mixing bowl until well blended. Pour egg mixture over bacon and cheese. Bake at 375°F. for 35 minutes or until quiche tests done. Allow quiche to stand for 5 minutes before serving.

# ASPARAGUS QUICHE

**Makes 6 servings**

    **9-inch baked pie shell**
**1 cup shredded Swiss cheese**
**1 cup, cooked, chopped asparagus**
**6 eggs**
**1 cup half-and-half**
**1/2 teaspoon chopped basil**
**1/2 teaspoon salt**

Sprinkle cheese and asparagus into pie shell. In a large mixing bowl combine remaining ingredients, blend. Pour egg mixture over asparagus and cheese. Bake at 375°F. for 35 minutes or until quiche tests done. Allow quiche to stand for 5 minutes before serving.

# VEGETABLE QUICHE

**Makes 6 servings**

9-inch baked pie shell
2 tablespoons butter
½ pound mushrooms, sliced
6 green onions, minced
1 cup shredded Cheddar cheese
4 eggs, slightly beaten
1 cup half-and-half
¼ cup freshly grated Parmesan cheese
½ teaspoon
¼ teaspoon white pepper

In a large skillet over medium heat, melt butter. Cook mushrooms and green onions until tender, stirring often. Spread vegetables in baked pie shell, reserve. Sprinkle cheese over vegetable mixture. In a mixing bowl blend together remaining ingredients. Pour over mushrooms and cheese. Bake at 375°F. for 35 minutes or until tests done. Allow quiche to stand 5 minutes before serving.

# MILK
# AND
# CHEESE

# MILK AND CHEESE

## Milk

The historians cannot tell us for sure when dairy foods became an important part of the human diet. The world's earliest written records found in the Sanskrit of ancient India, date back nearly 6,000 years, but milk had already become an important food. To the early people of central Asia the cow was so important that wealth was measured in numbers of cattle. Later the cow was worshipped in India, in Babylonia, and in Egypt. There are many references to cows and milk in the Old Testament.

From ancient times until 1850 few changes in milk production occurred. Due to the lack of refrigeration and transportation,

# MILK

## What Is Really in Milk?

Milk is about 87 percent water and 13 percent solids. The solids consist of fat and the fat-soluble vitamins it contains and the solids not fat, which include protein, carbohydrate, water-soluble vitamins, and minerals. The minimum amounts of fat and the solids not fat in milk that is shipped in interstate commerce are specified by federal standards.

The bar graph shows the major nutrients in the fat and the solids not fat as percentages of the U.S. Recommended Daily Allowances (U.S. RDA). The U.S. RDA are the amounts of nutrients that are recommended for healthy adults and children over four years of age.

## Milk

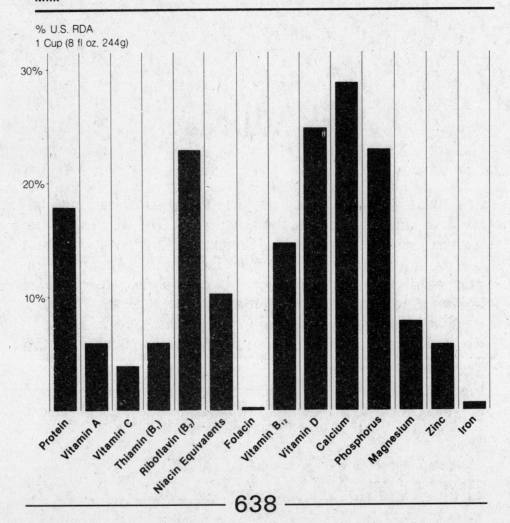

% U.S. RDA
1 Cup (8 fl oz, 244g)

most milk was consumed within a few miles of where it was produced. But with the rapid growth of cities came many changes; sanitation regulation, modern milking equipment, mechanical refrigeration, pasteurizing and bottling plants, the cream separator, and special milk trains and tank trucks. With these innovations, there was a shifting of the processing and delivery of milk from the farms to processing plants. With increased markets, the scientific study of cattle breeding and feeding became important for greater milk production.

**SHOPPING POINTERS**

It's easy to pick out the kind of milk you want. The main panel of the container includes:

• The product name

• The word "Pasteurized," if so processed

• The word "Homogenized," if so processed

• Ingredients, if any are added, such as vitamins or nonfat milk solids

• Pull date (open dating) which indicates when the product should be withdrawn from retail sale. This date allows for additional storage life in the consumer's refrigerator.

The following chart shows how long milk's freshness will last when it is stored and transported at the recommended temperature.

| Product | Approximate Storage Life at Specific Temperatures | Recommended Temperatures |
|---|---|---|
| Fresh, fluid, pasteurized milks | 8-20 days | 4°C (39°F) |
| Evaporated milk | 1 month at | 32°C (90°F) |
| | 12-24 months at | 21°C (70°F) |
| | 24 months at | 4°C (39°F) |
| Condensed milk | 3 months at | 32°C (90°F) |

|                           |                 |               |
|---------------------------|-----------------|---------------|
|                           | 9-24 months at  | 21°C (70°F)   |
|                           | 24 months at    | 4°C (39°F)    |
| Nonfat dry milk           | 6 months at     | 32°C (90°F)   |
|                           | 16-24 months at | 21°C (70°F)   |
|                           | 24 months at    | 4°C (39°F)    |
| Ultra high temperature    |                 |               |
| milk, unopened            | 3 months at     | 21°C (70°F)   |

Federal, state, and local agencies are involved in regulating the production and processing of milk. Consumers can rely on many safeguards to protect the milk they buy. But after purchasing it, consumers have the responsibility to protect the high quality and flavor of their milk.

## STORAGE TIPS

Keep milk fresh and good tasting by following these recommendations:

•When shopping, pick up the milk just before checking out.

•Refrigerate fresh milk as soon as possible after purchase or delivery to the home.

•Use milk in the order of purchase.

•Chill UHT milk before serving. After it is opened, keep it refrigerated.

•Once reconstituted, dry milk should be refrigerated.

•After pouring the milk you need, return the remainder to the refrigerator.

•If you don't use all the poured milk, refrigerate the unused milk separately. Don't pour it back in the original container.

•Close containers to prevent from absorbing flavors from other foods in the refrigerator.

•Store canned milk in a cool, dry place. After opening, pour the unused milk into a clean container and refrigerate.

•Store dry milk in a cool, dry place. Reseal the container after opening. Humidity causes dry milk to lump and may change the color and the flavor. If this occurs, the milk should not be used.

•Freezing milk changes its consistency but not its nutritional value. If milk freezes, thaw it in the refrigerator and stir gently.

## USE MILK OFTEN

For convenience, milk can't be beat. Just pour it—no cooking, stirring, or shaking is needed—and drink it with meals and as a snack.

Milk is not just a refreshing, nutritious drink, it is a basic ingredient in countless recipes—appetizers, beverages, main dishes, desserts, and snacks.

In cooking and baking, follow recipe directions. Milk should be heated just until bubbles form around the sides of the pan and steam escapes. Boiling milk will coagulate some of its protein which will form a film on the surface.

Cream sauces and soups, cereals cooked in milk, milk on cereal, fluffy bavarians, puddings, custards, pies, cocoa made with milk, milkshakes and party punches are just a few of the dishes that begin with milk.

| Milk | Fat % | Calories per cup |
|---|---|---|
| Buttermilk | 0.88 | 99 |
| Chocolate, 2% lowfat | 2.00 | 179 |
| Milk, whole | 3.25 | 150 |
| 2% lowfat | 2.00 | 121 |
| 1% lowfat | 1.00 | 102 |
| Skim | 0.25 | 86 |
| Lactose-free, whole | 3.25 | 150 |
| 2% lowfat | 2.00 | 121 |
| Nonfat dry, instant, reconstituted | 0.17 | 82 |

# BUTTER AND CREAM

From food remnants in vessels found in early tombs, we know that ancient Egyptians cooked with butter and cheese. For many centuries, buttermaking and cheesemaking were the only known means of preserving milk and cream. In many parts of the world, butter has long been prized as a flavorful food. More than a thousand years ago, Mongolians and Tibetans savored steaming cups of tea laced with golden melting butter—a custom still popular in northern China.

Since April 1, 1977, all fluid cream products shipped from one state to another must comply with one of the following general standards of identity;

**HEAVY CREAM** or heavy whipping cream pasteurized or ultra-pasteurized cream which contains not less than 36 percent milkfat.

**LIGHT WHIPPING CREAM** or whipping cream pasteurized or ultra-pasteurized cream containing not less than 18% but less than 30% milkfat.

**HALF-AND-HALF**, a mixture of pasteurized or ultra-pasteurized milk and cream which contains not less than 10.5% but less than 18% milkfat.

Federal standards established U.S. grades for butter, based on flavor plus body, color, and salt characteristics:

**U.S. GRADE AA** has a delicate sweet flavor, with a fine, highly pleasing aroma; is made from fresh sweet cream; has a smooth, creamy texture with food spreadability; has salt completely dissolved and blended in just the right amount.

**U.S. GRADE A** has a pleasing flavor; is made from fresh cream; is fairly smooth in texture.

**U.S. GRADE B** has a fairly pleasing flavor; is generally made from selected sour cream; is well accepted by many consumers.

Cream and butter have long held places of honor in the cuisines of the world. Many gourmet and not-so-fancy cooks favor butter for its distinctive flavor and its excellent cooking qualities.

## CALORIES

Half-and-half 1 T (15g) . . . . . . . . . . . . . . . . . . . . . . . . . . . . . . . . . . . . . 20
Light cream 1 T (15g) . . . . . . . . . . . . . . . . . . . . . . . . . . . . . . . . . . . . . 29
Coffee whitener, liquid—
    $\frac{1}{2}$ fluid oz. (15g) . . . . . . . . . . . . . . . . . . . . . . . . . . . . . . . . . . . . . 20
Coffee whitener, powder 2 tsp (4g) . . . . . . . . . . . . . . . . . . . . . . . . . 22
Butter 1 pat (5g) . . . . . . . . . . . . . . . . . . . . . . . . . . . . . . . . . . . . . . . . 36
Margarine 1 pat (5g) . . . . . . . . . . . . . . . . . . . . . . . . . . . . . . . . . . . . 36
Salad/cooking oil 1 T (13.6g) . . . . . . . . . . . . . . . . . . . . . . . . . . . . 120
Vegetable shortening 1 T (12.5g) . . . . . . . . . . . . . . . . . . . . . . . . . 111

Keep cream refrigerated at 39° in its closed carton. Cream stays fresh for at least one week after processing. Ultra-pasteurized keeps well up to 6-8 weeks. Freezing damages texture, so do not freeze.

Keep opened butter in a covered dish. Refrigerate in butter compartment. Keep unopened butter for several weeks in refrigerator shelf at 39°, or lower. Or wrap each package in foil or plastic wrap and freeze. Keeps well 6-9 months at 0° or lower.

# BUTTERMILK

History does not tell us what lucky person had the very first sip of that tangy concoction we call buttermilk. All we know is that buttermilk dates back many centuries. It evolved from the process of making butter, and butter has been consumed for 5,000 years. Ancient Hindus base the market value of their cows on the amount of butter churned from their milk. Early colonists brought buttermaking and buttermilk to America. Inventive American homemakers found many ways to utilize the butter-flecked fluid left over from home buttermaking, in cakes, pies, Boston brown bread and pancakes. For many decades, rural homemakers made their own butter and buttermilk. Factory production of butter began about 1860, but most butter was churned on farms until the 1920's. Creameries began to dry the churned buttermilk in the 1940's for more efficient use in baked goods, candy, ice cream mixes, and other dried mixes. Milk processors then started producing cultured buttermilk to meet consumer demand.

Today's buttermilk is made by fermentation, a process known to the ancient populations of southern Russia and the eastern Mediterranean countries. They found that milk left in a warm place developed a tart flavor and thicker body. We know that these changes are caused by bacterial action. Specially selected strains of bacteria are grown, or cultured, under laboratory conditions. Once added to fluid milk, these beneficial bacteria multiply and convert some of the milk sugar lactose to lactic acid. This lactic acid gives cultured milk products their tart flavor. The thickness is the result of bacterial action on milk protein.

Buttermilk, like all fluid milk, should be kept clean, cool and covered. Refrigerate buttermilk in its closed container at 45° F. or lower to protect its fresh acid flavor, aroma, and texture. Return any unused portion to the refrigerator promptly. Buttermilk's acidity retards growth of spoilage bacteria. Thus buttermilk will keep for as long as two weeks after purchase if stored properly. A date stamped on the container indicates when it should be withdrawn from retail sale. The date is set to allow additional storage time in the consumer's home. For peak flavor, buttermilk should be used within the first week after purchase. Freezing buttermilk is not advised because it causes separation of the watery portion of buttermilk from the solids. Thus freezing may alter the taste. If frozen, buttermilk can be thawed in the refrigerator, gently stirred, and best used in cooked products.

Imaginative cooks have long valued buttermilk as a cooking ingredient and as a thirst-quenching beverage. Its slight acidity makes for light and tender cakes, biscuits, and pancakes, and helps tenderize meats. The gaminess of a meat like venison for example, is offset by marinating it overnight in buttermilk. Creative cooks who have buttermilk on hand can explore its versatility in many tempting recipes.

For example:

Blend and chill buttermilk, egg yolks, sugar, lemon juice and grated rind, and vanilla. Serve as a chilled soup for a flavor surprise.

Substitute the same amount of buttermilk in recipes calling for soured milk.

Below is a bar graph that shows the percentages of the U.S.

Recommended Daily Allowances (U.S. RDA) for eight nutrients as contained in an eight-ounce glass of buttermilk. The U.S. RDA are the amounts of nutrients needed everyday by most healthy people, plus an excess of 30 to 50 percent to allow for individual variations. The quantities of nutrients in a food serving are expressed as percentages of the U.S. RDA in nutrition labeling of foods. As the graph shows, buttermilk supplies protein, riboflavin (B₂) and calcium in the highest amounts.

The nutrient and caloric content of buttermilk are similar to those of the fluid milk from which it is made. The caloric value for most buttermilk sold in the United States is about 90 calories for eight ounces. This buttermilk is made with skim milk, which contains less than 0.5 percent fat. The caloric value increases to 120 calories for eight ounces of buttermilk with 2 percent milkfat and to 150 calories for eight ounces of buttermilk made from whole milk with a fat content of at least 3.25 percent.

# YOGURT

The discovery of yogurt seems locked in the annals of history. People in the Middle East discovered yogurt when they left milk in a warm place. Although the beginnings of yogurt seem sketchy, there is little doubt that yogurt has been around for many centuries. Now yogurt is known in almost every part of the world. However, it met with limited success in the United States until flavors and fruits were added. Today three main types are produced.

1. Flavored, containing no fruit, vanilla, coffee, lemon and so forth.

2. Flavored, containing fruit; Sunday-style fruit at the bottom of the container and plain or flavored yogurt on top, usually stirred or inverted onto a dish before eating. Blended style, Swiss, French, and so forth, fruit blended throughout plain or flavored yogurt.

3. Unflavored, the natural or basic style of ancient times.

From ancient times to the present, yogurt has been made by fermentation. In this process, desirable bacteria convert lactose, milk sugar, to lactic acid. The acid thickens the milk and creates the tangy aroma and flavor characteristic of yogurt.

The earliest method of making yogurt was simply to provide the warmth that encouraged fermentation of the bacteria naturally present in milk. Modern manufacturing differs greatly from the old method. Processing is continuous and automated. Standards are high and quality is rigidly controlled.

Federal standards of identity define and regulate the ingredients of yogurt.

Yogurts are mixtures of milk, skim milk and/or cream and lactobacillus bulgaricus and Streptococcus thermophilus bacteria. Each type of yogurt must contain at least 8.25 percent nonfat milk solids and 0.9 percent acid.

The difference among yogurts is the amount of milkfat. Yogurt, sometimes referred to as whole milk yogurt, must contain at least 3.25 percent milkfat. Lowfat yogurts contain between 0.5 and 2 percent milkfat. Nonfat yogurt must contain less than 0.5 percent milkfat. Responding to Americans' weight consciousness, most of the yogurt in supermarkets is a lowfat product. Optional ingredients permitted in yogurts are: other dairy products, such as nonfat dry milk to increase firmness; sweeteners, such as sugar and honey; flavorings, as vanilla or fruit-flavored extracts, fruit preserves and purees; colorings; and stabilizers, such as gelatin for firmer texture.

# ICE CREAM

For many Americans, young and old, the words ice cream have pleasant and nostalgic connotations. They remind us of good food and the good times. The popularity of this frosty family of foods is due not only to its ready-to-eat convenience, its widespread availability and its nutritive value, but also to its appealing forms, colors, and flavors. Choices abound; from bricks, cones, bars, and sandwiches to delicate party molds, from creamy ivory to rainbow hued swirls to dusky chocolate, from avocado flavor to almond. Though they come in many variations, ice cream and a group of similarly frozen foods are made in much the same way and have many of the same ingredients. These foods include:

**ICE CREAM, FROZEN CUSTARD, FRENCH CUSTARD ICE CREAM.** Highest in milkfat and milk solids. Ice cream and frozen custard are made similarly. Ice cream may contain egg yolk solids. If they are in excess of 1.4% by weight, the product is called frozen custard, French ice cream or French custard ice cream.

**ICE MILK** Less milkfat, protein and total food solids distinguish ice milk from ice cream. Ice milk usually has more sugar than ice cream.

**SOFT ICE MILK OR ICE CREAM** These products are soft and ready to eat when drawn from the freezer. About three-fourths of the soft serve products are ice milks.

**FROZEN YOGURT** So new that no federal standards exist for it. Frozen yogurt has less milkfat and higher acidity than ice cream and less sugar than sherbet. The distinctive characteristic of frozen yogurt is whether soft or hard frozen is the culturing of the pasteurized mix with selected strains of bacteria. The bacteria convert some of the milk sugar, lactose, to lactic acid which produces the characteristic flavor.

**SHERBET** Sherbet is low in both milkfat and milk solids. It has more sugar than ice cream. The tartness of fruit sherbet comes from added fruit and fruit acid. Nonfruit sherbet is flavored with such ingredients as spices, coffee or chocolate.

**WATER ICES** Water ices are nondairy frozen foods. They contain neither milk ingredients nor egg yolk. Ices are made just as sherbet. Water ices are high in water and sugar and have a tart flavor.

In the fourth century B.C. Alexander the Great enjoyed sipping ice-chilled drinks. Marco Polo brought already ancient recipes for flavored ices to Italy from the Orient in the thirteenth century A.D. Ice cream may have been first made by freezing milk and honey. In the eighteenth century George Washington's household inventory listed "two pewter ice cream pots." Ice cream was made by jiggling the pot of ingredients inside the larger pot of ice and salt and beating the creamy mixture fiercely until it froze. This pot freezer method lasted until 1846 when an American woman, Nancy Johnson invented the hand crank freezer.

Commercial ice cream production in the United States was started by a Baltimore dairy owner, Jacob Fussell, in 1851. The advent of electricity in the early 1900s led to the development of mechanical refrigeration and freezers.

Now, ice cream is manufactured in modern, scientifically engineered, sanitary facilities. Rigid government standards assure consumers of the food's purity, healthfulness and quality.

# ICE CREAM

**Table I**
**Standards for Frozen Desserts**

| Product | Milkfat | Vegetable or animal fat | Nonfat milk solids | Total milk solids | Egg yolk solids | Acidity | Product weight | Total food solids |
|---|---|---|---|---|---|---|---|---|
| | Minimum percentage based on final product weight | | | | | | Pounds per gallon | |
| Ice cream | 10* | | 10 | 20 | (1.4 max) | | 4.5 | 1.6 |
| Bulky flavored | 8 | | 8 | 16 | | | 4.5 | 1.6 |
| Frozen custard | 10* | | 10 | 20 | 1.4 | | 4.5 | 1.6 |
| Bulky flavored | 8 | | 8 | 16 | 1.12 | | 4.5 | 1.6 |
| Ice milk | 2* | | 9 | 11 | | | 4.5 | 1.3 |
| Bulky flavored | 2 | | 7 | 11 | | | 4.5 | 1.3 |
| Sherbet | 1 | | 1 | 2 | | | 6 | |
| Fruit flavored | 1 | | 1 | 2 | | 0.35 | 6 | |
| Water ice | — | | | | | 0.35 | 6 | |
| Mellorine** | — | 6 | *** | | | | 4.5 | 1.6 |
| Bulky flavored | | 4.8 | | | | | 4.5 | 1.6 |

\* For richer products, when the milkfat is increased above the minimum, nonfat milk solids may be decreased, within defined limits.

\*\* 40 IU Vitamin A per gram of fat added

\*\*\* Sufficient nonfat milk solids added to provide 2.7 percent protein with a protein efficiency ratio not less than that of whole milk

**Table II**
**Calories and Nutrient Values***

| Dessert | Serving | Calories | Protein | Calcium | Riboflavin |
|---|---|---|---|---|---|
| | | | Percentage of U.S. RDA | | |
| Vanilla ice cream | ½ cup | 130 | 7.5 | 10 | 7.5 |
| Ice milk (hardened) | ½ cup | 100 | 7.5 | 10 | 7.5 |
| Ice milk (soft-serve) | ½ cup | 135 | 10 | 12.5 | 12.5 |
| Sherbet | ½ cup | 130 | 1 | 2 | 2 |
| Water ices | ½ cup | 125 | 1 | † | † |
| Brownie with nuts | 1 brownie (20 g) | 100 | 2 | † | 2 |
| Plain cake with chocolate icing | 1 piece (123 g) | 450 | 8 | 8 | 6 |
| Apple pie | 4¾-inch sector (158 g) | 400 | 6 | 2 | 2 |

\*Source  USDA Agriculture Information Bulletin No. 382  Nutrition Labeling—Tools for Its Use  1975.

†None or less than 1 percent

# CHEESE

Cheese was shown on stone tablets as early as 4000 B.C. Legend tells that the first cheese was made accidentally by a shepherd carrying milk in a pouch made from a sheep's stomach. Rennet from the lining of the pouch combined with the sun's heat caused the milk to separate into curds, solid portion and whey, liquid. From Asia to Europe to the United States, the cheesemaker's art has constantly improved. Cheesemaking evolved from a farm to a business with the first cheese factory at Rome, New York in 1851. Many cheeses were named from their places of origin, Cheddar, England, Muenster, Germany; Swiss and American. Today, virtually all foreign types of cheese are made in the United States with American cheesemakers among the finest in the world. Approximately $1/5$ of U.S. milk produced goes for cheese.

Making natural cheese is an art. It consists of removing most of the milk solids from the milk by coagulating with rennet or a bacterial culture or both, and separating the curd from the whey by heating, draining, and pressing. Most cheeses in this country are made from whole milk. Both milk and cream are used for certain types of cheeses and for other types, skim milk, whey and mixtures of these are used. The distinctive flavor, body and texture characteristics of the various cheeses on the market are determined by:

1. The kind of milk used.

2. The methods used for coagulating the milk; cutting, cooking and forming the curd.

3. Type of culture used.

4. Salting.

5. Ripening conditions.

After cheese has been formed into its characteristic shape, it is coated with wax or wrapped and aged. Cheese may be classified as: very hard, hard, semi-soft or soft.

TERMS

CURED Flavor and texture characteristics are determined by the time allowed enzymes and micro-organisms to develop. Mild, medium or sharp indicate ripening (time).

NATURAL CHEESE is the solid or casein portion of milk (curds) separated from the liquid portion (whey). Coagulation is caused and controlled by the action of rennet or lactic acid or both.

> Mild Cheese is cured two to three months; has little flavor development; softness and open texture.

> Medium Aged Cheese is cured up to six months; mellow bodied, smooth textured with characteristic nutty flavor of aged cheese more apparent.

> Sharp or Aged Cheese is cured over six months; has richer flavor than cheeses cured less time; is preferred for cooking because it melts easily and blends well with other ingredients.

PASTEURIZED PROCESS CHEESE is a blend of fresh and aged natural cheeses which have been shredded, mixed with an emulsifier and heated. Pasteurization stops the ripening, allows the cheeses to blend and develop a uniform flavor, body and texture. Blend may consist of 1 or more varieties of natural cheese and may contain vegetable or meat.

PASTEURIZED PROCESS CHEESE FOOD is prepared like Process Cheese, except it contains less cheese and more nonfat milk or whey solids and water. It has a slightly higher moisture and lower milk fat content than Process Cheese.

PASTEURIZED PROCESS CHEESE SPREAD is made like Process

Cheese Food, but contains slightly higher moisture and has lower milk fat content.

UNRIPENED, FRESH CHEESE is not cured, so is normallly quite bland and has a mild flavor, i.e., COTTAGE CHEESE, made from pasteurized skimmed milk has a mild flavor, moist texture and large or small curds; CREAM CHEESE is a mixture of whole cow's milk and cream which is pasteurized and coagulated by a lactic acid starter, has a mild flavor and a buttery texture. NEUFCHATEL CHEESE is similar to cream cheese but contains less fat and more moisture.

NUTRITIONAL VALUE OF CHEESE Cheese, in its concentrated form, contains many of milk's nutrients — especially the complete protein, casein, calcium, phosphorous and vitamin A. It is one of nature's most versatile foods, nutritious and readily digested. •To make 1 pound of Cheddar cheese it takes approximately 10 lbs. of milk or almost 5 quarts. •Nearly $1/2$ of the total solids of whole milk remain in the cheese curd and approximately $4/5$ of the milk's original protein. •Butter fat content is about 20-30% of its total weight.

•One and one-half oz. of Cheddar contains about the same calcium as 1 cup of whole, skim or buttermilk.

•Three oz. of Cheddar have about the same protein as 3 large eggs or 3 oz. meat patty.

In a well-balanced diet, cheese is almost completely digested and doesn't interfere with bodily functions.

CALORIES IN 1 OUNCE OF FAMILIAR CHEESES:

Cheddar: 113; Cream: 106; Blue: 104; Swiss: 105; Parmesan: 111; American Pasteurized Process Cheese: 105; American Pasteurized Process Cheese Spread: 81.

## COOKING AND SERVING SUGGESTIONS

When you cook cheese, add it to other ingredients in small pieces so that it will blend evenly and cook in a shorter time. Keep the heat LOW, with just enough heat to melt and blend the cheese. High heat or long cooking makes cheese tough and stringy. Add Cheese as the last ingredient when making a sauce and heat just until melted. • When topping a casserole, do not add cheese until the last few minutes of cooking.

COOKING EQUIVALENTS:

> 4 oz. Cheddar or Swiss yield 1 cup shredded cheese •4 oz. Blue yield 1 cup crumbled cheese •4 oz. Parmesan or Romano yield 1 cup grated cheese.

To slice cheese, use a cheese cutter for slices of uniform thickness. Heavy thread or thin wire can also be used, especially when cutting Blue cheese.

SERVING SUGGESTIONS FOR CHEESE: snacks, dips, appetizers, desserts, sandwiches, sauces for vegetables, toppings for fruit, seasonings, casseroles, salads, etc. • Cheese tastes best at room temperature, except for cottage cheese and cream cheeses, so take the portion you need out of the refrigerator 30 to 60 minutes before serving time. However, cheese can be shredded more easily when it's chilled.

CHEESE STORAGE

REFRIGERATOR:

Cured cheeses keep well in the refrigerator for several weeks. Long holding will result in some additional curing and a sharper flavor.

Cheese should not be kept outside of the refrigerator for extended periods. Exposed to air and heat, cheese dries out, "oils-off" and might become moldy. Proper storage at 40°F. preserves the original flavor and appearance and insures full use of the cheese without waste. Original wrapping, waxed paper, transparent wrap, aluminum foil and plastic bags are all satisfactory wrapping for refrigerator storage. Cover tightly to exclude air if large pieces are to be stored for any extended period of time.

Natural cheeses when improperly wrapped or under moist conditions may develop mold spots. This harmless mold can be scraped off and no change in flavor will be noticed unless the mold had penetrated deeply into cracks in the cheese. In such cases the molding portion should be discarded. With Blue cheese, however, its unique flavor comes from the molding process. Cheese that has dried out may be grated and kept in a covered container in the refrigerator. Pasteurized Process Cheese should be refrigerated after opening to prevent drying and unattractive "oiling-off."

FREEZER: Most natural cheese can be successfully frozen for 6 weeks to 2 months if unopened in the original package. Neufchatel does not freeze well. Partially used packages of natural cheese should be rewrapped and kept frozen only for 6 weeks; Pasteurized Process Cheeses can be frozen for 4 months. When freezing cheese, have pieces of 1 pound or less, not over 1-inch thick and wrap them tightly (in) moisture-vapor-proof wrap to help prevent loss of moisture and subsequent drying. After removing cheese from the freezer, let it thaw in the refrigerator for 24 hours and serve it soon after thawing.

# CHEESE

Name, Origin, Characteristics, and Mode of Serving of Commonly Used Varieties of Cheese[a]

| Name | Origin | Consistency and Texture | Color and Shape |
|---|---|---|---|
| American pasteurized process[b] | United States | Semisoft to soft; smooth, plastic body | Light yellow to orange; square slices |
| Asiago, fresh, medium, old | Italy | Semisoft (fresh), medium, or hard (old); tiny gas holes or eyes | Light yellow; may be coated with paraffin, clear or colored black or brown; round and flat |
| Bel paese | Italy | Soft; smooth, waxy body | Slightly gray surface, creamy yellow interior; small wheels |
| Blue[b], Bleu | France | Semisoft; visible veins of mold on white cheese, pasty, sometimes crumbly | White, marbled with blue-green mold; cylindrical |
| Breakfast, Frühstück | Germany | Soft; smooth, waxy body | Cylindrical, 2½ to 3 inches diameter |
| Brick[b] | United States | Semisoft; smooth, open texture; numerous round and irregular-shaped eyes | Light yellow to orange; brick-shaped |
| Brie[b] | France | Soft, thin edible crust, creamy interior | White crust, creamy yellow interior; large, medium, and small wheels |
| Caciocavallo | Italy | Hard, firm body; stringy texture | Light tan surface, interior; molded into distinctive shapes, typically spindle-shaped or oblong |
| Camembert[b] | France | Soft, almost fluid in consistency; thin edible crust, creamy interior | Gray-white crust, creamy yellow interior; small wheels |
| Cheddar[b] | England | Hard; smooth, firm body, can be crumbly | Nearly white to orange; varied shapes and styles |
| Colby[b] | United States | Hard but softer and more open in texture than Cheddar | White to light yellow, orange; cylindrical |
| Cottage, Dutch, Farmers, Pot[b] | Uncertain | Soft; moist, delicate, large or small curds | White; packaged in cuplike containers |
| Cream[b] | United States | Soft; smooth, buttery | White; foil-wrapped in rectangular portions |
| Edam[b] | Holland | Semisoft to hard; firm, crumbly body; small eyes | Creamy yellow with natural or red paraffin coat; flattened ball or loaf shape, about 4 pounds |
| Feta[b] | Greece | Soft, flaky, similar to very dry, high-acid cottage cheese | White |
| Gammelost | Norway | Semisoft | Brownish rind, brown-yellow interior with a blue-green tint; round and flat |
| Gjetost[b] | Norway | Hard; buttery | Golden brown; cubical and rectangular |
| Gorgonzola | Italy | Semisoft, less moist than blue | Light tan surface, light yellow interior, marbled with blue-green mold; cylindrical and flat loaves |
| Gouda[b] | Holland | Hard, but softer than cheddar; more open mealy body like edam, small eyes | Creamy yellow with or without red wax coat; oval or flattened sphere of about 10 to 12 pounds |
| Gruyere[b] | Switzerland | Hard, tiny gas holes or eyes | Light yellow; flat wheels |
| Limburger[b] | Belgium | Soft; smooth, waxy body | Creamy white interior, brownish exterior; rectangular |
| Monterey, Jack[b] | United States | Semisoft (whole milk), hard (lowfat or skim milk); smooth texture with small openings throughout | Creamy, white; round or rectangular |
| Mozzarella[b] | Italy | Semisoft; plastic | Creamy white; rectangular and spherical, may be molded into various shapes |
| Muenster[b] | Germany | Semisoft; smooth, waxy body, numerous small mechanical openings | Yellow, tan, or white surface, creamy white interior; cylindrical and flat or loaf shaped, small wheels and blocks |
| Neufchatel[b] | France | Soft; smooth, creamy | White; foil-wrapped in rectangular retail portions |
| Parmesan, Reggiano[b] | Italy | Very hard (grating), granular, hard brittle rind | Light yellow with brown or black coating; cylindrical |
| Port du salut, Oka[b] | Trappist Monasteries | Semisoft; smooth, buttery | Russet surface, creamy white interior; small wheels, cylindrical flat |
| Primost | Norway | Semisoft | Light brown; cubical and cylindrical |
| Provolone[b] | Italy | Hard, stringy texture; cuts without crumbling, plastic | Light golden-yellow to golden-brown, shiny surface bound with cord; yellow-white interior. Made in various shapes (pear, sausage, salami) and sizes |
| Queso blanco, White cheese | Latin America | Soft, dry and granular if not pressed; hard, open or crumbly if pressed | White; various shapes and sizes |
| Ricotta[b] | Italy | Soft; moist and grainy, or dry | White; packaged fresh in paper, plastic, or metal containers, or dry for grating |
| Romano[b] | Italy | Very hard, granular interior, hard brittle rind | Round with flat sides various sizes |
| Roquefort[b] | France | Semisoft, pasty and sometimes crumbly | White, marbled with blue-green mold; cylindrical |
| Sap Sago | Switzerland | Very hard (grating), granular frequently dried | Light green, small, cone-shaped |
| Schloss, Castle cheese | Germany, Northern Austria | Soft, small, ripened | Molded in small rectangular blocks 1½" square by 4" long |
| Stirred Curd, Granular | United States | Semisoft to hard | Varied shapes and styles |
| Stilton | England | Semisoft-hard; open flaky texture, more crumbly than blue | White, marbled with blue-green mold; cylindrical |
| Swiss, Emmentaler[b] | Switzerland | Hard; smooth with large gas holes or eyes | Pale yellow, shiny; rindless rectangular blocks and large wheels with rind |
| Washed Curd | United States | Semisoft to hard | Varied shapes and styles |

# CHEESE

| Flavor | Basic Ingredient | Normal ripening period[c] | Mode of Serving |
|---|---|---|---|
| Mild | Cheddar, washed, colby, or granulated (stirred curd) or mixture of two or more | Unripened after cheese(s) heated to blend | In sandwiches; on crackers |
| Piquant, sharp in aged cheese | Cow's milk, whole or lowfat | 60 days minimum for fresh (semisoft), 6 months minimum for medium, 12 months minimum for old (grating) | Table cheese (slicing cheese) when not aged; as seasoning (grated) when aged |
| Mild to moderately robust | Cow's milk, whole | 6-8 weeks | As such (dessert); on crackers; in sandwiches; with fruit |
| Piquant, tangy, spicy, peppery | Cow's milk, whole or goat's milk | 60 days minimum; 3-4 months usually; 9 months for more flavor | As such (dessert); in dips, cooked foods; salads and dressings |
| Strong, aromatic | Cow's milk, whole or lowfat | Little or none (either) | As such (dessert); on crackers; in sandwiches |
| Mild but pungent and sweet | Cow's milk, whole | 2-3 months | As such; in sandwiches, salads Slices well without crumbling |
| Mild to pungent | Cow's milk, whole, lowfat, or skim | 4-8 weeks | As such (dessert) |
| Sharp, similar to provolone | Sheep's, goat's or cow's milk (whole or lowfat) or mixtures of these | 3 months minimum for table use, 12 months or longer for grating | As such; as seasoning (grated) when aged |
| Mild to pungent | Cow's milk, whole | 4-5 weeks | |
| Mild to sharp | Cow's milk, whole | 60 days minimum; 3-6 months usually; 12 or longer for sharp flavor | As such; in sandwiches, cooked foods |
| Mild to mellow | Cow's milk, whole | 1-3 months | As such; in sandwiches, cooked foods |
| Mild, slightly acid, flavoring may be added | Cow's milk, skim; cream dressing may be added | Unripened | As such; in salads, dips, cooked foods |
| Mild, slightly acid, flavoring may be added | Cream and cow's milk, whole | Unripened | As such; in salads, in sandwiches, on crackers |
| Mild, sometimes salty | Cow's milk, lowfat | 2 months or longer | As such; on crackers; with fresh fruit |
| Salty | Cow's, sheep's, or goat's milk | 4-5 days to 1 month | As such; in cooked foods |
| Sharp, aromatic | Cow's milk, skim | 4 weeks or longer | As such |
| Sweet, caramel | Whey from goat's milk | Unripened | As such; on crackers |
| Piquant, spicy, similar to blue | Cow's milk, whole or goat's milk, or mixtures of these | 3 months minimum, frequently 6 months to 1 year | As such (dessert) |
| Mild, nutlike, similar to edam | Cow's milk, lowfat but more milkfat than edam | 2-6 months | As such; on crackers, with fresh fruit; in cooked dishes |
| Mild, sweet | Cow's milk, whole | 3 months minimum | As such (dessert); fondue |
| Strong, robust, highly aromatic | Cow's milk, whole or lowfat | 1-2 months | In sandwiches; on crackers |
| Mild to mellow | Cow's milk, whole, lowfat or skim | 3-6 weeks for table use, 6 months minimum for grating | As such; in sandwiches, grating cheese if made from lowfat or skim milk |
| Mild, delicate | Cow's milk, whole or lowfat; may be acidified with vinegar | Unripened to 2 months | Generally used in cooking, pizza; as such |
| Mild to mellow, between brick and limburger | Cow's milk, whole | 2-8 weeks | As such; in sandwiches |
| Mild | Cow's milk, whole or skim, or a mixture of milk and cream | 3-4 weeks or unripened | As such; in sandwiches, dips, salads |
| Sharp, piquant | Cow's milk, lowfat | 10 months minimum | As such; as grated cheese on salads and soups |
| Mellow or mild to robust. Similar to gouda | Cow's milk, whole or lowfat | 6-8 weeks | As such (dessert); with fresh fruit; on crackers |
| Mild, sweet, caramel | Whey with added buttermilk, whole milk or cream | Unripened | As such; in cooked foods |
| Bland acid flavor to sharp and piquant, usually smoked | Cow's milk, whole | 6-14 months | As such (dessert) after it has ripened for 6 to 9 months; grating cheese when aged |
| Salty, strong, may be smoked | Cow's milk, whole, lowfat or skim or whole milk with cream or skim milk | Eaten within 2 days to 2 months or more; generally unripened if pressed | As such or later grated |
| Bland but semisweet | Whey and whole or skim milk or whole and lowfat milk | Unripened | As such; in cooked foods; as seasoning (grated) when dried |
| Sharp, piquant if aged | Cow's (usually lowfat), goat's milk, or mixtures of these | 5 months minimum; usually 5-8 months for table cheese; 12 months minimum for grating cheese | As such; grated and used as a seasoning |
| Sharp, spicy (pepper), piquant | Sheep's milk | 2 months minimum; usually 2-5 months or longer | As such (dessert); in salads; on crackers |
| Sharp, pungent, flavored with leaves; sweet | Cow's milk, skim, slightly soured with buttermilk and whey | 5 months minimum | As such; as seasoning (grated) |
| Similar to, but milder than, limburger | Cow's milk, whole or lowfat and/or casein | Less than 1 month; less intensively than limburger | In sandwiches; on crackers |
| Similar to mild cheddar | Cow's milk | 1-3 months | Usually used to make pasteurized process cheese |
| Piquant, spicy, but milder than roquefort | Cow's milk, whole with added cream | 4-6 months or longer | As such (dessert); in cooked foods |
| Mild, sweet, nutty | Cow's milk, lowfat | 2 months minimum, 2-9 months usually | As such; in sandwiches; with salads; fondue |
| Similar to mild cheddar | Cow's milk | 1-3 months | Usually used to make pasteurized process cheese |

# CHEESE RABBIT ____

**Makes 8 servings**

- 1 pound shredded sharp processed American cheese
- 1 cup milk
- 1 teaspoon dry mustard
- 2 teaspoons Worcestershire sauce
- 1/4 teaspoon cayenne
- 1 egg slightly beaten
- 8 slices toast
- 1 pound bacon, fried, drained

In the top of a double boiler over simmering water and medium heat, cook cheese and milk until cheese has melted and a smooth sauce is formed. Blend in remaining ingredients except toast and bacon. Continue cooking until mixture thickens and is smooth. Arrange one slice of toast on each plate, pour cheese sauce over toast, top with strips of bacon.

# FONDUE FROM PIEDMONT

**Makes 6 servings**

     2 cloves garlic, minced
     1 pound Bel Paese cheese, cut into cubes
    3/4 cup dry white wine
     1 tablespoon butter
    1/2 teaspoon nutmeg, salt
     1 tablespoon green peppercorns
     1 Italian bread, tear into 1-inch pieces

Combine all ingredients except bread pieces in the top of a double boiler over simmering water. Stir often, cook until the mixture is smooth and the cheese has melted. If the mixture seems too thick add more wine, by the tablespoonful. Serve fondue in a serving dish over a warming candle. Have chunks of the Italian bread available with fondue forks. Vegetable crudities are a pleasant alternative to using bread.

# SWISS CHEESE FONDUE

**Makes 8 servings**

>     1 **pound Swiss cheese, diced**
>     2 **tablespoons all-purpose flour**
>     3 **cloves garlic, peeled, minced**
>     2 **cups dry white wine**
>  ¹/₄ **teaspoon ground pepper**
>     1 **French bread, tear into bite-sized pieces**
>       **Fondue forks**

In a fondue pot or in a heavy, medium saucepan combine Swiss cheese and flour as it heats, over medium-low heat. Blend in garlic, white wine, and pepper, stirring often, do not bring to a boil. When cheese melts it is ready to serve. Spear a bread cube onto a fondue fork and dip it into the cheese fondue until it is coated with cheese.

# CHOCOLATE CHEESE CAKE _____

**Crust**

- 2 cups chocolate cookie crumbs
- 6 tablespoons melted butter
- 1/2 teaspoon cinnamon

**Filling**

- 3 packages, 8 ounces each, cream cheese, room temperature
- 1/2 pound creamed cottage cheese
- 1 1/2 cups sugar
- 2 teaspoons vanilla
- 1/4 teaspoon salt
- 6 eggs
- 12 ounces melted semi-sweet chocolate pieces, cool
- 1 cup heavy cream, whipped
- Chocolate curls, optional, for garnish

**Crust**

Combine crumbs, butter and cinnamon in a large mixing bowl. Press mixture into the bottom and up the sides of a 9-inch springform pan, chill.

**Filling**

Combine cream cheese, cottage cheese, sugar, vanilla, salt in the large bowl of an electric mixer. Beat for 6 minutes. Add melted chocolate; continue beating until mixture is combined. Fold in whipped cream. Mound filling into prepared cookie crust. Cover with plastic wrap. Freeze until firm. Allow cheesecake to stand at room temperature for 1 hour before serving. Remove rim, garnish with chocolate curls.

# MARBLED CHEESECAKE

**Makes 8-10 servings**

**Crust**

1½ **cups crushed vanilla wafers**
¼ **cup melted butter**

**Filling**

4 **packages, 8 ounces each, cream cheese, room temperature**
1¾ **cups sugar**
5 **eggs**
1 **cup heavy cream**
1 **tablespoon vanilla**
6 **tablespoons melted butter**
5 **tablespoons all-purpose flour**
2 **cups commercial sour cream**
2 **ounces melted semi-sweet chocolate**

**Crust**
The Marbled Cheesecake should be prepared the day before it is needed. Combine crushed wafers and butter in a medium mixing bowl. Press into the bottom and up the sides of a 9-inch springform pan. Set aside. Prepare filling.

**Filling**
In the large bowl of an electric mixer beat cream cheese until

light and fluffy, about 6-8 minutes. Gradually beat in sugar. Beat in eggs, cream, vanilla and butter. Continue beating until mixture is smooth. In a separate bowl, sprinkle flour over sour cream, stir well. Add sour cream mixture to cheese batter. Beat well. Remove 2 cups of batter to a medium mixing bowl. Stir in cooled chocolate. Pour remaining vanilla batter into prepared crust. Drop chocolate with a tablespoon over vanilla filling. Marble chocolate and vanilla together with a knife. Bake cheesecake at 325°F. for 1 hour and 10 minutes. Shut off heat, do not open oven door for 2 hours, allowing cake to cool slowly. Remove from oven. Leave cheesecake at room temperature until cool. Refrigerate for 24 hours.

# CHEESE BALL WITH PINEAPPLE _____

2 packages cream cheese, room temperature, cut into
  cubes
1 small onion, minced
1 small green bell pepper, seeded, chopped
1 cup crushed pineapple, drained
2 cups chopped walnuts

In a large mixing bowl, combine all ingredients except 1 cup
chopped walnuts. Shape into a ball, cover with waxed paper,
chill. When cheese ball is firm, roll in remaining nuts. Serve
with crackers and sliced fruit.

# STUFFED CELERY ___

1 package, 3 ounces, cream cheese, room temperature
$1/2$ teaspoon Worcestershire sauce
$1/2$ teaspoon freshly squeezed lemon juice
4 tablespoons pistachio nuts, minced
2 dozen long stalks celery, peel strings, trim

In a medium mixing bowl combine all ingredients except pistachio nuts and celery. Fill each piece of celery with cheese mixture. Sprinkle with pistachio nuts.

# CHEESE COOKIES

**Makes 12 servings**

### Crust

   1/4 cup butter
   1/4 cup firmly packed light brown sugar
     1 cup all-purpose flour
   1/2 cup shredded coconut

### Filling

   1/2 cup sugar
     1 package, 8 ounces, cream cheese, room temperature
     1 egg
     2 tablespoons milk
     1 tablespoon freshly squeezed lemon juice
   1/2 teaspoon vanilla

In a large bowl cream butter with brown sugar. Blend in flour and coconut making a crumb mixture. Press 1/2 of crumb mixture into bottom of a greased 8-inch square baking pan, reserve remaining crumbs for topping. Bake at 350°F. for 10-12 minutes, cool. In a large mixing bowl blend sugar and cream cheese until smooth. Mix in egg, combine. Add milk, lemon juice and vanilla, beat well. Spread cheese mixture over crumb mixture. Sprinkle with reserved crumbs. Bake at 350°F. for 25 minutes. Cool, cut into squares, refrigerate.

# CURRY-WALNUT CHEESE MOLD

**Makes 8 servings**

 1 package, 8 ounces, cream cheese, room temperature
 1/2 pound shredded Swiss cheese
 3 tablespoons cream or milk
 1 1/2 teaspoons curry powder
 1/2 teaspoon Worcestershire sauce
 1 cup chopped walnuts
 3 tablespoons minced parsley

Place cream cheese, Swiss cheese, cream, curry powder, Worcestershire sauce into a large mixing bowl. Combine all ingredients until well blended. Mix in 3/4 cup of the walnuts. Spoon mixture into a lightly oiled mold or bowl. Cover with a double layer of aluminum foil. Chill overnight. Unmold onto a serving dish. Sprinkle remaining walnuts and parsley over mold, pressing into place. Serve with sliced apples and grapes.

# COUNTRY STYLE HERB CHEESE

**Makes 8 servings**

  1 **pound small curd creamed cottage cheese**
  5 **tablespoons commercial sour cream**
12 **ounces cream cheese, room temperature, cubed**
  4 **medium shallots, minced**
$1/2$ **teaspoon salt, white pepper, tarragon, basil**
$1/2$ **cup fresh chopped parsley**

Drain cottage cheese, place in a large mixing bowl. Beat until smooth. Add sour cream, cream cheese, shallots, salt, pepper, tarragon and basil. Beat until combined and mixture is smooth. Gather cheese together into a ball shape with wet hands. Place in triple layer of cheesecloth. Place suspended, so that excess moisture is able to drain in a colander with a bowl underneath. Refrigerate for 24 hours. Unmold from cheesecloth. Place parsley on a plate, roll cheese in parsley. Serve with thin slices of rye bread.

# FRESH STRAWBERRY CUSTARD ICE CREAM

**Makes 6 servings**

    4 egg yolks, slightly beaten
    2 cups milk
1 1/4 cups sugar
  1/8 teaspoon salt
    4 cups heavy cream
    1 tablespoon vanilla
1 1/2 cups strawberries, hulled, crushed
    2 teaspoons freshly squeezed lime juice

In the top of a double boiler over simmering water combine egg yolks, milk, sugar and salt. Cook over medium heat, stirring occasionally until custard thickens and it coats a spoon; cool. Blend in heavy cream and vanilla. Pour mixture into ice cream maker and use according to manufacturers' directions. Blend in crushed strawberries and lime juice; combine. Place in covered container, freeze until ready to serve.

# INDIVIDUAL GRAND MARNIER SOUFFLES

**Makes 6 servings**

    4 egg yolks
  1/2 cup sugar
    1 tablespoon orange zest
    3 tablespoons Grand Marnier liqueur
    1 cup heavy cream

In a medium mixing bowl beat egg yolks and sugar together until light and fluffy. Blend in orange zest and Grand Marnier, continue beating for 2 minutes, reserve. In a separate bowl beat cream until firm peaks form. Fold in orange mixture. Clip a double layer, buttered and sugared aluminum foil collar around 6 souffle ramekins. Mound filling into ramekins, freeze. Place ramekins at room temperature 10 minutes before serving.

# BISCUIT TORTONI __

**Makes 10 servings**

    1 cup ground almond macaroons
    1/4 cup dry sherry
    1 cup half-and-half
    1/2 cup sugar
    1 cup heavy cream, whipped
    10 cupcake papers
    1/2 cup blanched, ground almonds
    10 candied cherries

In a medium bowl, soak macaroons in sherry for 20 minutes. Add half-and-half and sugar, combine. Place covered bowl in freezer until the mixture begins to harden. Remove from freezer, fold in whipped cream. Mound into cupcake papers. Place on a cookie sheet, freeze. Leave at room temperature for 10 minutes before serving. When about to serve sprinkle with ground almonds and place cherry on top.

# MANDARIN ORANGE ICE ————

**Makes 5-6 servings**

2 tablespoons orange zest
1 cup sugar
1 cup water
2 cups canned mandarin oranges, drained, pureed
3 tablespoons freshly squeezed lemon juice

In a small saucepan bring orange zest, sugar and water to a boil, stirring until the sugar is dissolved. Boil for 5 minutes, stirring often; cool. Stir in mandarin oranges and lemon juice. Pour mixture into a covered container, freeze. Place in a deep bowl, soften and stir, refreeze in covered container until ready to serve.

# BANANA ICE CREAM

**Makes 8 servings**

    2 cups milk, scald, cool
    2 tablespoons cornstarch
1½ cups sugar
    2 eggs, separated
    1 teaspoon vanilla
    1 quart heavy cream
    2 cups banana pulp
    5 tablespoons freshly squeezed lemon juice

In a medium heavy saucepan combine milk, whisk in cornstarch, sugar. Cook over medium heat for 8 minutes, stirring occasionally. Stir in well beaten egg yolks, continue cooking until custard thickens, cool. Mix in cream and stiffly beaten egg yolks and vanilla. In a separate bowl combine banana pulp with lemon juice. Process cream mixture in an ice cream maker according to manufacturers' directions. When partially chilled blend in banana mixture, continue until ice cream is finished. Place in a covered container and freeze until ready to serve.

# SANDWICH COOKIE ICE CREAM

**Makes 5-6 servings**

    4 cups light cream or half-and-half
    1 cup sugar
1½ teaspoons vanilla
    1 cup chocolate sandwich cookies, crumbled

In a large deep bowl blend cream and sugar, 3 minutes. Pour mixture into an ice cream maker and process according to manufacturers' directions. Fold in crumbled sandwich cookies. Place ice cream in a covered container, freeze until ready to serve.

# PINEAPPLE ITALIAN ICE

**Makes 4 servings**

    2 cups water
1¼ cups sugar
    1 cup pineapple juice
½ cup crushed pineapple, drained

In a small saucepan bring water and sugar to a boil, stirring until the sugar is dissolved. Boil for 5 minutes, stirring often; cool. Stir in juice and crushed pineapple. Pour mixture into a covered container, freeze 3 hours, stirring twice before it freezes. Scrape mixture into paper cups or dessert cups.

# VANILLA
# ICE CREAM ROLL ___

**Makes 8 servings**

      5  **eggs, separated**
    ¹/₂  **cup sugar**
      1  **teaspoon vanilla**
      1  **cup cake flour**
    ¹/₂  **cup sugar**
      1  **quart vanilla ice cream**

In a large mixing bowl, beat egg whites until stiff peaks form, set aside. In a separate bowl, beat egg yolks, sugar and vanilla until light and fluffy. Sprinkle flour over egg yolk mixture, incorporate. Fold in egg whites. Spread over a jelly-roll pan, 15¹/₄ x 10¹/₂ x 1 inches, lined with buttered and floured wax paper. Bake at 350°F. for 18-20 minutes, or until cake tests done. Remove cake from oven, unmold onto a clean, sugared dish towel, roll jelly-roll style. Unroll and spread with softened ice cream, reroll. Cover ice cream roll with aluminum foil and freeze until ready to serve. Serve with a chocolate or strawberry sauce.

# BREADS

# —Breads—

## General Yeast Bread Information

When combining yeast directly with liquid, the temperature should be from 105°F. to 115° F. If the yeast is mixed with the dry ingredients before the liquid is added, the liquid should be warmer, 120° F. to 130° F. Usually a little sugar is added to give the yeast something on which to feed.

Flour is usually added and incorporated. Knead dough on a lightly floured board so as not to add too much extra flour. Form dough into a ball. To knead, fold edges of the dough toward center. Push dough down and away from you with heels of both hands. Give dough a quarter turn. Repeat folding, pushing and turning until the dough is smooth and elastic.

Place dough in a large greased bowl to rise. Turn dough so that it becomes lightly greased on all sides. Cover and let rise in warm area, about 80° F. to 85° F. The inside of an unlit oven is a good safe area for bread rising. To test to see if the bread has risen sufficiently, poke a finger into the dough. If the dent remains, then the dough has risen to the proper size. When the dough has doubled, push with your fist into the center of the dough. Let dough rest about 5 to 10 minutes. Roll or shape according to recipe directions. Place in pan or mold; cover lightly; let rise, bake. Individual recipes may differ but in general these are the basic bread baking guidelines.

When you bake your next loaf of bread, be creative, add some raisins, nuts, or other interesting ingredients to the batter. And be sure to keep a baker's eye on your oven's temperature.

## BREAD BAKING EQUIPMENT

Cookie sheets; Select several sizes of cookie sheets.

Baking pans; Purchase what best fits your baking needs. Pans are available in a variety of sizes. For example:

black steel loaf pans

heavy aluminum pans

glass pans, pyrex

clay loaf pans

Pullman loaf pan

miniature pans

cast iron pans

popover pans

French bread pans

Baking pans; Always buy the best baking equipment, the initial investment is high but will turn out to be a better value. Try to shop at restaurant supply houses if available.

## BREAD MAKING INGREDIENTS

Yeast is a delicate living organism composed of tiny cells. In order to grow, it needs food, sugar, warmth, moisture and air. When yeast is activated, carbon dioxide is released, causing the dough to rise, become light, and develop the porous structure characteristic of all yeast breads. Yeast is temperature sensitive. Too hot a temperature will destroy it and not enough heat will stop the growth of the yeast.

Flour is the main ingredient in bread. It forms the structural framework of all bread. Bread flour, with its high gluten content, is the best flour for bread-making. All-purpose flour, bleached and unbleached, is the flour most readily available and quite acceptable for bread. It is a blend of hard and soft wheat. Whole wheat flour is made by grinding the whole wheat berry. It has less gluten than white flour and produces a heavier and more compact loaf.

Cornmeal is milled from corn and may be white or yellow. Both give good results.

Water gives a nutty flavor and a hard, crisp crust. Milk makes a more nutritious loaf, and gives a softer crust and texture. Other liquid may be used and whatever liquid it is, it should be warm unless otherwise stated.

A loaf is made tender by the addition of shortening. It also makes for a finer texture and improves the keeping quality of bread. Butter, margarine, vegetable oil or solid vegetable shortening are used.

Eggs produce a loaf rich in flavor and color. Eggs improve the texture of the bread.

Salt is used for flavor and to control the growth of the yeast.

Sweeteners help the yeast to grow and add flavor. White or brown sugar, honey or molasses may be used.

## BAKING TERMS

**BEAT**: to combine and make smooth by rapid, vigorous motion using an electric mixer, rotary beater, wire whisk or spoon.

**BLEND** to mix thoroughly two or more ingredients.

**COMBINE** to make smooth, light and fluffy by beating with a spoon or mixer.

**GLAZING** is done with a brush. Egg white makes the crust shiny, whole egg makes it golden and shiny, water or milk makes it hard and non-shiny.

## BREAD MAKING HINTS

Dough should rise in a warm, draft-free area unless the recipe states otherwise. Use a warm, large bowl for dough rising.

Before adding fruit and nuts to dough, toss with a small amount of flour. This procedure will keep them from sinking to the bottom of the loaf.

Breads bake faster in a glass pan than in a metal one, so remember to lower the temperature 25° when using glass pans. Breads baked in shiny metal pans may require more browning.

When bread loaves are baked, place on a wire rack to cool. Cool completely before wrapping for storage.

Bread flour absorbs more moisture than all-purpose flour. Flours will absorb less of the liquid in hot, humid months than in the cool, dry months.

Since different flours vary in the amount of moisture they can absorb, it is not usually possible to determine the exact amount of flour required. In general, for yeast breads, sufficient flour should be used to make the dough stiff enough to knead.

Baking temperatures for yeast breads vary from moderate, 325° F. to 350° F. The lower temperatures are used for rich doughs to prevent excessive browning. Rolls are usually baked at 400°F. to 425° F, then the temperature is reduced about 15 minutes to 350° F. If it is baked the entire time at 400° F. to 425° F. a browner crust results.

Bread enjoys even temperature. An oven thermometer is helpful. Allow bread to bake 15 minutes before peeking in the oven, this will avoid the dough falling. If the crust needs extra browning turn oven up to 400° F. a few minutes. Cover areas that are brown enough with patches of aluminum foil. Always preheat your oven.

# FRENCH BREAD ____

**Makes 2 loaves**

- 2 packages dry yeast
- 4 teaspoons sugar, divided
- 1¹/₃ cups warm water, divided (105°-115°F.)
- 4 cups all-purpose flour
- ¹/₂ teaspoon salt
- 2 tablespoons butter, melted, cooled
- Cornmeal
- 1 egg white, slightly beaten
- 1 tablespoon water

Dissolve yeast with ¹/₃ cup water and 1 teaspoon of the sugar in a large bowl; stir in ¹/₂ cup of the flour, mix well. In a small bowl, combine remaining sugar, salt and remaining flour. Mix in remaining water and melted butter to yeast mixture, stirring well. Add flour mixture and incorporate all ingredients with your hands. Dough will be slightly sticky. Knead dough on a lightly floured board until it is smooth. Place dough in a large greased bowl, turn to grease dough. Set bowl in a warm place, about 85° and let rise until doubled in bulk, about 1¹/₂ hours. Punch dough down, divide in half. Form each part into a long rectangle and fold the long side to the center. Pinch the seams together and set the loaves, seam side down on a cookie sheet that has been well buttered and sprinkled with corn-meal. Make diagonal slashes on loaves about ¹/₄ inch deep and 2 inches apart. Cover loaves lightly and let rise until double in bulk. In a small bowl combine egg whites and water. Brush top of loaves with mixture. Place backing sheet in a 375°F. oven and lower heat immediately to 350°F. Place a pan of boiling water in the bottom of the oven. Bake 45 minutes. Cool on wire rack.

# RYE BREAD WITH CARAWAY SEEDS

**Makes 1 loaf**

  1 **package dry yeast**
  ½ **cup warm water, 105°-115°**
  ½ **cup milk, scalded, cooled**
  ¼ **cup molasses**
  3 **tablespoons butter, melted, cooled**
  ½ **teaspoon salt**
1½ **cups bread flour**
1½ **cups rye flour**
  2 **tablespoons caraway seeds**
  1 **egg, slightly beaten**

Dissolve yeast with warm water in a small bowl. Combine warm milk, molasses, shortening and salt in a large bowl; blend well. Stir in yeast. Mix in flours and caraway seeds. Gather dough together and knead on a lightly floured surface until dough is smooth, about 6-7 minutes. Place dough in a large greased bowl, turn to grease dough. Set bowl in a warm place, about 85°, and let rise until doubled in bulk, about 1½ hours. Punch down, let dough rest for 10 minutes. Knead 1 minute; shape into loaf, place on greased cookie sheet. Cover; let dough rise in warm area until doubled in bulk, about 1 hour. Brush loaf with egg. Bake at 350°F. for 45 minutes or until done. Cool on rack.

# GREEK BREAD

**Makes 1 loaf**

  1 package dry yeast
$1/4$ cup warm water, 105°-115°
$1/2$ cup milk
$1/4$ cup sugar
$1/4$ cup butter, cut into pieces
$1/2$ teaspoon salt
$1/4$ teaspoon anise oil
$1/2$ teaspoon ground cinnamon
  3 cups all-purpose flour
  1 egg, slightly beaten

Dissolve yeast in water in a large mixing bowl, in a warm area, 85°. In a small saucepan scald milk with sugar and butter over medium heat, stirring occasionally; cool to room temperature. Mix in salt, anise, cinnamon and 1 cup of the flour. Add yeast, combine. Mix in remaining flour. Gather dough together and knead on a lightly floured board for 5-6 minutes until dough is smooth. Place dough in a lightly oiled bowl, turn dough to oil sides. Cover, place in a warm area, let dough double in bulk, about $1^1/2$ hours. Punch dough down. Knead for 1 minute, return to bowl, let rise again for 45 minutes. Divide dough into three pieces. With hands form a sausage-shaped dough with each piece, about 1 foot long.

Attach the three pieces at one end; braid bread. Place on a greased cookie sheet. Cover; let rise again about 45 minutes. Brush with beaten egg. Bake at 375°F. for 25 minutes or until bread tests done. Cool on wire rack.

# LIMPA BREAD

**Makes 2 loaves**

5½ cups self-rising flour
2 packages dry yeast
2 cups water
½ cup firmly packed light brown sugar
2 tablespoons vegetable oil
1 tablespoon orange zest
½ teaspoon anise seed
1 teaspoon fennel seed
2 eggs
2 cups rye flour
Oil

In a large bowl mix together 3 cups self-rising flour and yeast. In a small saucepan boil water, sugar, oil, zest, anise and fennel seeds, 2 minutes. Cool to lukewarm; stir into flour-yeast mixture and combine until mixture is smooth, about 2 minutes in an electric mixer. Mix in eggs. Add 1 cup of the self-rising flour; beat 1 minute on medium speed. Stir in rye flour and enough self-rising flour to make a stiff dough. Turn dough out onto a lightly floured surface; knead until the dough is smooth and elastic, about 7-8 minutes. Gather dough into a ball; place in a lightly greased bowl. Turn to grease all sides. Cover; let rise in a warm draft-free place, about 85° until dough has doubled in volume, about 1½ hours. Punch down. Divide dough in half; shape into balls. Let rest 10 minutes. Shape loaves. Place in 2 greased 4 ½ x 8 ½-inch loaf pans. Brush with oil. Let rise in warm place until double, about 1 hour. Bake in preheated 400°F. oven for 35 minutes, or until bread tests done. Remove bread from pans; cool.

# DILLY BREAD

**Makes 1 loaf**

```
    1 package dry yeast
 1/4 cup warm water, 105°-115°
    1 teaspoon sugar
    1 cup creamed cottage cheese
    2 tablespoons minced onion
    2 tablespoons chopped dill weed
    1 teaspoon baking powder
 1/2 teaspoon salt
    1 tablespoon sugar
    1 egg, slightly beaten
2 1/2-3 cups all-purpose flour
```

Dissolve yeast in warm water in a large mixing bowl, stir in sugar. In a separate bowl combine cottage cheese, onion, dill weed, baking powder, salt, sugar and egg. Stir in yeast mixture and blend. Stir in flour making a stiff dough. Gather dough into a ball, knead on a lightly floured board until smooth, about 4-5 minutes. Shape dough into a ball; place in a lightly greased bowl. Turn to grease all sides. Cover; let rise in a warm place, about 85°, until doubled in volume. Punch down. Turn out onto a lightly floured surface and knead 1 minute. Shape into a loaf and place in a greased loaf pan. Bake at 350°F. for 30 minutes. Remove from pan, cool on wire rack.

# MEXICAN HOLIDAY BREAD

**Makes 1 loaf**

- 1/3 cup warm water, 105°-115°
- 1 package dry yeast
- 1 teaspoon sugar
- 2 cups all-purpose flour
- 1/2 cup sugar
- 6 tablespoons butter, melted, cooled to room temperature
- 1/2 teaspoon salt
- 2 eggs, slightly beaten
- 3/4 cup raisins
- 1/2 cup all-purpose flour
- 3 tablespoons butter, melted, cooled
- 1 cup confectioners' sugar
- 5 tablespoons milk
- 1/2 teaspoon vanilla
- 1/4 cup red and green cherries, drained
- 1/4 cup blanched, sliced almonds

Dissolve yeast in warm water with sugar in a warm area, about 85°. In a large bowl combine flour, sugar, butter, salt and eggs. Coat raisins with the half cup flour in a small mixing bowl. Add yeast to flour mixture, combine. Mix in raisins. Turn dough out onto a lightly floured board. Knead until dough is smooth and elastic, about 5 minutes. Place dough in a lightly greased bowl; turn dough. Cover, let stand until doubled in bulk. Turn dough onto a lightly floured board. Knead until smooth and elastic, about 2 minutes. Shape dough into a circle shape on a buttered cookie sheet. Make 1-inch slits around the outside loosely. Place in a warm area to double in bulk. Brush bread lightly with melted butter. Bake at 350°F. for 30 minutes. Combine confectioners' sugar, milk and vanilla. Drizzle icing over bread while it is still warm. Decorate with cherries and almonds.

# BREAD IN A COFFEE CAN

**Make 2 loaves**

1 package dry yeast
$^1/_2$ cup warm water, 105°-115°
$^1/_2$ teaspoon ground ginger
2 tablespoons sugar
1 can, 13 ounces, evaporated milk
1$^1/_2$ teaspoons salt
3$^1/_2$-4 cups all-purpose flour
2 tablespoons vegetable oil
2 tablespoons butter, melted

Dissolve yeast in warm water in a large mixing bowl, with ginger and sugar. Add warm evaporated milk, salt, 3 cups of the flour and oil. Gather into a ball and knead on a lightly floured board until smooth, about 5 minutes, incorporating remaining flour. Divide dough in half, arrange in two greased 1-pound coffee cans. Cover and let rise in a warm place, about 85° until doubled in volume, lids will pop off. Bake at 350°F. for 45 minutes. Remove from oven and brush top of bread with butter; remove from can, cool on rack.

# BRIOCHE

**Makes 1 loaf**

- 1 package dry yeast
- 1/2 cup warm water, 105°-115°
- 1 teaspoon sugar
- 1/2 cup butter, room temperature, cut into 1/2-inch pieces
- 3 tablespoons sugar
- 1/2 teaspoon salt
- 2 eggs
- 2 1/4 cups all-purpose flour
- 1 egg
- 1 tablespoon water

Dissolve yeast in water with sugar in a large mixing bowl, in a warm area, 85°. In a separate bowl cream butter, sugar and salt. Add yeast mixture, eggs and 1 1/4 cups of the flour, combine. Mix in remaining flour. Knead on a lightly floured board until smooth. Place dough in a greased bowl, turn dough to grease all sides. Cover, place in a warm area, let double in bulk, about 1 1/2 hours. Punch dough down. Grease a 6-cup brioche pan. Tear off walnut size piece of dough. Place remaining dough in the prepared pan. Place the small piece of dough in the top of the brioche for the traditional topknot. Cover dough and allow to rise for 1 1/2 hours in a warm area. Combine egg and water, brush top of brioche. Bake at 375°F. for 45 minutes, cool on wire rack.

# OATMEAL BREAD ___

**Makes 1 loaf**

- 1/2 cup quick cooking oatmeal
- 1 cup boiling water
- 1 package dry yeast
- 4 tablespoons warm water, 105°-115°
- 1 teaspoon sugar
- 1 teaspoon salt
- 1/4 cup molasses
- 1/3 cup firmly packed light brown sugar
- 1 egg, slightly beaten
- 3 cups all-purpose flour

Combine oatmeal and boiling water in a medium bowl, let stand 30 minutes. Dissolve yeast in warm water with sugar, in a warm area, about 85°. In a large bowl, combine salt, molasses, brown sugar and oatmeal and mix well. Gradually beat in flour until dough forms a ball. Knead on a lightly floured surface until smooth, about 4 minutes. Place dough in an oiled bowl, turn dough; cover. Let dough rise in a warm area until double in bulk, about 1 1/2 hours. Punch dough down; knead for 1 minute; shape into a loaf. Place in a greased loaf pan, 9x5x3 inches. Let dough rise for approximately 1 hour or until dough doubles in bulk. Bake at 375°F. for 45 minutes; cool on wire rack.

# EGG BRAID BREAD _

**Makes 1 loaf**

- 1 package dry yeast
- 1 teaspoon sugar
- 3/4 cup warm water, 105°-115°
- 1/4 cup shortening
- 1/2 teaspoon salt
- 1 egg, slightly beaten
- 1/4 cup sugar
- 3 cups all-purpose flour
- 1 cup cake flour
- 1/4 cup wheat germ
- 1 egg, slightly beaten
- 1 tablespoon poppy seeds

Dissolve yeast in warm water with sugar in a large mixing bowl, in a warm area, about 85°. Blend shortening, salt, egg and sugar together; mix with yeast. Mix in flours and wheat germ. Gather together and knead on a lightly floured board until smooth, about 4 to 5 minutes. Place dough in a greased bowl, turn to coat all surfaces. Cover and let rise, until double in bulk, about 1 1/2 hours. Punch down. Let dough rest 10 minutes. Divide dough into thirds, form each third into a rope about 14 inches long. Attach the three pieces together at one end, braid. Place bread on a lightly greased cookie sheet. Cover lightly, let rise about 45 minutes until double in bulk. Brush lightly with egg, sprinkle with poppy seeds. Bake at 375°F. for 45 minutes or until baked. Cool on wire rack.

# TOMATO BREAD ___

**Makes 1 loaf**

  1 package yeast
  1 cup warm water, 105°-115°
  2 teaspoons sugar
  $1/2$ teaspoon salt
$2^{1}/_{2}$-$3^{1}/_{4}$ cups all-purpose flour
  $1/4$ pound Italian sausage, break into small pieces
  4 canned, well drained Italian tomatoes, chopped

Dissolve yeast in warm water with sugar in a large mixing bowl. Stir in remaining ingredients; gather dough together into a ball and knead for 4-5 minutes on a lightly floured board until smooth. Place dough in a lightly oiled bowl; turn bread so that it will coat all sides. Cover with a cloth, let rise for 1 hour, 20 minutes or until double. In a large skillet, cool sausage and tomatoes until sausage is cooked, stirring occasionally. Punch dough down. Roll dough out to a 9 x 6-inch form. Sprinkle with cooled sausage mixture; roll dough jelly-roll style. Place dough into a greased loaf pan. Cover, let rise until double in bulk. Bake at 350°F. for 45 minutes. Unmold bread, cool on wire rack.

# HERB BREAD

**Makes 1 loaf**

- 1 package dry yeast
- 1/2 cup warm water 105°-115°
- 1 tablespoon sugar
- 1/2 cup milk
- 1/2 teaspoon salt
- 3 tablespoons butter
- 3 cups all-purpose flour
- 1/4 cup crushed basil, minced fresh parsley, crushed tarragon

Dissolve yeast in water with sugar, in a large mixing bowl, in a warm area about 85°. In a small saucepan scald milk with salt and butter stirring occasionally as butter melts; cool to room temperature. Mix in 1 cup of the flour, combine. Add milk mixture, combine. Mix in remaining flour. Gather dough into a ball, knead on a lightly floured board until smooth, about 5 minutes. Place dough in a greased bowl, turn dough to oil all sides. Cover, let double in bulk in a warm area, about 1 3/4 hours. Turn dough out on a lightly floured board, roll into a rectangle, about 8 inches x 12 inches and 1/4 inch to 1/2 inch thick. Sprinkle herbs over bread, roll jelly-roll style. Fit into a buttered loaf pan, 9 x 5 x 3 inches. Allow to rise for 45 minutes. Bake at 375°F. for 35-45 minutes.

# MONKEY BREAD

**Makes 1 loaf**

1½ packages yeast
¼ cup warm water 105°-115°
1 tablespoon sugar
1 cup milk
½ cup butter
3 eggs, slightly beaten
3½- 4 cups all-purpose flour
½ teaspoon salt
Melted butter

Dissolve yeast in warm water with sugar, in a large mixing bowl. Scald milk and add butter; stir to melt, cool to lukewarm. Stir eggs and cooled milk-butter into yeast. Mix in flour and salt. Gather dough together and knead on a lightly floured board until dough is smooth, about 4-5 minutes. Gather dough into a ball; place in a lightly greased bowl. Turn to grease all sides. Cover; let rise in a warm place, about 85° until dough has doubled in volume. Punch down. Shape into a loaf, place in a greased and floured loaf pan. Let rise in warm place until doubled, about 45 minutes. Roll dough about ⅓ inch thick and cut with diamond-shaped cookie cutter. Place in a 6-cup greased ring mold. Brush each diamond with butter and place overlapping in mold. Add second layer and continue until the dough is used or mold is ¾ filled. Allow dough to rise until double in bulk. Bake at 375°F. for 45 minutes or until bread tests done. Unmold, cool on wire rack.

# PITA BREAD

**Makes 6 pita breads**

- 1 package dry yeast
- 1 cup warm water, 105°-115°
- 1 teaspoon honey
- 2 cups all-purpose flour
- 1 cup whole wheat flour
- 1 teaspoon salt
- 2 tablespoons oil

Dissolve yeast in warm water in a large mixing bowl, stir in honey. Mix in remaining ingredients until well blended. Gather dough together and knead on a lightly floured board for 5 minutes or until smooth. Place in a lightly oiled bowl, turn dough around, oiling on all surfaces. Cover and let rise in a warm area, about 85°, until double in volume, about 1½ hours. Punch dough down, knead again for 2-3 minutes. Divide dough into six equal parts. Form each part into a smooth round ball. Cover the balls with a clean towel and let stand for 15 minutes. Preheat oven to 475°F. Roll each ball into ½ inch in thickness. Arrange pita breads on an ungreased cookie sheet, evenly spaced. Bake on the lowest oven rack for 10 minutes or until they are puffed and turn a light brown. Wrap the pita breads in a towel, as they cool, 10 minutes.

# SOURDOUGH BREAD —————————

**Makes 1 loaf**

  1 **package dry yeast**
1¼ **cups warm water, 105°-115°**
  1 **teaspoon sugar**
  1 **cup starter, see next page**
  3 **cups all-purpose flour**
  1 **teaspoon salt**
  1 **teaspoon baking soda**
1½ **cups all-purpose flour**

In a large mixing bowl dissolve yeast in warm water with sugar, in a warm area, about 85°. Blend in starter. Mix in 3 cups flour and salt, blend together. Cover dough, let rise until double in bulk, about 1½ hours. Mix in remaining ingredients, gather dough together. Knead on a lightly floured board, about 4 to 5 minutes. Gather dough together into a round shape. Place in a greased 9-inch round baking pan. Cover, let dough rise in a warm area for 45 minutes. Bake at 375°F. for 45 minutes or until it tests done.

# SOURDOUGH STARTER

**2 cups all-purpose flour**
**1 package dry yeast**
**2 cups warm water**

In a large mixing bowl combine all ingredients. Let mixture stand uncovered in a warm area, about 85° for 48 hours; stirring occasionally. Stir mixture well before using. Ladle out amount required in recipe. Replenish the remaining starter by mixing in 1 cup flour and 1 cup warm water. Let stand uncovered in a warm area for 4 hours or until it begins to bubble. Cover loosely, refrigerate. Use and replenish every two weeks.

# CROISSANTS

**Makes 12 croissants**

1 package dry yeast
1 tablespoon sugar
4 tablespoons warm water, 105°-115°
1/2 cup all-purpose flour
2 cups all-purpose flour
1/2 teaspoon salt
3/4 cup milk, scald, room temperature
1 cup butter

Dissolve yeast in water with sugar in a warm area, about 85°. Stir in the 1/2 cup flour, leaving in the warm area to rise. In a separate bowl combine the 2 cups flour, salt and milk. When the sponge is light, mix in the flour and milk mixture. Let stand 15 minutes. Dust 2 sheets of wax paper with flour; put the cup of butter between them. With a rolling pin flatten to 1/2 inch; chill. Take the dough and on a floured board, roll into an oblong strip. Put 1/2 of the butter in the middle of the strip and fold one end over the butter. Put the other piece of butter on the folded dough and fold the second end over the butter. Roll out again and fold into 4 layers. Wrap in wax paper and chill 4-5 hours or overnight. An hour and a half before baking, remove the dough from the refrigerator and make 2 more turns, that is, roll it in a strip, fold 4 times and repeat. Chill 1/2 hour; roll in 2 strips, 1/8 inch thick, 4 1/2 inches wide, cut into triangles. Roll and place on cookie sheet and curve into crescents. Brush with egg yolk mixed with cream. Let rise. Preheat oven to 400°F. Bake 5 minutes. Reduce heat to 375°F. Bake 10 minutes or until golden.

# BREAD STICKS _____

**Makes 18 bread sticks**

<pre>
  1 package dry yeast
1¼ cups warm water, 105°-115°
  1 tablespoon sugar
 ½ teaspoon salt
  4 tablespoons vegetable oil
  3 cups all-purpose flour
  1 egg white, slightly beaten
  4 tablespoons poppy seeds
</pre>

Dissolve yeast with warm water and sugar in a large mixing bowl. Add salt, vegetable oil and 2 cups of the flour, combine. Sprinkle remaining flour over batter and combine. Gather dough together and knead on a lightly floured board, until dough is smooth, about 4-5 minutes. Roll dough into a sausage shape. Tear dough into 18 equal sized balls. With your hands roll each ball into a pencil shape about 5 inches long. Arrange on a greased cookie sheet. Cover loosely with a towel, 25 minutes. Brush bread sticks with beaten egg, sprinkle with poppy seeds. Bake at 375°F. for 30 minutes or until golden brown.

# BUTTERMILK ROLLS

**Makes 1½ dozen**

- 1 package dry yeast
- ¼ cup warm water, 105°-115°
- ¾ cup buttermilk
- ¼ teaspoon baking soda
- 2 teaspoons sugar
- ½ teaspoon salt
- 3 tablespoons butter, room temperature
- 2½ cups all-purpose flour

Dissolve yeast in warm water in a large mixing bowl. Stir in remaining ingredients with half of the flour, combine. Sprinkle flour over batter, incorporate. Gather dough into a ball, knead on a lightly floured board for 4 minutes or until elastic. Break off large walnut-sized pieces, roll into balls. Place rolls in greased muffin tin, cover, let rise until double, about 1½ hours. Bake at 400°F. for 15-20 minutes or until baked. Turn rolls out of pan, cool on wire rack.

# ENGLISH MUFFINS _

**Makes 18 muffins**

5½- 6 cups all-purpose flour
  2 cups milk
  ½ cup sourdough starter
  1 tablespoon sugar
  1 teaspoon salt
  1 teaspoon baking soda
  2 tablespoons vegetable oil
  1 package dry yeast
    Cornmeal
    English muffin rings, available at gourmet stores

In a large deep bowl combine 2 cups of the flour, milk, starter, sugar, salt and baking soda; mix until smooth. Cover loosely with waxed paper, let stand in a warm area about 85° for overnight. Stir in oil and yeast; combine. Mix in enough flour to make a stiff dough. Turn dough out onto a lightly floured board and knead until dough is smooth, about 6-8 minutes. Sprinkle the board with cornmeal. Roll dough ½ inch thick. Cut out muffins and place on a lightly greased skillet with ring around muffin. Cook, turning once, 10 minutes on each side or until done. To serve split and toast, butter.

# POTATO ROLLS _____

**Makes 3 dozen**

  1 **cup milk**
  1 **cup hot mashed potatoes**
  ½ **cup shortening**
  ¼ **cup sugar**
  ½ **teaspoon salt**
  2 **packages dry yeast**
  ¼ **cup warm water, 105°-115°**
  5 **eggs, slightly beaten**
3½ **cups all-purpose flour**

In a small saucepan scald milk, over medium heat. Combine milk with mashed potatoes, shortening, sugar and salt, cool. Dissolve yeast with warm water. Add yeast to potato mixture with eggs and 2 cups of the flour, combine. Cover and let mixture rise about 1 hour. Stir in remaining flour making a stiff dough. Knead on a lightly floured surface until smooth. Place dough in a greased bowl, turn to oil all sides. Cover and place in refrigerator. Two and one-half hours before serving time, shape dough into rolls. Place in greased pan and let stand until double in bulk, about 1½ hours. Bake at 400°F. for 15 minutes.

# HOT-CROSS BUNS

**Makes 1 dozen**

- 1 package active dry yeast
- 1/4 cup warm water, 105°-115°
- 1 teaspoon sugar
- 1/2 cup milk
- 4 tablespoons butter, cut into pieces
- 1/2 teaspoon salt
- 3 tablespoons orange zest
- 1/4 cup sugar
- 1 egg, slightly beaten
- 2 1/4 cups all-purpose flour
- 1/2 cup golden raisins
- 1/2 cup candied fruit, chopped

Dissolve yeast in water with sugar in a large mixing bowl, in a warm area, about 85°. In a small saucepan scald milk with butter, salt, orange zest and sugar; cool to room temperature. Mix cooled milk mixture and egg into yeast, combine. Sprinkle in flour, raisins and fruit, knead together. Gather dough into a ball. Knead on a lightly floured board for 5 minutes or until smooth. Dough will be soft. Place dough in an oiled bowl, turn dough, cover. Let double in bulk in a draft-free area, about 1 1/2 hours; punch dough down. Place on a lightly floured board, knead 1 minute. Divide dough into 12 even pieces. Shape into round balls. Place on a buttered large cookie sheet. Cover lightly and allow to double in bulk, about 45 minutes. Combine egg and water. Brush buns with egg wash. Bake at 375°F. for 35 minutes or until tests done. Cool on wire rack.

# PIZZA CRUST

**Makes 2 crusts**

   1 **package dry yeast**
   1 **cup warm water, 105°-115°F.**
2¹/₂ **cups all-purpose flour**
   1 **teaspoon salt**
 ¹/₂ **cup all-purpose flour**
    **Cornmeal**

Dissolve yeast in warm water in a large mixing bowl, in a warm area about 85°. Blend together with 2¹/₂ cups flour and salt. If dough is sticky, add flour by tablespoons from the ¹/₂ cup of flour. Gather dough together and knead on a lightly floured board until smooth. Place dough in an oiled bowl, turn, oiling all sides of dough. Cover and let rise until double in bulk about 1¹/₂ hours. Punch down. Divide dough into two pieces. Grease a cookie sheet or 2 14-inch pizza pans. Sprinkle with cornmeal. Roll out each piece of dough or push out dough to cover pan. Cover dough with tomato sauce, ¹/₂ pound melting cheese and garnish with peppers, mushrooms and/or anchovies. Bake in a 400°F. oven for 20 minutes or until done.

# CHEESE BREAD ____

**Makes 1 loaf**

    3 tablespoons butter
    1 cup milk
 1/2 cup grated Cheddar cheese
 1/4 cup chopped pimiento, drained
    1 package dry yeast
    1 teaspoon sugar
 1/4 cup water, 105°-115°
2 1/2 to 3 cups all-purpose flour

Place butter and milk in a medium saucepan, cook over medium heat, scald; remove from heat; add cheese and pimiento and stir until the cheese melts. Combine yeast, sugar and water in a cup; stir to dissolve yeast. Combine flour, yeast and milk mixture in a large mixing bowl; mix well. Turn dough out onto a lightly floured board and knead until dough is smooth and elastic. Place dough in a greased bowl; turn bread dough to oil. Cover, let rise in a draft-free area for about 1 hour or until doubled in bulk. Punch down. Place dough onto a lightly floured board, knead for 1 minute. Butter a loaf pan, 9 x 5 x 3 inches. Place dough in pan, cover, let rise until it has doubled in bulk, about one hour. Bake at 375°F. for 40 minutes or until baked. Cool on a wire rack.

# ONION BAGELS

**Makes 1 dozen**

- 1 package dry yeast
- 1 cup warm water, 105°-115°F.
- 1 teaspoon sugar
- 3¼ cups all-purpose flour
- 1 teaspoon salt
- 1 egg, slightly beaten
- ¾ cup minced onion
- 4 tablespoons poppy seeds

Dissolve yeast in water with sugar in a large mixing bowl, in a warm area, 85°. Mix in flour and salt. Knead dough on a lightly floured board for 5 minutes or until smooth. Place dough in a greased bowl, turn to oil all sides. Cover, place in a warm area and let dough double in bulk. Punch dough down, divide into 12 equal pieces. Work one piece at a time, keep the remaining bagels covered. Roll dough between hands into an 8-inch length. Pinch ends together to form a circle. Cover and let rise 15 minutes. Fill a large skillet ¾'s full with water, bring to a boil. Reduce heat to simmer. Float 4-5 bagels at a time, simmer, for 3 minutes on each side. Cool on paper toweling, place on a lightly greased cookie sheet. Brush with beaten egg, sprinkle with minced onion and poppy seeds. Bake at 375°F. for 25 minutes.

# RAISIN BAGELS

**Makes 1 dozen**

   1 **package dry yeast**
1½ **cups warm water, 105°-115°F**
   3 **tablespoons sugar**
   1 **teaspoon ground cinnamon**
  ½ **teaspoon salt**
   1 **cup raisins**
3½- 4 **cups flour**
   1 **egg white**
   1 **teaspoon water**

Dissolve yeast in water with 1 tablespoon of the sugar, in a large mixing bowl, in a warm area about 85°. Mix in remaining ingredients and 3 cups of the flour, combine. Sprinkle remaining flour, incorporate. Knead dough on a lightly floured board for 6 minutes or until smooth. Place dough in a greased bowl, turn to oil all sides, cover, place in a warm place, and let double in bulk. Punch dough down, divide into 12 equal pieces. Work one piece at a time, keep the remaining bagels covered. Roll dough between hands into an 8-inch length. Pinch ends together to form a circle. Cover and let rise 15-20 minutes. Fill a large skillet ¾'s full with water, bring to a boil. Reduce heat to simmer. Float 4 bagels at a time, simmer for 3 minutes on each side. Cool on paper toweling, place on a lightly greased cookie sheet. Bake at 400°F. for 10 minutes. Combine egg and water in a small bowl. Brush bagels with egg wash. Return to oven and bake 20 minutes.

# CHOCOLATE-DIPPED PRETZELS

**Makes 32 pretzels**

1 package dry yeast
1½ cups warm water, 105°-115°
1 tablespoon sugar
1 teaspoon salt
3½- 4 cups flour
1 egg
1 teaspoon water
Coarse salt
½ pound white coating chocolate

Dissolve yeast with warm water and sugar in a large mixing bowl. Add salt and 3 cups of the flour, mix well. Gather dough together and knead on a lightly floured board, incorporating remaining flour. Gather dough into a ball, place in a greased bowl, turn to grease all sides. Cover, let rise in a warm place, 85°, until double in bulk, about 1½ hours. Punch down. Divide dough into 32 equal pieces. Work on one piece at a time, keeping the remaining dough covered with a towel. Roll dough between hands into a 5-inch length. Place on lightly greased cookie sheets. Dough does not have to have a second rising. In a small bowl combine egg and water. Brush each pretzel with egg glaze and coat with coarse salt. Bake at 425°F. for 12 minutes or until lightly brown. Melt coating chocolate in top of a double boiler over simmering water, melt. Dip ends of pretzels into chocolate, place on a sheet of waxed paper to dry.

# CHRISTMAS STOLLEN

**Makes 1 loaf**

  1 package dry yeast
$1/4$ cup warm water, 105°-115°
  1 teaspoon sugar
  3 cups all-purpose flour
$1/2$ cup milk, scalded, cooled
  4 tablespoons butter, melted, cooled
$1/2$ teaspoon salt
$1/4$ cup sugar
  1 teaspoon vanilla
  1 egg, slightly beaten
$1/4$ cup candied orange peel, golden raisins
  1 cup candied cherries
$1/4$ cup flour
  1 egg, slightly beaten
  Confectioners' sugar

Dissolve yeast with water and sugar in a large bowl; stir in 2 cups of the flour, mix well. In a small bowl combine milk, butter, salt, sugar, vanilla and egg. Mix milk mixture into yeast-flour. In a small bowl combine candied fruit with $1/4$ cup flour, mix into dough. Mix in remaining flour. Gather dough together, knead on a lightly floured board until smooth, about 6 minutes. Place dough in a large greased bowl, turn to grease dough. Set bowl in a warm place, about 85°, and let rise until double in bulk, about $1 1/2$ hours. Punch dough down. Roll out dough into a 10-12 inch rectangle. Roll up dough from the short side, jelly-roll style. Place on a greased baking sheet. Brush with egg. Cover and let rise for 1 hour. Bake at 375°F. for 45 minutes. Cool on rack. Sprinkle liberally with Confectioners' sugar.

# SALLY LUNN

**Makes 1 Sally Lunn**

- ³/₄ **cup milk**
- ¹/₄ **cup sugar**
- ¹/₂ **teaspoon salt**
- ¹/₄ **cup butter**
- 1 **package dry yeast**
- ¹/₂ **cup warm water, 105°-115°**
- 3¹/₂ **cups all-purpose flour**
- 2 **eggs, slightly beaten**
- 2 **teaspoons orange zest**

In a medium saucepan scald milk with sugar, salt and butter; cool. Dissolve yeast with warm water in a small bowl, in a warm area about 85°. Mix flour into milk mixture; stir in yeast and eggs. Add orange zest, beat for 2 minutes. Gather dough together place in a greased bowl, turn. Let dough rise until double in bulk about 1¹/₄ hours. Punch down, knead for 1 minute. Mound dough into a well buttered 9-inch tube pan. Let batter rise until it is at the top of the pan. Bake at 375°F. for 45-50 minutes. Cool on rack.

# KUGELHUPH

**Makes 1 kugelhuph**

   1 package dry yeast
1/4 cup warm water, 105°-115°
3 1/2 cups all-purpose flour
   3 eggs, slightly beaten
   6 tablespoons butter, room temperature, cut into small pieces
1/4 cup sugar
1/2 teaspoon salt
   2 tablespoons lemon zest
1/4 cup candied cherries, chopped
1/4 cup currants
1/4 cup slivered almonds

Dissolve yeast in warm water, let stand in a warm area. Place flour in a large mixing bowl, add yeast mixture and eggs, combine. Mix until smooth. Place in a greased bowl, turn dough greasing as you turn. Let dough rise until it is double in bulk, about 45 minutes. Punch down. Cream butter, sugar and salt. Mix into batter as you knead on a lightly floured board. Mix in lemon zest, cherries, and currants. Butter a kugelhuph mold. Scatter almonds on the bottom of pan. Mound dough into pan, cover lightly. Let rise for 45 minutes. Bake at 375°F. for 45 minutes. Cool on rack.

# BLUEBERRY MUFFINS

**Makes 24 muffins**

> 3 cups all-purpose flour
> 1 cup sugar
> 4 teaspoons baking powder
> 1/2 teaspoon salt
> 1/2 cup butter, room temperature
> 1 cup milk
> 2 eggs, slightly beaten
> 2 teaspoons vanilla
> 1 can, 16 1/2 ounces, blueberries, drained
> 1/2 cup chopped walnuts
> 1/2 teaspoon cinnamon
> 4 tablespoons sugar

Combine flour, sugar, baking powder and salt in a deep bowl. With a pastry knife cut butter into flour mixture. Mix in milk, eggs and vanilla. Stir to combine. Mix in drained blueberries and walnuts. Fill paper-lined muffin tins 2/3's full. Combine cinnamon and sugar; sprinkle over muffins. Bake at 400°F. for 20 minutes or until muffins test done.

# ZUCCHINI BREAD

**Makes 1 loaf**

    3 eggs
    1 cup sugar
 1/2 cup firmly packed light brown sugar
    1 cup vegetable oil
    2 cups grated, drained, zucchini
    2 teaspoons vanilla
    2 cups all-purpose flour
    2 teaspoons baking soda
    1 teaspoon baking powder
    3 teaspoons ground cinnamon
    1 teaspoon salt
 1/2 cup golden raisins

In a deep bowl beat eggs and sugars until light. Mix in vegetable oil. Blend in zucchini. Add remaining ingredients. Mound mixture into a greased loaf pan 9 x 5 x 3 inches. Bake at 375°F. for 50 minutes or until bread tests done. Cool on wire rack.

# STRAWBERRY AND CREAM BREAD

**Makes 1 loaf**

1³/₄ cups all-purpose flour
  1 teaspoon baking powder
  1 teaspoon baking soda
 ¹/₂ teaspoon salt
  2 teaspoons ground cinnamon
  1 cup sugar
  1 package, 10 ounces, frozen strawberries, strained, room temperature
  1 egg, slightly beaten
  4 tablespoons vegetable oil
 ¹/₂ cup commercial sour cream
 ¹/₂ cup chopped walnuts

In a large bowl combine dry ingredients. Mix in remaining ingredients. Blend well. Pour batter into a greased loaf pan, 9 x 5 x 3 inches. Bake at 350°F. for 55 to 60 minutes or until the bread tests done. Cool on wire rack. Serve with strawberry jam.

# CORN BREAD ————

**Makes 9 servings**

   1 egg
   1 cup milk
 1/2 cup sugar
   1 cup yellow cornmeal
   1 cup all-purpose flour
   2 teaspoons baking powder
 1/2 teaspoon baking soda
 1/2 teaspoon salt
   3 tablespoons melted butter

In a large bowl beat together egg, milk and sugar. Add all remaining ingredients, blend well. Spread mixture into a buttered 8-inch square pan. Bake at 425°F. for 20 minutes. Cool, cut into squares.

# CARROT BREAD

**Makes 1 loaf**

- 3 eggs
- 1 cup sugar
- 3/4 cup commercial sour cream
- 2 cups grated carrots
- 1 3/4 cups all-purpose flour
- 1 1/2 teaspoons baking powder
- 1 1/2 teaspoons baking soda
- 1/2 teaspoon ground cinnamon and salt
- 1/2 cup grated coconut

In a deep bowl beat eggs and sugar until light. Mix in sour cream and carrots. Add remaining ingredients, blend together. Mound mixture into a greased loaf pan, 9 x 5 x 3 inches. Bake at 375°F. for 50 minutes or until bread tests done. Cool on wire rack.

# GLAZED LEMON BREAD

**Makes 1 loaf**

- ¼ cup butter or shortening
- 1 cup sugar
- 2 eggs, well beaten
- 1 cup milk
- 1 teaspoon salt
- 2 tablespoons lemon zest
- 2½ cups all-purpose flour
- 3 tablespoons baking powder
- ½ cup chopped walnuts
- ¼ cup sugar
- 1 tablespoon lemon zest
- ⅓ cup freshly squeezed lemon juice

In a large mixing bowl beat butter and sugar until light. Mix eggs, milk and salt, combine. Mix in remaining ingredients, except sugar, zest and lemon juice. Stir until combined. Mound mixture into a greased loaf pan, 9 x 5 x 3 inches. Bake at 350°F. for 55-60 minutes or until baked. Leave bread in pan. While bread is baking, in a small saucepan combine sugar, zest and lemon juice; cook over medium heat until sugar dissolves, stirring occasionally. Drizzle over hot bread after it is removed from oven. Cool bread in pan for 30 minutes, cool remaining time on wire rack. Bread is better after a day or two.

# APPLESAUCE BREAD WITH CURRANTS

**Makes 1 loaf**

- 6 tablespoons butter
- 1/2 cup firmly packed brown sugar
- 1/4 cup granulated sugar
- 1 egg, well beaten
- 1 teaspoon vanilla
- 3/4 cup applesauce
- 1 teaspoon ground cinnamon
- 1/2 teaspoon ground nutmeg
- 1/4 teaspoon ground cloves
- 2 cups unbleached all-purpose flour
- 2 teaspoons baking soda
- 1 teaspoon baking powder
- 1 cup dried currants

In a large deep mixing bowl cream butter and sugars. Mix in egg and vanilla. Blend in applesauce and spices. Add remaining ingredients. Mound mixture into a greased loaf pan, 9 x 5 x 3 inches. Bake at 350°F. for 55-60 minutes or until bread is done. Cool on a wire rack. Slice and serve with sweetened whipped cream cheese.

# STEAMED BROWN BREAD

**Makes 3 breads**

1 teaspoon baking soda
3/4 cup molasses
1 cup yellow cornmeal
1 cup all-purpose flour
1 cup milk
1/2 teaspoon salt
1 cup raisins

In a large bowl stir baking soda into the molasses until it is dissolved. Mix in remaining ingredients. Mound mixture into a 4-quart pudding mold or fill buttered cans, 3/4's full. Butter aluminum foil and attach to tops of cans. Steam in a Dutch oven on a rack, or in a kettle, over water, simmering for 3 hours. Open cans, cool bread in cans before removing.

# PRUNE BREAD

**Makes 1 loaf**

2 1/2 cups all-purpose flour
1 cup sugar
1 1/4 teaspoons baking powder
1 1/4 teaspoons baking soda
1/2 teaspoon salt
1 teaspoon lemon zest
3 tablespoons salad oil
3/4 cup prune juice
1/2 cup milk
1 egg, slightly beaten
1 cup drained, chopped, cooked prunes
1/2 cup slivered almonds

Combine all ingredients in a large mixing bowl. Blend well. Mound mixture into a greased loaf pan or ring mold. Bake at 350°F. for 55-60 minutes or until bread tests done. Unmold, cool on wire rack.

# BANANA NUT BREAD

**Makes 1 loaf**

- ¹/₄ cup shortening
- ³/₄ cup sugar
- ¹/₄ cup firmly packed light brown sugar
- 1 egg, slightly beaten
- 3 bananas, mashed
- 4 tablespoons sour cream
- 1³/₄ cups all-purpose flour
- 1¹/₂ teaspoons baking powder
- 1¹/₂ teaspoons baking soda
- ¹/₄ teaspoon salt
- ³/₄ cup chopped hazelnuts
- 1 teaspoon vanilla

In a large bowl cream shortening and sugar until light and fluffy. Beat in egg, bananas and sour cream. Stir in remaining ingredients, blend well. Mound into a greased loaf pan, 9 x 5 x 3 inches. Bake at 350°F. for 55-60 minutes or until bread tests done. Unmold, cool on wire rack.

# PUMPKIN BREAD

**Makes 2 loaves**

3½ cups all-purpose flour
2 teaspoons baking soda
1 teaspoon salt
3 cups sugar
1 teaspoon ground nutmeg
1 teaspoon ground cinnamon
4 eggs, slightly beaten
¾ cup water
1 cup salad oil
2 cups canned pumpkin
¾ cup chopped walnuts
½ cup golden raisins

In a large bowl mix together flour, soda, salt, sugar, nutmeg and cinnamon. In a separate bowl combine eggs, water, salad oil and pumpkin puree. Add pumpkin mixture into flour mixture, mix only until well-blended. Fold in nuts and raisins. Mound batter into 2 greased and floured loaf pans. Bake at 350°F. for 1 hour or until a toothpick inserted into the center comes out clean. Cool on a wire rack.

# IRISH SODA BREAD

**Makes 1 bread**

2 tablespoons butter, room temperature
2½- 3 cups all-purpose flour
1½ teaspoons baking soda
½ teaspoon salt
2 tablespoons sugar
1 cup buttermilk
¾ cup golden raisins

In a deep bowl cut butter into flour with pastry knife. Stir in baking soda, salt and sugar. Beating constantly add buttermilk, and raisins. Form dough into a smooth ball, kneading on a lightly floured board for 3-5 minutes. Flatten dough into a circle shape about 2 inches high on a greased cookie sheet. Cut a cross ½ inch deep in the center. Bake at 425°F. for 35-40 minutes. Cool slightly on rack.

# APRICOT NUT BREAD

**Makes 1 bread**

- 1 cup sugar
- 3 tablespoons vegetable oil
- 1 egg, slightly beaten
- 1/2 teaspoon salt
- 3/4 cup freshly squeezed orange juice
- 1 tablespoon orange zest
- 2 1/2 cups all-purpose flour
- 3 teaspoons baking powder
- 2 cups dried apricots, finely chopped
- 1/2 cup chopped pecans

In a large mixing bowl combine sugar and oil. Mix in egg, salt, orange juice and zest. Add remaining ingredients, blend together. Pour into a greased and floured loaf pan. Bake at 350°F. for 55-60 minutes or until bread tests done. Remove from pan, cool on wire rack.

# SOUTHERN SPOON BREAD

**Makes 8-9 servings**

- 4 cups milk
- 1 cup yellow cornmeal
- 2 tablespoons butter, melted
- $\frac{1}{2}$ teaspoon salt
- 1 teaspoon baking powder
- 4 eggs, separated

In a medium saucepan warm milk over medium heat; as the milk warms, stir in cornmeal slowly. When mixture begins to thicken, add the melted butter, salt and baking powder. Do not let mixture boil. Remove from heat; stir in egg yolks. Fold in stiffly beaten egg whites. Mound mixture into a buttered 1 $\frac{1}{2}$-quart baking dish. Bake at 400°F. for 30 minutes or until center is firm and lightly brown. Serve warm. Cut into squares.

# CORNBREAD WITH BACON

**Makes 8-9 servings**

- 4 strips bacon
- 1 cup yellow cornmeal
- 1 cup all-purpose flour
- 4 tablespoons sugar
- 4 tablespoons baking powder
- 1/4 teaspoon salt
- 1 cup milk
- 1 egg
- 1/4 cup bacon drippings

Fry bacon in a skillet over medium heat; crumble bacon, reserve drippings. In a mixing bowl combine cornmeal, flour, sugar, baking powder and salt. Mix in remaining ingredients, blend well. Grease an 8-inch square baking pan with drippings. Bake at 425°F. for 20 minutes or until cornbread tests done. Cool, cut into squares.

# SOPAIPILLAS

**Makes 32**

- 2 cups all-purpose flour
- 1/4 teaspoon salt
- 1 1/2 tablespoons baking powder
- 4 tablespoons vegetable shortening
- 2/3 cup water
- 3 cups vegetable oil for frying
- 1/2 cup sugar

Combine flour, salt, baking powder and shortening and mix until shortening is blended. Add water and mix well. Turn out onto a lightly floured board. Knead until smooth, about 2 minutes. Roll into a ball. Cover and refrigerate for 20 minutes. Cut dough in half. Roll out one ball on a lightly floured board, into a 12-inch square. Cut into 3-inch pieces. Heat oil to 375°F. in a medium skillet. Fry sopaipillas, 2 at a time, for 25 seconds on each side, or until golden brown. Remove with a slotted spoon. Drain on paper toweling. Sprinkle sugar on top. Serve warm or cool.

# APPLE MUFFINS

**Makes 14-16 muffins**

- $1/4$ cup sugar
- $1/4$ cup firmly packed light brown sugar
- 4 tablespoons butter, room temperature
- 1 egg, well beaten
- $3/4$ cup commercial sour cream
- $1/2$ teaspoon salt, ground nutmeg, ground cinnamon
- 3 teaspoons baking powder
- 2 cups all-purpose flour
- $1/2$ cup cake flour
- $1/2$ cup golden raisins
- 3 large firm apples, peeled, cored, grated.

In a large deep bowl beat sugars and butter until light. Mix in egg and sour cream. Blend in remaining ingredients. Mound mixture into lined muffin tins, $2/3$'s full. Bake at 400°F. for 20 minutes or until muffins test done.

# ENGLISH SCONES

**Makes 22 scones**

4 cups all-purpose flour
4 teaspoons baking powder
1 cup sugar
$^1/_2$ teaspoon salt
$^3/_4$ cup shortening
1 cup golden raisins
$^1/_2$ cup candied chopped fruit
1 cup milk

In a deep mixing bowl combine flour, baking powder, sugar and salt. With a pastry blender, cut in the shortening. Stir in raisins and chopped fruits. Blend in milk. Gather dough together and knead on a lightly floured board until smooth, about 2-3 minutes. Roll dough out to a $^1/_2$-inch thickness. Cut into circles with a $2^1/_2$-inch or 3-inch floured cookie cutter. Bake on a cookie sheet at 375°F. for 10 minutes.

# SURPRISE MUFFINS _

**Makes 12 muffins**

 2 cups all purpose flour
 2 teaspoons baking powder
 1/2 teaspoon salt
 1 teaspoon ground cinnamon, ground nutmeg
 1/2 cup sugar
 1 egg
 1 cup milk
 1 cup cooked, mashed yams
 1/4 cup butter, melted
 3/4 cup chopped pecans
 1 tablespoon lemon zest
 4 tablespoons sugar
 1/2 teaspoon cinnamon

In a large bowl combine flour, baking powder, spices and sugar. In a small bowl beat egg; add milk, yams and butter, blend well. Stir egg mixture into flour mixture. Blend in pecans and lemon zest. Batter will be combined but lumpy. Spoon into greased muffin tin, 2/3's full. Combine sugar and cinnamon, sprinkle over muffins. Bake at 425°F. for 25 minutes.

# POPOVERS ——————————

**Makes 1 dozen**

- 4 **eggs**
- 1 **cup milk**
- 1 **cup all-purpose flour**
- 1/2 **teaspoon salt**
- 4 **tablespoons melted butter**

In a large bowl beat together eggs and milk. Mix in flour and salt. Beat with a fork until the mixture is smooth. Heat oven to 375°F. Preheat the muffin tin in the oven for 5 minutes. Brush the cups generously with melted butter. Fill each muffin cup 2/3's full with batter; working quickly so that the muffin tin stays hot. Bake for 35 minutes without opening the oven. Prick each popover with a fork, to let steam escape. Serve immediately.

# RICE
# AND
# PASTA

# Rice
# And Pasta

## TYPES OF RICE

**LONG GRAIN RICE**

Rice that is long and slender in shape, as much as 4 to 5 times long as it is wide. When cooked, the grains tend to remain separate and are light and fluffy.

**MEDIUM GRAIN RICE**

Rice that is plump in shape, but not round. When cooked, these grains are more moist and tender than long grain.

**SHORT GRAIN RICE**

Rice that is almost round in shape. Short grain rice tends to cling together when cooked.

**ROUGH (PADDY) RICE**

Rice as it comes from the field. The hull that surrounds the grain must be removed before consumption.

**BROWN RICE**

Whole or broken kernels of rice from which only the hull has been removed. Brown rice may be eaten as is or milled into regular-milled white rice. Cooked brown rice has a slightly chewy texture and a nut-like flavor. The light brown color of brown rice is caused by the presence of the seven bran layers which are rich in minerals and vitamins, especially the B-complex group.

## PARBOILED RICE

Rough rice soaked, steamed, and dried before milling. This procedure gelatinizes the starch in the grain, and ensures a separateness of grain. Parboiled rice is favored by consumers and chefs who desire a fluffy, separate cooked rice. It also retains more nutrients than unenriched regular-milled white rice, but it takes a few minutes longer to cook.

## PRE-COOKED RICE

Rice that has been cooked and dehydrated after milling. This reduces the time required for cooking.

## REGULAR-MILLED WHITE RICE

The rice product after it has been through the entire milling process is sometimes called milled rice, milled white rice. The hulls, bran layers, and germ all have been removed and the rice is sorted according to size. The cultivation of rice is older than recorded history. As far back as 2800 B.C. tales of rice and its significance to mankind dot the pages of history of the Eastern Hemisphere from China to ancient Greece and from Persia to the Nile Delta. The history of rice in North America began with colonization of the fertile new land. The most favorable area for agriculture during America's colonial period was considered to be the Carolinas.

# HOW TO PREPARE RICE

Most rice packages have easy-to-follow directions for preparing perfect rice. In the absence of package directions, the same high quality product can be obtained by using the following method(s):

1 cup regular-milled rice

2 cups liquid (water, broth, consomme, juice)

1 teaspoon salt

1 tablespoon butter or margarine is an optional ingredient

For drier, fluffier rice, decrease liquid by 2 to 4 tablespoons.

The amount of liquid and cooking time do vary slightly when cooking with different rices:

| 1 Cup Uncooked Rice | Liquid | Cooking time | Yield |
|---|---|---|---|
| Regular-milled white | 1¾ to 2 cups | 15 min. | 3 cups |
| Regular-milled white medium or short grain | 1½ cups | 15 min. | 3 cups |
| Brown | 2 to 2½ cups | 45 to 50 min. | 3 to 4 cups |
| Parboiled | 2 to 2½ cups | 20 to 25 min. | 3 to 4 cups |
| Pre-cooked | follow package directions | | |
| Flavored or seasoned mixes | follow package directions | | |

**REFRIGERATING RICE** When refrigerating rice, be sure to cover the rice tightly so the grains will not dry out or absorb the flavors of other foods.

**REHEATING RICE** For each cup of cooked rice, add 2 tablespoons liquid. Cover and heat 4 to 5 minutes on top of range or in oven. In microwave, cook about 1½ minutes per cup, using high setting.

**TOP OF THE RANGE** Combine rice, liquid, salt, and butter or margarine in a 2 to 3-quart saucepan. Heat to boiling. Stir once or twice. Lower heat to simmer. Cover with a tight-fitting lid or heavy duty foil. Cook 15 minutes. If rice is not quite tender or liquid is absorbed, replace lid and cook 2 to 4 minutes longer. Makes about 3 cups.

**RICE COOKERS** There are several reliable brands available, both automatic and non-automatic. Care should be taken to follow individual manufacturer's directions. In general, however, all ingredients are combined using ¼ to ½ cup less liquid than the top-of-the-range method.

**OVEN METHOD** It's an efficient use of energy when other foods are baking. Use boiling liquid. Combine ingredients in a baking dish or pan; stir. Cover tightly and bake at 350° F. for 25 to 30 minutes (30 to 40 minutes for parboiled rice).

**MICROWAVE** The microwave saves energy and cleanup time too. Use 2 cups liquid for regular-milled, parboiled, and brown rice. Combine all ingredients in a microproof baking dish. Cover and cook on HIGH (maximum power) 5 minutes or until boiling. Reduce setting to 50% power and cook 15 minutes (for brown rice reduce setting to 30% power and cook 45 minutes). Fluff with fork.

# ORIENTAL FRIED RICE

**Makes 8 servings**

1/4 cup peanut oil
2 eggs, slightly beaten
5 green onions, chopped
3 cups cooked, salted rice
3 tablespoons light soy sauce
1 cup cubed or shredded cooked pork
1 small carrot, grated
1/2 cup water chestnuts, sliced
1 cup cooked green peas

Heat half of the oil in a heavy skillet, over medium heat. Cook eggs into an omelet, cut into strips, reserve. Heat remaining oil in the skillet, stir-fry, cooking quickly in a stirring motion, the green onions, until tender. Mix in rice, soy sauce, pork, carrot and water chestnuts, stirring well after each addition. Add eggs, toss lightly, remove fried rice to a serving dish. Sprinkle the peas over and serve hot.

# SAFFRON RICE I ____

**Makes 2-3 servings**

- 1/2 teaspoon saffron
- 3 tablespoons hot water
- 1 cup rice
- 2 cups water
- 1/2 teaspoon salt

Combine saffron and water in a cup, let stand for 10 minutes. Strain liquid and pour into a 1-quart saucepan. Wash rice and drain. Combine rice, water and salt in the saucepan. Bring rice to rolling boil; stir, cover. Remove from heat. Let stand for 20 minutes. Serve.

# SAFFRON RICE II ____

**Makes 8 servings**

- 3 cups strong chicken stock
- 1 cup dry white wine
- 1 onion, minced
- 2 teaspoons fresh parsley, minced
- 1/2 teaspoon saffron
- 1/2 teaspoon coriander
- 1/2 teaspoon fennel
- 1/4 teaspoon mace
- 2 cups long grain rice

Combine all ingredients except rice in a medium saucepan with a tight fitting cover. Bring mixture to a boil over medium heat. Add rice, cover, do not stir, reduce heat to simmer, cook 30 minutes, serve.

# GREEN RICE

**Makes 4-5 servings**

- 2 cups cooked rice
- 3/4 cup Cheddar cheese, grated
- 5 tablespoons melted butter
- 1 onion, minced
- 3 egg yolks
- 3/4 cup fresh parsley, minced
- 1/2 cup fresh spinach, minced
- 1/2 teaspoon salt
- 1/2 teaspoon white pepper
- 3 egg whites, beat stiff

In a large bowl combine rice, cheese, butter, onion, egg yolks, parsley, spinach, and seasonings. Fold in stiffly beaten egg whites. Mound mixture into a buttered 1½-quart casserole. Bake at 350° F. for 25 minutes.

# RICE PUDDING ———

**Makes 8 servings**

- 1 quart milk
- 1 cup uncooked rice, washed and drained
- 1 cup sugar
- 4 eggs, slightly beaten
- 1/2 teaspoon salt
- 1 teaspoon vanilla
- 1 cup golden raisins
- 1/2 teaspoon ground cinnamon
- 1/4 teaspoon ground nutmeg

Combine milk and rice in a medium saucepan, let stand for one-half hour. Stir rice; cover and simmer for 20 minutes, or until the rice is tender. Place rice in a large mixing bowl; add remaining ingredients and blend together. Butter a 2-quart souffle dish. Pour rice pudding mixture into the prepared dish. Set souffle dish in a larger pan and add one inch of hot water to the outer pan. Bake at 375° F. for 50 minutes, or until it tests done. Cool in oven. Serve warm or chilled.

# RICE WITH CHEESE _

**Makes 8 servings**

   2 cups cooked rice
   2 large tomatoes, peeled, seeded, and chopped
 1/4 cup raisins
   1 large onion, chopped
   1 green bell pepper, seeded, and chopped
 1/2 pound Cheddar cheese, grated
   1 cup cream-style corn
   2 cups bread crumbs

Combine all ingredients except bread crumbs, in a large mixing bowl. Butter a 2-quart casserole. Top with bread crumbs. Bake at 350° F. for 1 hour.

# MEXICAN RICE _____

**Makes 5-6 servings**

    3 tablespoons lard or vegetable oil
 1 1/2 cups long grain rice, washed and drained
    2 cloves garlic, peeled and minced
    1 large onion, minced
    1 large tomato, peeled and chopped
    3 cups chicken stock

Heat oil in a medium skillet. Add rice and cook, until the rice begins to brown, stirring constantly. Add garlic, onion and tomato; mix well. Saute for 1 minute. Stir in stock, cover and simmer for 15 minutes.

# RISOTTO

**Makes 3-4 servings**

- 3 tablespoons butter
- 1 tablespoon olive oil
- 1 cup rice
- 1 large onion, minced
- 1/2 teaspoon salt
- 1/2 teaspoon ground pepper
- 1 cup dry white wine or water
- 3/4 cup chicken stock

In a large skillet, heat butter and olive oil over medium heat. Add rice, and onion, cook, stirring constantly. Season with salt and pepper. When the rice begins to turn a golden brown stir in the wine or water, stirring continuously. When the liquid is absorbed add chicken stock, stirring continuously, for 5 minutes or until the rice is tender and still firm. Serve.

# RICE AND VEGETABLE CASSEROLE

**Makes 6 servings**

1 green bell pepper, seeded, sliced
5 green onions, minced
4 tablespoons butter
3 cups cooked rice
1 can (17 ounces) whole kernel corn, drained
1 can (14½ ounces) tomatoes, crushed, drained
1¼ cups Cheddar cheese, grated
4 eggs, slightly beaten
1 cup cream-style cottage cheese
¼ cup milk
½ teaspoon salt
½ teaspoon white pepper

Heat butter in a large saucepan, saute peppers and onions, until tender, stirring occasionally. Mix in rice, corn, tomatoes, and cheese. Combine remaining ingredients; mix into rice mixture. Mound into a buttered 2-quart casserole. Bake at 350° F. for 45 minutes. Let stand 5 minutes before serving.

# SEAFOOD-RICE SALAD

**Makes 6 servings**

- 3 cups cooked rice, room temperature
- 1/4 cup cooked crab meat, shredded
- 1/2 cup shrimp, cooked, shelled, and deveined
- 1 can mandarin oranges, drained
- 2 apples, cored, chopped
- 5 stalks celery, sliced
- 3/4 cup commercial sour cream
- 1/4 cup mayonnaise
- 4 tablespoons freshly squeezed orange juice

Toss rice, crab meat, shrimp, oranges, apples and celery. Combine remaining ingredients in a small bowl. Toss lightly with rice mixture, chill until ready to serve.

# RICE NEW ORLEANS STYLE

**Makes 6-8 servings**

- 3 tablespoons vegetable oil
- 1/4 pound chicken gizzards, chopped
- 1/4 pound ground pork
- 2 bay leaves
- 1 onion, chopped
- 4 stalks celery, chopped
- 1 green bell pepper, chopped
- 2 cloves garlic, peeled and minced
- 1/2 teaspoon Tabasco sauce or to taste
- 1/2 teaspoon salt
- 1/2 teaspoon ground cumin
- 1/4 teaspoon ground pepper
- 2 tablespoons butter
- 2 cups chicken stock
- 1/4 pound chicken livers, ground
- 1 cup uncooked long grain rice

In a large skillet heat oil over medium heat; saute gizzards and pork until cooked, stirring occasionally. Stir in vegetables and seasonings, blend well. Add butter, mix until melted, cook for 4-5 minutes, stirring often. Mix in stock and liver, cook about 1 minute. Mix in rice, stir thoroughly; cover, reduce heat to simmer, cook 5 minutes. Remove from heat, leave covered about 15 minutes or until rice is cooked. Discard bay leaves.

# RICE PILAF

**Makes 8 servings**

 5 tablespoons butter
 1/2 cup thin egg noodles, crumbled into pieces
 2 cups uncooked long grain rice
 4 cups chicken stock

In a medium skillet heat butter; over medium heat. Saute noodles until lightly browned. Add rice and stir to coat with butter. Add stock, simmer, stirring occasionally, until the stock is absorbed and the rice is tender, about 15-20 minutes. Cover and let set for a few minutes before serving.

# PASTA

Although pasta is consumed worldwide, the true pasta country is in that area of Italy from Naples southward. Besides the ordinary spaghetti and lasagne, there are orecchietti, little ears; laganelle, small rectangles; ricci di donna, ladies' curls; fusille, pulled out spirals; stracsinati, little rectangles with one side ribbed, and so forth. Pasta identifies the multitude of products made from flour, semolina, water and/or eggs and then shaped and dried in various shapes and forms. Each pasta has its own descriptive name. Each region of Italy has its special shape of pasta and the variations on it are limited only by the imagination of the individual chef.

## POPULAR PASTAS

Pastas that can be stuffed include manicotti, cannelloni, ravioli and tortellini.

Pasta that is selected for baking are lasagne, curly lasagne, green lasagne, macaroni, tortiglioni and a faralle.

Pasta that should be boiled are tagliatelle, capellini, spaghetti, spaghettini, ziti, malfadine and zitoni.

Pasta for soups may be anellini and semini de Melo.

## PASTA TYPES

**ACIMI DE PEPE** Tiny shapes of round or square pasta that are used in soups.

**ANELLI** Little rings used in soup.

**ANGNOLOTTI** Round ravioli that are filled with meat.

**CANNELLONI** Flat squares of pasta rolled around a stuffing.

**CAPPELLETTI** Delightful little hats, can be flat or round squares with filling.

**CAVATELLI** A short noodle, formed into a shell-like pasta.

**FARFALLE** Butterflies or bows; can be small, medium, or large.

**FETTUCCINE** Ribbon pasta, usually about $1/4$ inch in width.

**FUSILLI** Spiral, curly spaghetti made in a twisted shape.

**LASAGNE** Very wide, flat pasta. Sometimes prepared as spinach pasta or with curly edges.

**MACARONI** Popular hollow pasta available in many styles and shapes.

**RAVIOLI** Pasta squares of different sizes, stuffed with a variety of foods.

**RIGATONI** Large, ribbed, tubular pasta usually cut in abou 3-inch lengths.

**SPAGHETTI** Pasta that is dried in long, thin round strands.

**TAGLIATELLE** Narrow egg noodle, also called gettucine.

**TORTELLINI** Small twists of pasta for stuffing.

**VERMICELLI** Very thin spaghetti, but not sold in solid straight shapes but in twisted forms.

# EGG PASTA

**Makes 6 servings**

1³/₄ **cups unbleached all-purpose flour**
 ³/₄ **cup instant flour**
 ¹/₂ **teaspoon salt**
 3 **eggs**
 2 **tablespoons olive oil**

Arrange flours in a mixing bowl with a well in the center; add remaining ingredients and place in the well. Mix together with fingers until the dough can be gathered into a ball. Knead dough on a lightly floured board until smooth and elastic, about 8 minutes. Add more flour if dough seems sticky. Gather dough together, wrap in waxed paper; let dough rest 15 minutes before rolling out. Divide dough into 2 balls. Cover one ball and flatten out other dough ball with your hand. Dust dough with flour, using a rolling pin, roll dough paper-thin. Roll up dough from the long end, jelly-roll style. Cut into ¹/₄-inch wide strips. Unroll each strip and spread on waxed paper or on a pasta dryer to dry.

**When ready to cook:**

 5 **quarts water**
 3 **tablespoons salt**
 3 **tablespoons vegetable oil**

Bring water to a boil in a large pot. Add salt and oil; add noodles. Cook until just tender, 2 to 3 minutes, drain. Transfer to a heated platter.

# WHOLE WHEAT PASTA

**Makes 2-3 servings**

1½ **cups whole wheat flour**
  3 **eggs**
  2 **tablespoons olive oil**
  1 **teaspoon salt**

Arrange flour in a mixing bowl with a well in the center; add remaining ingredients, place in the well. Mix together with fingers until the dough can be gathered into a ball. Knead dough on a lightly floured board until smooth and elastic, about 8 minutes. Add more flour if dough seems sticky. Gather dough together, wrap in waxed paper; let dough rest 10 minutes before rolling out. Divide dough into 2 pieces. Cover one piece and flatten out other dough ball with your hand. Dust dough lightly with flour. Using a rolling pin, or pasta machine, roll dough paper-thin. Roll up dough from the long end, jelly-roll style. Cut dough into ¼-inch wide strips. Unroll each strip and spread on waxed paper or on a pasta dryer to air dry.

**To cook:**

  5 **quarts water**
  3 **tablespoons salt**
  2 **tablespoons cider vinegar**
  2 **tablespoons oil**

Bring water to a rapid boil in a large pot. Add salt, oil and vinegar; add noodles. Cook until just tender, al dente, 2 to 3 mintes; drain. Transfer to a heated platter. Toss with butter.

# GREEN PASTA (SPINACH)

 2 cups all-purpose flour
 2 eggs
 5 ounces cooked spinach, drained and pureed
 1/2 teaspoon salt
 1 tablespoon vegetable or olive oil

Arrange flour in a mixing bowl with a well in the center; add remaining ingredients, place in the well. Mix together with fingers until the dough can be gathered into a ball. Knead dough on a lightly floured board until smooth and elastic, about 8 minutes. Add more flour if dough seems sticky. Gather dough together, wrap in waxed paper; let dough rest 10 minutes before rolling out. Divide dough into 2 pieces. Cover one piece and flatten out other dough ball with your hand. Dust dough lightly wih flour. Using a rolling pin, or pasta machine, roll dough paper-thin and cut into the desired shape by hand or with a pasta machine.

**To cook:**

 5 quarts water
 3 tablespoons salt
 2 tablespoons cider vinegar
 2 tablespoons oil

Bring water to a rapid boil in a large pot. Add salt, vinegar and oil; add noodles. Cook until just tender, al dente, 2 to 3 minutes; drain. Use as directed in recipe.

# SPINACH LASAGNA

**Makes 8-10 servings**

- 1/4 **cup butter**
- 3 **cloves garlic, peeled, minced**
- 1 **large onion, minced**
- 1 **small carrot, grated**
- 2 **stalks celery, sliced**
- 1 1/4 **pounds ground beef**
- 1 **large can (28 ounces) tomato puree**
- 1 **cup beef stock**
- 1 **teaspoon basil**
- 1 **teaspoon oregano**
- 1/2 **teaspoon salt**
- 1 **teaspoon honey**
- 3 **tablespoons butter**
- 3 **tablespoons all-purpose flour**
- 2 **cups milk or half-and-half**
- 1 **cup heavy cream**
- 3/4 **pound green lasagna noodles, cooked according to package directions and drained**
- 1 **cup Parmesan cheese, grated**

Melt butter in a large skillet over medium heat; sauté garlic, onion, carrot and celery until tender, stirring occasionally. Stir in beef, cook until lightly browned, stirring occasionally. Stir in tomato puree, beef stock, seasonings and honey, blend ingredients, reduce heat to simmer and continue cooking for 40 minutes.

In a medium saucepan heat butter; whisk in flour until it is absorbed. In a slow steady stream pour in milk and heavy cream, stirring until mixture thickens, set aside.

## To Assemble

Spoon ⅙ of the cream sauce over bottom of a 13x9-inch baking pan. Arrange a layer of the noodles, the meat sauce and then the cream sauce. Continue until all ingredients have been used. Sprinkle with Parmesan cheese. Bake at 375° F. for 40 minutes.

# DOROTHY'S PINK PASTA

**Makes 4 servings**

- 1 cup all-purpose flour
- 1 cup instant flour
- 2 tablespoons canned beets, drained and pureed
- ½ teaspoon salt
- 2 eggs
- 2 teaspoons olive oil

Arrange flours in a mixing bowl with a well in the center; add remaining ingredients and place in the well. Mix together with fingers until the dough can be gathered into a ball. Knead dough on a lightly floured board until smooth and elastic, about 8 minutes. Add more flour if dough seems sticky. Gather dough together, wrap in waxed paper; let dough rest 10 minutes before rolling out. Divide dough into 2 pieces. Cover one piece and flatten out other dough ball with your hand. Dust dough lightly with flour. Using a rolling pin, (or pasta machine) roll dough paper-thin. Roll up dough from the long end, jelly-roll style. Cut dough into ¼-inch wide strips. Unroll each strip and spread on waxed paper or on a pasta dryer to air dry.

**To cook**

- 5 quarts water
- 3 tablespoons salt
- 2 tablespoons cider vinegar
- 2 tablespoons vegetable oil

Bring water to a rapid boil in a large pot. Add salt, vinegar and oil; add noodles. Cook until just tender, al dente, 2 to 3 minutes; drain. Transfer to a heated platter. Toss with basil sauce.

# BASIL SAUCE

**Makes 4 servings**

- 6 tablespoons butter
- 3 tablespons chopped basil
- 1/4 teaspoon salt
- 1/4 teaspoon pepper
- 2 tablespoons cider vinegar
- 1 to 2 tablespoons vegetable oil

Melt butter in a small saucepan. Stir in basil, salt and pepper. Cook over simmering heat, 2-3 minutes. Drizzle over pink pasta, gently toss.

# NOODLES ALFREDO

**Makes 8 servings**

- 1 pound fettucine, cooked, drained
- 1/2 cup butter, room temperature, cut into small pieces
- 1/2 cup freshly grated Parmesan cheese
- 1/2 cup light cream
- 1/4 cup freshly grated Parmesan cheese for garnish

Arrange noodles in a hot serving bowl. Add butter, cheese and cream. Toss gently until all ingredients are combined. Serve at once topped with freshly grated Parmesan cheese.

# MACARONI AND MEAT CASSEROLE

 3 tablespoons butter
 1 tablespoon vegetable oil
 2 cloves garlic
 1 large onion, sliced thin
 2 pounds ground beef
 1/2 teaspoon ground cinnamon
 1/2 teaspoon Greek seasoning (available at specialty
    food stores)
 1 teaspoon salt
 1/4 teaspoon ground pepper
 1 can (16 ounces) tomatoes, quartered, include juice
 6 tablespoons catsup
 1/2 pound elbow macaroni, cooked according to pack-
    age directions, drained, and kept warm
 6 ounces Parmesan cheese, grated

Heat butter and oil in a large heavy skillet over medium heat.
Sauté garlic and onion until tender, stirring occasionally. Add
beef; brown, stirring occasionally. Sprinkle cinnamon, Greek
seasoning, salt and pepper over beef; mix lightly. Stir in tomatoes and catsup. Remove from heat. Toss beef mixture with
macaroni, mound into a buttered 9-inch baking dish. Sprinkle
with cheese. Bake at 350° F. for 45 minutes.

# SPAGHETTI WITH MEAT SAUCE

**Makes 8 servings**

- 4 tablespoons olive oil
- 2 cloves garlic
- 1 large onion, sliced thin
- 1 pound ground beef
- 2 cans (16 ounces each) tomatoes, drained, reserve juice, puree
- 1 can (6 ounces) tomato paste
- 2 cups water
- 1/2 teaspoon sugar
- 1/2 teaspoon crushed oregano
- 1/2 teaspoon salt
- 1/2 teaspoon pepper
- 1 teaspoon crushed basil
- 1 pound thin spaghetti, cooked according to package directions

Heat oil in a large saucepan; sauté garlic and onion over medium heat until tender, stirring occasionally. Add beef; sauté until lightly browned, stirring occasionally. Stir in remaining ingredients. Simmer, uncovered, for 45 minutes, stirring occasionally. Adjust seasonings.

**To serve**

Divide spaghetti onto 8 heated plates. Spoon sauce over pasta.

# MANICOTTI _____

**Makes 12 servings**

**Crepes**

　2 **eggs, slightly beaten**
¼ **teaspoon salt**
　2 **tablespoons melted butter, cooled**
　1 **cup milk**
　1 **cup water**
　2 **cups all-purpose flour**

Beat eggs with salt; add remaining ingredients. Cover and allow to stand at room temperature for 20 minutes. Use a seasoned crepe pan. Butter pan, pour in just enough batter to cover bottom of the pan. Cook over medium-low heat until the crepe is dry, turn over. Cook until lightly brown. Invert crepe onto a clean kitchen towel. Continue until all the batter has been used. If batter seems too thick, add water, 2 tablespoons at a time. When crepes are cool, stack with a piece of waxed paper or aluminum foil between them.

**Filling**

¼ **cup minced fresh parsley**
¾ **pound Mozzarella cheese, grated**
½ **pound Parmesan cheese, grated**
1¾ **pounds ricotta cheese**
　3 **eggs, slightly beaten**
¼ **teaspoon salt**
¼ **teaspoon white pepper**

Combine all ingredients in a deep bowl, set aside.

## Sauce

  3 tablespoons olive oil
  1 onion, minced
  3 cloves garlic, peeled, minced
  1 can tomatoes (16 ounces), reserve juice
  1 can (6 ounces) tomato paste
  1 teaspoon honey
 $1/2$ teaspoon salt
  2 teaspoons crushed oregano

Heat oil in a medium saucepan; sauté garlic and onion over medium heat until tender, stirring occasionally. Add tomatoes, juice, tomato paste, honey and spices, blend together; simmer 15 minutes.

## To assemble

Fill each crepe with cheese filling, roll. Arrange filled crepes, seam side down in a buttered pan, 13 x 9 x 2 inches. Drizzle sauce over crepes, to cover. Bake at 375° F. for 20 minutes.

# PASTA SHELLS A LA FORIENZA

**Makes 8 servings**

    4 large red bell peppers, seeded, sliced
 1/2 cup vodka
    1 pound pasta shells, cooked according to package
       directions, drained
 1/2 teaspoon salt
 1/2 teaspoon pepper
    1 can (16 ounces) tomatoes including juice, pureed
    6 stalks celery, sliced
    6 ounces grated Parmesan cheese
    1 cup heavy cream

Place peppers into a deep bowl; mix in vodka, toss. Allow mixture to marinate for 3 hours. Arrange hot noodle shells in a large serving bowl. Sprinkle with salt and pepper. Add tomato puree and celery. Combine grated Parmesan cheese and heavy cream in a small bowl; drizzle over pasta, toss gently. Mix in peppers, toss. Serve warm, divide into 8 deep bowls.

# EASY COLD PASTA SALAD

**Makes 8 servings**

 2 red bell peppers, seeded, and chopped
 1 Spanish onion, chopped
 1 can artichoke bottoms, drained and quartered
 1/2 cup pepperoni or salami, diced
 1 pound small pasta, cooked al dente
 1 cup mayonnaise
 3 tablespoons wine vinegar
 1/2 teaspoon salt
 1/2 teaspoon ground pepper
 1/2 teaspoon powdered garlic
 1 teaspoon Worcestershire sauce
 3/4 cup sliced black olives

In a large deep mixing bowl toss vegetables with pepperoni. Add cooked, drained pasta, toss. In a small bowl, combine mayonnaise, wine vinegar, and seasonings. Drizzle over salad, toss well. Chill until ready to serve. Top with sliced black olives before serving.

# MEATLESS ENTREES

# Meatless Entrees

## GOLDEN CASSEROLE _____

**Makes 6 servings**

  2 cups hot cooked salted rice
10 hard-boiled eggs, shelled, chopped
  ½ cup mayonnaise
  ½ cup commercial sour cream
  ⅓ cup chopped onion and green bell pepper
  3 tablespoons chopped pimiento
  1 tablespoon freshly squeezed lemon juice

In a large mixing bowl combine all ingredients. Mound mixture into a greased 1½-quart casserole; bake at 350°F. for 30 minutes.

# ZITI

**Makes 6 servings**

  3  **tablespoons butter**
  3  **tablespoons olive oil**
  2  **cloves garlic, peeled, minced**
  1  **large onion, chopped**
  1  **carrot, grated**
  2  **stalks celery, sliced**
  1/2  **teaspoon salt**
  1/2  **teaspoon oregano**
  1/2  **teaspoon chopped basil**
  1/4  **teaspoon pepper**
  1  **pound ziti, cooked according to package directions, drained**
  1  **can (28 ounces) Italian tomatoes, finely chopped, include juice**
  1  **cup Romano cheese, grated**

In a large saucepan, heat butter and oil over medium heat; sauté garlic, onion, carrot and celery until tender, stirring occasionally. Mix in spices and tomatoes, simmer for 20 minutes, stirring occasionally. Toss ziti with tomato sauce. Arrange in a buttered baking dish. Sprinkle with cheese, stir. Bake at 450°F. for 12 minutes.

# STUFFED GRAPE LEAVES ____

**Makes 8 servings**

- 16 ounce jar grape leaves (available at specialty food stores)
- 3 tablespoons vegetable oil or olive oil
- 1 onion, minced
- 2 cups uncooked rice
- 1 cup currants
- 1 teaspoon chopped dried mint leaves
- 2 teaspoons minced fresh dill weed
- 1/2 teaspoon ground cinnamon
- 1/2 teaspoon salt
- 1/4 teaspoon pepper
- 2 tablespoons butter
  Juice of 1 lemon

Carefully unfold the vine leaves and rinse under cold water. Line a large heavy skillet with one layer of the broken leaves. Heat the oil in a separate skillet over medium heat; sauté onion until tender, stirring occasionally. Stir in rice and cook until coated. Stir in currants and spices. Remove from heat. Arrange about 1 tablespoon of the rice mixture on a vine leaf and roll up jelly-roll style, tucking edges under making the stuffed grape leaf securely wrapped. Continue until all the stuffing is used. Arrange a layer of stuffed grape leaves over bottom of prepared skillet; continue stacking until all stuffed grape leaves have been placed. Drizzle 2 cups hot water over all, add butter and lemon juice. Place a plate, to weigh down the food, over stuffed grape leaves.

Bring mixture to a boil, reduce heat to a simmer, continue simmering for 45-60 minutes or until cooked. Remove to serving platter. Good warm or cold.

# MUSHROOM PATÉ

**Makes 4 servings**

  4-5 tablespoons butter
  1 pound mushrooms, chopped
  1 onion, minced
  1/3 cup minced fennel, bulb only
  2 eggs
  1 clove garlic, peeled, minced
  3 ounces cream cheese, room temperature
  3/4 cup bread crumbs
  1/2 teaspoon oregano
  1/2 teaspoon salt
  1/4 teaspoon ground pepper

Melt butter in medium saucepan, over medium heat; sauté mushrooms and onion until tender, stirring occasionally. In a separate bowl beat egg until light. Blend in cream cheese. Mix in vegetables, bread crumbs and seasonings, stir until smooth. Butter a 1-quart loaf pan; line with waxed paper. Mound mixture into pan, smooth top out with back of spoon. Cover with aluminum foil. Bake at 400°F. for 1 1/2 hours or until it tests done. Let paté come to room temperature, unmold.

# SPECIAL POACHED EGGS ____

**Makes 4 servings**

  1 can (10³/₄ ounces) condensed cream of chicken
    soup, undiluted
1¹/₂ cups milk
  1 package (10 ounces) peas and carrots
  1 small onion, minced
  1 teaspoon crushed basil
  8 eggs
  4 French rolls, split, buttered
    Grated Parmesan Cheese

Combine soup and milk in a medium skillet, over medium heat. Add vegetables and seasonings, stirring occasionally, until mixture begins to simmer. Reduce heat to low, continue simmering. Poach eggs, cover and cook 8 minutes, or until done. Remove with a slotted spoon. Sprinkle rolls lightly with cheese. Broil about 6 inches from heat until cheese is melted and the cut edges are lightly browned, about 2 minutes. For each serving, place 1 roll in each of 4 individual soup bowls. Arrange 2 eggs onto each roll. Ladle soup mixture over eggs.

# EGG ON A POTATO

**Makes 2 servings**

1½ tablespoons butter
1½ tablespoons all-purpose flour
   1 small onion, minced
   ½ teaspoon salt, prepared mustard
   ¾ cup milk
   ⅓ cup Cheddar cheese, shredded
   2 cups cooked sliced carrots, cauliflower
   2 large potatoes, baked
   2 eggs, poached

In a medium saucepan over medium heat, melt butter. Blend in flour, onion and salt. Cook, stirring constantly, until mixture is smooth and bubbly. Stir in milk all at once. Cook and stir until mixture boils and is smooth and thickened. Remove from the heat. Stir in cheese and mustard until cheese is melted. Stir in vegetables. Cut cross in top of each potato and press open. Fluff or mash. Spoon about ¾ cup vegetable sauce over each potato. Top each with 1 egg.

# PUFFED EGGS ———

**Makes 4 servings**

  4 **eggs**
 1/4 **teaspoon cream of tartar**
  1 **cup grated Swiss cheese**
  4 **teaspoons minced fresh parsley**
 1/4 **cup mayonnaise**

Separate eggs, keeping the egg yolk in egg shell halves set upright in egg carton for easy handling. In a small mixing bowl beat egg whites and cream of tartar until stiff, but not dry. Reserve 2 tablespoons cheese and 1/2 teaspoon parsley for topping, fold remaining cheese, remaining parsley and mayonnaise into egg whites. Place about 3/4 cup egg white mixture in each of four 1 1/2-cup individual, shallow baking dishes or custard cups. Bake at 350°F. for 15 minutes. With a spoon make a well in the center of each and slip a reserved yolk into each well. Sprinkle with reserved cheese and parsley. Bake until yolks are desired degree of doneness, about 5 to 8 minutes. Serve immediately.

# STUFFED PEPPERS __

**Makes 8 servings**

16 sweet finger peppers, slit, seeded
1/2 pound Monterey Jack cheese, cut into 1/2-inch strips
3 eggs, separated
4 tablespoons all-purpose flour
2 cups vegetable oil for frying
   Flour
4 large tomatoes, peeled and chopped
1 onion, minced
1 chicken bouillon cube
1/2 teaspoon crushed oregano
1/2 teaspoon salt
1/2 teaspoon pepper
4 ounces Cheddar cheese, shredded

Stuff each pepper with Monterey Jack cheese, dividing cheese evenly among peppers. Beat egg whites until soft peaks form. Beat egg yolks until light; add to egg whites. Sprinkle flour over egg mixture; fold together. Heat oil in a heavy, medium-size skillet. Coat peppers with flour. Dip peppers into egg batter. Fry in oil until golden on all sides. Drain on paper toweling. In medium-sized saucepan, combine tomatoes, onion, bouillon, oregano, salt and pepper. Simmer, covered, for 3 minutes, stirring occasionally. Place peppers in a shallow baking dish. Spoon sauce over tops of peppers. Sprinkle cheese over sauce. Bake at 350°F. for 15 minutes or until cheese melts. Serve hot.

# ZUCCHINI PANCAKES

**Makes 6-8 servings**

    3 cups grated zucchini
    1 onion, minced
    1 small carrot, grated
  3/4 cup all-purpose flour
  3/4 teaspoon baking powder
    2 eggs, slightly beaten
  1/2 teaspoon salt
  1/2 teaspoon white pepper
  .1/2 teaspoon oregano
    3 tablespoons butter
    3 tablespoons vegetable oil

Combine all ingredients, except butter and oil, in a large mixing bowl; blend together. Heat butter and oil in a large skillet. Shape zucchini mixture into pancakes with a tablespoon. Fry until golden brown on each side, turning with a spatula.

# SCRAMBLED EGGS WITH POTATOES

**Makes 6 servings**

    3  tablespoons shortening
    3  tablespoons bacon drippings
    2  large potatoes, diced
  1/2  teaspoon salt
  1/4  teaspoon ground pepper
    1  large onion, minced
    1  red bell pepper, seeded, chopped
    6  eggs, well beaten

Heat shortening and bacon drippings in a large heavy skillet. Stir in potatoes and seasonings. Cover, cook over low heat for 20 minutes, stirring often, do not brown. Stir in onion and pepper, sauté until tender over medium heat. Blend in eggs stirring often until eggs are cooked. Serve with hot sauce and warm flour tortillas.

# ENCHILADAS WITH SOUR CREAM

**Makes 8 servings**
**Filling**

> 4 cups refried beans
> 1 large onion, chopped
> 1 cup heavy cream

Combine all ingredients in a large mixing bowl, set aside.

**Tortillas**

> 1/2 cup vegetable oil
> 16 corn tortillas

Heat oil in a small skillet. Using tongs to turn tortillas, fry for 5-10 seconds on each side. Drain on paper toweling.

**Sauce**

> 2 cloves garlic, peeled, minced
> 4 large tomatoes, peeled, seeded
> 2 teaspoons crushed oregano
> 1/2 teaspoon sugar, black pepper, ground cumin
> 1 cup commercial sour cream

Combine garlic, tomatoes, spices and sour cream. Place in a covered container and refrigerate until ready to use.

**To Assemble**

**1 cup sour cream**

Dip each tortilla in sauce; place 3 tablespoons filling on each tortilla, roll. Arrange seam side down, in a shallow 9 x 13 x 1³/₄-inch baking dish. Pour remaining sauce over enchiladas. Bake uncovered, at 350° F. for 20 minutes. Garnish with sour cream.

# TORTILLAS AND CHEESE

**Makes 8-10 servings**

8 large flour tortillas
$1/4$ pound butter, room temperature
8 ounces Monterey Jack cheese, shredded
1 pound Chedder cheese, shredded

Brush each tortilla generously with butter. Arrange tortillas on cookie sheet. Bake at 400°F. for 2 minutes. Combine cheeses. Sprinkle cheeses over tortillas. Bake 10 minutes, or until cheese has melted. Place tortillas on serving dishes, cut into pie-shaped wedges with kitchen shears.

# BURRITOS WITH REFRIED BEANS AND CHEESE

**Makes 8 servings**

3 cups Monterey Jack cheese
3 cups refried beans
8 10-inch flour tortillas
1 large onion, minced

Combine cheese and 1 cup of the beans in a bowl. Divide filling between the tortillas; spread evenly. Fold one inch of the bottom and top edges toward the center. Fold sides into the center. Arrange seam side down, on a baking sheet. Bake at 350°F. for 10 minutes, or until the burritos are heated through. Place one burrito on each plate. Top with refried beans, sprinkle with onion.

# CHEESE TACOS WITH SAUCE ____

**Makes 8 servings**

  3 tablespoons vegetable oil
  1 onion, minced
  3/4 pound Monterey Jack cheese, shredded
  5 ounces cream cheese, cut into small pieces
  8 corn tortillas or taco shells
    Shredded lettuce
    Commercial sour cream
    Refried beans
    Taco sauce

Heat oil in large heavy skillet over medium heat; sauté onion until tender, stirring occasionally. Add cheeses; blend thoroughly. Remove from heat. Fill each taco shell with two tablespoons of the cheese mixture. Serve garnished with lettuce, sour cream, beans and taco sauce.

**Taco Sauce**

  3 tablespoons vegetable oil
  3 cloves garlic, peeled, minced
  1 can (13 ounces) tomato sauce
  6 tablespoons red wine vinegar
  1/2 teaspoon salt
  1/2 teaspoon red pepper flakes
  1/2 cup water

Heat oil in a small saucepan; sauté garlic, cook until lightly browned, stirring often. Add remaining ingredients. Simmer for 3-4 minutes. Store in a covered container, refrigerate until ready to serve.

# MUSHROOM CHEESE NO-FAIL SOUFFLE __

**Makes 8 servings**

  4 **tablespoons butter**
  1 **small onion, sliced thin**
  1 **pound mushrooms, sliced**
12 **slices white bread, crust removed**
  ³/₄ **pound Cheddar cheese, crumbled**
  6 **eggs, well beaten**
3¹/₂ **cups milk or half-and-half**
  ¹/₂ **cup minced fresh parsley**

Melt butter in a heavy skillet over medium heat; sauté onion and mushrooms until tender, stirring occasionally, reserve. Tear bread into strips, arrange one layer in the bottom of a 6-cup souffle dish. Cover with a cheese layer, top with a vegetable layer, continue until all the ingredients have been used. Combine remaining ingredients in a bowl, pour over souffle. Cover; refrigerate overnight. Bake, uncovered at 325°F. for 50 minutes or until souffle tests done. Let stand 5 minutes before serving.

# GREEK CHEESE PIE

**Makes 12 servings**

- 30 sheets phyllo dough, available at specialty food stores
- 1 cup butter, melted
- 4 eggs, well beaten
- 1 cup feta cheese, crumbled
- 1 cup ricotta cheese
- 2 cups small curd cottage cheese
- 2 tablespoons milk
- 1/2 teaspoon crushed dill weed
- 1/2 teaspoon tarragon
- 3 tablespoons minced fresh parsley

Brush the bottom of an 11 x 7-inch baking dish. Cut phyllo dough so it will fit into baking dish, layer ten sheets of phyllo dough on the bottom of the pan, brushing quickly, each sheet. Covering unused portion of dough with a damp towel to prevent drying. Combine remaining ingredients in a mixing bowl. Spread half of the cheese mixture over the phyllo. Top with buttered phyllo dough, continue until all the ingredients have been used. Brush remaining butter on top layer of phyllo. Bake at 350°F. for 1 hour or until phyllo is golden brown. Cut into squares.

# VEGETABLE NOODLE PIE

**Makes 12 servings**

- 1 pound medium egg noodles, cooked according to package directions, drain
- 3 tablespoons butter, room temperature
- 1 pound creamed cottage cheese
- 1/2 cup commercial sour cream
- 1 large Spanish onion, sliced thin
- 2 carrots, grated
- 4 stalks celery, sliced
- 1/2 teaspoon garlic powder
- 1/2 teaspoon salt
- 1/2 teaspoon tarragon
- 1/4 cup Parmesan cheese, grated

Arrange noodles in a deep bowl, toss with butter, set aside. In a separate bowl combine cottage cheese, sour cream, vegetables and seasonings, mix until well blended. Mound into 2 well greased 9½-inch pie plates. Sprinkle with Parmesan cheese. Bake at 350°F. for 45 minutes or until done.

# CARROT PATTIES ___

**Makes 4 servings**

  2 eggs
  1 cup cooked, mashed carrots
  ¹/₂ teaspoon salt
  ¹/₄ teaspoon white pepper
  3 tablespoons chopped fresh parsley
  ¹/₂ cup all-purpose flour
  4-5 tablespoons butter
  3 onions, sliced thin

Beat eggs until light in a large bowl. Mix in carrots, salt, pepper, parsley. Sprinkle flour over batter, incorporate. Set aside. In a large heavy skillet heat butter over medium heat; sauté onions until tender, stirring occasionally. Remove fried onions to serving plate. Reheat skillet adding more butter if necessary. Fry carrot cutlets, until golden brown on both sides. Arrange over onions.

# CHEESE BLINTZES

**Makes 4 servings**
**Batter**

```
   2  eggs
1¹/₂  cups milk
   1  cup all-purpose flour
   2  tablespoons melted butter, cool
```

Beat eggs until light; mix in remaining ingredients, blend until smooth. Cover, let stand for 20 minutes. Use a seasoned crepe pan. Butter pan, pour in just enough batter to cover bottom of the pan. Cook over medium-low heat until the crepe is dry, turn over. Cook until lightly brown. Invert crepe onto a clean kitchen towel. Continue until all the batter has been used. If batter seems too thick, add water, 2 tablespoons at a time. When crepes are cool, stack with a piece of waxed paper or aluminum foil between them.

## Filling

```
³/₄  pound dry cottage cheese
¹/₄  cup commercial sour cream
  2  tablespoons sugar
  1  egg, slightly beaten
  2  teaspoons orange zest
¹/₂  teaspoon vanilla or ground cinnamon
```

## To Assemble

Fill each crepe with cheese filling, roll tucking ends under, envelope style. Heat 3 tablespoons of butter in a large skillet. Heat blintzes until cooked and lightly brown on both sides.

# BREAD AND CHEESE FRITTERS

**Makes 3-4 servings**

- 6 eggs, well beaten
- 1/2 cup milk
- 1 cup bread crumbs
- 1/2 cup Romano cheese, grated
- 3 tablespoons chopped fresh parsley
- 3 cloves garlic, peeled and minced
- 1/2 teaspoon salt
- 1/2 teaspoon white pepper
- Vegetable oil for frying

Combine eggs, and milk, reserve. In another smaller bowl mix together bread crumbs, cheese, parsley, garlic, salt and pepper. Pour this mixture into the egg-milk mixture, combine. Heat oil to 375°F. in a medium skillet or use a deep-fryer, using medium heat. With a tablespoon slide mixture into the oil by spoonfuls; cook about 4 at a time, over medium heat. Cook until lightly brown on both sides, drain on paper toweling.

# ARTICHOKE DUMPLINGS

**Makes 3-4 servings**

1¹/₂ cups all-purpose flour
  4 eggs, well beaten
 ¹/₂ cup milk
 ¹/₂ teaspoon salt
 ¹/₂ teaspoon chopped basil
 ¹/₄ teaspoon white pepper
  2 packages (10 ounces) artichokes, cooked according to package directions and drained
  8 anchovy filets, minced
   Oil for deep frying

In a deep bowl combine flour with remaining batter ingredients, blend well. Cover, let stand 20 minutes. Mix artichokes and chopped anchovies into batter. Heat oil in a medium skillet with high sides, to 375°F. or use a deep fryer. With a tablespoon slide mixture into the oil by spoonfuls; cook about 4 at a time. Cook until lightly brown on both sides, drain on paper toweling.

# EGGS POACHED IN RED WINE ——————

**Makes 6 servings**

- 2 tablespoons butter
- 1 cup dry red wine
- 6 eggs
- 1/4 teaspoon salt and white pepper

In a medium skillet melt butter, add wine, over medium heat. Break eggs gently into simmering water, poach. Remove with slotted spoon. Serve with buttered English muffins.

# BAKED CHEESE MEXICAN SYLE ——————

**Makes 6 servings**

- 1 1/2 pounds Monterey Jack cheese or sharp Cheddar cheese, sliced thin
- 1 large onion, minced
- 6 tablespoons pimiento, chopped

Butter six small baking dishes. Divide evenly the cheese among the dishes. Bake at 350°F. for 10 minutes. Sprinkle cheese with onions and pimiento. Serve hot.

# PASTA WITH ROQUEFORT CHEESE

**Makes 8 servings**

  1 **cup half-and-half**
1/2 **pound Roquefort cheese, broken into pieces**
1/4 **teaspoon salt**
1/4 **teaspoon white pepper**
1/4 **teaspoon ground nutmeg**
  1 **pound ziti, cooked according to package directions, keep warm**
  4 **tablespoons butter**
1/4 **cup Parmesan cheese, grated**

In a medium saucepan heat the half-and-half; blend in Roquefort cheese, whisk until combined. Season with salt, pepper and nutmeg. Toss with ziti and butter, continue cooking over medium heat until warm. Arrange on serving plates. Sprinkle with Parmesan cheese.

# CHICAGO-STYLE PIZZA

**Makes 1 pizza**

> 1 package dry yeast
> 1 cup warm water
> 1 teaspoon sugar
> 1/2 teaspoon salt
> 1 tablespoon olive oil
> 2 3/4 cups all-purpose flour
> Cornmeal
> Filling
> 12 ounces sliced Mozzarella cheese
> 1 can (28 ounces) tomatoes, drained, chopped
> 2 teaspoons oregano
> 1/2 teaspoon salt
> 1 teaspoon fennel seeds, crushed
> 1/2 cup Parmesan cheese, grated

Dissolve yeast in water with sugar. Stir in salt and oil. In a large bowl combine flour and yeast, gather dough together, turn out onto a lightly floured pastry board; knead until the dough is smooth, about 5 minutes. Place dough in a greased bowl, turn to coat all sides. Cover and let rise until double in bulk, about 1 1/2 hours. Punch dough down. Brush a 14-inch deep dish pizza pan with oil. Sprinkle pan with cornmeal, just to lightly coat bottom. Press dough into the bottom and up the sides of the pan. Let dough rise about 20 minutes. Layer the cheese over dough. Combine tomatoes with seasonings, drizzle tomato around cheese. Sprinkle cheese over top of pizza. Bake at 450°F. 35-40 minutes.

# VEGETABLE PIZZA

**Makes 2 pizzas**

- 1 package dry yeast
- 1 cup warm water
- 1 teaspoon sugar
- 1/2 teaspoon salt
- 1 tablespoon olive oil
- 2 3/4-3 1/4 cups all-purpose flour

Dissolve yeast in the water with sugar. Stir in salt and oil. In a large bowl combine flour and yeast, gather dough together; turn dough onto a lightly floured pastry board; knead until the dough is smooth, about 5 minutes. Place dough in a greased bowl, turn to coat all sides. Cover and let rise until double in bulk, about 1 1/2 hours. Punch dough down, cut in half. Roll each half into a ball and press to fit two pizza pans, about 14 inches each. Brush with olive oil.

**Filling**

- 12 ounces Mozzarella cheese
- 4 tablespoons butter
- 1/2 pound mushrooms, sliced
- 1/2 teaspoon salt, pepper
- 1 teaspoon oregano
- 1 large onion, sliced thin
- 2 bell peppers, red and green, seeded, sliced
- 1/4 cup Parmesan cheese, grated

Layer cheese over crust. Heat butter in medium skillet; sauté onion and mushrooms until tender, season. Scatter over cheese. Arrange peppers on pizza. Sprinkle with cheese. Bake at 450°F. 15-20 minutes.

# PASTA SPINACH ROLL

**Makes 8 servings**

3/4 pound all-purpose flour
2 eggs
4 tablespoons warm water
Salt

**Filling:**
1 pound spinach
Salt
3/4 cup ricotta cheese
3/4 cup grated Parmesan cheese
2 eggs
Grated nutmeg
Tomato sauce
Grated Parmesan cheese

Sift flour onto a board, make a well in the center and add the eggs, water and salt. Work ingredients together until well blended, form the dough into a ball, cover with plastic wrap and chill for 30 minutes.

Filling: Clean and wash spinach and cook, with a small amount of salt, without water. Drain thoroughly and work through a sieve with ricotta cheese, or process with steel blade. Mix Parmesan cheese, eggs, salt and nutmeg. Roll out the dough in a thin rectangle, cover with the spinach mixture and roll up jelly-roll style. Roll in a clean cloth and tie both ends with kitchen string. Place in cheesecloth for easy handling. Cook in simmering salted water for 45-50 minutes. Transfer to a warm serving dish and serve, sliced with tomato sauce and grated Parmesan cheese poured over the spinach roll.

# TORTELLINI WITH CHEESE ____

**Makes 6 servings**

- 2 **cups all-purpose flour**
- 3 **eggs**
- 8 **tablespoons water**

**Filling**
- ³/₄ **cup ricotta cheese, sieved**
- 6 **tablespoons grated Parmesan cheese**
- 2 **eggs**
- 2 **tablespoons freshly minced parsley**
- **Salt and ground nutmeg**

Prepare filling: in a large mixing bowl mix the cheeses together. Blend in eggs, parsley, salt and nutmeg, reserve.

Prepare pasta: Sift the flour onto a board; make a well in the center, beat in the eggs and add the water. Work ingredients together until dough is smooth. Roll out dough into a thin sheet and cut into circles with pasta or biscuit cutter. Put a ¹/₂ teaspoon of filling in each circle. Fold dough over pressing the edges together and press the corners together to form tortellini. Cook the tortellini in boiling salted water for a few minutes and remove them with a slotted spoon as they rise to the surface. Toss tortellini in melted butter and Parmesan cheese and serve immediately.

# SPINACH GNOCCHI _

1½ pounds fresh spinach, trimmed, washed, cooked, drained well
1½ cups ricotta cheese
  2 eggs
  2 egg yolks
 ¾ cup sifted all-purpose flour
 ½ cup grated Parmesan cheese
    Salt and ground nutmeg to taste
  3 tablespoons butter
  1 clove garlic, minced

Puree spinach in food processor fitted with steel blade. Blend together with cheese and eggs. Mix in flour, cheese and seasonings. Shape mixture into small balls and sprinkle with flour. Slide into a large pot of boiling water and remove with a slotted spoon as they rise to the surface. Place on individual plates and sprinkle with grated Parmesan cheese to taste. Heat butter in small saucepan with garlic, stirring often. Drizzle over gnocchi.

# LARGE STUFFED SHELLS

**Makes 6 servings**

10 ounces giant pasta shells
1 tablespoon olive oil
2 tablespoons butter
2 tablespoons all-purpose flour
2 cups milk
Salt and ground nutmeg to taste
4 ounces Fontina cheese, diced
2 egg yolks
1 tablespoon butter, room temperature
Parmesan cheese, freshly grated

Cook giant pasta shells in boiling salted water with 1 table-spoon oil until they are al dente and drain on paper toweling, reserve. Prepare sauce; heat butter in a medium saucepan over medium heat; stir in flour until flour is absorbed. Mix in milk, salt, nutmeg and cheese. Whisk until mixture thickens. Mix in egg yolks and whisk until well blended. Fill the shells and place filled side up in a buttered ovenproof casserole. Dot with butter, sprinkle with grated Parmesan cheese. Bake in a 400°F. oven for 20 minutes or until golden brown. Serve immediately.

# EGG FOO YUNG ____

**Makes 4 servings**

  4 **green onions, chopped**
½ **cup water chestnuts, sliced**
  1 **cup bean sprouts**
  4 **stalks celery, sliced**
  6 **eggs, well beaten**
  4 **tablespoons peanut oil**

Combine vegetables in a bowl. Mix in eggs. Heat oil in a large heavy skillet or wok. Ladle mixture into skillet, forming a pancake shape. Cook until lightly brown on both sides.

# STRAW AND HAY NOODLES

**Makes 6 servings**

- 1/4 **pound green spinach noodles**
- 1/4 **pound egg pasta noodles**
- 1/2 **cup butter**
- 1 **cup heavy cream**
- 4 **tablespoons grated Parmesan cheese**
- **Salt and ground nutmeg to taste**

Cook pasta in a large pot of boiling salted water until it is al dente. Drain. In a large pan cook the butter, cream cheese, salt and nutmeg over medium heat until warm and thick, stirring constantly. Toss pasta in pan with sauce, mixing gently. Transfer mixture to a warm serving dish, serve immediately with extra Parmesan cheese. Recipe can easily be doubled or tripled.

# EGGS ON ARTICHOKE HEARTS

**Makes 4 servings**

- 4 **artichoke hearts**
- **Olive oil**
- **Lemon juice**
- **Salt and pepper to taste**
- 4 **eggs**
- 1/2 **cup mayonnaise**
- **Parsley sprigs for garnish**

Cook the artichoke hearts in boiling salted water. If using canned or frozen artichokes cook according to package directions. Season the inside with oil, lemon juice and salt and pepper to taste. Cook 4 eggs for 6 minutes. Shell and cool. Place 1 egg in each artichoke heart. Cover with mayonnaise and garnish with parsley sprigs.

# EGGS IN TOMATO ASPIC

**Makes 4 servings**

  4 eggs
  1 tablespoon tomato sauce
  1 cup aspic, commercial or home-made
  $\frac{1}{2}$ cup butter or margarine
  $\frac{1}{2}$ teaspoon anchovy paste
  4 anchovy fillets, rinsed, drained
  4 capers
  1 hard-boiled egg, peeled, quartered

Mix the tomato sauce into the cool but liquid aspic and let stand until almost set. Put the eggs in salted cold water, bring to a boil and continue cooking for 6 minutes. Put the eggs in cold water for a few minutes, shell. Melt the butter or margarine over medium heat with the anchovy paste and dip the eggs into this mixture. Pour into 4 individual molds a $\frac{1}{2}$-inch layer of aspic, let stand until completely set. Place 1 egg in each mold. Cover with remaining aspic and let stand in the refrigerator until aspic is completely set. Unmold onto a serving dish, top each with an anchovy fillet rolled around a caper and garnish dish with egg quarters.

# POACHED EGGS IN MUSHROOM CAPS

**Makes 4 servings**

    4 large mushroom caps
    1 egg, slightly beaten
    1/2 cup seasoned bread crumbs
    4 tablespoons butter
      Salt and pepper to taste
    4 eggs

    Sauce:
    1/2 cup dry white wine
    1 shallot, minced
    2 tablespoons beef stock
    1 tablespoon butter
    1/2 teaspoon freshly squeezed lemon juice
    1 tablespoon fresh minced parsley

Dip mushroom caps into a mixture of beaten egg and bread-crumbs. Heat butter in a medium skillet over medium heat, brown mushroom caps and season with salt and pepper. Arrange mushrooms inverted, onto a hot serving dish. Poach eggs and place drained eggs onto mushroom caps. Serve immediately accompanied by sauce.

In a small saucepan combine wine and shallot and simmer until mixture is reduced by half. Mix in stock, butter and lemon juice. Simmer 1 minute, stir in parsley. Drizzle over mushrooms.

# TOMATO FLAN _____

**Makes 6-8 servings**
**Pastry**

    **All-purpose flour**
1/2 **teaspoon salt**
1/2 **cup commercial sour cream**
5 **tablespoons butter, cut into pieces**

In a deep bowl combine all ingredients with pastry knife. Gather dough together into a ball, cover and refrigerate for 30 minutes. Roll out the dough and use it to line a 9 1/2 or 10-inch flan pan.

**Filling**

    5 **firm tomatoes, sliced**
6 **ounces Monterey Jack cheese, sliced**
8 **thin slices, French bread**
1/2 **cup heavy cream**
1/2 **cup commercial sour cream**
4 **eggs**
1/2 **teaspoon paprika**
1/4 **teaspoon ground nutmeg**
1 **tablespoon butter, room temperature**

Cover the bottom of the flan pan with tomatoes. Arrange the cheese on top. Cover the cheese with the 8 thin slices of French bread. Lightly beat the cream and sour cream together with eggs and seasonings. Pour mixture into the flan pan. Dot with butter. Bake at 400°F. for 30-40 minutes or until flan is firm and golden brown.

# TOMATO WITH CHEESE _____

**Makes 8 servings**

- 8 firm medium tomatoes, wash, dry
- 1 teaspoon salt
- 4-5 tablespoons butter
- 2 tablespoons all-purpose flour
- 1/2 cup half-and-half
- 1/2 teaspoon dried tarragon
- 3/4 cup grated Gruyere cheese, about 4-5 ounces
- 3 eggs, separated

Cut small 1/2-inch slice off stem ends, scoop out pulp, leaving the shell intact. Sprinkle inside of shell with salt. Invert onto paper toweling, drain 10 minutes. Melt butter in a medium saucepan and whisk in flour. Cook until butter is absorbed, stirring constantly. Stir in half-and-half and whisk until sauce thickens. Remove from heat, whisk in tarragon, cheese and egg yolks. Beat egg whites until stiff. Fold egg whites into cool sauce. Mound souffle into the drained tomatoes and mound some of the mixture on top. Arrange tomatoes on a cookie sheet. Bake at 275°F. for 30 minutes, serve immediately.

# MEAL IN A POTATO _

**Makes 6 servings**

- 2 large firm tomatoes, peeled, chopped
- 1 cup chopped zucchini
- 1 cucumber, peeled, chopped
- 1 red onion, sliced
- ½ cup grated Cheddar cheese
- 1 cup bottled mild taco sauce
- 6 baking potatoes, washed
- 3 tablespoons butter or margarine, melted
- 1½ cups Ricotta cheese

Combine chopped vegetables and cheese in a large mixing bowl. Blend in taco sauce, let stand for 1 hour. Prick potatoes with tines of a fork. Bake at 350°F. for 1 hour, or until fork tender. Slit potatoes lengthwise down the center and push together at the ends, creating a well. Place potatoes in a baking casserole. Brush insides of potatoes with butter. Fill potato with Ricotta cheese and spoon vegetables over the cheese. Bake 10-15 minutes. Serve hot.

# SUMMER STIR-FRY _

**Makes 6 servings**

    4  **tablespoons peanut oil**
    1  **large red onion, sliced**
    2  **cloves garlic, minced**
    3  **carrots, sliced thin**
    2  **cups fresh pea pods**
    1  **cup celery, sliced on diagonal**
    2  **cups broccoli, broken into flowerettes**
        **Salt and pepper**
    3  **tablespoons light soy sauce**

In a wok or large heavy skillet heat oil. Stir-fry onion and garlic for 30 seconds. Add carrots and pea pods, stir-fry 1 minute. Add remaining vegetables, stir-fry for 2 minutes or until vegetables are cooked but still crisp to the bite. Season with salt, pepper and light soy sauce. Serve with white fluffy rice.

# CAKES AND FROSTINGS

# Cakes
## and
# Frostings

To assemble a layer cake, place the bottom layer so that its top side is down, on the serving platter. Frost the first layer using a spatula. Spread to the edge of the cake unless the filling is very soft, a whipped cream frosting for example. Place the second layer over the first layer so that the top side, with its slightly rounded edge, is up. The edges of the cake layers should align.

To frost the cake, first brush away any loose crumbs. The cake should be completely cooled. Use a cake plate that is at least 2 inches larger than the cake itself. The top layer will slide easily into place when the icing dries, forming a slight crust before the top layer is added. If the top layer is positioned while the icing is soft, it cannot be moved. Spread a thin layer of frosting on the sides of the cake, using long strokes of a spatula held perpendicular to the cake. Frost the top of the cake, sealing in any loose crumbs. Frost roughly after the icing has formed a crust, first on the sides, then on the top of the cake. Continue using long, firm strokes to smooth the icing.

## FOR PERFECT CAKES EVERY TIME

Follow the recipe directions exactly.

Fill the cake pans one-half to two-thirds full.

Bake in a preheated oven at the temperature specified in the recipe.

Space oven racks so that the cake will be almost in the middle of the oven. Stagger layer pans so no pan is directly over another and they do not touch each other or the sides of the oven.

Test for doneness at the end of the minimum baking time. Do not open the oven door before this time.

Cool cakes completely before frosting.

The size of the pan is important. If a cake is baked in a pan that is too big it will be shrunken, flat and pale. If the pan is too small or shallow, the cake will bulge over and lose its shape. Always use the pan size recommended in the individual recipe.

Grease the bottom of baking pans for any cake made with shortening except chiffon types. Line the pan with waxed paper that has been cut to fit the bottom exactly. Grease the paper. Do not grease the baking pan for sponge and angel food cakes. If the pans are greased the batter cannot cling to the sides of the pan.

# WHAT WENT WRONG?

If butter-type cake falls

Causes may be;
•too much sugar, liquid, leavening or shortening
•underbaking
•temperature too low
•not enough flour

If sponge-type cake falls

Causes may be;
•egg whites overbeaten
•egg yolks underbeaten
•greased pans were used
•too much sugar
•underbaking

If hard top crust forms with butter-type cake

Causes may be
•too much baking
•oven temperature too hot

If hard top crust forms with sponge-type cakes

Causes may be
•too much flour or sugar
•oven temperature too hot

If cake is heavy (butter)

Causes may be:
•too many eggs
•too little leavening or flour
•too much mixing

|  |  |
|---|---|
|  | •too much shortening or liquid |
|  | •oven temperature too hot |
| If cake is heavy (sponge) | Causes may be: |
|  | •egg yolks underbeaten |
|  | •too much mixing |
|  | •egg whites overbeaten |

# WHIPPED CREAM FROSTING _____

  1 egg
3/4 cup sugar
1/4 cup butter, melted
  1 cup heavy cream, whipped
  1 teaspoon rum extract
    Ground nutmeg

In a large bowl beat egg and sugar until light. Mix in butter. Slowly add whipped cream and vanilla. Chill until ready to use. Serve over warm cake. Sprinkle with nutmeg to taste.

# CREAM CHEESE FROSTING _____

  4 tablespoons butter, room temperature
  1 box  Confectioner's sugar
  1 package (8 ounces) cream cheese, room temperature
  1 teaspoon vanilla

In a large mixing bowl combine all ingredients and blend together until smooth. Add food coloring to match cake if desired.

# ORANGE CHIFFON CAKE

**Makes 10-12 servings**

2¹/₂ cups cake flour
1¹/₂ cups sugar
  2 teaspoons baking powder
¹/₂ teaspoon baking soda
¹/₂ teaspoon salt
¹/₂ cup vegetable oil
  5 egg yolks
³/₄ cup freshly squeezed orange juice
  1 tablespoon grated orange peel
  1 cup egg whites
¹/₂ teaspoon cream of tartar

Combine dry ingredients in a large bowl. Make a well in center of mixture; add oil and egg yolks. Stir in orange juice and peel; blend with wooden spoon until smooth. In a separate bowl, beat egg whites and cream of tartar just until stiff peaks form. Fold in orange juice mixture. Pour into ungreased 10-inch tube pan. Bake at 325°F. for 55 minutes. Raise temperature to 350°F. for 10 minutes or until cake tests done. Invert cake until cool. Unmold onto serving platter.

## ORANGE GLAZE

³/₄ cup sifted Confectioners' sugar
3-4 tablespoons orange juice

Combine ingredients and drizzle over warm cake.

# CHOCOLATE CHIFFON CAKE WITH WHIPPED CREAM

**Makes 10-12 servings**

1½ cups cake flour
1¼ cups sugar
¾ cup cocoa
2 teaspoons baking powder
½ teaspoon baking soda
½ teaspoon salt
½ cup vegetable oil
5 egg yolks
¾ cup water
5 egg whites
1½ teaspoons vanilla
1 cup heavy cream
4 tablespoons sugar
1 teaspoon vanilla

Combine dry ingredients in a large deep bowl. Make a well in center of the mixture; add oil and egg yolks. Mix in water; continue mixing with a wooden spoon until mixture is well blended. In a separate bowl beat egg whites and cream of tartar just until stiff peaks form. Fold chocolate mixture into egg whites. Pour into ungreased 10-inch tube pan. Bake at 325°F. for 55 minutes. Raise temperature to 350°F. for 10 minutes or until cake tests done. Invert cake; cool. Unmold onto serving platter. Beat heavy cream with sugar and vanilla until soft peaks form. Serve with cake.

# HONEY CHIFFON CAKE

**Makes 8-10 servings**

3¹/₂ cups all-purpose flour
2¹/₂ teaspoons baking powder
1 teaspoon baking soda
¹/₂ teaspoon salt
³/₄ teaspoon cinnamon
¹/₄ teaspoon ground nutmeg
¹/₄ teaspoon ground ginger
1 cup sugar
3 egg yolks
¹/₄ cup vegetable oil
1¹/₃ cups honey
1¹/₃ cups warm strong coffee
1 tablespoon orange peel
3 egg whites, stiffly beaten

Combine dry ingredients in a large mixing bowl. Make a well and add egg yolks, oil, honey, coffee, and peel, mix well. Fold in egg whites. Pour mixture into ungreased 10-inch tube pan. Bake at 350°F. for 1 hour or until cake tests done. Invert cake on a funnel until cool. Loosen cake and unmold. Sprinkle with confectioners' sugar.

# RAISIN POUND CAKE

**Makes 8 servings**

- 1 cup butter
- 1 cup sugar
- 4 eggs
- 3 cups all-purpose flour
- 3 teaspoons baking powder
- 1/2 teaspoon salt
- 1 cup golden raisins

Cream together butter and sugar until the mixture is light and fluffy. Add eggs, 1 at a time, beating well after each addition. Blend in dry ingredients. Mix in raisins. Pour mixture into greased loaf pan. Bake at 300°F. for 2 hours. Cool before removing from pan.

# PECAN POUND CAKE

**Makes 8-10 servings**

      1 cup butter
2³/₄ cups sugar
      6 eggs
      3 cups all-purpose flour
  ¹/₄ teaspoon baking soda
  ¹/₂ teaspoon salt
      1 teaspoon lemon extract
      1 cup sour cream
      1 cup chopped pecans

Cream butter and sugar. Add eggs, 1 at a time. Beat well after each addition. Combine dry ingredients and add alternately with the sour cream. Blend until batter is smooth. Mix in pecans. Pour into a greased and floured 10-inch tube pan. Bake at 350°F. for 1 hour, 20 minutes. Cool, unmold. Sprinkle with confectioners' sugar.

# FLOURLESS CHOCOLATE CAKE

**Makes 8 servings**

    6 ounces dark sweet chocolate
    2 tablespoons strong coffee
    2 tablespoons coffee liqueur
    6 eggs, room temperature, separated
    2/3 cup sugar, plus 6 tablespoons
    1/4 teaspoon salt
    1 cup heavy cream, whipped for garnish, optional

Melt chocolate and coffee in top of double boiler over simmering water. Remove from heat; stir until smooth. Set aside. Beat yolks with 2/3 cup sugar until thick and light. Beat egg whites with salt until stiff but not dry. Mix chocolate with egg yolk mixture. Fold chocolate mixture into egg whites. Place one-third of the batter into a small bowl; refrigerate covered. Pour remaining batter into a buttered 9-inch springform pan. Bake at 350°F. for 25 minutes. Turn off oven; leave cake in oven 5 minutes. The center of the cake will fall and edges will form a rim. Cake will be 1 to 1½ inches in height. While the cake is still hot, place on serving platter. Spread chilled uncooked batter over top of cooled cake. Refrigerate 1 hour. When ready to serve, whip cream until it begins to thicken. Sprinkle remaining sugar over cream. Beat until soft peaks form. Decorate top of cake with whipped cream using a pastry bag fitted with a No. 4 star tip.

# CHOCOLATE ANGEL FOOD CAKE

**Makes 10-12 servings**

- ³/₄ cup cake flour
- ¹/₄ cup cocoa
- ¹/₂ cup sugar
- 1¹/₄ cups egg whites
- 1 teaspoon cream of tartar
- ¹/₄ teaspoon salt
- 1 cup sugar
- 1¹/₂ teaspoons vanilla

Measure and sift together cake flour, cocoa, and sugar; set aside. In a large deep bowl of electric mixer, beat egg whites until soft peaks form. Sprinkle cream of tartar and salt over egg whites; continue beating just until stiff peaks form. Fold in flour-sugar mixture with vanilla. Pour batter into ungreased tube pan. Bake at 325°F. for 1 hour or until cake tests done.

# CHOCOLATE SOUR CREAM CAKE

**Makes 6-8 servings**

- 1 teaspoon baking soda
- ¼ cup commercial sour cream
- ¼ cup butter, room temperature
- 1-ounce square unsweetened chocolate
- 1 cup sugar
- 1 egg
- 2 teaspoons creme de cocoa liqueur
- 1 cup cake flour
- ½ cup hot water

Stir baking soda into sour cream; set aside. In a small saucepan, melt butter and chocolate, stirring constantly over very low heat. In a separate bowl, whisk together sugar and egg until light and fluffy. Mix in creme de cocoa. Whisk in chocolate mixture. Add flour alternately with water, mixing thoroughly after each addition. Pour mixture into a greased and floured 8-inch layer pan. Bake at 350°F. for 30 minutes. Sprinkle with confectioners' sugar. Cut into squares.

# DARK CHOCOLATE POUND CAKE

**Makes 10-12 servings**

- 1/2 **pound butter, room temperature**
- 2 **cups sugar**
- 4 **eggs**
- 2 **teaspoons vanilla**
- 4 **ounces semi-sweet chocolate, melted**
- 3 **cups all-purpose flour**
- 1/2 **teaspoon salt**
- 1/2 **teaspoon baking soda**
- 1 **cup buttermilk**

Cream together butter and sugar until light. Add eggs, 1 at a time, beating well after each addition. Blend in vanilla and chocolate. Mix together flour, salt and baking soda. Add dry ingredients alternately with buttermilk until all ingredients have been used; blend well. Pour into a greased and floured 10-inch tube pan. Bake at 325°F. for 1 hour 20 minutes or until cake tests done. Cool before removing from pan.

# CHOCOLATE PAN CAKE

**Makes 10-12 servings**

  1 cup boiling water
$^2/_3$ cup unsweetened cocoa
  1 tablespoon instant coffee
  4 tablespoons butter, room temperature
$^1/_2$ cup shortening
  2 eggs
  1 cup sugar
$2^1/_2$ cups all-purpose flour
$1^1/_2$ teaspoons baking powder
$1^1/_2$ teaspoons baking soda
$^1/_4$ teaspoon salt
  1 cup sour milk*
  1 cup miniature marshmallows

Pour boiling water into cocoa and coffee; cool to room temperature. In a separate bowl cream butter, shortening, and sugar until light. Add eggs, 1 at a time, beat well after each addition. Mix in vanilla. Add dry ingredients alternately with buttermilk and cocoa. Mix in marshmallows. Mound mixture into a greased 13 x 9-inch pan. Bake at 350°F. for 1 hour or until cake tests done. Frost and cut into squares.

*To sour milk: place 1 tablespoon vinegar into 1 cup milk.

# ANGEL FOOD CAKE

**Makes 16 slices**

1³/₄ cups egg whites (12 eggs), room temperature
1¹/₂ teaspoons cream of tartar
¹/₄ teaspoon salt
1¹/₄ cups sugar
1¹/₄ cups sifted cake flour
1 teaspoon vanilla
¹/₂ teaspoon almond extract

Preheat oven to 350°F. Beat egg whites in large bowl of electric mixer at medium speed with cream of tartar and salt until soft peaks form. Incorporate sugar, ¹/₄ cup at a time. Continue beating just until stiff peaks form. Gently sprinkle flour over egg whites; fold in. Mix in vanilla and almond extract. Mound into ungreased 10-inch tube pan, bake on lowest rack in oven, 25-40 minutes or until done. Invert on a funnel for 1 hour to cool.

# FILLED CHOCOLATE CUPCAKES

**Makes 18 cupcakes**

1½ cups all-purpose flour
 1 teaspoon baking powder
½ teaspoon baking soda
½ teaspoon salt
½ cup cocoa
¾ cup buttermilk
 1 egg
 3 tablespoons butter
 1 teaspoon vanilla
18 Cherries

Combine dry ingredients in a mixing bowl. Mix in buttermilk, egg, butter, and vanilla. Pour batter into cupcake tins fitted with paper cups, ⅔ full. Bake at 400°F. for 16-20 minutes; cool. Cut off the tops and remove 1 teaspoonful of the center. Fill the center with Filling; replace tops. Frost tops of cupcakes with cocoa frosting. Garnish with cherries or sprinkle with chopped nuts.

**Filling**

 1 cup heavy cream
 4 tablespoons sugar
 1 teaspoon vanilla

Beat heavy cream. Sprinkle sugar over cream; fold in. Mix in vanilla; beat until soft peaks form.

**Cocoa Frosting**

   **1 pound confectioners' sugar**
   **½ cup cocoa**
   **½ cup butter, melted, cooled**
   **¼ cup milk**

Combine sugar and cocoa in a mixing bowl. Blend in butter and enough milk to make frosting spreading consistency.

# PRALINE APPLE BREAD PUDDING

**Makes 6 servings**

 ¾ cup apple juice
 ½ cup sugar
 1 teaspoon cinnamon
 ¼ teaspoon nutmeg
2½ pounds cooking apples, peeled, sliced
 2 tablespoons cornstarch
 3 tablespoons water
 1 tablespoon vanilla
 4 tablespoons butter
 ½ cup firmly packed light brown sugar
 6 slices dry white bread, crusts removed, quartered
 ½ cup sliced almonds

In medium saucepan, mix apple juice, sugar, cinnamon, nutmeg, and apple slices. Simmer until apples are tender, about 6 minutes, stirring occasionally. Combine cornstarch and water. Blend into apple mixture. Continue cooking until apples thicken. Mix in vanilla; cool. Combine butter and sugar in a large heavy skillet. Heat until mixture begins to bubble. Add bread pieces and almonds; toss to coat with butter mixture. Remove from heat. Lightly butter a 1-quart casserole. Layer one-half of the bread mixture in the bottom of the casserole. Arrange half of the apple sauce over the crumbs. Add remaining crumbs and top with apple sauce. Refrigerate at least 4 hours before serving. Can be made the day before serving.

# BANANA CAKE

**Makes 6-8 servings**

    1/2 cup butter
    1/4 teaspoon salt
    1/2 teaspoon ground ginger
    1 1/2 teaspoons vanilla
    1 cup sugar
    2 eggs
    2 cups all-purpose flour
    3/4 teaspoon baking powder
    1/2 teaspoon baking soda
    1/4 cup sour milk
    1 cup mashed bananas
    2 cups heavy cream
    2 teaspoons vanilla
    1 cup confectioners' sugar

In a deep bowl combine shortening, salt, ginger, and vanilla. Blend in sugar until light and fluffy. Mix in eggs, 1 at a time, beating thoroughly after each addition. Combine flour, baking powder and baking soda in a separate bowl. Add one-third of the flour mixture to creamed mixture, together with milk and bananas. Beating well after each addition, continue until all ingredients have been used. Mound batter into two 8-inch greased layer pans. Bake at 350°F. for 25-30 minutes. Beat heavy cream with vanilla and sugar until soft peaks form. Frost layers, sides and top of cake. Chill until ready to serve.

# CARROT CAKE ____

**Makes 3 cakes**

- 2 cups all-purpose flour
- ³/₄ cup sugar
- ³/₄ cup firmly packed light brown sugar
- 1¹/₂ teaspoons baking soda
- 1¹/₂ teaspoons baking powder
- 1 cup vegetable oil
- 4 eggs
- 3 cups grated carrots
- 1 teaspoon cinnamon
- ¹/₂ cup golden raisins

In a large deep bowl, combine dry ingredients. Blend in oil. Add eggs, 1 at a time, mixing well after each addition. Stir in remaining ingredients. Pour mixture into 3 buttered and floured, 8-inch baking pans or 10-inch tube pan. Bake at 350°F. for 25-30 minutes or until cake tests done. Cool on rack.

# APPLE NUT CAKE __

**Makes 8 servings**

     3 large baking apples (Granny Smith) peeled, coarsely
        chopped
 3/4 cup hazelnuts, chopped
     1 cup firmly packed light brown sugar
     6 tablespoons butter, room temperature
     2 eggs
     2 cups all-purpose flour
     1 teaspoon baking powder
     1 teaspoon baking soda
 1/2 teaspoon salt
     1 cup commercial sour cream

Combine chopped apples, hazelnuts and half of the sugar. Sprinkle over the bottom of a greased 9x9-inch square baking pan; set aside. In a mixing bowl, beat remaining sugar and butter until light. Mix in eggs and continue beating until combined. In a separate bowl combine dry ingredients; add alternately with sour cream until all ingredients have been used. Carefully mound mixture over apples. Bake at 350°F. for 45 minutes or until done. Serve with sweetened whipped cream.

# WHITE LAYER CAKE

**Makes 8 servings**

- 3 cups cake flour
- 3 tablespoons baking powder
- 1/4 teaspoon salt
- 3/4 cup butter, room temperature
- 1 cup sugar
- 1/2 cup water
- 1 teaspoon vanilla
- 6 egg whites, stiffly beaten

In a deep bowl combine flour, baking powder, and salt. In a separate bowl, cream butter with sugar until light. Combine milk, water, and vanilla. Add alternately with dry ingredients to creamed mixture, beat well after each addition. Fold egg whites into batter. Pour into 3 greased and floured 9-inch layer cake pans. Bake at 350°F. for 25 minutes or until cake tests done. Cool on wire rack.

# GERMAN APPLE CAKE

**Makes 6-8 servings**

1/4 pound butter, room temperature
1 cup all-purpose flour
1 egg
1/4 cup sugar
1/2 teaspoon vanilla

**Filling**

3 pounds Granny Smith apples, peeled, coarsely chopped
1 teaspoon cinnamon
1/4 teaspoon ground nutmeg
1 cup golden raisins
1/2 cup chopped walnuts

**Topping**

2 eggs, separated
4 tablespoons sugar
1/2 teaspoon vanilla
1 tablespoon flour
1 cup commercial sour cream

In a mixing bowl crumble butter into flour with pastry knife. Mix in egg, sugar and vanilla; knead until combined. If mixture is sticky, add 2 tablespoons flour and blend together. Press dough into bottom and halfway up sides of a 9-inch springform pan; set aside. Toss apples with sugar, cinnamon, raisins, and chopped nuts. Arrange apple mixture in the springform pan. Mix together egg yolks, sugar, vanilla, flour, and sour cream. Beat egg whites until stiff peaks form. Fold egg yolk mixture into egg whites. Spoon over apples. Bake at 350°F. for 1 hour; cool.

# COFFEE CAKE WITH NUTS

**Makes 8-10 servings**

- 1/4 pound butter
- 1 cup sugar
- 2 eggs
- 2 cups cake flour
- 1 teaspoon baking powder
- 1 teaspoon baking soda
- 1/2 teaspoon salt
- 1 cup commercial sour cream
- 1 teaspoon vanilla
- 1 1/4 cups chopped walnuts
- 1/4 cup firmly packed light brown sugar
- 2 tablespoons all-purpose flour

In a large bowl cream butter with sugar until light. Mix in eggs, 1 at a time, beating well after each addition. Combine flour, baking powder, baking soda, and salt. Add dry ingredients alternately with sour cream. Blend well. Butter and flour a 10-inch tube pan. Spoon 1/3 of the nut mixture over batter. Continue until all the ingredients have been used, ending with nut mixture. Bake at 350°F. for 45 minutes or until cake tests done. Cool on rack.

# HAZELNUT TORTE

**Makes 8 servings**

6 egg yolks
1¼ cups sugar
2 cups ground hazelnuts
¼ cup all-purpose flour
¼ teaspoon salt
1 teaspoon baking powder
6 egg whites, stiffly beaten

Lightly butter two 8-inch layer cake pans. Line the pans with waxed paper. Butter waxed paper, set aside. Beat egg yolks and sugar until light. Mix in hazelnuts, flour, salt, and baking powder. Fold egg whites into the hazelnut mixture. Pour batter into the prepared pans. Bake 25 minutes or until the cakes test done. Invert cakes on a wire rack to cool. Remove waxed paper.

**To Assemble**

1½ cups heavy cream, chilled
5 tablespoons sugar
1 teaspoon vanilla

Whip cream in a large mixing bowl until soft peaks form, beating in 1 tablespoon sugar at a time. Mix in vanilla. Place one of the layers top-side up on a serving plate. Spread whipped cream over top and sides. Place the second layer, top-side down, over the bottom layer. Frost with remaining whipped cream. Chill until ready to serve.

# RUM SPONGE CAKE ____

**Makes 8 servings**

    4 eggs, separated
  1/2 cup cake flour
  1/2 cup sugar
  1/4 teaspoon salt

Beat egg whites just until stiff peaks form. Sprinkle flour over egg whites; gently fold into egg whites. Beat egg yolks until lemon colored. Add sugar and salt; mix lightly. Fold egg yolks into egg whites. Pour batter into a lightly buttered 9-inch springform pan. Bake for 40 minutes. Prepare syrup. Remove cake from oven and cool for 5 minutes. Place on a serving plate. Prick top of cake with a toothpick. Ladle syrup over cake.

**Syrup**

    1 cup sugar
  3/4 cup water
    1 3-inch cinnamon stick
  1/3 cup rum

Place sugar, water and cinnamon stick in a small saucepan and bring mixture to a boil. Reduce heat and simmer for 3 minutes. Remove cinnamon stick. Add rum, mix well; cool.

# CHOCOLATE SPONGE CAKE ____

**Makes 8-10 servings**

 6 **egg yolks**
 1 **cup sugar**
 1 **cup cake flour**
 1/2 **teaspoon salt**
 1/4 **cup butter, melted, cooled**
 4 **ounces semi-sweet chocolate, melted, cooled**
 2 **tablespoons orange-flavored liqueur**
 6 **egg whites, stiffly beaten**

Beat egg yolks; blend in sugar and mix until light and fluffy. Sprinkle flour and salt over mixture; fold in. Blend butter, chocolate, and liqueur into batter. Fold egg whites into mixture. Pour batter into greased and floured 9 1/2-inch springform pan. Bake at 325°F. for 50 minutes, or until cake tests done. Cool on rack.

# BABAS AU RHUM __

¼ cup warm water, 105°-115°F.
1 teaspoon sugar
1 package dry yeast
¼ cup milk
6 tablespoons butter, cut into pieces
4 tablespoons sugar
¼ teaspoon salt
3 eggs
2 cups all-purpose flour
½ cup cake flour
8 baba molds, available at gourmet stores

Pour water into a measuring cup; sprinkle yeast and sugar over water, stirring to combine. Place in a draft-free area until dissolved, about 5 minutes. Heat milk to scalding. Add butter; stir until the butter melts. Mix in sugar and salt; cool. Beat eggs until light; mix into yeast mixture. Blend in milk mixture. Slowly beat in flour, blending until batter is smooth. Pour batter into well buttered baba molds. Let rise in a warm area until almost double in bulk. Arrange molds on a cookie sheet. Bake at 350°F. for 20-25 minutes. Remove babas from the mold, prick with a fork, place on wire rack over cookie sheet. Baste with Rum Syrup. Cool before serving.

**Rum Syrup**

  1 **cup sugar**
  2 **teaspoons lemon peel**
$1/2$ **cup water**
$1/4$ **cup rum**

Combine sugar, lemon peels and water in a small saucepan. Bring to a boil, reduce heat to simmer, and continue cooking for 5 minutes. Remove saucepan from heat and blend in rum.

# JELLY ROLL

**Makes 8 servings**

4 eggs, room temperature
1 teaspoon baking powder
¼ teaspoon salt
¾ cup sugar
1 teaspoon vanilla
¾ cup cake flour
2 jars (12 ounces each) raspberry jam
Confectioners' sugar

In a large bowl beat eggs, baking powder, and salt until light. Beat in sugar and vanilla and continue beating until lemon-colored and fluffy. Sprinkle flour over egg mixture; fold in. Grease and line a jelly roll pan with waxed paper; grease waxed paper. Spread mixture over pan. Bake at 400°F. for 15 minutes. Turn out of pan onto a towel that has been sprinkled with sugar. Slowly peel off paper and roll up cake. Cool. Unroll, spread raspberry jam over cake; reroll. Place cake on serving dish. Sprinkle top with confectioners' sugar.

# PRUNE SPICE CAKE

**Makes 8 servings**

- 2 cups all-purpose flour
- 1/2 teaspoon salt
- 1 teaspoon baking soda
- 1 teaspoon baking powder
- 2 teaspoons ground cinnamon
- 1/4 teaspoon ground nutmeg
- 1/4 teaspoon ground allspice
- 1/2 cup shortening
- 1 1/2 cups sugar
- 3 eggs
- 1 cup sour milk or buttermilk
- 1 cup pitted, chopped, drained prunes

In a large bowl combine flour, salt, baking soda, baking powder and spices. Cream shortening and sugar until light. Add eggs, 1 at a time, beating well after each addition. Add dry ingredients alternately with sour milk, beat only until blended. Add prunes and stir until well blended. Pour into two 9-inch layer cake pans. Bake at 350°F. for 35 minutes or until cake tests done. Cool on rack. Frost and serve.

# COCOA FROSTING

**Makes 3 cups frosting**

2³/₄ **cups confectioners' sugar**
¹/₄ **cup cocoa**
6 **tablespoons butter, room temperature, cut into pieces**
4 **tablespoons milk**
1¹/₂ **teaspoons vanilla**

In a large bowl combine sugar and cocoa. Mix in butter, milk and vanilla.

# CANDY CANE FROSTING

**Frosts three 8 or 9-inch cake layers**

¹/₂ **cup crushed candy canes (crush between 2 sheets of waxed paper with rolling pin)**
³/₄ **cup milk or half-and-half**
1³/₄ **pounds confectioners' sugar**

In a small saucepan, melt candy with milk over medium heat, stirring occasionally. Place confectioners' sugar in mixing bowl, blend in milk and candy mixture.

# CARAMEL FROSTING

**Makes 3 cups frosting**

- ¹/₂ cup sugar
- 2 cups sugar
- ³/₄ cup milk
- ¹/₂ cup butter
- 1 egg, slightly beaten
- 1 teaspoon vanilla

Melt ¹/₂ cup sugar in a small heavy skillet over low heat. In a small saucepan combine 2 cups sugar, milk, butter, and egg. Stir over low heat until butter melts. Increase heat and cook until mixture boils rapidly. When the sugar in skillet is a golden brown, pour it into the saucepan and stir continuously. Cook until a soft ball stage is reached on a candy thermometer. Mix in vanilla. Beat until frosting is spreading consistency.

# COCONUT FROSTING

**Frosts 3-layer cake**

  2 cups sugar
  1 cup milk
  1/4 teaspoon salt
  1 tablespoon butter
  1 teaspoon vanilla
  2 cups grated coconut

In a small saucepan combine sugar, milk, and salt; bring mixture to a boil over medium heat, stirring occasionally. Continue cooking 7 minutes. Remove from heat. Mix in butter, vanilla, and half of the coconut. Spread on cake while the cake and frosting are warm. Sprinkle cake with remaining coconut.

# DECORATOR'S ICING _____

4 **cups confectioners' sugar**
1 **teaspoon vanilla extract**
4 **tablespoons light cream**

In a large bowl combine all ingredients until they are of spreading consistency. Tint portions as desired. Frost cookies.

# SABAYON SAUCE ____

8 **egg yolks**
1/4 **teaspoon salt**
1 **cup sugar**
**Juice of 1/2 lemon**
1 **cup dry sherry**
2 **tablespoons brandy**
1 **cup heavy cream, chilled, whipped**

In the top of a double boiler over warm water whisk together egg yolks, salt, sugar and lemon juice. When sauce thickens whisk in sherry and brandy. Remove from heat, fold in whipped cream. Serve immediately.

# COCOA-RUM SAUCE _____

**¹/₂ cup plus 2 tablespoons heavy cream**
**2 tablespoons cocoa**
**¹/₂ cup sugar**
**1 tablespoon butter**
**2 tablespoons dark rum or 1 teaspoon rum extract**

Combine cream, cocoa, sugar and butter in a small saucepan. Cook over medium heat until mixture comes to a boil, about 3 minutes, stirring often. Stir in rum. Serve cold.

# SHERRY SAUCE _____

**2 eggs, separated**
**4 tablespoons sugar**
**4 tablespoons dry sherry**
**2 egg whites**
**1 cup heavy cream, chilled and whipped**
**Zest of 2 lemons**

Beat egg yolks and sugar until light. Stir in sherry, 2 well beaten egg whites, and cream. Fold in lemon zest. Serve immediately.

# ORANGE RUM SAUCE

**Makes 1³/₄ cups sauce**

> Juice of 2 oranges
> ¹/₂ cup sugar
> ¹/₂ cup water
> 1 teaspoon cornstarch
> Salt
> ¹/₄ cup rum
> 1 teaspoon orange zest

Combine orange juice, water with sugar, cornstarch and salt. Cook in top of double boiler over warm water, until thickened. Add rum and orange zest which has been allowed to drain on paper toweling. The sauce is served cold and should be the consistency of heavy cream.

# LIME FLUFF FROSTING

**Topping for angel cake**

- 1/2 cup sugar
- 1/4 teaspoon salt
- 1/2 cup thawed limeade concentrate
- 2 egg yolks, slightly beaten
- 1 tablespoon grated lime peel
- 1 1/2 cups heavy cream, beaten to soft peaks

Combine sugar, salt and limeade concentrate in a small saucepan. Simmer until sugar melts, stirring often. In a mixing bowl add egg yolks in a slow steady stream. Return mixture to saucepan. Add lime peel. Simmer until frosting is slightly thickened, stirring occasionally; cool.

# FUDGE ICING _____

4 cups granulated sugar
¼ pound butter
1 cup evaporated milk
1 pint marshmallow creme
12 ounces semi-sweet chocolate chips
2 cups chopped pecans
1 teaspoon vanilla extract

Combine sugar, milk and butter in medium saucepan. Cook over medium heat to 236° on candy thermometer, or about 8 to 10 minutes. Remove from heat, stir in chocolate chips, creme and stir until chocolate has melted. Stir in pecans and vanilla.

# HARD SAUCE _____

¼ cup butter, room temperature
1 teaspoon rum extract
1½ cups confectioners' sugar
2 tablespoons milk

In a large bowl cream butter until light and fluffy. Mix in sugar a little at a time; then beat in the rum extract and milk until mixture is smooth. Place in a covered container and chill. Spoon onto warm fruit pies and/or bread pudding.

# COFFEE FILLING

- 1/4 cup coffee liqueur
- 1 tablespoon granulated sugar
- 1 tablespoon water
- 2 teaspoons instant coffee
- 1 cup heavy cream, chilled, whipped

In a medium bowl combine all ingredients together and brush over individual cake layers. For a fluffy filling blend mixture into the heavy cream. Good with crepes.

# MINT CHOCOLATE FILLING

- 1 package (12 ounces) semi-sweet chocolate chips
- 1/2 pound butter, cut into pieces
- 2 cups confectioners' sugar
- 3 tablespoons Creme-de-menthe

In a medium heavy skillet melt chocolate chips and butter over low heat stirring constantly. Remove mixture from heat. Cool. Add confectioners' sugar until smooth. Blend in Creme-de-menthe.

# PIES
# AND
# PASTRIES

# Pies
## and
# Pastries

## PASTRY HINTS

Chilled ingredients are important for best results, unless otherwise stated.

Spoon dry ingredients lightly into measuring cup; do not pack. Level off the flour with spatula or a knife. Combine the flour with the salt. Use a large mixing bowl.

When cutting the shortening into the flour use a pastry knife or a food processor fitted with a steel blade. The dough will resemble coarse cornmeal.

Liquid should be added 1 or 2 tablespoons at a time. Incorporate and then continue sprinkling the water and blending until the dough holds together. Do not add too much liquid, just enough to hold the ingredients together.

If the filling is juicy, a steam vent should be provided so that the steam and juice can escape. Paper funnels can be used. Toss fruit with tapioca, flour, or cornstarch as directed in the recipe.

Bring dough together and shape into a ball; cover with waxed paper or plastic wrap, chill 30 minutes to 1 hour before rolling. If dough is very cold it will have to stand at room temperature for 20-30 minutes in order to warm up. Pounding with a rolling pin is also a way of softening hard, cold pastry.

Pastry dough should be rolled on a lightly floured pastry cloth or a pastry board. If the dough is for a double crust, divide dough in half before rolling out. Roll crust lightly from the center. Do not use too much pressure during rolling as the dough may stick to the rolling pin or the dough may roll out too thin. If the dough tears during rolling, pinch together and reroll. Roll dough $1/8$ inch thick and about $1 1/2$ - 2 inches larger than the size of the pan. Fold dough in half and then in half again. Place dough in the center of the pie plate. Unfold dough and fit it into the bottom and up the sides of the pie pan. Don't stretch the dough as it may tear.

Trim a single crust pie leaving a $3/4$ - 1 inch overhang. Fold the dough under to make a high rim, or flute. Fill and bake according to the recipe. If baking without a filling, prick the bottom and sides of the dough with a fork. Chill crust for 20-30 minutes. Line crust with aluminum foil. Cover bottom of pan with uncooked dry beans or rice. Bake at 450°F., for 12 minutes. Remove the foil and beans. Continue baking 4-5 minutes or until the crust is dry and a light golden brown. Cool.

Double crust pies are fitted with a bottom crust as in a single crust pie. Do not prick bottom. Fill as directed in the individual recipe. Roll the top crust, arrange it over the filling. Make a steam vent or prick with a fork. Press the edges of the two crusts together, fluting as desired. Cover the edges with foil to prevent browning too rapidly. Remove foil during the last 15-20 minutes of baking.

A lattice top is made by rolling the top crust and cutting it into 1/2-inch strips, using a sharp knife or a pastry wheel. Arrange half of the strips in one direction, attaching to the crust and trimming. Arrange the remaining necessary strips in the opposite direction. Press edges to seal. For variety, the second set of strips can be woven and then attached to the edge of the crust in the following manner. Lay the opposite set of strips and weave the strip through the other strips on the pie. Continue weaving the strips until the lattice is complete. Moisten edges and attach.

# FLAKY PASTRY DOUGH

**Makes a single crust**

1¼ cups all-purpose flour
¼ teaspoon salt
3 tablespoons butter
2 tablespoons vegetable shortening
4-5 tablespoons ice water

Combine flour and salt in a large mixing bowl. Cut butter and vegetable shortening into flour with a pastry knife. Sprinkle water over dough; mix together until dough forms a ball. Turn out onto a lightly floured board; knead for 1 minute. Cover with a plastic wrap or waxed paper and refrigerate for 30 minutes. Roll out on lightly floured board.

# HOT WATER PASTRY

**Makes a double 9-inch pie crust**

2 cups all-purpose flour
½ teaspoon baking powder
¼ teaspoon salt
⅓ cup boiling water
½ cup vegetable shortening

Combine flour, baking powder, and salt in a large mixing bowl. Blend together the boiling water and shortening in a small bowl. Blend into the flour mixture. Gather into a dough ball, cover with waxed paper, and chill 1 hour.

# BASIC PIE CRUST __

**Makes 2 pie crusts or 1 pie with top pastry**

1½ **cups all-purpose flour**
 ½ **teaspoon salt**
 ½ **cup vegetable shortening**
 ¼ **cup ice water**

Sift together flour and salt. Cut in shortening, with a pastry knife. Add ice water and mix with hands until dough forms a ball. The ball should be easy to handle, neither too sticky because of too much water or too crumbly because of too little water. Roll out dough and place in pie pan. Fill or bake as a pie crust.

# OLD-FASHIONED PIE CRUST

**Makes one double crust or 2 single crusts**

- 2 cups all-purpose flour
- $1/8$ teaspoon salt
- $1/2$ teaspoon baking powder
- $1/2$ cup butter
- $1/2$ cup shortening
- 4 to 6 tablespoons freshly squeezed orange juice
- 1 teaspoon orange zest

Combine dry ingredients in a deep bowl. Cut in butter and shortening until mixture resembles small peas. Add orange juice and zest, mix with a fork until mixture clings together. Form into 2 balls. Chill for 30 minutes. Roll between two sheets of wax paper. Add flour as necessary if dough is sticky.

# LARD PASTRY FOR 2-CRUST PIE

**Makes 9¹/₂-inch crusts**

2 cups all-purpose flour
¹/₂ teaspoon salt
4 tablespoons lard
4 tablespoons butter
5-7 tablespoons ice water

Place flour in a deep bowl with salt. Cut lard and butter into flour with pastry knife. Sprinkle 2 tablespoons of water over flour; toss to mix. Add enough water to make mixture hold together. Gather dough into a ball. Wrap in waxed paper or place in a plastic bag; store in refrigerator until you are ready to use. Divide dough in half. Roll on lightly floured pastry board. Fold circle of pastry dough into quarters, lift into pie plate, unfold and trim.

# GINGERSNAP CRUST

**Makes 1 crust**

1¹/₄ cups gingersnaps, crushed
¹/₄ cup butter, melted

Mix crushed gingersnaps with melted butter in a deep bowl. Pat into a 9- or 9¹/₂-inch pie pan. Bake at 325°F. for 10 minutes; cool.

# PIE CRUST WITH VINEGAR

**Makes 4 pie crusts or 2 pies with top pastry**

| | |
|---|---|
| 1/2 | teaspoon salt |
| 3 | cups all-purpose flour |
| 1 3/4 | cups shortening |
| 1 | egg |
| 5 1/2 | tablespoons water |
| 1 | teaspoon vinegar |

In a deep bowl combine salt with flour. Cut in shortening with pastry knife unitl crumbly. Reserve. Beat egg, water and vinegar together slightly. Add to the flour mixture and mix until it forms a ball. Divide into four balls. Cover and chill 30 minutes. Roll out one at a time on well floured surface and place in pie plate. Fill with desired filling, or bake as pie crust.

# FRESH COCONUT CRUST

**Makes 1 crust**

    2  cups fresh coconut
 1/4  cup butter, room temperature
    1  tablespoon all-purpose flour

In a deep mixing bowl combine all ingredients. Press firmly into the bottom and up the sides of a 9-inch pie plate. Bake at 325°F. for 10 minutes or until the crust is lightly browned. Cool.

# NUT CRUST

**Makes 1 crust**

 1/2  cup butter
 1/2  cup chopped almonds
 1/2  cup sugar
    1  cup all-purpose flour
 1/4  teaspoon ground cinnamon, ground nutmeg

Melt butter in medium heavy skillet. Mix almonds and stir fry until golden. Remove pan from heat. Stir in sugar, flour, cinnamon and nutmeg. Continue stirring until mixture is crumbly and lightly brown. Press crust into a 9-inch pie pan. Chill 1 hour before filling.

# ANGEL PIE SHELL __

**Makes 1 pie shell**

 3 egg whites
1/2 teaspoon cream of tartar
3/4 cup sugar
3/4 cup chopped pecans
3/4 cup sugar
 1 teaspoon vanilla

Beat egg whites until foamy and add cream of tartar and salt. Beat until soft peaks form. Sprinkle sugar gradually and continue beating until stiff, but not dry peaks form. Mound meringue into a buttered 9-inch pie plate and make a nest-like shell with the back of a tablespoon. Bring the side up 1/2 inch above the edge of the plate. Bake at 250°F. for 1 hour. Do not overbake.

# CREAM CHEESE CRUST

**Makes 3 dozen tart shells**

- 1/2 cup butter, room temperature
- 1 package, 3 ounces, cream cheese, room temperature
- 2 tablespoons milk
- 1 1/4 cups all-purpose flour

Cream butter, cream cheese and milk in a large deep mixing bowl. Blend in flour. Divide mixture into 3 sections. Wrap in plastic, chill 20 minutes. Roll each ball into a rectangle 6 x 8 inches and 1/8-inch thick. Cut each rectangle into 12 2-inch squares; press dough squares into muffin tins. Trim as desired. Chill 15 minutes. Bake at 350°F for 10-12 minutes.

# CRUMB CRUST FOR SPRINGFORM PAN

**Makes 1 crust**

- 2 cups graham cracker crumbs
- 1/2 teaspoon cinnamon
- 4 tablespoons brown sugar
- 8 tablespoons melted butter

In a large deep mixing bowl blend crumbs, brown sugar and cinnamon. Mix in melted butter. Press mixture evenly over the bottom and up the sides of a 9 1/2-inch springform pan. Chill until ready to use.

# PASTRY SHELL _____

1½ cups all-purpose flour
½ teaspoon salt
½ cup shortening
1 egg yolk
4 to 5 tablespoons ice water
2 teaspoons lemon juice

In a large bowl stir together flour and salt. Cut in shortening until pieces are size of small peas. Blend together egg yolk, 4 tablespoons ice water, and lemon juice with fork. Add liquid to flour mixture, mixing lightly with fork until dough just sticks together. Add more water, if necessary. Press into a ball. On lightly floured surface or pastry cloth, rolling from center to edge, roll into a ⅛-inch thick circle about 10 inches in diameter. Fit loosely into 9-inch pie pan or plate. Trim edge and flute, as desired. For baked shell, prick bottom and sides with fork. If using metal pie pan, bake shell in preheated 350°F. oven until golden brown, 8 to 10 minutes. If using pie plate, bake shell at 425°F. Cool on wire rack.

# PATÉ SUCUREE
# Sweet Crust _____

**Makes 1 crust**

1½ **cups all-purpose flour**
  1 **tablespoon sugar**
½ **cup butter**
  1 **egg yolk**
  2 **tablespoons ice water**

In a large deep bowl mix flour and sugar together. With a pastry knife cut in butter until mixture is crumbly or the size of small peas. Mix egg yolk with 1 tablespoon water; add to the flour mixture. With your hands combine remaining water making a smooth dough ball. Wrap in plastic wrap, chill 20 minutes. Roll dough on a lightly floured circle. Fold dough in half and then into quarters. Gently arrange in the bottom of a 9½-inch pie plate. Unfold dough; gently pressing dough against the bottom and up the sides of the pan; trim. If baking unfilled crust, cover with aluminum foil and add 1 cup of uncooked beans as a weight. Bake at 350°F. for 1 minute; remove foil and beans. Continue baking for 15 minutes or until crust is lightly browned.

# GRASSHOPPER PIE _

**Makes 8 servings**

1¹/₃ cups honey graham crackers, crumbled
 ¹/₄ cup sugar
 ¹/₄ cup cocoa
 ¹/₄ cup margarine, melted
 ¹/₄ cup green creme de menthe
  1 9-ounce jar marshmallow creme
  2 cups heavy cream, whipped

Combine first 4 ingredients thoroughly. Press into a 9-inch pie pan. Reserve 2 tablespoons of mixture for topping. Bake at 375°F. for 8 minutes.

Gradually add creme de menthe to marshmallow creme. Beat until well blended. Fold whipped cream into marshmallow mixture. Pour into crust. Sprinkle with reserved crumbs around edge and center of pie. Freeze until firm.

# MINCEMEAT PIE ——

1½ cups flour
1 teaspoon salt
⅔ cup lard
5 to 6 tablespoons ice water

Sift flour and salt into bowl. Mix in lard and blend with a pastry blender until mixture resembles fine cornmeal. Add ice water, tossing lightly until dough holds together in a ball, cleaning sides of bowl. Roll out on a floured pastry mat to a circle 1 inch larger than an inverted 9-inch pie pan. Fit loosely into the pan, trim off excess dough. Pour in the following filling. Add dots of butter and sprinkle with nutmeg. Add the top crust (make slits to let steam escape). Fold top edge under lower crust. Pinch edges to seal. Sprinkle top crust with sugar and drops of milk to make a brown glaze. Bake at 425°F. for 35 minutes.

## FILLING

2 cups mincemeat
½ cup orange marmalade
2 tablespoons flour
1 tablespoon lemon juice
¼ teaspoon nutmeg

Combine all ingredients.

# SPECIAL CHOCOLATE PIE ____

        3 squares unsweetened chocolate
    3¹/₂ cups milk
        1 egg or 2 egg yolks, slightly beaten
      ³/₄ cup sugar
        2 tablespoons butter
      ²/₃ cup sifted cake flour
    1¹/₂ teaspoon vanilla
      ³/₄ teaspoon salt
      ¹/₂ cup cream, whipped
        1 cup chopped raisins or dates
      ¹/₄ cup chopped nutmeats
        1 baked 9-inch piecrust

Add chocolate to milk and heat in a double boiler. When chocolate is melted, beat with rotary egg beater until blended. Combine sugar, flour and salt. Add a small amount of chocolate mixture, stirring until smooth. Return to double boiler and cook until thick, stirring constantly. Then continue cooking 10 minutes, stirring occasionally.

Add a small amount of mixture to the egg, stirring vigorously. Return to double boiler and cook 2 more minutes, stirring constantly. Remove from boiling water, Add butter and vanilla. Cool slightly and turn into piecrust. Chill. Before serving cover with sweetened whipped cream to which raisins or dates have been added. Top with nutmeats.

# NESSELRODE PIE ___

3 eggs, separated
1 cup milk
1/4 teaspoon salt
2/3 cup sugar
1 tablespoon unflavored gelatin
2 tablespoons cold water
2 tablespoons rum extract
1/4 cup chopped maraschino cherries
1/2 cup heavy cream, whipped
1 8-inch baked piecrust

In the top of a double boiler, place the slightly beaten egg yolks, milk, salt and 1/2 cup of the sugar. Stir, then set over hot (not boiling) water until thick. Stir constantly, then remove. Soak gelatin in the water a few minutes, then stir into hot mixture until dissolved. Chill until syrupy.

Whip egg whites until stiff peaks form. Gradually add remaining sugar. Fold whipped cream into egg whites. Stir cherries and rum extract into gelatin mixture, then fold in whipped cream and egg whites. Pile into baked piecrust, garnish with grated sweet chocolate. Chill until firm.

# BOSTON CREAM PIE

### Cake

    3 egg yolks
    1/2 cup sugar
    1 cup all-purpose flour
    1/2 teaspoon salt
    1 teaspoon vanilla
    3 egg whites, stiffly beaten

In a large bowl, beat egg yolks until light. Blend in sugar; beat until fluffy. Mix in flour, salt, and vanilla. Fold in egg whites. Pour mixture into a greased and floured 9-inch layer cake pan. Bake at 350°F. for 35-40 minutes. Cool on rack.

### Custard

    2 cups milk
    3 tablespoons cornstarch
    1/2 cup sugar
    3 egg yolks, well beaten
    1 teaspoon vanilla

In a medium saucepan, heat milk over medium heat. Combine remaining ingredients and slowly stir into milk. Continue whisking until mixture thickens. Cool.

### Chocolate Glaze

    5 tablespoons cocoa
    3 tablespoons water

**1/2 teaspoon vanilla or rum**
**2 teaspoons light corn syrup**
**2 tablespoons butter, cut into pieces**

Combine all ingredients in a small saucepan over medium heat. Stir constantly until mixture thickens.

**To Assemble**

Split cake in half using a serrated knife or by pulling a thread through cake. Fill with custard. Drizzle chocolate glaze over top of cake. Refrigerate until ready to serve.

# APPLE CHARLOTTE _

**Makes 6 servings**

10 slices white bread, crust removed
1/2 cup butter, melted
4 cups applesauce
2/3 cup apricot jam
1 teaspoon vanilla

Butter a 6-cup Charlotte mold or a souffle dish. Cut 1 slice of bread into a circle to fit bottom of mold. Cut remaining slices in half. Dip both sides of each bread into butter. Place the round shape in the bottom of the mold. Place overlapping slices of bread around and up the sides of mold; set aside. Place applesauce in a medium saucepan. Heat over medium heat. Mix in apricot jam and vanilla; simmer for 4-5 minutes, stirring often. Cool. Mound applesauce into the prepared Charlotte mold. Bake at 375°F. for 30 minutes. Cool for 2 hours; unmold.

# DEEP-DISH APPLE PIE

**Makes 8 servings**

   1 **deep 10-inch pie crust**
2¾-3 **pounds firm cooking apples, peeled, sliced**
   4 **tablespoons all-purpose flour**
 ¾ **cup sugar**
   2 **teaspoons ground cinnamon**
 ½ **teaspoon ground nutmeg**
 ½ **cup golden raisins**
   1 **tablespoon butter, cut into pieces**
 ½ **cup firmly packed light brown sugar**
   1 **cup all-purpose flour**

In a deep bowl toss apple slices, flour, sugar, spices, and raisins. Arrange in pie crust. Combine butter, light brown sugar and flour; sprinkle over pie. Bake at 350°F. for 30-35 minutes. Serve with slice of Cheddar cheese or rich vanilla ice cream.

# APPLE CUSTARD PIE

      **9-inch pie shell, unbaked (recipe follows)**
**1 cup thinly peeled, sliced apples**
**¹/₃ cup sugar**
**¹/₂ teaspoon ground cinnamon**
**¹/₄ teaspoon ground nutmeg**
**4 eggs, slightly beaten**
**2 cups milk, scalded**
**1 teaspoon vanilla**
**¹/₄ teaspoon salt**

Arrange apple slices on bottom of pie shell. Combine 1 tablespoon of the sugar with cinnamon and nutmeg. Sprinkle over apples. Beat together eggs, remaining sugar, milk, vanilla and salt. Place prepared pie on oven rack. Pour egg mixture over apples in pie shell. Bake in preheated 400°F. oven until a knife inserted halfway between center and edge comes out clean, about 30 minutes. Cool or chill pie before serving.

# TARTE TATIN _____

**Single crust of dough**

**¹/₂ cup butter**
**1¹/₄ cups sugar**
**2¹/₂ pounds Granny Smith apples, peeled, sliced**
**Sweetened whipped cream**

Roll dough to ¹/₈ thickness and into a 10¹/₂-inch circle. Place dough on a plate and prick with a fork; refrigerate. Melt butter and sugar over low heat in a deep 10-inch metal pie pan. Arrange apples in an attractive, overlapping pattern in pie pan, building up successive layers. Continue cooking until apples have caramelized, about 5 minutes. Place pan in a 400°F. oven for 5 minutes. Remove and cover with prepared crust. Crimp edges to seal. Raise temperature to 450°F. Bake pie 20 minutes, or until the crust is browned. Invert onto a serving platter. Serve warm with sweetened whipped cream.

# BANANA CREAM PIE

**Makes 8 servings**
**Crust**

1¼ cups all-purpose flour
½ teaspoon salt
¼ cup butter, room temperature
3 tablespoons vegetable shortening, room temperature
5 to 7 tablespoons ice water

Combine flour and salt in a large mixing bowl. Cut butter and vegetable shortening into flour with a pastry knife or use food processor fitted with steel blade. Dough will resemble crumbs. Sprinkle water over dough, mix until a dough holds together in a ball. Knead on a lightly floured board for 1 minute. Gather dough together, cover with plastic wrap, and chill for 30 minutes. Roll dough on a lightly floured board. Fit dough into 9-inch pie plate. Preheat oven to 400°F. Cover crust with aluminum foil, fill with uncooked beans. Bake for 10 minutes. Remove foil and beans, bake for 7 minutes, cool.

**Filling**

2 cups milk
½ cup sugar
4 tablespoons cornstarch
¼ teaspoon salt
3 egg yolks

**2 teaspoons butter**
**1 teaspoon vanilla**
**4 large, ripe bananas**
**1 cup heavy cream**
**6 tablespoons sugar**

Scald milk, remove from heat, cool. Combine sugar, cornstarch, and salt. Add to egg yolks and beat until light and fluffy. Add egg yolk mixture to milk; blend well. Place in top of double boiler over simmering water. Cook, stirring often, until mixture thickens. Add butter and vanilla. Stir until butter melts. Cool. Slice bananas into prepared pie crust. Pour cooled custard over bananas. Refrigerate until set. When ready to serve, beat heavy cream, sprinkle with sugar, and continue beating until soft peaks form. Cover top of pie with whipped cream.

# KIWI FRUIT TART

**Makes 8 servings**

- 1 9½-inch tart shell, baked, cooled
  Custard Filling
- 5 egg yolks
- 1 cup sugar
- 4 tablespoons all-purpose flour
- 2 cups milk, scalded and cooled
- 1 tablespoon butter
- 1½ teaspoons vanilla

Combine egg yolks and sugar; beat until lemon colored. Mix in flour. Slowly in a steady stream, add mixture to milk. Pour mixture into a medium saucepan and cook over medium-low heat until custard thickens, stirring often. Remove from heat, mix in butter and vanilla, chill.

**To Assemble**

- 1 jar (12 ounces) apricot jam
- 6 kiwi fruit, peeled, sliced

Place apricot jam in a small saucepan. Add 4 tablespoons water and heat until the mixture comes to a boil, stirring occasionally. Brush jam on bottom of pie crust. Pour cooled custard into tart shell. Arrange kiwi fruit attractively over custard. Brush with apricot glaze.

# PLUM TART

**Makes 8 servings**

**9½-inch sweet pie crust**
**2½-3 pounds fresh plums, cut in half and pitted, or
  canned plums drained and pitted**
 **¾ cup sugar**
  **3 tablespoons all-purpose flour**
 **¾ cup heavy cream**
  **1 teaspoon vanilla**
 **½ teaspoon cinnamon**
  **3 tablespoons sugar**

Arrange plums in a circular design in pie crust. Combine sugar, flour, cream, and vanilla. Sprinkle flour mixture over plums. Combine cinnamon and sugar; sprinkle over top of tart. Bake at 400°F. for 30 minutes or until plums are tender. Cool; serve with sweetened whipped cream.

# COUNTRY BLUEBERRY PIE

**Makes 6-8 servings**

- 1 **recipe double crust**
- 4 **cups fresh blueberries or 2 cans (21 ounces) blueberry pie filling**
- 3 **tablespoons tapioca or all-purpose flour**
- 3/4 **cup sugar**
- 1/4 **teaspoon salt**
- 2 **tablespoons grated lemon peel**

Line a 9 or 9½-inch pie plate with half of the pastry; set aside remaining pastry. Wash fresh blueberries; drain. Sprinkle tapioca over berries. Arrange berries in the bottom of the pie plate. Combine sugar, salt, and lemon peel; sprinkle over blueberries. Roll out remaining pastry. Cover pie with pastry; seal edges by pinching together. Prick crust with a fork. Cut a ½-inch steam vent in the top of the pie crust. Bake at 450°F. for 10 minutes. Reduce heat to 350° and continue baking for 35 minutes or until crust is brown. Serve warm with vanilla ice cream.

# PEACH TOPPED PIE _

**Makes 6-8 servings**

   1 **package (8 ounces) cream cheese, room temperature**
   1/3 **cup sugar**
   2 **teaspoons vanilla**
   1/2 **cup heavy cream**
     **9-inch pie shell, baked and cooled**
   6 **large peaches, peeled and sliced**
   1/2 **cup orange marmalade**
   2 **tablespoons water**

In a mixing bowl combine cream cheese, sugar, and vanilla. Spoon cheese mixture into cooled pie shell; refrigerate for 45 minutes. Arrange peach slices over cheese mixture, overlapping slices slightly. Heat marmalade in a small saucepan with water; stir until the marmalade has melted and the mixture is smooth. Drizzle over peaches.

# RASPBERRY CHIFFON PIE

**Makes 6-8 servings**

- 1 9-inch cookie crumb crust
- 1 package (8 ounces) cream cheese, room temperature
- 1 tablespoon milk
- 3 packages, 10 ounces, frozen raspberries, thawed and drained
- 4 tablespoons cornstarch
- 1/4 cup water
- 1/4 cup sugar
- 1 tablespoon freshly squeezed orange juice
- 1 teaspoon grated orange peel
- 1 cup heavy cream, whipped

In a large bowl, blend cream cheese with milk; beat until smooth and light. Heat raspberries, cornstarch mixed with water, sugar, orange juice and orange peel over medium heat until mixture thickens; cool. Blend in cream cheese mixture. Fold in whipped cream. Mound into pie crust. Chill.

# STRAWBERRY TART

**Tart Shell**

1¹/₄ cups all-purpose flour
  3 tablespoons sugar
 ¹/₂ teaspoon salt
  4 tablespoons vegetable shortening, room temperature
  2 tablespoons butter, room temperature
  2 eggs
  4 to 6 tablespoons ice water

**Filling**

  1 cup sugar
  5 egg yolks
¹/₃ cup all-purpose flour
  2 cups scalded milk, cooled
  1 tablespoon butter
  3 tablespoons dark rum

Combine flour, sugar and salt. Cut shortening and butter into flour mixture with pastry blender. Combine eggs with water. Gradually blend egg mixture into flour mixture until the dough holds together. Knead 1 minute. Gather dough into a ball. Cover with plastic wrap, refrigerate for 1 hour before using. Roll dough between two pieces of wax paper and fit into pan or pat dough into a 9-inch fluted tart pan with removable bottom. Cover with tin foil, fill with uncooked beans. Preheat oven to 400°F. Bake 10 minutes. Remove foil and beans. Bake 7 minutes. Have filling, topping, and glaze ready for a last-minute assembly. Beat sugar and egg yolks for 2 minutes or until lemon colored. Blend in flour. Continue beating while adding the milk in a slow steady stream. Pour filling into top of a double boiler over hot water. Heat until mixture thickens, whisking often. Remove from heat. Blend in butter and rum. Cool. Pour into prepared pie shell.

### Topping

**3 pints fresh, firm strawberries, washed, drained, hulled**
**1 pint blueberries, washed, drained**

Arrange strawberries with the largest berries in the center, putting the smallest berries around the edges. Sprinkle blueberries around the top of the pie into the spaces between strawberries.

### Glaze

**12-ounce jar apricot jam**
**6 tablespoons water**

Heat jam and water, stirring occasionally until jam melts and begins to boil. Drizzle glaze over fruit topping using a pastry brush or a teaspoon. Serve within an hour.

# BLUEBERRY PIE _____

**Crust**

  2  **cups all-purpose flour**
$1/4$  **teaspoon salt**
$1/2$  **cup butter, room temperature, cut into $1/2$-inch chunks**
  3  **tablespoons vegetable shortening, room temperature**
  5  **to 7 tablespoons ice water**

**Filling**

  1  **quart fresh, ripe blueberries, washed and drained**
  4  **tablespoons tapioca**
$1/2$  **cup sugar**
$1/4$  **teaspoon salt**
  3  **tablespoons milk**
  4  **tablespoons sugar**

**Crust**

Combine flour and salt in a large mixing bowl. Cut in butter and vegetable shortening with a pastry knife or a food processor until the mixture resembles crumbs. Add water and mix until the dough holds together. Gather dough into a ball. Wrap dough in plastic wrap and refrigerate for 1 hour. Divide pastry in half. Roll 1 half of pastry on a lightly floured surface. Fit into a $9^1/2$-inch pie plate. Preheat oven to 450°F.

**Filling**

Toss blueberries with tapioca, sugar and salt. Heap berries into crust in pie plate. Mound berries slightly at the center. Roll remaining dough into a circle 10 to 11 inches in diameter. Cover top of the pie, crimp edges. Make a ½-inch steam vent on the top of the pie. Brush milk over top of the pie. Sprinkle sugar over top crust. Bake at 450°F. for 10 minutes. Reduce heat to 375°F. Continue baking for 25 minutes or until the crust is golden brown and juice runs from the berries. Cool on a baking rack to room temperature. Serve with vanilla ice cream.

# STRAWBERRY CREAM PUFFS

**Makes 12 large puffs**

  1 **cup water**
1/4 **teaspoon salt**
1/4 **pound butter, room temperature, cut into 1/2-inch pieces**
  1 **cup all-purpose flour**
  2 **tablespoons sugar**
  4 **eggs**

Combine water, salt and butter in a medium saucepan. Bring mixture to a boil over medium heat; stir until the butter melts. Remove saucepan from heat. Add flour and sugar; beat with a wooden spoon until the mixture pulls away from the sides of the pan and forms a ball. Add eggs, 1 at a time, beating well after each addition. Lightly butter a cookie sheet. Preheat oven to 425°F. Drop batter by tablespoonfuls onto the cookie sheet, or use a pastry bag to shape puffs. Leave 2 inches between puffs. Reduce heat to 350°F., bake for 15 minutes or until the puffs are a golden brown and puffed. Cut tops off puffs; shut heat off and allow puffs to dry in oven. Remove any excess uncooked dough. Fill puffs 1 hour before serving.

**Strawberry Cream Filling**

1/2 **cup confectioners' sugar**
  1 **pint strawberries, hulled and chopped**
  1 **cup heavy cream, whipped**

In a large bowl, sprinkle sugar over berries. Blend in whipped heavy cream. Fill cooled puffs with strawberry cream filling. Sprinkle with confectioners' sugar.

# COCONUT CUSTARD PIE _____

**Makes 6 servings**

- 1 9-inch partially baked crust
- 4 eggs
- 1/2 teaspoon salt
- 1/2 cup sugar
- 3 cups milk, scalded and cooled
- 1 teaspoon vanilla
- 1 cup grated coconut
- Fresh grated nutmeg for garnish

Beat eggs in mixing bowl; blend in salt, sugar, milk, vanilla, and coconut. Pour custard mixture into pie shell. Garnish with grated nutmeg. Bake at 350°F. for 10 minutes. Reduce heat to 325°F., continue baking 35 minutes or until pie tests done.

# CHOCOLATE CHEESE PIE _____

**Makes 8 servings**

- 1 10-inch chocolate cookie crumb crust
- 1 package (8 ounces) cream cheese, room temperature
- 1/2 pound creamed cottage cheese
- 3/4 cup sugar
- 2 teaspoons vanilla
- 1/4 teaspoon salt
- 3 eggs
- 12 ounces semisweet chocolate pieces, melted and cooled
- 1 cup heavy cream, whipped
  Chocolate curls, optional

In a large, deep mixing bowl, combine cream cheese, cottage cheese, sugar, vanilla, salt and eggs; beat until smooth and light, about 5 minutes. Stir in melted chocolate. Continue mixing until completely blended. Fold in whipped cream. Mound filling into prepared cookie crust. Freeze until set. Allow pie to stand at room temperature for 1 hour before serving. Garnish with chocolate curls or dollops of sweetened whipped cream if desired.

# SOUTHERN PECAN PIE _____

**Makes 6-8 servings**

> 1 9-inch unbaked pastry shell
> 4 eggs
> ½ cup firmly packed dark brown sugar
> ¾ cup dark corn syrup
> ¼ teaspoon salt
> 2 teaspoons orange zest
> 1 teaspoon vanilla
> 1½ cups pecan halves

Beat eggs and sugar until light in mixing bowl. Add syrup, blend together. Beat in salt, orange zest and vanilla. Spread pecans evenly over the bottom of the pie shell. Pour filling in shell. Bake at 350°F. for 50 minutes or until done. Cool on rack.

# MINIATURE PECAN PIES

1 package (3 ounces) cream cheese, softened
1/2 cup margarine, softened
1 cup flour

Combine cream cheese and margarine; blend well. Add flour and mix thoroughly. Chill overnight. Divide pastry into 24 balls and press into miniature muffin tins, covering bottom and sides. Spoon pecan filling into shells. Bake at 325°F. for 25 minutes. Cool in pans; turn out onto waxed paper.

**Pecan Filling**

1 egg, lightly beaten
3/4 cup firmly packed light brown sugar
1 tablespoon margarine, melted
1 teaspoon vanilla extract
1/4 teaspoon salt
2/3 cup coarsely broken pecans

Combine all ingredients; mix well.

Note: For variety use coconut and dates in place of pecans. Pastry shells can be baked and then filled with jellies or marmalade.

# COOKIES

# Cookies

## MACAROONS _____

**Makes 3 dozen**

   1 cup almond paste, room temperature
   1 cup confectioners' sugar
   3 egg whites
  1/4 teaspoon salt
  1/2 teaspoon vanilla

Soften almond paste in a large mixing bowl. Blend in sugar. Add egg whites, 1 at a time, mixing after each addition. A soft dough will form. Mix in salt and vanilla. Drop batter by tea-spoonfuls onto greased cookie sheet. Bake at 300°F. for 20 minutes. Cool on rack.

# BIRTHDAY GREETING CARD COOKIE

**Makes 2 birthday cookies**

1½ cups butter
1 cup firmly packed light brown sugar
1 cup granulated sugar
3 eggs
1 teaspoon vanilla
3½ cups all-purpose flour
1 teaspoon baking soda
¼ teaspoon salt
Packaged tubes of icing in various colors or Royal Icing

Cream butter and sugars together in a large mixing bowl until light and fluffy. Blend in eggs and vanilla. In a separate bowl, combine flour, baking soda and salt. Add flour to the creamed mixture, blend together. To make 2 large cookies use 1 cookie sheet for each cookie. Divide dough in half, arrange dough into a circle or heart shape on cookie sheet. Bake at 350°F. for 20 minutes or until the cookies are golden brown. Cool completely on rack. Decorate cookies with birthday message with tube frosting.

# CHOCOLATE DIPPED COOKIES _____

**Makes 24 cookies**

  5 tablespoons butter, cut into small pieces
$1/3$ cup sugar
  1 egg yolk
$1/2$ cup canned chestnut puree, available at gourmet stores
$1/2$ teaspoon vanilla
$1/4$ teaspoon salt
$1^1/4$ cups all-purpose flour
  1 egg white, slightly beaten
  1 cup sugar
$3/4$ cup semi-sweet chocolate chips
  3 tablespoons boiling water

Cream butter and sugar until light. Mix in egg yolk. Blend in chestnut puree, vanilla, salt and flour. Roll 1 tablespoon of batter into a finger shape. Dip into the egg white, roll in sugar. Place cookies on buttered cookie sheet. Bake 20 minutes or until cookies are firm and lightly browned. Melt chocolate with boiling water. Dip ends of cookie into the chocolate; let cookies dry on a sheet of waxed paper.

# MOLASSES COOKIES

**Makes 1½ dozen**

```
  4 cups all-purpose flour
 ½ teaspoon salt
1½ teaspoons ground ginger
 ½ teaspoon ground cloves
 ½ teaspoon nutmeg
 ½ teaspoon allspice
  1 cup dark molasses
  1 teaspoon baking soda
  2 tablespoons rum
 ⅓ cup water
  1 cup sugar
 ½ cup butter
```

Combine dry ingredients in a large mixing bowl. Combine molasses and baking soda. Mix rum and water together. Cream sugar and butter. Add half dry ingredients and half water mixture and half molasses mixture, blending well after each addition. Repeat. Wrap dough in aluminum foil, waxed paper or plastic wrap and chill for 1 hour. Roll dough on lightly floured surface ¼ inch thick; cut wih 4-inch cookie cutter or use the bottom of a 1 pound coffee can as a cutter. Place cookies on a greased cookie sheet. Bake at 375°F. for 10-12 minutes. Allow cookies to cool 5 minutes, remove from cookie sheet to rack.

# HERMITS —————

**Makes 4½ dozen cookies**

  ¾ **cup butter or margarine, room temperature**
1½ **cups firmly packed dark brown sugar**
  2 **eggs**
2½ **cups all-purpose flour**
  1 **teaspoon baking soda**
  1 **teaspoon ground cinnamon**
  ¼ **teaspoon salt**
  ¼ **teaspoon allspice**
  ¼ **teaspoon ground cloves**
  ¾ **cup golden raisins**
  ¾ **cup chopped walnuts**

Cream butter and sugar in a large mixer bowl until light and fluffy. Beat in eggs. In a separate bowl combine flour, baking soda and spices. Add it to the creamed mixture, blend well. Mix in raisins and walnuts. Drop by rounded teaspoonfuls onto a greased baking sheet. Bake at 375°F. for 8 to 10 minutes or until golden brown. Cool on rack.

# FRUIT DROP COOKIES

**Makes 5¹/₂ dozen cookies**

1¹/₄ cups all-purpose flour
¹/₄ teaspoon baking soda
1 teaspoon ground cinnamon
¹/₂ teaspoon ground cloves
¹/₄ teaspoon salt
¹/₂ cup butter or margarine, room temperature
1 cup firmly packed light brown sugar
2 eggs
¹/₂ cup buttermilk
1 cup raisins, currants
¹/₄ cup candied diced pineapple
¹/₂ cup candied diced citron
¹/₂ cup chopped walnuts

Combine flour, baking soda, cinnamon, cloves and salt, set aside. Cream butter and sugar until light and fluffy. Add eggs, beating until light. Alternately add flour mixture and buttermilk, beat well after each addition. Mix in fruit and nuts. Drop from teaspoon, 2 inches apart onto a greased cookie sheet. Bake at 350°F. for 12 to 15 minutes, or until the edges are lightly browned.

# OATMEAL COOKIES

**Makes 4 dozen cookies**

 3/4 cup butter or margarine
 1 cup firmly packed light brown sugar
 2 eggs
 1 teaspoon vanilla
 2 cups all-purpose flour
 1 teaspoon baking soda
 3/4 teaspoon ground cinnamon
 1 cup raisins
 3/4 cup rolled oats

Cream butter and sugar until light. Add eggs, beat well. Combine dry ingredients, blend into butter mixture. Mix in raisins. Drop by teaspoonfuls onto a greased cookie sheet. Bake at 375°F. for 15 minutes. Cool on rack.

# APRICOT SQUARES

**Makes 16 squares**

  1 **cup dried apricots**
    **Water**
$1/2$ **cup butter**
$1/4$ **cup firmly packed brown sugar**
  1 **cup all-purpose flour**
$1/3$ **cup all-purpose flour**
$1/2$ **teaspoon baking powder**
  3 **eggs**
  1 **cup firmly packed brown sugar**
  1 **teaspoon vanilla**
    **Confectioners' sugar**

Cook apricots in water to cover until apricots are tender, about 10 minutes. Drain, cool and puree. Mix butter into sugar and 1 cup flour until mixture resembles crumbs. Press into the bottom of greased 9x9-inch pan. Bake at 350°F. for 20 minutes. Combine $1/3$ cup flour and baking powder. Beat eggs until light. Mix in brown sugar and flour mixture. Mix in vanilla and apricots. Spread over baked layer. Bake for 25-30 minutes. Sprinkle with confectioners' sugar. Cut into squares.

# PUMPKIN COOKIES _

**4 cups all-purpose flour**
**2 cups quick or old-fashioned oats, uncooked**
**2 teaspoons baking soda**
**2 teaspoons ground cinnamon**
**1 teaspoon salt**
**1½ cups butter, room temperature**
**2 cups firmly packed brown sugar**
**1 cup granulated sugar**
**1 egg**
**1 teaspoon vanilla extract**
**1 can, 16 ounces, pumpkin**
**1 cup semi-sweet chocolate pieces**
**Peanut butter**
**1 cup raisins**
**1 cup peanuts**

Preheat oven to 350°F. Combine flour, oats, soda, cinnamon and salt; set aside. Cream butter; gradually add sugars, beating until light and fluffy. Add egg and vanilla; mix well. Alternate additions of dry ingredients and pumpkin, mixing well after each addition. Stir in chocolate pieces. For each cookie, drop ¼ cup dough onto lightly greased cookie sheet; spread into pumpkin shape using a thin metal spatula. Add a bit more dough to form stem. Bake at 350°F. for 20-25 minutes, until cookies are firm and lightly browned. Remove from cookie sheets; cool on racks. Decorate using icing or peanut butter to affix raisins and peanuts.

# PFEFFERNUSSE

1³/₄ **cups all-purpose flour**
  1 **teaspoon baking powder**
  1 **teaspoon cinnamon**
¹/₂ **teaspoon cloves**
¹/₂ **teaspoon mace**
¹/₄ **teaspoon pepper**
  2 **eggs**
  1 **cup sugar**
³/₄ **cup chopped candied citron**
  1 **teaspoon grated lemon peel**
   **Confectioners' sugar**

In a mixing bowl, blend together flour, baking powder, cinnamon, cloves, mace and pepper; set aside. Beat eggs unti light. Gradually beat in sugar. Stir in dry ingredients. Stir candied citron and lemon peel; mix well. Shape into 1-inch balls. Place on greased cookie sheets. Cover with wax paper and let stand overnight. Bake at 350°F. for 20 minutes. Roll in confectioners' sugar. Cool on wire rack. Store in tightly covered container for 1 week before serving.

# BUTTER COOKIES __

**Makes 3¹/₂ dozen cookies**

   **¹/₂ cup butter**
    **1 cup confectioners' sugar**
    **1 egg**
     **Grated peel of I lemon**
   **¹/₄ teaspoon mace**
   **¹/₂ teaspoon salt**
**2¹/₂ cups all-purpose flour**
   **¹/₂ teaspoon baking powder**

Cream butter and sugar until light and fluffy. Beat in egg and lemon peel. Add dry ingredients, work with hands to a smooth dough. Chill several hours. Roll to ¹/₈-inch thickness on a lightly floured board; cut with floured cookie cutter. Bake at 350°F. for 15 minutes; cool.

# WALNUT CRESCENTS

**Makes 4¹/₂ dozen cookies**

  1 **cup ground walnuts**
  1 **cup butter**
 ³/₄ **cup sugar**
2¹/₂ **cups all-purpose flour**
1¹/₂ **teaspoons vanilla**

**Vanilla Sugar**

  2 **vanilla beans, cut into 1-inch pieces**
  2 **cups confectioners' sugar**

Combine all cookie ingredients in a large mixing bowl; knead to a smooth dough. Shape dough into 1¹/₂-inch long crescents, using 1 teaspoon of the dough for each cookie. Bake on cookie sheets at 350°F. for 15 minutes. Cool slightly; while cookies are still warm roll in vanilla sugar. Cool cookies and re-roll in vanilla sugar.

**Vanilla Sugar**

Combine vanilla beans and confectioners' sugar in a covered jar. Allow vanilla sugar to stand for 2 days. Remove beans.

# APRICOT BARS ————

1 cup butter, room temperature
2 cups all-purpose flour
1/2 cup sugar
2 cups (12 ounces) dried apricots
1 cup water
2 cups packed light brown sugar
4 eggs, well beaten
2/3 cup all-purpose flour
1/4 teaspoon salt
1 teaspoon baking powder
1 teaspoon vanilla
1 cup chopped pecans
Confectioners' sugar

Combine butter, flour and sugar together in a large mixing bowl. Spread mixture into 11 3/4 x 7-inch baking pan. Pat mixture firmly into pan. Bake at 350°F. for 35 minutes or until the crust is a light brown. Prepare filling: Combine dried apricots and water in a small saucepan. Bring mixture to a boil and continue boiling, uncovered, 10 minutes. Remove from the heat, cool, drain, puree. Beat brown sugar and eggs until light and fluffy. In a separate bowl combine dry ingredients. Gradually add to sugar and eggs. Mix in vanilla, nuts and apricots. Spread mixture over baked crust. Bake at 350°F. for 30 minutes. Cool in pan; cut into bars. Sprinkle apricot bars wth confectioners' sugar.

# LACE COOKIES

**Makes 5 dozen**

- ¼ cup butter
- ¼ cup vegetable shortening
- ½ cup light corn syrup
- ¾ cup packed light brown sugar
- 1 cup unsifted all-purpose flour
- ¾ cup ground pecans
- 1 cup semi-sweet chocolate pieces

Combine butter, vegetable shortening, corn syrup and sugar in a medium saucepan; bring to a boil. Remove from heat. Mix in flour and nuts. Drop batter by rounded teaspoon onto a greased and floured cookie sheet, 3 inches apart. Bake at 325°F. for 8 to 10 minutes. Cool 1 minute, remove from cookie sheet with a spatula. Melt chocolate in the top of a double boiler over hot (not boiling) water, stirring until smooth. Brush each cookie with chocolate.

# DARK CHOCOLATE DROP COOKIES

**Makes 4¹/₂ dozen cookies**

- ¹/₂ cup butter or margarine
- 1 cup packed light brown sugar
- 1 egg
- 1 teaspoon vanilla
- 2 squares, 1 ounce each, unsweetened chocolate, melted, cooled
- 2 cups unsifted, all-purpose flour
- ¹/₂ teaspoon baking soda
- ¹/₄ teaspoon salt
- ³/₄ cup commercial sour cream
- ¹/₂ cup chopped pecans

Cream butter and sugar until light and fluffy in large mixer bowl. Beat in egg and vanilla. Stir in cooled chocolate. In a separate bowl combine dry ingredients. Add to chocolate mixture alternately with the sour cream, combine. Stir in pecans. Drop from teaspoon, 2 inches apart onto a greased and floured cookie sheet. Bake at 350°F. for 10 minutes or until done. Remove from sheet, cool. Frost with mocha frosting.

**Mocha Frosting**

- ¹/₄ cup butter, room temperature
- 2 tablespoons cocoa
- 2 teaspoons instant coffee
- ¹/₄ teaspoon salt

**3** cups confectioners' sugar
**3** tablespoons milk
**1¹/₂** teaspoons vanilla

Cream butter, cocoa, instant coffee, salt in medium mixer bowl until smooth. Blend in confectioners' sugar. Add enough milk to bring mixture to spreading consistency.

# NUT SLICES ————————

**Makes 3¹/₂ dozen**

- 1 package dry yeast
- ¹/₄ cup warm water
- 1 teaspoon sugar
- 2 cups all-purpose flour
- ¹/₂ teaspoon salt
- ³/₄ cup butter or margarine
- 2 eggs, separated
- ¹/₂ cup sugar
- 1 teaspoon vanilla
- ¹/₂ cup chopped pecans
  Confectioners' sugar

Sprinkle yeast over warm water in cup. Add 1 teaspoon sugar, allow to stand 15 minutes or until yeast foams. Combine flour and salt. Cut in butter until mixture resembles cornmeal. Blend in egg yolks and yeast. Mix until a smooth ball is formed. Beat egg whites until stiff but not dry. Beat in ¹/₂ cup sugar. Continue beating until stiff peaks form. Fold in vanilla. Divide dough in half. Roll out each half on lightly floured surface into a 9 inch x 13-inch rectangle. Spread with egg white mixture and sprinkle with nuts. Roll up as a jelly roll, starting at the long side. Place rolls on a greased cookie sheet. Make ¹/₂-inch deep cut down center of each roll lengthwise. Bake at preheated oven at 375°F. for 20-25 minutes. When still warm, sprinkle with confectioners' sugar. Cool. Slice diagonally.

# PECAN BUTTER BALLS

**Makes 3 dozen**

- 1 cup butter
- $1/2$ cup confectioners' sugar
- $1/2$ teaspoon vanilla
- $13/4$ cups all-purpose flour
- $1/2$ cup chopped pecans

Cream butter and sugar. Blend in vanilla, flour and nuts. Wrap dough in aluminum foil, waxed paper or plastic wrap and chill several hours. Form dough into 1-inch balls. Place cookies on greased cookie sheets, 2 inches apart. Bake in preheated 350°F. oven for 20 minutes or until the bottoms turn brown. Set cookies on a wire rack and sprinkle with confectioners' sugar.

# NEW ENGLAND GINGERSNAPS

**Makes 3½ dozen**

    ¾ **cup butter or margarine**
    ¾ **cup sugar**
    ¼ **cup molasses**
     1 **egg**
     2 **cups all-purpose flour**
    ½ **teaspoon salt**
     2 **teaspoons baking soda**
     1 **teaspoon cinnamon**
     1 **teaspoon cloves**
     1 **teaspoon ginger**
     3 **tablespoons sugar**

Cream butter and sugar. Add egg and molasses; continue beating until blended. Combine dry ingredients; add to creamed mixture. Wrap dough in aluminum foil, waxed paper or plastic wrap and chill two hours. Use a level tablespoon of dough for each cookie. Shape dough into balls, dip it into the sugar and place on greased cookie sheets, 2 inches apart. Bake in preheated 375°F. oven 10-12 minutes.

# GINGER COOKIES ___

**Makes 8 dozen cookies**

  3 eggs
1/2 cup packed light brown sugar
3 1/4 cups unsifted all-purpose flour
1/2 teaspoon baking powder
1/2 teaspoon salt
  1 teaspoon cinnamon, ground cloves
  1 teaspoon orange zest
3/4 cup diced candied ginger

Beat eggs until light; gradually beat in sugar. In a separate bowl combine flour, baking powder, salt, and spices; add to egg mixture. Cover and chill 2 hours. Turn out onto a sugared board, shape dough into a 2-inch roll; cut into 2-inch lengths and roll each to 4 inches long. Cut in half and place onto greased cookie sheets. Bake at 300°F. 8 to 10 minutes.

# JELLY COOKIES

**Makes 2 dozen**

- 1/2 cup butter, soften
- 1/3 cup sugar
- 1 egg
- 1 1/4 cups unsifted all-purpose flour
- 1/2 teaspoon salt
- 1/4 cup blanched ground almonds
- 1/2 cup sugar
- Grape jelly

Cream butter and sugar until light. Separate egg; mix in yolk, and continue creaming. In separate bowl, combine flour and salt; gradually add to creamed mixture. Roll dough out on a lightly floured surface or between 2 pieces of waxed paper to 1/8 inch thick. Cut with a 2 1/2-inch round cookie cutter. Cut an equal number of cookies with a scalloped cookie cutter, about 2 inches in diameter. Remove the center with a thimble. Beat egg white slightly. Combine ground almonds and sugar on a sheet of waxed paper. Brush each scalloped cookie with egg and dip into almond-sugar mixture. Place cookies almond side up on a greased and floured cookie sheet. Bake at 375°F. 6 minutes. Cookies should not brown. Cool on racks and assemble scalloped cookie on top of round cookie with a teaspoonful of grape jelly in the center of each cookie.

# CHOCOLATE AND PEANUT DROP COOKIES

**Makes about 35 cookies**

- ⅓ cup walnuts
- ¼ cup chilled butter, cut into ½-inch chunks
- ¼ cup peanut butter
- ½ cup sugar
- 1 extra large egg
- ¼ cup milk
- ½ teaspoon vanilla
- ½ cup all-purpose flour
- ¼ teaspoon baking powder
- ¼ teaspoon baking soda
- ½ teaspoon salt
- ½ cup rolled oats
- 3 ounces semi-sweet chocolate chips

Preheat oven to 475°F. Into a food processor, insert steel blade. Add walnuts to bowl, chop. It will be very noisy. Remove from bowl and reserve. Replace steel blade into processor, add butter and peanut butter, combine, start with two on and off motions, and then process until combined. Add sugar, egg, milk and vanilla, combine. Place flour, baking powder, baking soda, salt and oats in a mixing bowl. Place flour mixture into processor bowl, mix well. Add chocolate chips and walnuts, process to combine. Drop by teaspoonful onto an ungreased baking sheet. Bake for 10 to 12 minutes, until cookies are golden brown.

# CANDY

# Candy

When making candy you should always follow the recipe directions closely. Use the correct equipment, measure carefully and make accurate tests for the finished product of the candy.

Use standard measuring spoons and cups. A long handled wooden spoon, spatula, wire whisk and a candy thermometer are essential. To measure, dip and level sugar and firmly pack brown sugar before leveling off are important steps.

Cold water test is a fairly accurate test for the experienced candy maker but is best used in combination with the candy thermometer. Fill a cup with cold water; drip about $\frac{1}{2}$ teaspoon of the boiling candy into the cold water. Form into a ball with your fingers keeping the candy under water. Pick up the ball to judge its consistency as to the state of cooking.

The candy thermometer gives the most accurate results. Under normal conditions water boils at 212° F. The altitude and atmospheric pressure affects candy making.

Candy is kneaded to make it creamier, however, it must not be overkneaded. Press the candy into a buttered pan or dish; cover with waxed paper and let stand until firm.

Avoid hard, tough caramels by increasing the amount of fat in cream or butter and by not overcooking.

# CHOCOLATE TRUFFLES

**Makes 36 truffles**

  1 package (12 ounces) chocolate chips
$^3/_4$ cup sweetened condensed milk
  1 teaspoon vanilla
1$^1/_2$ cups vanilla wafer crumbs
  2 tablespoons creme de cafe coffee liqueur
    Powdered cocoa

Melt chocolate chips in top of double boiler over hot water using medium heat. Stir in condensed milk, vanilla, vanilla wafer crumbs and liqueur. Beat until smooth and all ingredients are combined. Refrigerate mixture about 45 minutes or until cool and easy to shape. With buttered hands, shape mixture into $^3/_4$-inch balls. Roll balls in cocoa.

# MINT MARSHMALLOWS

**Makes 36 pieces**

- 2 tablespoons unflavored gelatin
- ¾ cup cold water
- 2 cups sugar
- ¼ teaspoon salt
- ¾ cup boiling water
- 3 drops green food coloring
- ½ teaspoon peppermint flavoring
- Flaked coconut for coating

In a small saucepan soften the gelatin in cold water, about 5 minutes; stir. Cook over medium heat until dissolved, stirring often, set aside. Combine sugar, salt, boiling water and food coloring in medium saucepan, cook until sugar dissolves. Blend sugar mixture in with gelatin and beat in large bowl of electric mixer until mixture is creamy and fluffy. Stir in peppermint flavoring. Pour mixture into an 8 x 8-inch pan, dusted with sugar. Cool 30 minutes or until set; cut into squares. Roll in coconut. Store in refrigerator.

# BUTTER-RUM FUDGE

**Makes 3 dozen pieces**

- 4 cups sugar
- 1 can (13 ounces) evaporated milk
- 1 cup butter
- 12 ounces semi-sweet chocolate pieces
- 2 cups marshmallow
- 1 teaspoon rum flavoring
- 1 cup chopped pecans

Combine sugar, milk and butter in a medium saucepan; cook over medium heat to soft ball stage 236°F. on candy thermometer, stirring occasionally. Remove from heat; mix in chocolate, marshmallow, rum flavoring and nuts. Beat until chocolate is melted and all ingredients are well blended. Pour fudge mixture into a well buttered 9 x 9-inch pan. Score into squares. When fudge has cooled cut into squares.

# MEXICAN PECAN CANDY

**Makes 24 pecan candies**

- 2 cups brown sugar
- 2 cups chopped pecans
- 1/2 cup milk
- 1 1/2 tablespoons butter

Cook all ingredients in a heavy saucepan over medium heat to soft ball stage, 236°F. on candy thermometer. Beat with a wooden spoon until mixture begins to thicken and is creamy. Drop by teaspoonfuls onto greased cookie sheet.

# PRALINES

**Makes 15 patties**

- 3 cups sugar
- 1 cup evaporated milk
- 1/4 teaspoon salt
- 1 tablespoon butter
- 2 cups pecan halves

Mix all ingredients except pecans in a heavy saucepan; cook over medium heat, stirring until mixture comes to a full boil. Continue boiling, about 4 minutes, stirring often, until candy reaches soft ball stage, 236°F. Remove from heat; add pecans. Beat until candy begins to thicken but still looks shiny. Drop mixture by tablespoonfuls onto buttered cookie sheet to form 2-inch patties.

# PEANUT BRITTLE

**Makes 2 pounds**

- 1/2 cup water
- 2 cups sugar
- 1 cup light corn syrup
- 2 cups Spanish peanuts
- 2 teaspoons baking soda
- 1/4 teaspoon salt
- 2 tablespoons butter
- 1 teaspoon vanilla

Bring water to a boil in a medium saucepan over medium heat; stir in sugar and corn syrup, stirring to combine. Continue cooking, stirring constantly until sugar is dissolved and mixture reaches soft ball stage, 236°F. on candy thermometer. Stir in peanuts, cook until mixture turns golden brown and reaches to hard crack stage. Add remaining ingredients, stir to combine. Pour onto 2 large buttered cookie sheets. When candy is cold break into pieces.

# PRUNES WITH FONDANT

**Makes 30 stuffed prunes**

> 1 **cup confectioner's sugar**
> 1/3 **cup butter**
> 1/2 **cup light corn syrup**
> 1 **teaspoon vanilla**
> 1 **package (12 ounces) pitted prunes**

In a medium heavy saucepan combine half of the sugar, butter and corn syrup. Cook over low heat, until mixture comes to a full boil, stirring constantly. Stir in remaining ingredients, remove saucepan from the heat. Stir with wooden spoon only until the mixture holds its shape. Pour the fondant into a well buttered 9 x 9-inch pan. Set aside until cool enough to handle; and then knead until smooth. Slit each prune, stuff fondant in center. Arrange decoratively on candy dish.

# MARSHMALLOW FUDGE

**Makes 3 dozen pieces**

- 4 cups sugar
- 3/4 cup milk
- 4 tablespoons cocoa
- 1 cup marshmallow
- 4 tablespoons butter
- 1 teaspoon vanilla

Combine sugar and milk in a medium saucepan; cook over medium-low heat to soft ball stage 235°F. on candy thermometer, stirring occasionally. Remove from heat and working quickly stir in remaining ingredients, blend together. Pour fudge mixture into a well buttered 9 x 9-inch pan. Score into squares. When fudge has cooled cut into squares.

# ENGLISH TOFFEE

**Makes 1 pound toffee**

1 cup butter
1 cup sugar
2 tablespoons water
1 tablespoon light corn syrup
1/2 cup finely chopped walnuts
4 ounces (4 squares) semi-sweet chocolate, melted

Melt butter over low heat in a medium heavy saucepan. Mix in sugar; cook over low heat, stirring constantly until the mixture comes to a rolling boil. Add water and corn syrup, combine. Continue to cook and stir until mixture reaches the soft crack stage 290°F. on candy thermometer. Butter a 13 x 9-inch pan. Sprinkle half of the nuts over bottom of pan. Pour candy into pan and spread evenly. When cool, spread chocolate over toffee. Sprinkle with remaining nuts. Refrigerate. When chocolate hardens, break toffee into regular pieces.

# CANDIED ORANGE PEEL

**6 medium navel oranges, quartered**
**3 cups sugar, divided**

Separate orange pulp and peel; set pulp aside for other use. In a saucepan place peel, cover with cold water. Simmer peel for 10 minutes; drain and set aside to cool enough to handle. With a spoon, scrape off white inner part of peel; discard. Cut peel into strips. In a saucepan over medium heat, simmer 2½ cups sugar and 2 cups of water until the mixture reaches 238°F. on thermometer. In a large skillet, place syrup and orange peel. Cook over medium heat, stirring often, until peel is glazed. Transfer peel to rack over a pan to drain and cool. In a bowl, place remaining sugar. Toss glazed cooled peel in sugar; arrange on rack to dry.

# JAMS, JELLIES, AND PRESERVES

# Jams, Jellies, And Preserves

To preserve fruits and vegetables, you will need a large kettle, jelly bag or cheesecloth, a thermometer, a measuring cup and spoons, knives, bowls, colander, long handled wooden spoon and a scale.

Use standard canning jars or jelly glasses with two-piece vacuum seal lids. For the paraffin method, sterilize jelly containers in boiling water for 10 minutes. Jars should be hot when filled to prevent cracking. Keep containers hot, until they are ready for use. Wash and rinse all lids and bands. Seal according to manufacturer's direction.

When the food is to be canned, lift jars or glasses with tongs, place on counters; fill jars to $1/8$ inch from the top of the jar and to $1/2$ inch from lid. Seal at once. Pour a thin layer of hot paraffin, use only enough paraffin to make a layer ⅛ inch thick. Prick air bubbles in paraffin. Use a double boiler for melting paraffin and for keeping it hot. Better still, omit paraffin seal and process in a hot boiling water bath.

Pectin: Many people prefer the added-pectin method for making jams and jellied fruit products because fully ripe fruit can be used and cooking time is shorter. Some kinds of fruits have enough natural pectin to make high quality products. Others require added pectin, particularly when they are used for making jellies, which should be firm enough to hold their shape. Fruit has more pectin when underripe. Pectin should be stored in a cold, dry area. Do not use last year's supply.

Fresh prepared jelly should be stored undisturbed overnight to avoid breaking the gel. Cover jelly glasses with metal or paper lids. Label and store in a cool, dry area, the shorter the storage time the better.

Pickle and relish recipes usually call for finishing the preserving process with a water bath. Place the filled and sealed jars, next to each other on a rack in a canner or deep kettle. Pour in enough hot, but not boiling, water to immerse the jars by at least 1 inch, securely cover the pot, bring water to a boil over medium heat. Boil for 12-15 minutes. Carefully with tongs, remove jar, cool overnight. Test the seal of ring-top lids by pressing the center of each lid with forefinger. If the flat inner lid remains indented, remove the outer ring, leaving the seal intact. If the inner lid pops up, the jar is not properly sealed; refrigerate and serve the food within a week. Never eat any pickles or foods that are slimy, bad smelling or that are soft or frothy. Do not even taste them. Throw them away.

Fix jar covers as per manufacturer directions and place the filled jars on a rack in a kettle containing boiling water. Add hot, not boiling, water to bring water an inch from the tops of containers. Cover the kettle. With medium heat when the water returns to a rolling boil, begin to count processing time. Boil gently and steadily for the processing time recommended for the food that you are processing. Remove jars from the kettle and seal according to manufacturer's directions.

# CANTALOUPE PRESERVE

**Makes 4 jars**

- 2 large ripe cantaloupes, peeled, seeded, diced
- 2 cups sugar
- 1 cup water
- 1/2 cup cider vinegar
- 4 cinnamon sticks
- 6 whole cloves

Combine all ingredients in a large saucepan; bring mixture to a boil over medium heat, simmer until melon is tender. Remove the melon with a slotted spoon and place into hot, sterilized jelly jars or Mason jars. Simmer syrup 6 minutes, pour over melon pieces. Seal jars according to manufacturer's directions. Process in water bath 10 minutes, cool.

# BLUEBERRY-APPLE PRESERVE

**Makes 3 jars**

   2  **tart apples, peeled, chopped**
   1  **quart blueberries, washed, picked over to remove any stems or undesirable fruit**
      **Zest from 1 lemon**
   4  **tablespoons freshly squeezed lemon juice**
   4  **cups sugar**

In a large saucepan combine apples, blueberries, zest and lemon juice, bring mixture to a boil over medium heat, reduce to simmer, continue cooking for 10 minutes, stirring occasionally. Mix in sugar, continue cooking over medium heat for 15-20 minutes, or until thermometer registers 220°. If not using a thermometer, drop a half teaspoon of preserves onto a cold plate, it should gel. Pour preserves into hot sterilized jelly glasses or Mason jars. Seal according to manufacturer's directions.

# LEMON AND LIME MARMALADE

**Makes 12 jars**

8 **large lemons**
8 **large limes**
**Water**
**Sugar**

Grind lemons and limes, discard seeds; measure pulp. For each cup pulp add 3 cups water, arrange in a large glass bowl overnight. Place in a large kettle, bring mixture to a boil over medium heat, simmer 15 minutes. Again, let mixture stand overnight. Measure the lemon-lime mixture into a large kettle, add 1 cup sugar for each cup pulp. Bring mixture to a boil, over medium heat, stirring constantly until sugar melts, and measures 220°, on candy thermometer. Let cool about 5 minutes, pour into hot sterilized jelly jars or Mason jars. Place a thin layer of paraffin over marmalade. Adjust caps and seal according to manufacturer's directions. Cool.

# ORANGE MARMALADE _____

**Makes 3 jars**

     6  large seedless oranges, sliced thin
     1  medium lemon, sliced thin
   1/2  cup candied cherries
        Water
        Sugar

Place oranges and lemon slices in a large bowl. Mix in cherries. Measure fruit, add 1 1/2 cups water for each cup of fruit. Cover with plastic wrap. Refrigerate overnight. Place fruit in a large saucepan. Simmer for 1 1/2 hours or until the fruit is tender. If mixture is dry, add water, 2 tablespoons at a time. Cool to room temperature. Refrigerate overnight. Measure fruit. Add 1 cup sugar for each cup of fruit. Cook over medium heat for 30 minutes or until fruit begins to gel. Pour into hot sterilized jelly jars or Mason jars, seal according to manufacturer's directions.

# STRAWBERRY JAM _

**Makes 4 jars**

- 6 cups strawberries, hulled
- Zest from half lime
- 3 tablespoons freshly squeezed lime juice
- 6 cups sugar
- 1 bottom, 6 ounces, liquid pectin

In a large saucepan combine all ingredients; bring mixture to a boil over medium heat, reduce heat to a simmer. Continue cooking stirring occasionally for 10 minutes. Ladle mixture into hot sterilized jelly jars or Mason jars. Seal according to manufacturer's directions. If you wish, cover jam with a thin layer of paraffin according to the paraffin directions.

# PEACH JAM _____

**Makes 4 jars**

- 6 cups ripe peaches, peeled, pitted, pureed
- 1 lemon, sliced
- ½ cup water
- 4 cups sugar

Place peaches in a large saucepan with lemon slices. Stir in water, bring mixture to a boil over medium heat. Continue boiling and stirring occasionally for 10 minutes. Mix in sugar. Reduce heat to simmer, continue cooking, stirring occasionally for 20 minutes. The thermometer will register 220°. Pour peach mixture into hot sterilized jelly glasses or Mason jars, seal according to manufacturer's directions. If using paraffin, use according to directions.

# APPLE BUTTER ——

**Makes 6 jars**

- 5 pounds cooking apples, peeled, sliced
- 1½ cups cider or apple juice
- 2½ cups sugar
- 3 tablespoons ground cinnamon
- 1 teaspoon ground nutmeg
- 1 teaspoon ground cloves

Combine all ingredients in a large saucepan. Simmer uncovered for 45 minutes, stirring occasionally. Mash apples and continue simmering until apple butter is smooth, about 30 minutes. Pour apple butter into hot sterilized jars, or Mason jars, and seal according to manufacturer's directions.

# MANGO JAM ——

**Makes 6 jars**

- 4 large mangos (not completely ripe), peeled
- 6 cups sugar
- ½ cup freshly squeezed lime juice
- 1 tablespoon lime zest

In a large bowl chop mango fruit, makes about 7-8 cups pulp. In a large saucepan combine pulp, sugar, lime juice and zest. Simmer slowly for 1 hour, or until mixture becomes thick, stirring occasionally. Spoon jam into hot, sterilized jelly jars, or Mason jars, seal according to manufacturer's directions.

# APRICOT BUTTER __

**Makes 4 jars**

4½ pounds apricots, peel and pit
1½ cups freshly squeezed orange juice
  3 cups sugar
  1 teaspoon ground nutmeg
  5 tablespoons freshly squeezed lemon juice
1½ teaspoons ground cinnamon
  ½ teaspoon ground allspice

Mash apricots and place pulp in a large saucepan with orange juice. Simmer over low heat until tender, stirring occasionally. Sieve pulp. Add remaining ingredients. Place mixture into baking dish, bake at 300°F. for 45 minutes or until apricot butter is thick, stir occasionally. Ladle butter into hot sterilized jelly jars or Mason jars, and seal according to manufacturer's directions.

# PICKLED CRABAPPLES _____

**Makes 5-6 jars**

- 3 cups distilled white vinegar
- 3 cups water
- 6 cups sugar
- 1 tablespoon whole allspice
- 2 sticks cinnamon
- 1 cup raisins
- 2 quarts crabapples, wash well

Combine all ingredients except crabapples in a large saucepan; bring mixture to a boil over medium heat. Reduce heat to a simmer, continue cooking until syrup forms. Place apples in saucepan, simmer slowly until apples are tender, do not overcook. Place apples in hot sterilized jelly jars, or Mason jars, cover with boiling syrup. Seal according to manufacturer's directions. Process 15 minutes.

# PLUM JAM _____

**Makes 4 jars**

2¹/₂ pounds plums, pitted, leave skins on for a deep red
    color
  1 small seedless orange, sliced thin
¹/₂ cup water
3¹/₂ to 4¹/₂ cups sugar

In a large saucepan combine plums and orange; bring mixture
to a boil over medium heat, continue cooking 10 minutes, stirring occasionally. Place thermometer in pan. Add sugar. Reduce heat to medium; cook for 15-20 minutes, stirring
occasionally until thermometer reaches 220˚. Pour mixture
into hot sterilized jars or Mason jars and seal according to
manufacturer's directions.

# PRESERVED PEACHES

**Makes 8 small jars**

    1  **orange, chopped**
    7  **cups peaches, scalded, peeled, minced**
    5  **cups sugar**
  **¼  cup candied ginger, chopped**

Combine fruit in a large kettle, simmer 20 minutes, stirring occasionally, over medium heat. Add remaining ingredients, continue cooking until mixture is 220° on candy thermometer. Pour mixture into hot sterilized jars or Mason jars. Cover according to manufacturer's directions. Process in water bath for 10 minutes, cool.

# PICKLED ONIONS ___

**Makes 5-6 jars**

2 quarts small white onions
½ cup salt
1 quart distilled vinegar
1 cup sugar
½ cup mixed pickling spices

Place onions in a large glass bowl; cover with boiling water, let stand for 3 minutes, drain. Cover with cold water, peel. Place onions in glass bowl, cover with water, mix in salt, let stand overnight. Rinse, drain. Place onions in large pan, add remaining ingredients, bring mixture to a boil. Place onions in hot sterile jars or Mason jars, fill and cover with the remaining boiled liquid. Seal according to manufacturer's directions. Process 10 minutes in water bath.

# DILL PICKLES _____

**Makes 6 pints**

```
  2 quarts small cucumbers, wash well, drain
5-6 tablespoons salt
  3 cups vinegar
  3 cups water
 12 dill weed heads
  3 tablespoons mixed pickling spices
  1 teaspoon black peppercorns, crushed
```

In a medium saucepan combine salt, vinegar and water, heat to boiling point over medium heat. Arrange cucumbers in hot sterilized jars. Combine spices and divide into each jar; each jar should have 2 heads of dill. Fill with boiled vinegar mixture to 1/2 inch of the top of jar or Mason jars. Process 10 minutes in water bath.

# WATERMELON PICKLES

**Makes 5 pints**

4 quarts watermelon rind, cut into ³/₄-inch cubes, trim off outer rind, leave rim of red fruit
4 tablespoons salt
3 cups distilled white vinegar
7-8 cups sugar
4 cinnamon sticks
Juice of 1 lemon
Zest of 1 lemon
2 teaspoons whole cloves

Arrange watermelon rind in saucepan, cover with boiling water, stir in salt, simmer until tender. Drain, chill in cold water, 2 hours or overnight. Drain rind, place in saucepan. In a separate pan combine remaining ingredients, cook over medium heat until sugar has melted, stirring occasionally. Pour hot syrup over rind. Simmer until watermelon rind is clear and slightly transparent. Pack rind in hot, sterilized jelly jars or Mason jars, covering rind with boiling syrup. Seal according to manufacturer's directions. Process 5 minutes in water bath.

# BREAD AND BUTTER PICKLES ___

**Makes 3-4 jars**

      2 quarts small cucumbers
      4 onions, sliced
    1/4 cup salt
  2 1/2 cups cider vinegar
  2 1/2-3 cups sugar
      1 tablespoon mustard seeds
      1 tablespoon celery seeds
      1 teaspoon ground turmeric
    1/4 teaspoon ground cloves

In a large glass bowl combine cucumbers and onions, divided into rings. Sprinkle with salt, let stand 2-3 hours, drain. Place in large pan, add remaining ingredients. Bring mixture to a boil over medium heat; arrange immediately into hot sterilized jars or Mason jars. Seal according to manufacturer's directions. Cool. Test seal.

# OUTDOOR COOKING

# Outdoor Cooking

Score the edges of the steaks, ham or chops so that they won't curl.

Use long-handled tongs, instead of forks.

Trim excess fat from meat to prevent flare-ups.

A small new painter's brush is good for brushing on sauces and for basting.

Use a meat therometer to check doneness of large cuts of meat.

Get together all the pieces of equipment you will need.

Cooking time for meats will vary with the cut, thickness, shape, temperature, where placed over the coals and the arrangement of the charcoals.

When threading meats on rotisserie spit consider that they are balanced so that they will turn evenly. Thread spareribs onto spit by weaving rod in and out of ribs, forming accordion folds.

Foods may be basted during the entire cooking time or during the last half hour, depending upon the ingredients in the basting sauce. Sauces high in sugar, tomato sauce or other ingredients that burn readily should be applied during the last 15 to 30 minutes of cooking time.

For the average appetite allow;

Boneless, 1/4 to 1/2 pound of meat per person.

Bone-in, 3/4 to 1 pound of meat, depending upon the amount of bone.

Store briquets in a dry area. They absorb dampness readily, which will cause the fire to kindle slowly.

## COOKING METHODS

**Spit Roasting** Many meats and poultry which can be roasted in the kitchen oven adapt well to the spit. To shorten spit roasting time, food may be precooked in oven before placing on spit.

**Grilling** Many foods that can be broiled or fried in the kitchen can be grilled outside. Skillets and shish kebab skewers give versatility to your cooking.

# ROTISSERIE ROASTING GUIDE

| Type of roast | Approximate cooking time 4-6 pound roast at room temperature | Temperature |
|---|---|---|
| Beef | | |
| Rare | 2 to 2½ hours | 140° |
| Medium | 2½ to 3 hours | 160° |
| Well Done | 3 to 4 hours | 170° |
| Pork (fresh) | 2 to 3½ hours | 185° |
| Lamb | | |
| Medium | 1½ to 2 hours | 175° |
| Well Done | 2 to 2½ hours | 180° |

# CHUCK ROAST OVER COALS _____

**Makes 6-7 servings**

 ³/₄ **cup catsup**
 ¹/₄ **cup light soy sauce**
  3 **cloves garlic, minced**
4¹/₂- 5 **pound chuck roast, 1¹/₂ inches thick, remove fat**

Combine catsup, soy sauce and minced garlic. Brush sauce over chuck steak. Cook meat on grill, about 2 inches from hot coals, turn occasionally. When steak has cooked, remove to serving platter, slice against the grain. Serve with baked potatoes and salad.

# HAM STEAK _____

**Makes 3-4 servings**

  1 **center-cut ham steak, 1¹/₄ - 1¹/₂ pounds**
  1 **teaspoon prepared mustard**
  1 **tablespoon honey**
  1 **tablespoon tarragon vinegar**
  1 **tablespoon dry wine**
  1 **tablespoon sesame seeds**

Remove any extra fat on ham. Combine mustard, honey, vinegar, wine and sesame seeds. Cook ham steak on grill over hot coals, turn once. Brush liberally with sauce. Slice and serve.

# HAMBURGERS

**Makes 4 servings**

- 1 pound ground beef
- 1 small onion, minced
- 1 teaspoon prepared mustard
- 1 egg, slightly beaten
- 1/2 cup bread crumbs
- 1/4 teaspoon salt, pepper
- 4-5 hamburger rolls

In a large bowl, combine beef with onion and mustard. Add ingredients, 1 at a time, combine. Shape into 4 or 5 hamburger patties. Cook on grill, over hot coals, 4 inches from heat. Cook about 2 minutes on each side, turn with a spatula. Serve on hamburger rolls with catsup, mustard and pickles.

# BRATWURST ON THE GRILL

**Makes 4-6 servings**

- 8 bratwurst
- 1 can dark beer

Make slashes at 1½-inch intervals on bratwurst. Marinate overnight in dark beer; drain. Broil on grill over hot coals, turn as necessary. Place an aluminum foil boat under to catch any fat before it falls to the coals. Serve with rye bread and German mustard.

# HAM KABOBS

**Makes 4 servings**

6 carrots, cut into 1-inch pieces
1 package Brussels sprouts
1 pound fully cooked ham, cut into 1-inch cubes
1 can pineapple chunks, drained

**Marinade**

1/2 cup vegetable oil
1/4 cup red wine vinegar
1/4 teaspoon black pepper, garlic powder

Cook carrots in boiling, salted water until tender but still crunchy, drain. Place in deep glass bowl. Cook sprouts according to package directions, drain well. Place ham cubes in bowl. Combine oil, vinegar and spices; toss with vegetables and ham. Marinate overnight. Drain, thread ham, vegetables and pineapple chunks alternately on skewers. Broil over hot coals, 1 1/2 inches from heat, until cooked, turn once. Brush with more marinade.

# CORNISH HENS ON A SPIT

**Makes 4 servings**

- 4 1-pound Rock Cornish hens, rinsed, pat dry
- 4 tablespoons vegetable oil
  Garlic powder
- 1 teaspoon ground sage
  Salt and pepper

Rub hens with oil, sprinkle with spices, inside and outside. Truss hens, mount on the spit, hold in place with holding forks. Roast hens over coals for 1 hour until done. Brush occasionally with extra oil and/or melted butter.

# CHICKEN ON THE SPIT

**Makes 6-8 servings**

- ½ cup prepared mustard
- 4 tablespoons butter, melted
- 3 cloves garlic, minced
- ½ teaspoon salt, ground marjoram
- 2 broiler chickens

Combine mustard, butter and spices. Brush sauce over chickens. Truss the chickens, place on spit and fasten it securely. Roast chickens for about 2 hours, basting frequently. Place a pan under the chickens to catch drippings.

# LAMB RIBS _____

**Makes 5-6 servings**

　5　pounds lamb ribs, remove all fat, leave ribs in racks
　　　Salt, pepper
　1　cup catsup
　3　cloves garlic, minced
　1　onion, minced
　½　cup grape jelly, softened
　1　teaspoon Worcestershire sauce
　1　tablespoon vinegar

Brown lamb racks of ribs over hot coals, turn often, about 1 hour 20 minutes. Season with salt and pepper. Combine remaining ingredients. Place ribs in a skillet, cover with sauce, cover; simmer until ribs are cooked. Cut into serving pieces.

# SHORT RIBS ON THE GRILL

**Makes 4-5 serings**

**4¹/₂ pounds beef short ribs, 2¹/₂ inches long**

**Sauce**

  **¹/₂ cup light soy sauce**
  **2 teaspoons sugar**
  **¹/₂ teaspoon garlic powder, onion powder**
  **2 teaspoons orange zest**

Score meat side of the ribs, ¹/₂ inch apart. Combine sauce ingredients. Marinate ribs for 3 hours in a shallow dish. Remove and drain ribs. Arrange on a grill, 4 inches from heat, over hot coals. Grill until brown and cooked, about 20 minutes or until done, turning occasionally.

# HE-MAN SIRLOIN STEAK

**Makes 5-6 servings**

  2  **sirloin steaks, 1½ - 1¼ inches thick, 2 pounds each**

**Sauce**

  ¾  **cup catsup**
  ¼  **cup soy sauce**
  ¼  **cup firmly packed dark brown sugar**
  ¼  **cup tarragon vinegar**
  ½  **teaspoon garlic powder**

Arrange steaks in a shallow dish. Combine remaining ingredients, marinate at room temperature for 30 minutes, turn once. Remove meat, reserve marinade. Grill steaks over hot coals, 4-5 inches from heat. Cook about 8 minutes on each side, or to individual taste. Brush occasionally with marinade. Slice across the grain.

# OUTDOORS LEG OF LAMB ————————

**Makes 7-8 servings**

   1 leg of lamb, 5-6 pounds, boned, rolled

**Sauce**

   ½ cup vegetable oil
   2 tablespoons freshly squeezed lemon juice
   1 teaspoon lemon zest
   1 onion, minced
   2 cloves garlic, minced
   2 teaspoons curry powder
   ½ teaspoon salt, ground pepper

Center the leg of lamb on the spit. Secure with clamps. Place spit in position over hot coals. Simmer sauce for 5 minutes, brush over lamb. Roast 2½ hours, basting frequently with sauce, or until lamb is cooked according to individual taste.

# GRILLED SALMON WITH LEMON-BUTTER SAUCE

**Makes 4 servings**

      4  **salmon steaks, 3/4 inch thick**
    1/4  **cup vegetable oil**
      5  **tablespoons freshly squeezed lemon juice**
      2  **teaspoons lemon zest**

Grill salmon steaks on an oiled grill, about 4-5 inches from the hot coals, for 3 minutes. Brush with oil, juice and zest combined. Turn fish over, brush again. Cook 3 minutes longer or until cooked. (The fish can also be cooked in foil.)

**Lemon-Butter Sauce**

    1/2  **cup butter, melted**
      2  **tablespoons freshly squeezed lemon juice**
      2  **teaspoons lemon zest**
    1/4  **teaspoon salt, pepper**

Combine all ingredients and serve with salmon steaks.

# TROUT WRAPPED IN A BLANKET

**Makes 6 servings**

   6 trout, for individual servings, cleaned, scaled
   ½ teasoon salt, pepper
   4 green onions, minced
   6 bacon slices
      Toothpicks

Sprinkle salt, pepper and minced onion over trout. Wrap a bacon slice around each fish, secure with a toothpick. Grill over hot coals 3 inches from the heat, turn once, until fish is cooked and the bacon crisp, about 6-7 minutes.

# EARS OF CORN

**Makes 8 servings**

   8 ears of corn, husked, remove silk
   ½ cup butter, melted

Arrange each ear on a double layer of aluminum foil. Brush corn with melted butter. Wrap foil around ears of corn; twist ends to seal corn. Arrange foil-wrapped corn on grill over hot coals, grill, turn often, about 10-15 minutes or until cooked. Brush with butter, season to taste.

# STUFFED TENDERLOIN

**Makes 8 servings**

> 5 tablespoons butter
> 6 green onions, minced
> 1 pound mushrooms, chopped
> ¾ cup bread crumbs
> 1 egg
> ½ teaspoon salt, thyme
> ¼ teaspoon pepper
> ¼ cup chopped fresh parsley
> 5 pound tenderloin

**Sauce**

> 7 tablespoons butter
> ¼ cup prepared mustard
> ¼ cup brandy

In a large skillet heat butter; sauté onions and mushrooms until tender, stirring occasionally. Stir in bread crumbs, toss. Mix in egg, salt, thyme, pepper and fresh parsley. Cut a deep slit the length of the filet. Stuff lightly with dressing, tie with a string to secure. Broil, 2 inches from charcoals, turning occasionally. Baste occasionally. Cook 20 minutes or until done. Let meat rest 5 minutes, slice, serve.

# WESTERN RICE

**Makes 6 servings**

3 tablespoons butter
1 tablespoon oil
1 large onion, minced
2 cloves garlic, minced
1¼ cups uncooked rice
1 can, 16 ounces, tomatoes, include juice
1 green bell pepper, seeded, sliced
1½ cups chicken stock

Heat butter and oil in a medium saucepan; saute´ onion and garlic until tender over medium heat, stirring occasionally. Mix in rice, tomatoes and chicken stock, cover. Cook 10-15 minutes or until liquid is absorbed and rice is tender.

# BAKED BANANAS WITH COCONUT ____

**Makes 6-8 servings**

      8 bananas, cut into 1¹/₂-inch pieces
    ¹/₂ cup firmly packed light brown sugar
      2 tablespoons butter, cut in pieces
      4 tablespoons freshly grated coconut

Arrange bananas on a double sheet of aluminum foil made into a boat shape. Combine sugar and butter, sprinkle over bananas. Sprinkle coconut over bananas. Bake on grill over hot coals, secure aluminum foil. Cook until butter and sugar melts. Serve warm with rich vanilla ice cream.

# SOMEMORES _____

**Makes 5 Somemores**

    10 squares graham crackers
      5 chocolate bars
    20 large marshmallows

Arrange half of a chocolate bar on 1 graham cracker. Add 2 marshmallows, or to taste, over chocolate. Cover with remaining graham cracker, forming the classic sandwich. Press together lightly. Place on grill; cook until the chocolate and marshmallows have begun to melt. You will want some more.

# LOW CALORIE COOKING

# Low Calorie Cooking

## To Lose Weight

Eat smaller portions

Get daily exercise

Use a smaller plate

Eat fewer sweets and fats

Have regular meals

Eat slowly

Stop high-calorie snacking

Read labels carefully

Think before you drink

Eat out with food sense in mind

Trim back on saturated fats and cholesterol

Make a calorie trade-off

Moderation in everything makes a lot of sense

Give up the heavyweight title

Cut down on sugar

Shake the salt habit

Cooking tips for Lightening the Load of Calories and Fats

1. Trim excess fat from meat before cooking.

2. Roast and bril foods on a rack so fat can drain off.

3. Brown meats and poultry; then pour off fat before you continue cooking.

4. Baste meats with wine, tomato juice, or a corn oil-vinegar marinade rather than meat drippings.

5. Make pot roasts and stews a day ahead. Chill them and scrape off congealed fat; then reheat.

6. Use low-fat or skim milk, and skim and part skim milk cheese.

7. Limit sugary desserts, instead eat fruit.

8. If you add sugar to foods such as coffee, tea or cereal, add less each time; you may gradually eliminate it.

# VEGETABLE SOUP __

**Makes 4 servings**

3½ cups water
2 vegetable bouillon cubes
½ teaspoon garlic powder
¼ teaspoon pepper
1 onion, sliced thin
5 stalks celery, sliced
2 carrots, sliced
¼ head cabbage, shredded
1 cup canned tomatoes, chopped, include juice

In a large saucepan bring water to a boil over medium heat; stir in bouillon cubes, garlic powder and pepper. Add remaining ingredients and simmer until vegetables are tender stirring occasionally.

# BEET SOUP _____

**Makes 6 servings**

2 large cucumbers, pared, grated
3 cups buttermilk
1 cup beets, julienned
½ cup beet juice
½ cup imitation sour cream
Salt and pepper to taste
6 celery stalks for garnish

Combine all ingredients and stir unil smooth. Cover and chill for 3 hours. Serve in glass with a celery stalk.

# ZUCCHINI VINAIGRETTE _____

**Makes 4 servings**

- 4 cups sliced zucchini
- 1 large red onion, sliced
- 2 small oranges, peeled, sectioned
- 4 tablespoons corn oil
- 3 tablespoons red wine vinegar
- 3/4 teaspoon ground coriander
- Salt and pepper to taste

Arrange zucchini in vegetable steamer. Cover and steam over hot water, about 5 minutes or until cooked but still crisp. Remove from heat, cool. Combine remaining ingredients in a medium bowl, add zucchini, toss to combine. Refrigerate overnight. Divide evenly into 4 serving dishes.

# STEAMED ASPARAGUS _____

**Makes 6 servings**

- 2 pounds asparagus spears
- 1 lemon, cut into wedges for garnish

Remove lower part of asparagus spears. Wash and arrange in a shallow pan. Cover with just enough boiling water to cover asparagus. Cover with aluminum foil and cook over medium heat for 10 minutes or until tender. Drain and serve with lemon wedges.

# ASPARAGUS SOUFFLE

**Makes 6 servings**

  1 can, 10 $^3/_4$ ounces, condensed cream of chicken soup
  1 can, 14 ounces, asparagus, drained, pureed
$^1/_2$ cup shredded Swiss cheese
  1 small onion, minced
$^1/_2$ teaspoon crushed basil
  6 eggs, separated
$^1/_2$ teaspoon cream of tartar

Spray 6 individual souffle dishes or custard cups with vegetable coating spray. Combine soup, asparagus, cheese, onion and basil. In a medium saucepan; cook, over medium heat until cheese melts, stirring constantly. Beat egg yolks in a small bowl until light. Blend a small amount of the asparagus mixture into warm eggs. Stir yolk mixture into soup mixture. In a large bowl of electric mixer beat egg whites and cream of tartar until stiff but not dry. Fold asparagus into egg whites. Mound mixture into prepared dishes. Place dishes onto a cookie sheet. Bake at 350°F. until puffed and cooked, about 50-60 minutes. Serve immediately.

# OATMEAL MUFFINS

**Makes 12 muffins**

- ¾ **cup whole wheat flour**
- ¾ **cup white flour**
- 1 **cup uncooked oatmeal**
- 1 **tablespoon baking powder**
- 3 **tablespoons sugar**
- ¼ **teaspoon salt**
- 1 **egg**
- 1 **cup milk**
- ¼ **cup oil**

In a large mixing bowl combine flours, oatmeal, baking powder, sugar and salt; mix well. In a separate bowl, beat egg. Add milk and oil, blend together. Add liquid mixture to flour mixture. Stir until just blended; batter will be a little lumpy. Pour into paper-lined muffin tin, two-thirds full. Bake at 400°F., 15-20 minutes or until muffins are baked.

# BIBB SALAD VINAIGRETTE ____

**Makes 4 servings**

1¹/₂ tablespoons dehydrated onion flakes
 3 tablespoons red wine vinegar
 2 teaspoons freshly squeezed lemon juice
 3 green onions, chopped
 1 teaspoon capers
 1 medium dill pickle, sliced
¹/₂ cup water
 1 large head bibb lettuce
 2 tablespoons minced pimiento

Combine all ingredients except pimiento and lettuce. Let stand 2 hours. Break lettuce into bite-sized pieces. Divide lettuce on 4 chilled salad plates. Drizzle vinaigrette equally over lettuce. Garnish with pimiento.

# CREAMY SALAD DRESSING _____

**Makes 1³/₄ cups**

    1 cup lowfat cottage cheese
    ¹/₄ cup freshly squeezed lemon juice
    ¹/₂ cup tomato juice

Blend all ingredients with an electric mixer or a whisk until very smooth. Store dressing in a covered jar in refrigerator.

# FRENCH STYLE DRESSING _____

**Makes 1 cup**

    1 cup tomato juice
    2 tablespoons freshly squeezed lemon juice
    ¹/₂ teaspoon ground oregano
    2 cloves garlic, peeled, minced
    ¹/₄ teaspoon ground pepper

Place all ingredients in a covered jar, shake well to combine. Store in a covered jar in refrigerator. Shake before using.

# POACHED FLOUNDER

**Makes 6 servings**

- **4 cups skim milk**
- **2 tablespoons corn oil**
- **6 slices fillet of flounder**
- **¼ cup fresh dill weed**
- **¼ teaspoon salt, white pepper**

In a shallow baking pan combine milk and oil; bring mixture to scalding point. Arrange fish pieces in the milk and sprinkle with seasonings. Baste constantly until the fish flakes easily, about 8-10 minutes. Serve at once.

# BAKED FISH WITH TOMATO SAUCE ___

**Makes 4 servings**

1½ pounds whole fish, rinse fish in cold water, drain
  1 small onion, minced
  1 small green bell pepper, seeded, sliced
  1 can, 8 ounces, tomato sauce
 ½ teaspoon chili powder
 ¼ teaspoon salt, pepper

Arrange fish in baking dish. Combine remaining ingredients, pour over fish. Cover lightly with aluminum foil; bake at 350°F. for 30 minutes or until fish flakes easily.

# FISH LOAF ——————————

**Makes 4 servings**

   1 can, 12 ounces, salmon, flaked, remove bones, skin and liquid
  1/2 cup bread crumbs
  3/4 cup skim milk
   1 teaspoon freshly squeezed lemon juice
   2 eggs, well beaten
  1/2 teaspoon crushed basil
   1 small onion, minced
   3 stalks celery, chopped
    Salt and pepper to taste

In a large mixing bowl combine all ingredients. Mound into a loaf pan that has been sprayed with vegetable coating spray. Bake at 350°F. for 1 hour until firm and lightly golden brown.

# CHICKEN CACCIATORE ————

**Makes 4 servings**

- 1 small onion, chopped
- 1/4 cup water
- 1 cup canned tomatoes, chopped
- 1/2 cup tomato puree
- 1/2 teaspoon garlic powder
- 1/4 teaspoon ground pepper
- 4 chicken pieces

Simmer onion in water until tender, covered, in a small saucepan. Do not drain. Add tomatoes, tomato puree and spices to onion. Simmer 8-10 minutes, stirring occasionally. Arrange chicken pieces in a skillet. Pour tomato sauce over chicken. Cook, covered, over low heat until chicken is tender, about 45 minutes. Uncover and simmer 15 minutes.

# INDIAN-STYLE CHICKEN

**Makes 4 servings**

- 2 **cartons, 8 ounces each, unflavored low-fat yogurt**
- 1 **onion, minced**
- 1 **teaspoon tandoori spice, available at gourmet food stores, or to taste**
- ½ **teaspoon ground coriander**
- ¼ **teaspoon salt and pepper**
- 3½ **pounds chicken, cut up into serving pieces**

Combine all ingredients except chicken in a small bowl. Arrange chicken in a 3-quart baking dish. Spoon sauce over chicken. Bake, uncovered, in sauce about 1 hour or until chicken is tender. Baste often with sauce. Serve chicken with yogurt sauce.

# STUFFED ROCK CORNISH HENS

**Makes 3 servings**

- 3 rock cornish hens
- 1/2 teaspoon salt, white pepper
- 1 teaspoon oregano
- 3 tablespoons "low-cal" butter

**Stuffing**

- 1 tablespoon butter
- 3 tablespoons chicken bouillon
- 1 medium onion, sliced
- 1 cup celery, sliced
- 3 cups mushrooms, sliced
- 3 tablespoons fresh chopped parsley
- 1/2 teaspoon crushed thyme
- 1 teaspoon chopped basil
- 1/4 cup bread crumbs

**Sauce**

- 1 cup mushrooms, sliced
- 1/2 cup chicken stock

Wash and pat dry hens; season with salt, pepper and oregano, inside and out. Rub hens with butter. Prepare stuffing; heat the butter and chicken bouillon in a non-stick pan until hot. Sauté onion and celery until tender, stirring often. Add mushrooms and parsley, sauté for 1 minute. Add seasonings and bread crumbs, stir to combine. Divide, stuff the cavities of the hens. Place on a rack in a roasting pan; bake uncovered at 350°F. for 50 minutes or until hens are tender. While hens are roasting, prepare sauce. In a small saucepan heat mushrooms and chicken stock. Place hens on serving platter, drizzle with sauce.

# HOLIDAY TURKEY __

**Makes 6 servings**

12-14 pound turkey, wash, pat dry
 3 tablespoons oil
   Salt, pepper, paprika
 2 large onions, quartered
 4 stalks celery, sliced
 1 large apple, quartered

Brush turkey with oil and season to taste. Place onions, celery and apple into cavity of the turkey. Arrange turkey, breast side up in a roasting pan, cover tightly with aluminum foil. Cook at 325°F. for 20 minutes per pound. Remove foil 30 minutes before end of roasting time. Remove vegetables before serving. Slice, serve.

# STIR-FRIED STEAK __

**Makes 4-6 servings**

- 4 **tablespoons beef stock**
- 3/4 **pound skirt steak, sliced against the grain, 1/2-inch slices**
- 2 **slices fresh ginger, minced**
- 3 **cloves garlic, peeled, minced**
- 1/2 **teaspoon salt, pepper**
- 1/2 **pound snow peas, trimmed**
- 1/4 **cup beef stock**
- 1 **teaspoon catsup**

Heat beef stock in a wok or large heavy skillet. Stir-fry, cook quickly, until all color has gone from meat. Sprinkle with ginger, garlic, salt and pepper. Stir-fry snow peas briefly. Stir in beef stock and catsup. Serve over rice.

# VEAL SPARERIBS

**Makes 8 servings**

2¹/₂ pounds lean breast of veal
¹/₄ cup cider vinegar
5 tablespoons catsup
1 cup low cal crushed pineapple, include juice
3 tablespoons light soy sauce

Have the breast of veal trimmed of fat and cut into riblets. Arrange ribs in a roasting pan in a single layer. Bake, uncovered, in 425°F. oven for 20-25 minutes, to brown the meat and remove any excess fat. Pour off all accumulated fat. Combine the remaining ingredients and pour over ribs. Bake at 350°F. for 1¹/₂ hours or until tender.

# PINEAPPLE CHEESECAKE ____

**Makes 12 servings**

- 1 cup graham cracker crumbs
- 3 tablespoons margarine, melted
- 1 package, 3 ounces, lemon-flavored gelatin
- 1 cup boiling water
- 1½ pounds lowfat cottage cheese
- 2 tablespoons sugar
- 1 can, 8½ ounces, crushed pineapple, packed in natural juice
- 1 tablespoon water
- 2 teaspoons cornstarch

In a bowl mix crumbs and margarine together; press into bottom of an 8-inch square pan, chill. Dissolve gelatin in boiling water, cool to room temperature. Blend cottage cheese and sugar with a fork or electric mixer, slowly add the dissolved gelatin and combine. Pour cheese mixture into the crust, chill until firm. In a small saucepan blend together cornstarch and 1 tablespoon of water. Mix in pineapple and juice, bring mixture to a boil over medium heat, stirring constantly. Cool 15 minutes. Spread cooled pineapple mixture over cheesecake and chill 1 hour before serving.

# BERRY FLUFF _____

**Makes 6 servings**

- 2 **envelopes unflavored gelatin**
- 2 **cups crushed raspberries, fresh or frozen, thawed**
- 2 **tablespoons evaporated milk**
- 1 **cup boiling water**
- 1/4 **cup sugar**
- 2 **tablespoons freshly squeezed lemon juice**
- 2 **teaspoons lemon zest**
- 1 **cup imitation whipped cream**
- 3 **egg whites, beat stiff**

Dissolve gelatin in 1/4 cup cold water; add boiling water, stir to dissolve. In a large bowl mix together raspberries, lemon juice, zest, sugar, milk and gelatin; chill. Fold egg whites into whipped cream. Fold in raspberry mixture. Mound into sherbet glasses, serve.

# COTTAGE CHEESE CINNAMON TOAST

**Makes 4 servings**

    4 slices whole-grain bread
    1 cup lowfat cottage cheese
    1/2 teaspoon cinnamon

Toast bread; spread 1/4 cup of the cottage cheese over each slice of toast. Sprinkle lightly, or to taste with cinnamon. Place toast on cookie sheet under the broiler until cheese is warm.

# EGG CUSTARD

**Makes 6 servings**

    3 cups skim milk
    1 teaspoon vanilla
    6 eggs
    3 teaspoons sugar or sugar substitute
    1/2 teaspoon ground cinnamon, ground nutmeg

In a large deep bowl beat together all ingredients until well blended. Pour into lightly greased baking or custard dishes. Place dishes in a pie plate, fill halfway with warm water. Bake at 375°F. for 20-30 minutes or until done.

# STUFFED GRAPE LEAVES

**Makes 6-8 servings**

  1 **pound lean ground lamb**
¼ **cup rice, washed and drained**
  1 **tablespoon fresh minced parsley**
  1 **tomato, peeled, chopped**
  1 **tablespoon currants**
  1 **small onion, chopped, or onion flakes**
  1 **teaspoon cinnamon**
    **Salt and pepper to taste**
  1 **jar (1 pound) grape leaves**
    **Lemon slices for garnish**

Soak drained vine leaves for 15 minutes. Drain in colander. In a saucepan blanch the vine leaves in boiling water to cover for 5 minutes. In another bowl combine rice, meat, parsley, tomato, currants, onion, cinnamon and salt and pepper. Mix well. Put 1 tablespoon of the filling on the dull side of each leaf at the stem end. Fold in the sides and roll up the leaves, squeezing each one lightly in the palm of the hand. In a large heavy saucepan lined with slices of lettuce or extra grape leaves arrange the rolls seam side down in one layer and add ½ cup of water. Place a heavy plate on the top to prevent the stuffed grape leaves from unwinding. Simmer the leaves, covered adding water as necessary to keep them covered for 1½ hours or until they are tender. Cool in pan, serve hot or cold.

# SHRIMP SAUTÉ

**Makes 6 servings**

  2 **cups cooked shrimp**
 1/2 **cup blanched slivered almonds**
  2 **tablespoons vegetable oil**
    **Salt and pepper to taste**
 1/2 **teaspoon garlic salt**
  2 **tablespoons freshly squeezed lime juice**

In a non-stick skillet sauté almonds in oil until lightly browned. Remove almonds from skillet. Add shrimp and seasoning to non-stick skillet stirring until heated. Stir in lime juice and almonds. Serve over crisp lettuce leaves.

# CALORIE COUNTER

## BEVERAGES

| | PORTION | CALORIES | CARBO* Grams | CHOLESTEROL mg. |
|---|---|---|---|---|
| Coffee, plain | 1 cup | 0 c. | 0 | 0 |
| Tea, plain | 1 cup | 0 c. | 1/2 | 0 |
| Carbonated soft drinks | 8 oz. | 105 c. | 26 | 0 |
| Cocoa, all milk | 8 oz. | 235 c. | 20 | 62 |
| Lemonade | 8 oz. | 100 c. | 28 | 0 |
| Kool-Aid, pre-sweetened | 8 oz. | 90 c. | 1/2 | 0 |
| Beer | 12 oz. | 150 c. | 18 | 0 |

## BREADS, CRACKERS, GRAIN PRODUCTS

| | | | | |
|---|---|---|---|---|
| Corn Bread | 2" sq. | 200 c. | 18 | 70 |
| French Bread | 1 slice | 290 c. | 55 | N/A |
| Protein Bread | 1 slice | 40 c. | N/A | Low |
| Raisin Bread | 1 slice | 75 c. | 13 | Trace |
| Rye Bread | 1 slice | 75 c. | 12 | Trace |
| White Bread | 1 slice | 65 c. | 12 | Trace |
| Whole Wheat Bread | 1 slice | 65 c. | 11 | Trace |
| Biscuits | 1 average | 123 c. | 18 | 0 |
| Rolls | 1 medium | 140 c. | 20 | Low |
| Saltines | 2" sq. | 25 c. | 3 | 0 |
| Soda Crackers | 2" sq. | 25 c. | 4 | 0 |
| Graham Crackers | 1 medium | 28 c. | 5 | Low |
| Matzoth | 1 | 75 c. | N/A | N/A |
| Egg Noodles | 1 cup | 185 c. | 49 | 213 |
| French Toast | 1 slice | 125 c. | 14 | N/A |
| Pancakes | 4" dia. | 75 c. | 8 | 54 |
| Macaroni - Spaghetti | 1 cup | 200 c. | 80 | 0 |
| Rice | 1 cup | 125 c. | 32 | 0 |
| Waffles | 1 average | 225 c. | 30 | 119 |
| Frankfurter rolls | 1 average | 110 c. | 20 | Low |
| Hamburger rolls | 1 average | 170 c. | 20 | Low |
| Nut Bread | 1 slice | | 11 | N/A |

## CEREALS

| | | | | |
|---|---|---|---|---|
| Cream of Wheat | 3/4 cup | 100 c. | 21 | N/A |
| Corn Flakes | 1 cup | 100 c. | 18 | 0 |
| Bran Flakes | 3/4 cup | 100 c. | 23 | 0 |
| Oatmeal | 3/4 cup | 100 c. | 18 | 0 |
| Puffed Rice and Wheat | 3/4 cup | 50 c. | 8 | 0 |
| Rice Krispies | 1 cup | 110 c. | 25 | 0 |
| Shredded Wheat | 1 cup | 100 c. | 36 | 0 |
| Wheaties | 1 cup | | 23 | 0 |

## DESSERTS, SWEETS

| | | | | |
|---|---|---|---|---|
| Angel Food Cake | 1 average slice | 110 c. | 24 | 0 |
| Chocolate, 2 layer | 1 average slice | 400 c. | N/A | High |
| Cupcake, plain | 1 | 100 c. | 31 | Med. |
| Fruit cake | 1 average slice | 300 c. | N/A | 7 |
| Shortcake with fruit | 1 average slice | 350 c. | N/A | N/A |
| Pound cake | 1 average slice | 125 c. | 15 | High |

* Carbohydrate-grams

# Low Calorie Cooking

## DESSERTS, SWEETS

| | PORTION | CALORIES | CARBO Grams | CHOLESTEROL mg. |
|---|---|---|---|---|
| Caramel candy | 1 oz. | 250 c. | 8 | Med. |
| Fudge candy | 1 oz. | 110 c. | 18 | Med. |
| Chocolate cookies | 1 small | 18 c. | N/A | Med. |
| Chocolate Chip cookies | 1 small | 22 c. | 7 | Med. |
| Oatmeal cookies | 1 large | 100 c. | 16 | 0 |
| Chocolate bar with almonds | 1 average | 260 c. | N/A | N/A |
| Chocolate mints | 1 small | 41 c. | N/A | N/A |
| Doughnuts, jelly | 1 average | 250 c. | N/A | High |
| Doughnuts, plain | 1 average | 150 c. | 17 | High |
| Doughnuts, sugared | 1 average | 175 c. | 22 | High |
| Honey | 1 Tbsp. | 65 c. | 17 | 0 |
| Ice Cream | 1 cup | 400 c. | 28 | 85 |
| Ice Milk | 1 cup | 285 c. | 1/2 | 36 |
| Jello | 1/2 cup | 80 c. | 18 | 0 |
| Jellies, Jams | 1 Tbsp. | 50 c. | 14 | 0 |
| Pie, apple and other fruit | average slice | 330 c. | 50-54 | 0 |
| Pies, custard | average slice | 265 c. | 34 | 120 |
| Pies, cream | average slice | 400 c. | N/A | High ** |
| Pudding, bread | 1/2 cup | 125 c. | 21 | |
| Pudding, tapioca | 1/2 cup | 140 c. | 16 | 80 |
| Pudding, vanilla | 1/2 cup | N/A | N/A | 18 |
| Pudding, chocolate | 1/2 cup | N/A | N/A | 15 |
| Sherbet | 1/2 cup | 120 c. | 28 | 0 |
| Sugar, granulated and brown | 1 tsp. | 20 c. | 4 | 0 |
| Sugar, powdered | 1 Tbsp. | 90 c. | 8 | 0 |
| Syrup | 1 Tbsp. | 60 c. | 13 | 0 |

## DAIRY PRODUCTS, FATS, OILS, DRESSINGS

| | PORTION | CALORIES | CARBO Grams | CHOLESTEROL mg. |
|---|---|---|---|---|
| Butter | 1 Tbsp. | 50 c. | Trace | 35 |
| Cheese, American processed | 1 oz. | 75 c. | 1/2 | 25 |
| Cheese, cottage | 1 cup | 240 c. | 6 | 48 |
| Cheese, farmers, pot | 1 oz. | 25 c. | N/A | N/A |
| Cheese, Cheddar | 1 oz. | 100 c. | 1/2 | 28 |
| Cheese, Swiss | 1 oz. | 100 c. | 1 | 28 |
| Cream Cheese | 2 Tbsp. | 56 c. | 1/2 | 32 |
| Cream | 1 Tbsp. | 34 c. | 1 | 20 |
| Cream, whipped | 1 Tbsp. | 50 c. | 1/2 | Trace |
| Sour cream | 1 Tbsp. | 53 c. | 1/2 | 8 |
| Half & Half | 1 Tbsp. | N/A | 1 | 6 |
| Egg, whole | 1 large | 72 c. | Trace | 252 |
| white only | 1 large | 15 c. | Trace | 0 |
| yolk only | 1 large | 57 c. | Trace | 252 |
| Egg, boiled, poached | 1 medium | 75 c. | 0 | |
| Egg, fried | 1 medium | 100 c. | 0 | |
| Egg, scrambled | 1 medium | 125 c. | 1 | |
| Egg, omelet | 2 eggs | N/A | 1 | 526 |
| Milk, whole | 8 oz. | 165 c. | 12 | 34 |
| Milk, skim | 8 oz. | 85 c. | 13 | 5 |
| Milk, 2% low fat | 8 oz. | 120 c. | | 22 |
| Buttermilk | 8 oz. | 72 c. | 13 | 5 |
| Margarine, oleo | 1 Tbsp. | 50 c. | 0 | 0 |
| Oils, cooking & salad | 1 Tbsp. | 100 c. | 0 | 0 |
| Salad dressing, French | 1 Tbsp. | 100 c. | 2 | Low |
| Salad dressing, Roquefort | 1 Tbsp. | 125 c. | 1 | N/A |
| Salad dressing, Russian | 1 Tbsp. | 50 c. | 2 | Low |

** Depending on type of fruit

# CALORIE COUNTER

## DAIRY PRODUCTS, FATS, OILS, DRESSINGS

| | PORTION | CALORIES | CARBO Grams | CHOLESTEROL mg. |
|---|---|---|---|---|
| Salad Dressing, Italian | 1 Tbsp. | | 0 | Low |
| Salad Dressing, Mayonnaise | 1 Tbsp. | 93 c. | Trace | 8 |
| Vinegar and Oil | 1 Tbsp. | 130 c. | 0 | 0 |
| Salad Dressing, Thousand Island | 1 Tbsp. | 75 c. | 2 | Med. |
| | | (Most Dietary Dressings cut carbos 50%) | | |
| Yogurt | 1 cup | 165 c. | 10 | 17 |

## MEATS & POULTRY

| | | | | |
|---|---|---|---|---|
| Bacon, fried crisp | 1 slice | 47 c. | 1/2 | 7 |
| Beef, hamburger, lean broiled | 3 oz. | 200 c. | 0 | 80 |
| Beef, roast, lean | 4 oz. | 210 c. | 0 | 90 |
| Beef, round steak | 2 1/2 oz. | 147 c. | 0 | 4 |
| Beef, sirloin steak | 3 1/2 oz. | 206 c. | 0 | High |
| Beef, liver with onions | 3 1/2 oz. | 248 c. | 8 | 438 |
| Bologna | 1 slice | 85 c. | 1/4 | High |
| Chicken, whole, broiled | 3 lbs. | | 0 | 542 |
| Chicken, fried | 1/2 | | 5 | High |
| Chicken, fried | thigh or leg | 135 c. | N/A | 47 |
| Chicken, fried | breast | 150 c. | N/A | 80 |
| Frankfurter | 1 (2 oz.) | 125 c. | 1 | N/A |
| Ham, smoked | average slice | 450 c. | 0 | High |
| Ham, baked | 3 oz. | 320 c. | 0 | High |
| Ham, canned, lean | 2 oz. | 170 c. | 0 | High |
| Meatloaf | average slice | 225 c. | 4 | High |
| Pork, roast | 3 oz. | 200 c. | 0 | 76 |
| Pork, chops, fried | 1 medium | 325 c. | 0 | 76 |
| Pork, baked or broiled | 1 medium | 225 c. | 0 | N/A |
| Pork sausage | average patty | 170 c. | 0 | High |
| Veal cutlet, broiled | 3 oz. | 125 c. | 0 | 86 |
| Veal, roast | 3 oz. | 150 c. | 0 | 84 |

## FISH

| | | | | |
|---|---|---|---|---|
| Catfish | average serving | 100 c. | 0 | Med. |
| Codfish | 3 1/2 oz. | 100 c. | 1/2 | 50 |
| Gefilte fish | average serving | 150 c. | 0 | High |
| Haddock, fried | 3 1/2 oz. | 250 c. | 4 | 60 |
| Halibut | 3 1/2 oz. | 200 c. | 0 | 60 |
| Perch | average serving | 100 c. | 0 | High |
| Salmon, canned | 1/2 cup | 160 c. | 0 | 35 |
| Salmon, fresh | 3 1/2 oz. | 160 c. | 0 | 47 |
| Trout, fried | 3 1/2 oz. | 220 c. | 0 | 55 |
| Tuna, canned | 3 1/2 oz. | 250 c. | 0 | 65 |

## VEGETABLES

| | | | | |
|---|---|---|---|---|
| Asparagus, canned | 1/2 cup | 25 c. | 3 | 0 |
| Avocado | 1 small | 425 c. | 12 | Med. |
| Beans, baked | 1/2 cup | 100 c. | 3 | Low |
| Beans, string | 1 cup | 25 c. | 10 | 0 |
| Beets | 1/2 cup | 35 c. | 8 | 0 |
| Broccoli | 1 cup | 45 c. | 8 | 0 |
| Brussels sprouts | 1 cup | 60 c. | 12 | 0 |
| Cabbage, raw | 1 cup | 25 c. | 10 | 0 |
| Cabbage, cooked | 1 cup | 40 c. | 10 | 0 |
| Carrots, raw or cooked | 1/2 cup | 25 c. | 5 | 0 |
| Cauliflower | 1 cup | 30 c. | 6 | 0 |
| Celery | 2 stalks | 10 c. | 1 | 0 |

# CALORIE COUNTER

## VEGETABLES

| | PORTION | CALORIES | CARBO Grams | CHOLESTEROL mg. |
|---|---|---|---|---|
| Corn, fresh or frozen | 1 cup | 140 c. | 16 | 0 |
| Corn, canned | 1/2 cup | 70 c. | 20 | 0 |
| Cucumbers | 1/2 cup | 10 c. | 2 | 0 |
| Lettuce, shredded | 1 cup | 10 c. | 3 | 0 |
| Mushrooms | 1/2 cup | 15 c. | 5 | 0 |
| Onions, raw or cooked | 1/2 cup | 25 c. | 9 | 0 |
| Peas, fresh, frozen or canned | 1 cup | 110 c. | 32 | 0 |
| Potatoes, baked or broiled | 1 medium | 125 c. | 21 | Med. |
| Potatoes, French fried | 6 average | 100 c. | 12 | Med. |
| Potatoes, mashed with butter & milk | 1/2 cup | 73 c. | 15 | Med. |
| Radishes | 7 | 15 c. | 3 1/2 | 0 |
| Sauerkraut | 1/2 cup | 25 c. | 3 | 0 |
| Spinach & other greens | 1/2 cup | 25 c. | 3 | 0 |
| Sweet potatoes, baked | 1 medium | 200 c. | 36 | 0 |
| Sweet potatoes, candied | 1/2 medium | 150 c. | 30 | N/A |
| Tomato, raw | 1 medium | 50 c. | 6 | 0 |
| Tomato, stewed | 1 cup | 50 c. | 10 | 0 |
| Tomato, juice | 1 cup | 50 c. | 10 | 0 |

## FRUIT

| | | | | |
|---|---|---|---|---|
| Apple, raw | 1 medium | 75 c. | 18 | 0 |
| Applesauce, sweetened canned | 1/2 cup | 100 c. | 25 | 0 |
| Bananas | 1 medium | 100 c. | 23 | 0 |
| Cantaloupe | 1/2 medium | 50 c. | 9 | 0 |
| Cranberry sauce | 1 Tbsp. | 34 c. | 18 | 0 |
| Fruit cocktail | 1 cup | 100 c. | 50 | 0 |
| Grapefruit | 1/2 medium | 50 c. | 14 | 0 |
| Grapefruit juice | 1 cup | 100 c. | 24 | 0 |
| Grapes | 1 cup | 85 c. | 16 | 0 |
| Oranges | 1 medium | 75 c. | 16 | 0 |
| Orange juice | 1 cup | 100 c. | 24 | 0 |
| Peaches, fresh | 1 medium | 50 c. | 10 | 0 |
| Peaches, canned | 2 halves | 93 c. | 24 | 0 |
| Pears | 1 medium | 75 c. | 10 | 0 |
| Pineapple, canned | 1/2" slice | 37 c. | 13 | 0 |
| Plums | 1 medium | 30 c. | 7 | 0 |
| Prunes, cooked | 5 medium | 170 c. | 22 | 0 |
| Prune juice | 1/2 cup | 85 c. | 22 | 0 |
| Raisins, dried | 1/2 cup | 225 c. | 60 | 0 |
| Strawberries, frozen | 1/2 cup | 106 c. | 27 | 0 |
| Strawberries, fresh | 1 cup | 50 c. | 13 | 0 |
| Tangerines | 1 medium | 35 c. | 10 | 0 |
| Watermelon | 4 x 8" wedge | 100 c. | 29 | 0 |

## MISCELLANEOUS

| | | | | |
|---|---|---|---|---|
| Ketchup, chili sauce | 1 Tbsp. | 25 c. | 4 | 0 |
| Olives, green | 7 large | 63 c. | 1 | 0 |
| Olives, ripe | 7 large | 63 c. | 2 | 0 |
| Nuts, peanuts, roasted, shelled | | | | |
| Nuts, cashews | 1/2 cup | 375 c. | 18 | 0 |
| Nuts, pecans | 1/2 cup | 375 c. | 8 | Low |
| Nuts, English walnuts | 1/2 cup | 375 c. | 4 | 0 |
| Peanut butter | 1 Tbsp. | 100 c. | 3 | 0 |
| Pickles, dill | 4" | 15 c. | 2 | 0 |
| Pickles, sweet | 1 medium | 25 c. | 5 | 0 |
| Pizza | 5" wedge | 225 c. | 23 | High |

# Nutrition

## NUTRIENTS

**PROTEIN** Builds and repairs all body tissues; skin, bone, hair, blood, muscle, and so forth. It helps form antibodies to fight infection. It is a part of hormones and enzymes which are responsible for regulating body functions such as digestion and growth. May be used to furnish energy (calories). Good sources are meat; fish; poultry; eggs; dried peas and beans, especially soy beans, milk and milk products; peanut butter; and nuts.

**FATS** Supply a large amount of energy in a small amount of food. Some fats carry vitamins A, D, E and K needed for a healthy skin. Helps delay hunger feelings. Many medical authorities recommend that no more than 35% of the calories eaten in a day come from fat. Good sources are oil; shortening; butter, margarine; bacon; visible fat on meat; chocolate and nuts.

**CARBOHYDRATES** Supplies food energy. Helps the body make the best use of other nutrients. Good sources are cereal grains; sugar and sweets; rice; pastas; selected fruits as bananas and dried fruits; and selected vegetables as potatoes, corn and lima beans.

**THIAMIN** Promotes normal appetite and digestion. Necessary for a healthy nervous system. Needed in certain enzymes which help change food into energy. Good sources are liver; meat as pork; dried peas and beans; wheat germ; and whole grain and enriched bread and cereal.

**RIBOFLAVIN** Helps cells use oxygen. Helps maintain good vision. Needed for smooth skin. Helps prevent scaling and cracking of skin around mouth and nose. Needed in certain enzymes which help change food into energy. Good sources are liver; milk and milk products as cheese; green leaf vegetables; meat; eggs; whole grain and enriched bread and cereal.

**NIACIN** Promotes normal appetite and digestion. Necessary for a healthy nervous system. Needed in certain enzymes which help change food into energy. Good sources are liver; meat; fish; poultry; green vegetables; nuts as peanuts; whole grain bread and cereal except corn; and enriched bread and cereal.

**CALCIUM** Helps build strong bones and teeth. Helps blood clot. Helps muscles and nerves function normally. Needed to activate certain enzymes which help change food into energy. Good sources are milk and milk products as cheese; sardines and shellfish; green leafy vegetables as turnip, spinach, and mustard greens.

**PHOSPHORUS** Helps build strong bones and teeth. Needed by certain enzymes which help change food into energy. Good sources are meat; fish; poultry; dried peas and beans; milk and milk products; egg yolk; and whole grain bread and cereal.

**IRON** Combines with protein to make hemoglobin, the red substance in the blood that carries oxygen from lungs to cells and myoglobin which stores oxygen in muscles. Needed to prevent iron deficiency anemia. Good sources are liver; red meat; shellfish; egg yolk; dark green leafy vegetables; dried peas and beans; dried prunes, raisins and apricots; molasses; and whole grain and enriched bread and cereal.

**IODINE** Necessary for proper functioning of thyroid gland. Prevents some form of goiter. Good sources are seafoods and iodized table salt.

**VITAMIN C** Ascorbic Acid; Helps bind cells together and strengthens walls of blood vessels. Needed for healthy gums. Helps body resist infections. Promotes healing of wounds and cuts. Good sources are certain fruits and vegetables as citrus fruits and juices; broccoli; strawberries; tomatoes; cauliflower; cabbage; melons; green leafy vegetables and potatoes.

**VITAMIN A** Helps keep the skin healthy. Protects against night blindness. Needed for normal vision. Promotes growth and development. Helps build resistance to infection. Good sources are liver; fish liver oils; dark green leafy vegetables; deep yellow fruits and vegetables; egg yolk; butter; fortified Margarine; whole milk; and vitamin A fortified skim milk.

**VITAMIN D** Helps the body absorb calcium and phosphorus which build strong bones and teeth. Good sources are vitamin D fortified milk; liver; fish liver oils; and egg yolk.

Other important nutrients include; Vitamin $B_6$, Vitamin $B_{12}$, Folic Acid, Vitamin E, Vitamin K, Magnesium.

# NUTRIENTS

## GUIDE TO NUTRIENTS . . . and what they do

**Protein**
*(from animal &
plant foods)*

- essential for growth and life-long body maintenance
- builds resistance to disease

Other minerals are important. too. such as zinc. iodine. phosphorus and magnesium. Eating a wide variety of nutritious foods will provide them.

**Minerals -
Calcium**
*(from milk &
other dairy
products)*

- forms healthy bones and teeth
- aids in normal blood clotting
- helps nerves and muscles react normally

**Fats**

- carry vitamins A. D. E. & K
- source of energy (calories) best used in limited amounts

**Iron**
*(from liver.
meat. egg
yolks. dry
beans. dark
greens)*

- helps blood cells carry oxygen from the lungs to body cells
- protects against some forms of nutritional anemia

**Carbohydrates**

- inexpensive source of energy
- best when consumed as fruit sugar or starch (bread. cereal foods. potatoes)

---

**Vitamins**

**A**

- protects eyes and night vision
- helps keep skin healthy
- builds resistance to disease

**C**

- keeps body cells and tissues strong and healthy
- aids in healing wounds and broken bones

**B-complex**
*(Thiamin.
riboflavin.
folic acid.
niacin. $B_6$, $B_{12}$
are the
important ones.)*

- protects the nervous system
- keeps appetite and digestion in working order
- aids body cells in using carbohydrates. fat and protein for energy

**D**
*(especially
important for
children)*

- aids in absorption and use of calcium and phosphorous by body cells
- helps build strong bones and teeth

If children eat foods rich in vitamins A. B-complex & C and drink vitamin-D fortified milk. they will get the other vitamins they need, too.

# ──Index──

## Index